# The UK Stock Market
# Almanac
# 2007

HARRIMAN HOUSE LTD

43 Chapel Street
Petersfield
Hampshire
GU32 3DY
GREAT BRITAIN

Tel: +44 (0)1730 233870
Fax: +44 (0)1730 233880

Email: enquiries@harriman-house.com
Website: www.harriman-house.com

First edition published in Great Britain in 2004
2nd edition 2005, 3rd edition 2006
Copyright Harriman House Ltd

The right of Stephen Eckett to be identified as the author has been asserted in
accordance with the Copyright, Design and Patents Act 1988.

1-905641-08-7
978-1-905641-086

*British Library Cataloguing in Publication Data*
A CIP catalogue record for this book can be obtained from the British Library.

Printed and bound by Star Standard Industries Pte, Singapore.

# Contents

# Preface

Welcome to the 2007 edition of the UK Stock Market Almanac. The book where we celebrate the Efficient Market Theory – or rather, the failure of said theory. To briefly recap, Efficient Market Theory states that it is impossible to beat the markets, because prices already incorporate all known information. What a dull place the stock market would be if this was really true. Fortunately, the theory is tosh. At least, the strong version of the theory is (i.e. prices reflecting all known information), and it can safely be consigned to the What-do-academics-know-about-the market? bin.

This book could alternatively be titled, "The Inefficient Almanac" – as it revels in the trends and anomalies of the market that the Efficient Market Theory says shouldn't exist.

## Seasonality trends and anomalies

In this edition we look at answering questions such as:

- What stocks should you sell in December and buy in January?
- Should you buy or sell stocks after they are ejected from the FTSE100 Index?
- Does the market in January accurately predict the direction of the market for the whole year?
- If the market rises 5 days in a row, what is the probability of it rising for a sixth day?
- Which days of the week are the best for the FTSE100?
- Which are the strongest and weakest months in the year for the market?
- What sectors are the strongest (weakest) in each quarter?
- What type of companies become Ten Baggers?
- How has the daily volatility of the FTSE100 Index changed over the last 20 years?
- How does the FTSE100 behave in the days immediately following exceptionally large moves?

Besides that, we also take a look at some more whimsical topics, such as why UK investors should want Australia to win the Ashes and why they should buy companies whose CEOs have a first name Michael.

## What can we expect in 2007?

Well, we'll be celebrating the one thousandth anniversary of Aethelred buying two years of peace with the Danes for 36,000 pounds of silver (which, at today's rates, establishes a UK-Denmark peace rate of £1.8m per year). Elsewhere, in 1707 the UK market rose 21%, in 1807 it rose 3%, and in 1907 it fell 15%. Frankly, the trend doesn't look good.

However, whether the market goes up or down in 2007, the smart investor knows there are inefficiencies to be exploited and hopefully this book will help by identifying some of them.

Stephen Eckett

# I.

# Introduction

# Introduction

*Definition*

> *almanac (noun): an annual calendar containing dates and statistical information*

## What the book covers

Topics in the Almanac cover a wide spectrum. The diary includes essential information on upcoming company announcements and financial events such as exchange holidays and economic releases. There are also the results of a unique seasonality analysis of historic market performance for every day and week of the year. Besides this, there is information of a lighter nature, such as important social and sporting events and notable events in history.

Accompanying the diary is a series of articles about investing. Many of these articles focus on seasonality effects, such as the likely performance of the market in each month, momentum effects, and the difference in market performance between Summer and Winter.

The Almanac includes a reference section – invaluable for all investors. Ever wondered what a SEDOL code is; what time the morning opening auction starts or what the telephone number of the FSA is? It's all in the reference section. There's also information on market indices and performance.

At the back of the Almanac is a comprehensive directory of all UK listed companies and members of AIM, with information on their EPIC codes, sector, market capitalisation, NMS and expected dates of their AGM.

In short, the Almanac is a unique work providing everything from essential reference information to informative and entertaining articles on the UK stock market.

## How the book is structured

The Almanac has three major parts:

1. **Diary**

   This is in week per page format. There are 52 pages one for each week in the year. (See the next page for a detailed explanation of the layout of each diary page.) Opposite each Diary page is a short article about the stock market. The aim of these articles is to inform, educate and, hopefully, entertain.

2. **Reference**

   The central section of the book comprises a wide range of reference articles about the UK stock market.

3. **Company Directory**

   The final main section of the book is a comprehensive directory of all companies listed on the London Stock Exchange, and members of AIM.

## Supporting website

The website supporting this book can be found at www.harriman-house.com/almanac

# Understanding the diary pages

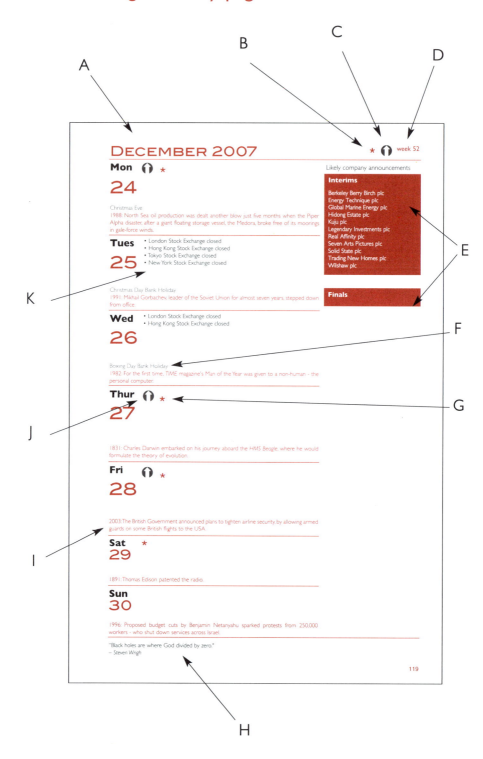

## DECEMBER 2007

★ 🎧 week 52

**Mon** 🎧 ★

### 24

Christmas Eve
1988: North Sea oil production was dealt another blow just five months when the Piper Alpha disaster, after a giant floating storage vessel, the Medora, broke free of its moorings in gale-force winds.

**Tues**
- London Stock Exchange closed
- Hong Kong Stock Exchange closed
- Tokyo Stock Exchange closed
- New York Stock Exchange closed

### 25

Christmas Day Bank Holiday
1991: Mikhail Gorbachev, leader of the Soviet Union for almost seven years, stepped down from office.

**Wed**
- London Stock Exchange closed
- Hong Kong Stock Exchange closed

### 26

Boxing Day Bank Holiday
1982: For the first time, *TIME* magazine's Man of the Year was given to a non-human - the personal computer.

**Thur** 🎧 ★

### 27

1831: Charles Darwin embarked on his journey aboard the *HMS Beagle*, where he would formulate the theory of evolution.

**Fri** 🎧 ★

### 28

2003: The British Government announced plans to tighten airline security, by allowing armed guards on some British flights to the USA.

**Sat** ★

### 29

1891: Thomas Edison patented the radio.

**Sun**

### 30

1996: Proposed budget cuts by Benjamin Netanyahu sparked protests from 250,000 workers - who shut down services across Israel.

"Black holes are where God divided by zero."
– Steven Wrigh

Likely company announcements

**Interims**
Berkeley Berry Birch plc
Energy Technique plc
Global Marine Energy plc
Hidong Estate plc
Kuju plc
Legendary Investments plc
Real Affinity plc
Seven Arts Pictures plc
Solid State plc
Trading New Homes plc
Wilshaw plc

**Finals**

119

## A – Diary page title

The calendar is a week per page format, so there are 52 pages with four pages to a month.

## B – Ten top and bottom weeks

Best and worst performing weeks are marked here. [See the next page for more information.]

## C – Weekly performance analysis (Sinclair numbers)

Results of the analysis on the historic performance of the market during this week. [See the next page for more information and the reference section for full tables.]

## D – Week number

The week number of the year is indicated at the top right of every diary page.

## E – Likely company announcements

The red boxes contain a list of companies expected to announce interim or final results during the week.

The list is only provisional, using the date of announcements in the previous year as a guide. Investors can check the updated situation regularly with reference to a number of forward diaries published on the internet (a good one can be found at www.digitallook.com).

## F – Social and sporting events

## G – Ten top and bottom days

Best and worst performing days are marked here. [See the next page for more information.]

## H – Quotation

## I – On this day

Events that happened on this calendar day in history. For example, on 29th December 1891, Thomas Edison patented the radio.

## J – Daily performance analysis (Sinclair numbers)

Results of the analysis on the historic performance of the market on this calendar day. [See the next page for explanation and the reference section for full tables.]

## K – Financial events

Indicates days of financial and economic significance. For example, exchange holidays and important economic releases.

### Glossary of terms

FOMC – Federal Open Market Committee

MPC – Monetary Policy Committee

# Sinclair numbers – daily, weekly and monthly performance analysis

## Sinclair Numbers

In the Reference Section (from page 123), there is a set of tables with the results of analysis of the historic performance of the market on each day and week of the year.

The analysis produces three numbers (Sinclair Numbers) for each day and week: Up(%), Avg Change(%), and StdDev. These numbers are explained below.

1. Up(%)

   The percentage of historic moves on this day that were up. For example, for 26th January, in our sample, the index increased 12 times on this day, and 3 times it decreased, so the Up(%) is 80%.

2. Avg Change(%)

   The average percentage change of the market on that diary day. For example, for 26th January, historically the market has risen 0.5% on this day.

3. StdDev

   This is the standard deviation of all the changes on this day away from the average. For example, for 26th January, the standard deviation is 0.8 – which means that 66% of all the market moves on 26th January fell between -0.3% and +1.3% (i.e. average -/+ standard deviation). Standard deviation measures how closely all the moves on this day cluster around the average. A high number for standard deviation suggests that clustering was not close, and therefore confidence in future moves being close to the average is decreased. Conversely, a low standard deviation figure suggests good clustering, and increases one's confidence in future moves being close to the calculated historic average.

The analysis was also carried out on weekly data.

## Sample data

The sample data used for analysis was the FTSE 100 Index from April 1984, when the Index was introduced.

## Diary pages

The figures for Up(%) are displayed for the respective days and weeks on the Diary pages employing the following symbols:

the Up(%) is over 70%

the Up(%) is 50% to 70%

the UP(%) is 50%

the Up(%) is 30% to 50%

the Up(%) is under 30%

## On the diary pages

The top ten days and weeks – with the highest Up(%) – are highlighted with a ★

The weakest ten days and weeks – with the lowest Up(%) – are highlighted with a ★

# 2.

# Diary

# The Ashes portfolio

The chart below plots the performance of two portfolios: the *Australia Portfolio* and the *England Portfolio*:

- **Australia Portfolio**: this portfolio invests in the UK market (as indexed by the FT All Share Index), only in those months when Australia is holding the Ashes. When Australia loses the Ashes, it liquidates its shares and holds cash.

- **England Portfolio**: the reverse of the above. This portfolio is fully invested in the UK market when England hold the Ashes, and is in cash when Australia holds them.

Both portfolios started with £1,000 in 1900.

Trades are made at the end of the month of the final test of the series (regardless of whether the series has already been decided at an earlier stage). For example, the final test match of the 2005 series took place 8-12 September 2005, and so at the close of the market on 30 September, the Australia Portfolio sold all its UK shares to hold cash and the England Portfolio invested fully in the UK market.

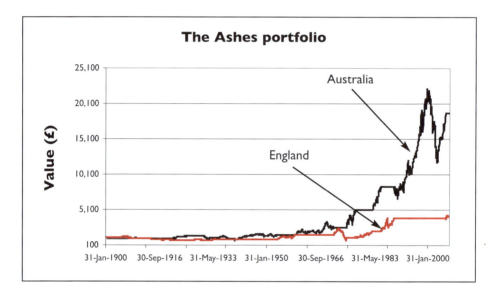

After the 106 years of investing, the value of the two portfolios in 2006 was:

- Australia Portfolio: £18,717

- England Portfolio: £4,025

It could be argued that the Australia Portfolio should obviously be the more successful as Australia has held the Ashes for longer than England, and the UK market has generally risen over the last century. This is true. Australia has held the Ashes for 65% of the months since 1900. So that certainly explains some out-performance – perhaps a 100% superior performance could be explained by this. But the actual out-performance was way above that – at 365%.

The lesson is inescapable: anyone investing in the UK market should be cheering on Australia in the 2006-7 test series.

# December 2006

## Mon
## 25

- London Stock Exchange closed
- Hong Kong Stock Exchange closed
- Tokyo Stock Exchange closed
- New York Stock Exchange closed

Christmas Day
1977: Charlie Chaplin, the comic genius of silent films, dies at his home in Switzerland at the age of 88.

## Tues
## 26

- London Stock Exchange closed
- Hong Kong Stock Exchange closed

Boxing Day
1861: Friedrich Engel (mathematician) was born.

## Wed
## 27

1960: France moved a step closer to developing a compact nuclear bomb after a third test in the Sahara desert.

## Thur
## 28

1895: The world's first cinema opened in Paris, France.

## Fri
## 29

1982: A Bob Marley postage stamp was issued in Jamaica.

## Sat
## 30

1986: The government announced that more than 200 canary birds were to be phased out of Britain's mining pits and replaced by hand-held gas detectors.

## Sun
## 31

1907: For the first time, a ball dropped at Times Square in New York to signal the new year.

Likely company announcements

**Interims**

Ardana plc

**Finals**

Acorn Income Fund Ltd
Defined Capital Return Hund Ltd
Ethical AIM VCT plc
Sportech

"The best way to keep money in perspective is to have some."
– Louis Rukeyser

# January market

## Market performance in the month

January is the 2nd best month for the market in the year. On average the market rises 2.7% this month - although the standard deviation (at 9.1) is the highest of all months, which means that returns in this month have diverged greatly from the average. The high standard deviation is no doubt affected by the extraordinary rise of 52.7% in January 1975.

However, despite the wild swings, January can be considered a good month for investors, with the market rising 69% of all years.

January is even better for mid-cap stocks. On average, the FTSE250 Index outperforms the FTSE100 by 1.4% in January – the best out-performance of all months.

Historic performance of the market in January

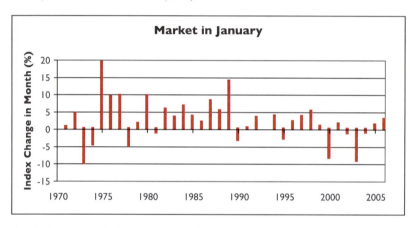

*Note:* In January 1975 the market rose 52.7%. As this distorts the chart, the Y-axis scale has been truncated at 20%.

## Company announcements

January is the quietest month in the year for company results.

Large companies reporting this month-

- *Finals:* AstraZeneca

## What to look out for this month

- Historic **strong sectors** in this first quarter are: Construction & Materials, Oil & Gas and Travel & Leisure.
- Historic **weak sectors** in this first quarter are: Technology Hardware & Equipment, Fixed Line Telecommunications, and Software & Computer Services.
- **7th strongest day** of the year: week 26 Jan; **10th weakest day** of the year: 23 Jan
- **7th strongest week** of the year for the market: week 4; **9th weakest week** of the year: week 3.
- For 26 of the past 35 years the **direction of the market in January** has predicted the direction of the market for the whole year. Although its predictive power has been getting weaker in recent years.
- The **FTSE250 is particularly strong relative to the FTSE100** in this month.
- The **MPC decision on interest rates** should be announced 12 noon on 10 January.
- **Holiday:** the LSE is closed 1 January.
- Don't forget: the last date to file your 2006 **tax return** is 31 January.

# JANUARY 2007

## Mon
# 1

New Year's Day Bank Holiday
1673: Regular mail delivery began between New York and Boston.

## Tues
# 2

Bank Holiday (Scotland)
5th Ashes Test v Australia, Sydney until 6th January
1980: Steel workers staged their first national strike for more than fifty years.

## Wed
# 3

1993: US and Russia agreed to halve the number of nuclear warheads.

## Thur
# 4

1967: Donald Campbell was killed attempting to break his own water speed record in Bluebird.

## Fri
# 5

1944: The *Daily Mail* became the first transoceanic newspaper.

## Sat
# 6

1914: Merrill Lynch was founded.

## Sun
# 7

1785: Blanchard and Jeffries became the first people to fly across the English Channel in a balloon.

"A bank is a place that will lend you money if you can prove that you don't need it."
– *Bob Hope*

---

Likely company announcements

**Interims**

AdEPT Telecom plc
Chariot (UK) plc
Cohort plc
Games Workshop Group plc

**Finals**

Britvic plc
South China Resources plc
Slimma plc
SCOTTY Group plc
Mercury Group plc

# Sector performance – first quarter

The table below shows the performance of sectors in the first quarter (31/12 – 31/3) of each year 2000-2006. The table is ranked by the final column – the average performance over the 7 years. For each year: the top 5 performing sectors are highlighted in red, the bottom 5 in grey.

| Sector | EPIC | 2000 | 2001 | 2002 | 2003 | 2004 | 2005 | 2006 | Average |
|---|---|---|---|---|---|---|---|---|---|
| Leisure Goods | NMX3740 | | | 7.4 | 11.3 | 24.6 | -5.7 | | 9.4 |
| Construction & Materials | NMX2350 | -9.1 | 2.2 | 14.6 | 1.7 | 9.1 | 8.4 | 15.1 | 6.0 |
| Tobacco | NMX3780 | 2.7 | 0.8 | 19.0 | -4.0 | 7.1 | 0.2 | 2.6 | 4.1 |
| Oil & Gas | NMX0530 | -5.2 | 4.9 | 15.3 | -6.5 | -2.0 | 8.3 | 6.0 | 3.0 |
| Travel & Leisure | NMX5750 | 3.9 | -0.7 | 7.5 | -0.6 | 8.6 | -0.6 | 2.5 | 2.9 |
| Electricity | NMX7530 | 0.6 | -3.5 | 5.6 | -1.7 | 3.7 | 2.9 | 12.9 | 2.9 |
| Personal Goods | NMX3760 | 2.7 | -2.6 | 15.4 | -13.9 | 6.3 | 6.0 | 6.6 | 2.9 |
| Real Estate | NMX8730 | -3.4 | 2.0 | 12.5 | -11.4 | 9.4 | -5.9 | 16.8 | 2.9 |
| Automobiles & Parts | NMX3350 | -21.6 | 0.4 | 27.3 | -11.6 | -0.2 | 4.3 | 15.5 | 2.0 |
| Mining | NMX1770 | -26.7 | 8.6 | 10.3 | -5.4 | -0.4 | 9.5 | 16.5 | 1.8 |
| Media | NMX5550 | 24.5 | -20.3 | 5.8 | -17.5 | 7.8 | 6.0 | 4.8 | 1.6 |
| Aerospace & Defence | NMX2710 | -11.6 | -8.2 | 10.8 | -10.9 | 14.2 | 6.7 | 5.8 | 1.0 |
| Industrial Transportation | NMX2770 | -19.5 | -10.7 | 11.9 | -6.0 | 4.1 | 3.6 | 20.1 | 0.5 |
| Industrial Engineering | NMX2750 | -19.2 | -7.5 | 13.2 | -7.4 | 3.4 | 5.1 | 14.1 | 0.2 |
| General Financial | NMX8770 | 1.3 | -18.4 | -0.1 | -9.4 | 8.4 | -2.6 | 22.5 | 0.2 |
| Beverages | NMX3530 | -6.5 | -4.1 | 13.5 | -10.0 | 0.6 | 0.3 | 7.4 | 0.2 |
| General Retailers | NMX5370 | -13.9 | 7.5 | 8.1 | -8.6 | 2.2 | -2.2 | 7.4 | 0.1 |
| Industrial Metals | NMX1750 | -36.6 | -11.3 | 19.4 | -66.4 | 37.5 | 6.9 | 49.2 | -0.2 |
| Equity Investment Instruments | NMX8980 | 3.6 | -10.3 | 1.6 | -10.5 | 0.5 | 2.2 | 9.1 | -0.5 |
| Food Producers | NMX3570 | -2.9 | -8.8 | 3.9 | -6.4 | 3.7 | 4.6 | 1.6 | -0.6 |
| Chemicals | NMX1350 | -2.5 | -11.6 | 7.2 | -24.6 | 3.8 | 5.9 | 13.9 | -1.1 |
| Pharmaceuticals & Biotechnology | NMX4570 | 3.4 | -2.2 | -0.1 | -5.4 | -11.5 | 2.8 | 2.8 | -1.5 |
| Support Services | NMX2790 | -9.1 | -13.2 | -3.8 | -13.2 | 3.6 | 5.8 | 12.3 | -2.5 |
| Food & Drug Retailers | NMX5330 | -0.8 | -5.2 | -0.6 | -9.0 | -3.1 | -0.1 | 0.4 | -2.6 |
| Health Care Equip & Services | NMX4530 | -6.4 | -7.4 | 7.3 | -12.7 | 7.8 | -6.0 | -3.7 | -3.0 |
| Electronic & Electrical Equipment | NMX2730 | 33.4 | -20.4 | -4.1 | -56.0 | 5.6 | 10.2 | 10.0 | -3.0 |
| Banks | NMX8350 | -10.6 | -4.7 | 0.2 | -8.2 | -4.2 | -3.9 | 6.2 | -3.6 |
| Life Insurance | NMX8570 | -13.1 | -17.3 | -6.8 | -25.7 | 2.1 | 5.4 | 16.2 | -5.6 |
| Software & Computer Services | NMX9530 | 9.3 | -28.6 | -13.0 | -20.0 | -1.0 | -1.4 | 1.0 | -7.7 |
| Fixed Line Telecommunications | NMX6530 | -1.3 | -23.8 | -23.4 | -3.1 | -4.6 | -0.3 | -0.5 | -8.1 |
| Nonlife Insurance | NMX8530 | -11.2 | -19.4 | -22.1 | -19.0 | 3.7 | 2.4 | 7.9 | -8.2 |
| Technology Hardware & Equip | NMX9570 | -22.1 | -48.1 | -28.4 | 6.7 | -0.3 | -7.4 | 12.5 | -12.4 |

## Observations

1. The general clustering of red highlights at the top of the table, and grey at the bottom, suggests that certain sectors consistently perform well (or badly) in this quarter. This effect is the strongest in the first quarter.

2. The **strong sectors** in this quarter are: Construction & Materials, Oil & Gas and Travel & Leisure.

3. The **weak sectors** in this quarter are: Technology Hardware & Equipment, Fixed Line Telecommunications, and Software & Computer Services.

# JANUARY 2007

## Mon
# 8

• Tokyo Stock Exchange closed

1656: The oldest surviving commercial newspaper was launched (Haarlem, Netherlands).

## Tues
# 9

1957: Sir Anthony Eden resigned as prime minister of Britain due to ill health, after one year and 279 days in the post.

## Wed
# 10

• MPC meeting (anticipated) until 11th January

1920: The League of Nations was instituted.

## Thur
# 11

1973: The first Open University degrees were awarded.

## Fri
# 12

1836: Charles Darwin in the HMS Beagle reached Sydney, Australia.

## Sat
# 13

1930: *Mickey Mouse* comic strip first appeared.

## Sun
# 14

1985: The British pound sunk to a record low of $1.11 .

Likely company announcements

### Interims
Abbey plc
HMV Group plc
Inter Link Foods plc
Jacques Vert plc
Northgate plc
Photo-Me International plc
Rotala plc
Vantis plc

### Finals
SThree plc
Romag Holdings plc
Mediasurface plc
Innovata plc
Driver Group plc
Deep-Sea Leisure plc
Contemporary Enterprises plc
Cobra Bio-Manufacturing plc

"A banker is a fellow who lends you his umbrella when the sun is shining, but wants it back the minute it begins to rain."
– *Mark Twain*

# Monthly performance of the FTSE100

The table below shows the monthly percentage performance of the FTSE100 Index for every year since 1970. The months where the Index fell are highlighted.

By scanning the vertical columns it is possible to get a feel for how the market moves in certain months. For example, in recent years the Index has been weak in March, May, and July, while it has been strong in the final three months of the year. In the last 20 years it can clearly be seen that the strongest month has been December (only down 4 times in 20 years). By contrast, in the 70s and 80s the strongest month was easily April (which increased every year from 1971 to 1985).

Looking across the table, it can be seen that the longest period of consecutive down months was April 2002 – Sep 2003. While the longest period of consecutive up months was Jul 1982 – Jun 1983 (the only time the FTSE100 Index has risen 12 months without break).

Monthly percentage changes for FTSE100 Index

| | Jan | Feb | Mar | Apr | May | Jun | Jul | Aug | Sep | Oct | Nov | Dec |
|---|---|---|---|---|---|---|---|---|---|---|---|---|
| 1970 | | -4.9 | 1.8 | -10.1 | -5.8 | 3.7 | 0.4 | -2.4 | 7.3 | -2.1 | -10.7 | 6.5 |
| 1971 | 1.0 | -7.6 | 9.1 | 11.3 | -0.6 | -1.2 | 5.8 | 2.5 | -0.6 | 0.2 | 6.3 | 9.4 |
| 1972 | 4.0 | 3.2 | -0.5 | 4.4 | -2.5 | -7.3 | 5.5 | 3.0 | -10.5 | 1.9 | 7.4 | -1.2 |
| 1973 | -8.4 | -3.5 | 2.1 | 1.6 | -0.2 | -2.7 | -4.9 | -3.3 | 3.6 | 0.7 | -15.8 | -5.5 |
| 1974 | -8.1 | 6.8 | -20.9 | 11.4 | -7.2 | -7.7 | -7.3 | -8.4 | -13.0 | 4.9 | -15.8 | -2.9 |
| 1975 | 46.8 | 27.4 | -7.1 | 16.7 | 5.5 | -15.4 | -2.9 | 15.6 | 0.6 | 6.6 | 1.7 | 5.2 |
| 1976 | 11.1 | -2.9 | -0.7 | 3.9 | -9.0 | 0.9 | -4.9 | -3.9 | -7.8 | -14.5 | 7.5 | 19.2 |
| 1977 | 10.1 | 5.2 | 2.1 | 3.2 | 3.6 | 1.7 | -3.5 | 13.8 | 4.0 | -2.9 | -4.9 | 0.9 |
| 1978 | -3.8 | -4.6 | 6.6 | 0.7 | 3.9 | -3.2 | 5.8 | 2.0 | -0.7 | -3.7 | 2.3 | -0.7 |
| 1979 | 0.6 | 7.0 | 12.9 | 5.3 | -7.2 | -4.8 | -4.4 | 3.7 | 3.7 | -6.3 | -1.3 | -2.1 |
| 1980 | 9.2 | 4.9 | -9.2 | 3.4 | -2.3 | 11.2 | 3.7 | 0.7 | 3.2 | 5.9 | 0.6 | -5.3 |
| 1981 | -1.5 | 4.3 | 0.4 | 6.9 | -5.0 | 1.9 | 0.4 | 5.0 | -16.6 | 3.2 | 10.5 | -1.1 |
| 1982 | 4.5 | -4.9 | 3.5 | 1.1 | 3.4 | -4.3 | 3.6 | 2.9 | 6.1 | 2.0 | 0.9 | 1.7 |
| 1983 | 3.1 | 0.6 | 1.8 | 8.1 | 0.2 | 2.8 | -2.1 | 2.6 | -2.6 | -3.4 | 5.7 | 1.9 |
| 1984 | 6.3 | -2.1 | 6.9 | 2.3 | -10.3 | 2.0 | -3.0 | 9.3 | 3.3 | 0.9 | 2.6 | 4.3 |
| 1985 | 3.9 | -1.6 | 1.4 | 1.1 | 1.7 | -5.9 | 2.2 | 6.3 | -3.8 | 6.8 | 4.5 | 1.8 |
| 1986 | 1.6 | 7.6 | 8.1 | -0.5 | -3.5 | 2.9 | -5.6 | 6.6 | -6.3 | 4.9 | 0.3 | 2.6 |
| 1987 | 7.7 | 9.5 | 0.9 | 2.6 | 7.4 | 3.7 | 3.4 | -4.7 | 5.2 | -26.0 | -9.7 | 8.4 |
| 1988 | 4.6 | -1.2 | -1.5 | 3.4 | -1.0 | 4.1 | -0.2 | -5.4 | 4.2 | 1.4 | -3.2 | 0.0 |
| 1989 | 14.4 | -2.4 | 3.6 | 2.1 | -0.2 | 1.7 | 6.8 | 4.0 | -3.7 | -6.8 | 6.3 | 6.4 |
| 1990 | 3.5 | -3.5 | -0.3 | -6.4 | 11.5 | 1.3 | -2.0 | -7.0 | -8.0 | 3.0 | 4.8 | -0.3 |
| 1991 | 1.3 | 9.7 | 3.2 | 1.2 | 0.5 | -3.4 | 7.2 | 2.2 | -0.9 | -2.1 | -5.7 | 3.0 |
| 1992 | 3.1 | -0.4 | -4.8 | 8.8 | 2.0 | -6.9 | -4.8 | -3.6 | 10.4 | 4.1 | 4.5 | 2.4 |
| 1993 | -1.4 | 2.2 | 0.4 | -2.3 | 1.0 | 2.1 | 0.9 | 5.9 | -2.0 | 4.4 | -0.1 | 7.9 |
| 1994 | 2.1 | -4.7 | -7.3 | 1.3 | -5.0 | -1.7 | 5.6 | 5.5 | -6.9 | 2.3 | -0.5 | -0.5 |
| 1995 | -2.4 | 0.6 | 4.3 | 2.5 | 3.2 | -0.1 | 4.5 | 0.4 | 0.9 | 0.6 | 3.8 | 0.7 |
| 1996 | 1.9 | -0.8 | -0.7 | 3.2 | -1.8 | -1.0 | -0.2 | 4.4 | 2.2 | 0.6 | 2.0 | 1.5 |
| 1997 | 3.8 | 0.8 | 0.1 | 2.9 | 4.2 | -0.4 | 6.6 | -1.8 | 8.9 | -7.7 | -0.2 | 6.3 |
| 1998 | 6.3 | 5.7 | 2.9 | -0.1 | -1.0 | -0.7 | 0.1 | -10.1 | -3.5 | 7.4 | 5.6 | 2.4 |
| 1999 | 0.2 | 4.7 | 1.9 | 4.1 | -5.0 | 1.5 | -1.4 | 0.2 | -3.5 | 3.7 | 5.5 | 5.0 |
| 2000 | -9.5 | -0.6 | 4.9 | -3.3 | 0.5 | -0.7 | 0.8 | 4.8 | -5.7 | 2.3 | -4.6 | 1.3 |
| 2001 | 1.2 | -6.0 | -4.8 | 5.9 | -2.9 | -2.7 | -2.0 | -3.3 | -8.3 | 2.8 | 3.3 | 0.3 |
| 2002 | -1.0 | -1.2 | 3.3 | -2.0 | -1.6 | -8.4 | -8.8 | -0.4 | -12.0 | 8.5 | 3.2 | -5.5 |
| 2003 | -9.5 | 2.5 | -1.2 | 8.7 | 3.1 | -0.4 | 3.1 | 0.1 | -1.7 | 4.8 | 1.3 | 3.1 |
| 2004 | -1.9 | 2.3 | -2.4 | 2.4 | -1.3 | 0.8 | -1.1 | 1.0 | 2.5 | 1.2 | 1.7 | 2.4 |
| 2005 | 0.8 | 2.4 | -1.5 | -1.9 | 3.4 | 3.0 | 3.3 | 0.3 | 3.4 | -2.9 | 2.0 | 3.6 |
| 2006 | 2.5 | 0.5 | 3.0 | 1.0 | -5.0 | 1.9 | -2.2 | | | | | |

## Mon
• New York Stock Exchange closed

# 15

Australian Tennis Open Begins
1535: Henry VIII declared himself head of the English Church.

## Tues

# 16

1868: The refrigerator car was patented by William Davis, a fish dealer in Detroit.

## Wed

# 17

1983: Britain's first breakfast news programme launched on BBC1.

## Thur

# 18

1644: Perplexed pilgrims in Boston reported America's first UFO sighting.

## Fri

# 19

1825: Ezra Daggett and nephew Thomas Kensett patented food storage in tin cans.

## Sat

# 20

1972: UK unemployment topped one million.

## Sun

# 21

1976: From London's Heathrow Airport and Orly Airport outside Paris, the first Concordes with commercial passengers simultaneously took flight.

"Economics is extremely useful as a form of employment for economists."
– *John Kenneth Galbraith*

---

Likely company announcements

### Interims

Bespak plc
Broker Network Holdings plc
DSG International plc
DTZ Holdings plc
Monsoon plc
Murgitroyd Group plc
Reflexion Cosmetics plc
PKL Holdings plcPace Micro
Technology plc
Scott Wilson Group plc
Spice Holdings plc
Twenty plc

### Finals

Wogen plc
Travelzest plc
SpaceandPeople plc
Sino-Asia Mining & Resources
Company plc
Reflexion Cosmetics plc
InvestinMedia plc
GW Pharmaceuticals plc
Galleon Holdings plc
Food & Drink Group (The) plc
Corporate Synergy Group plc

# Monthly comparative performance of the FTSE100 and FTSE250

The previous page showed the monthly changes of the FTSE100 Index. On this page, the table below shows the monthly out-performance of the FTSE100 Index over the mid-cap FTSE250 Index.

For example,

1. In Jan 1986, the FTSE100 Index increased 1.6%, while the FTSE250 Index increased 2.6%. The out-performance of the former over the latter was therefore -1.0%.

2. In Aug 1986, the FTSE100 Index increased 6.6%, while the FTSE250 Index increased 4.3%. The out-performance of the former over the latter was therefore 2.3%.

The cells are highlighted if the number is negative (i.e. the FTSE250 out-performs the FTSE100).

Monthly comparative performance of FTSE100 and FTSE250 indices

| | Jan | Feb | Mar | Apr | May | Jun | Jul | Aug | Sep | Oct | Nov | Dec |
|---|---|---|---|---|---|---|---|---|---|---|---|---|
| 1986 | -1.0 | -1.1 | 0.4 | -4.0 | -0.1 | -1.5 | -1.0 | 2.3 | -0.8 | -0.3 | -2.3 | 1.5 |
| 1987 | -1.8 | 2.6 | -2.1 | 1.3 | 1.3 | -4.8 | -2.7 | -0.1 | -1.3 | 2.6 | 1.0 | -4.1 |
| 1988 | -2.0 | -1.0 | -0.3 | -0.5 | -1.4 | -0.6 | -1.3 | 0.9 | 0.5 | -2.0 | 0.3 | 2.0 |
| 1989 | 1.3 | -3.6 | 1.5 | 2.8 | -1.3 | 2.6 | 0.1 | 3.2 | -2.1 | 2.2 | 2.6 | 1.8 |
| 1990 | -1.0 | 1.4 | 0.7 | -0.3 | 2.8 | -0.8 | 0.3 | 4.8 | 1.9 | -1.7 | 2.9 | -1.2 |
| 1991 | 2.7 | -4.8 | -1.4 | 1.6 | 2.2 | 0.0 | 2.0 | -1.9 | -1.9 | 0.4 | 0.4 | 4.0 |
| 1992 | -1.6 | -2.3 | -0.2 | -3.9 | -0.4 | 1.4 | 4.8 | 1.1 | 1.0 | -1.1 | -0.1 | -6.1 |
| 1993 | -4.6 | -0.6 | -2.0 | -3.1 | -0.1 | -0.1 | -1.3 | -0.3 | 0.2 | 1.6 | 1.1 | -0.9 |
| 1994 | -5.6 | -1.6 | -2.0 | 0.5 | 0.8 | 2.5 | -1.0 | 0.6 | 1.5 | 1.7 | 0.0 | -0.6 |
| 1995 | 1.3 | 0.2 | 2.8 | -0.3 | -0.3 | 1.5 | -2.0 | -1.9 | 0.0 | 2.0 | 2.2 | -0.9 |
| 1996 | -0.7 | -3.0 | -3.4 | -2.0 | -0.9 | 2.5 | 2.6 | 0.1 | 2.8 | -0.1 | 1.8 | 0.1 |
| 1997 | 1.5 | -0.5 | 1.8 | 4.5 | 4.2 | 1.1 | 5.2 | -4.3 | 3.9 | -3.8 | -0.5 | 3.5 |
| 1998 | 4.7 | -1.3 | -3.4 | -1.6 | -6.2 | 6.1 | 0.5 | 2.6 | 1.5 | 1.5 | 3.7 | 3.4 |
| 1999 | -3.3 | 0.3 | -2.4 | -2.8 | -1.4 | -2.4 | -3.3 | -0.6 | 2.0 | 4.9 | -4.7 | 1.0 |
| 2000 | -5.5 | -4.9 | 4.6 | 1.1 | 0.0 | -6.7 | -1.9 | 0.7 | -0.3 | 3.0 | -1.4 | -0.7 |
| 2001 | -1.7 | -4.7 | 3.5 | 0.8 | -5.4 | 1.5 | 1.4 | -3.9 | 8.1 | -2.0 | -5.8 | -1.3 |
| 2002 | 0.5 | -1.0 | -2.5 | -1.2 | -0.3 | 0.7 | 4.2 | -2.0 | -0.2 | 5.5 | 0.0 | -0.3 |
| 2003 | -2.5 | 1.9 | 0.8 | -2.2 | -6.6 | -3.5 | -4.2 | -4.9 | 0.7 | -0.1 | 1.5 | 1.5 |
| 2004 | -5.7 | -1.8 | -2.2 | 3.1 | 1.2 | -3.0 | 2.9 | 0.0 | -0.5 | 0.3 | -2.3 | -3.1 |
| 2005 | -2.5 | 1.2 | 0.2 | 3.7 | -2.3 | -0.6 | 0.1 | -1.6 | 0.8 | 0.1 | -6.0 | -2.0 |
| 2006 | -1.8 | -2.5 | -1.3 | 0.7 | 0.9 | 0.6 | -1.4 | | | | | |
| sum: | -1.4 | -1.3 | -0.3 | -0.1 | -0.6 | -0.2 | 0.2 | -0.3 | 0.9 | 0.7 | -0.3 | -0.1 |

## Observations

By looking at the clustering of the highlighted cells, it can be seen that:

1. The FTSE250 tends to out-perform the FTSE100 in the first half of the year, with the situation reversing in the second half.

2. The FTSE250 is particularly strong relative to the FTSE100 in January and February.

3. The FTSE100 is particularly strong relative to the FTSE250 in September and October.

## Mon
# 22

1979: A public sector strike paralysed the UK - the biggest mass stoppage since 1926.

## Tues  *
# 23

1973: US president, Richard Nixon, announced the Vietnam peace deal.

## Wed
# 24

1899: The rubber heel was patented by Humphrey O'Sullivan.

## Thur
# 25

Burns Night
1981: Dissident Labour MPs planned a new political party, to be called Social Democrats.

## Fri   *
# 26

1950: India became a republic.

## Sat
# 27
Holocaust Memorial Day
Australian Tennis Open, Women's Final
1710: Czar Peter the Great set first Russian state budget.

## Sun
# 28

Australian Tennis Open, Men's Final
1986: The American space shuttle, Challenger, exploded killing all seven astronauts on board.

Likely company announcements

### Interims

Aston Villa plc
Daejan Holdings plc
Fletcher King plc
Goodwin plc
Homestyle Group plc
IG Group Holdings plc
Misys plc
Renishaw plc
Stanley Leisure plc

### Finals

Beale plc
Bede plc
Crest Nicholson plc
Domino Printing Sciences plc
Howle Holdings plc
IONA Technologies plc
London Scottish Bank plc
Northern Rock plc
Porvair plc

"An economist is a surgeon with an excellent scalpel and a rough-edged lancet, who operates beautifully on the dead and tortures the living."

– Nicholas Chamfort

# The January predictor

Since 1971, in 26 years out of 35 (74%) the whole year followed the same direction as the market in January. Did this behaviour continue in 2005? The results can be seen in the table below. The columns are:

A:  FTSE100 change from 31 Dec (previous year) to 31 Jan.

B:  FTSE100 change from 31 Dec (previous year) to 31 Dec.

C:  Result of taking a position in the index on the first trading day after 31 January based on the direction of the market in January.

Performance of FTSE100 Index (1971-2005)

| Year | January change (%) | Year | | |
|---|---|---|---|---|
| change (%) | (A) | (B) | | (C) |
| 1971 | 1.0 | 39.9 | | 38.8 |
| 1972 | 4.0 | 6.1 | | 2.1 |
| 1973 | -8.4 | -31.9 | | 23.6 |
| 1974 | -8.1 | -53.1 | | 45.0 |
| 1975 | 46.8 | 132.8 | | 86.0 |
| 1976 | 11.1 | -5.6 | N | -16.7 |
| 1977 | 10.1 | 36.9 | | 26.8 |
| 1978 | -3.8 | 3.9 | N | -7.7 |
| 1979 | 0.6 | 5.2 | | 4.6 |
| 1980 | 9.2 | 27.1 | | 18.0 |
| 1981 | -1.5 | 5.7 | N | -7.2 |
| 1982 | 4.5 | 21.9 | | 17.4 |
| 1983 | 3.1 | 19.9 | | 16.8 |
| 1984 | 6.3 | 23.2 | | 16.9 |
| 1985 | 3.9 | 14.6 | | 10.7 |
| 1986 | 1.6 | 18.9 | | 17.3 |
| 1987 | 7.7 | 2.0 | | -5.7 |
| 1988 | 4.6 | 4.7 | | 0.1 |
| 1989 | 14.4 | 35.1 | | 20.7 |
| 1990 | -3.5 | -11.5 | | 8.0 |
| 1991 | 1.3 | 16.3 | | 15.1 |
| 1992 | 3.1 | 14.2 | | 11.0 |
| 1993 | -1.4 | 20.1 | N | -21.5 |
| 1994 | 2.1 | -10.3 | N | -12.5 |
| 1995 | -2.4 | 20.3 | N | -22.8 |
| 1996 | 1.9 | 11.6 | | 9.7 |
| 1997 | 3.8 | 24.7 | | 20.9 |
| 1998 | 6.3 | 14.5 | | 8.3 |
| 1999 | 0.2 | 17.8 | | 17.6 |
| 2000 | -9.5 | -10.2 | | 0.7 |
| 2001 | 1.2 | -16.2 | N | -17.4 |
| 2002 | -1.0 | -24.5 | | 23.5 |
| 2003 | -9.5 | 13.6 | N | -23.1 |
| 2004 | -1.9 | 7.5 | N | -9.5 |
| 2005 | 0.8 | 16.7 | | 15.9 |

## Observations

1.  The January Predictor has recently shown signs of failing (giving false signals in 2001, 2003 and 2004). However, the last signal in 2005 was good.

2.  Despite the strength of the signal it is difficult to profit from it, as often a large portion of the whole year's move occurs in January. A strategy of trading the signals every year from 1971 would have resulted in a total return of 1181% (not including transaction costs), against a total return in the FTSE100 Index of 1618% over the same period.

## Mon
# 29

1985: Oxford University delivered a stunning snub to the Prime Minister Margaret Thatcher, by refusing her an honorary degree.

## Tues
# 30

• FOMC meeting (tentative) until 31st January

1965: Thousands of people paid their last respects to Britain's greatest wartime leader, Sir Winston Churchill, who was buried after a full state funeral.

## Wed
# 31

1983: British drivers and front-seat passengers made to wear seatbelts, under a new law designed to reduce road deaths.

## Thur
# 1

1994: House of Commons MPs condemned the sale of Rover - the last major British car manufacturer.

## Fri
# 2

1802: First leopard was exhibited in Boston, US (admission 25¢).

## Sat
# 3

Rugby Union 6 Nations: Italy v France : England v Scotland
1988: Nurses across the UK took part in a day of industrial action, protesting for better pay.

## Sun
# 4

Rugby Union 6 Nations: Wales v Ireland
1920: First flight from London to South Africa took-off.

"Where facts are few, experts are many."
— *Donald R. Gannon*

---

Likely company announcements

### Interims

British Sky Broadcasting Group plc
BWA Group plc
Caffe Nero Group plc
City of London Investment Group plc
Core Business (The) plc
Filtronic plc
ITM Power plc
ISIS Medical Technology plc
Nadlan plc
SurfControl plc

### Finals

ARM Holdings plc
AstraZeneca plc
Chemring Group plc
Cosalt plc
Elan Corporation plc
Kensington Group plc
Rio Tinto plc
Royal Dutch Shell plc
Sanctuary Group (The) plc
Tadpole Technology plc
Wolfson Microelectronics plc

# February market

## Market performance in the month

February is a middling month for the market – ranking 8th of all months. On average the market rises 1.5% in the month which is strong, but there's also a fairly high standard deviation (meaning the returns vary a lot from year to year, as can be seen from the chart below). The market can be expected to show a positive return in February with a probability of 54%.

After January, February is the second best month for mid-cap stocks relative to the large caps. On average the FTSE250 Index outperforms the FTSE100 Index by 1.3% in this month.

Overall, a difficult market to call in any one year due to that large variation in returns. However, if an investor has been in the market to capture the good December and January months, and is waiting for the best month of all (April), then they would probably not gain much by selling out this month.

Historic performance of the market in February

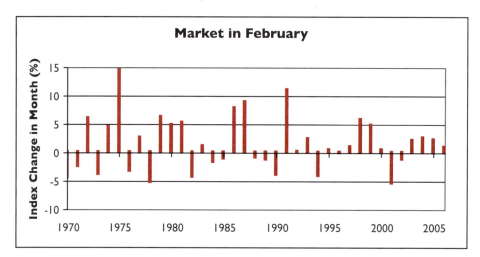

## Company announcements

Large companies reporting this month-

* *Finals*: Anglo American, BAE SYSTEMS, Barclays, BG Group, BP, Cadbury Schweppes, Centrica, GlaxoSmithKline, HSBC Holdings, Legal & General Group, Pearson, Reckitt Benckiser, Reed Elsevier, Rio Tinto, Rolls-Royce Group, Royal Bank of Scotland Group, Royal Dutch Shell, Standard Chartered, Unilever, WPP Group.

* *Interims*: BHP Billiton, British Sky Broadcasting Group, Diageo.

## What to look out for this month

* **9th strongest week** of the year for the market: week 5.

* The **FTSE250 is particularly strong relative to the FTSE100** in this month.

* The **MPC decision on interest rates** should be announced 12 noon on 7 February.

# FEBRUARY 2007

## Mon

# 5

1996: The first GM food went on sale in the UK.

## Tues

# 6

2005: Tony Blair marks 2,838 days in his post at Number 10, making him Labour's longest-serving PM.

## Wed

# 7

• MPC meeting (anticipated) until 8th February

1992: Maastricht treaties made the EU official.

## Thur

# 8

1952: Princess Elizabeth formally proclaimed herself Queen and Head of the Commonwealth and Defender of the Faith.

## Fri

# 9

1979: Football club Nottingham Forest clinched Britain's first £1m transfer deal.

## Sat

## 10

Rugby Union 6 Nations: England v Italy : Scotland v Wales
1952: Independent India's first general elections passed off peacefully and returned Prime Minister Jawaharlal Nehru to power.

## Sun

## 11

Rugby Union 6 Nations: Ireland v France
1975: The Conservative Party chose their first woman leader, Margaret Thatcher.

"An expert is a person who has made all the mistakes that can be made in a very narrow field."
– Niels Bohr

Likely company announcements

### Interims

Alumasc Group plc
Aquarius Platinum Ltd
Avingtrans plc
County Contact Centres plc
DICOM Group plc
EnCore Oil plc
McBride plc
Poole Investments plc
PZ Cussons plc
Regent Inns plc

### Finals

Alphameric plc
AMVESCAP plc
Autonomy Corporation plc
BG Group plc
BP plc
Carnival plc
GlaxoSmithKline plc
Imperial Chemical Industries plc
Pendragon plc
QA plc
Quantica plc
Randgold Resources Ltd
Reckitt Benckiser plc
Rolls-Royce Group plc
Smith & Nephew plc
Unilever plc
XP Power plc

# The quarterly sector strategy

The performance of the sectors in each quarter is analysed elsewhere in the Almanac. From the analysis it can be seen that the strongest sectors in the respective quarters are: Construction & Materials, Leisure Goods, Mining and Technology Hardware & Equipment.

The performance of these sectors, in their respective strong quarters, is shown in the table below.

|  | Sector | 1999 | 2000 | 2001 | 2002 | 2003 | 2004 | 2005 | 2006 |
|---|---|---|---|---|---|---|---|---|---|
| 1st Quarter | Construction & Materials |  | -9.1 | 2.2 | 14.6 | 1.7 | 9.1 | 8.4 | 15.1 |
| 2nd Quarter | Leisure Goods |  | 8.3 | 6.2 | 9.4 | 26.6 | 0.7 | -7.5 | 57.1 |
| 3rd Quarter | Mining | 8.3 | 0.9 | -19.9 | -19.7 | 17.6 | 17.2 | 31.1 |  |
| 4th Quarter | Technology Hardware & Equipment | 278.1 | -31 | 64.9 | -60.5 | 27.1 | 13.6 | 13.9 |  |

This behaviour suggests a strategy which cycles the portfolio through these four sectors throughout the year. In other words, the portfolio is 100% invested in the Construction & Materials sector from 31 December to 31 March, then switches into Leisure Goods to 31 June, then switches into Mining to 30 September, then switches into Technology Hardware & Equipment to 31 Dec, and then switches back into Construction & Materials and starts the cycle again.

The chart below illustrates the performance of such a strategy for the period 3rd Qtr 1999 to 2nd Qtr 2006, with a comparison to the FT All Share Index.

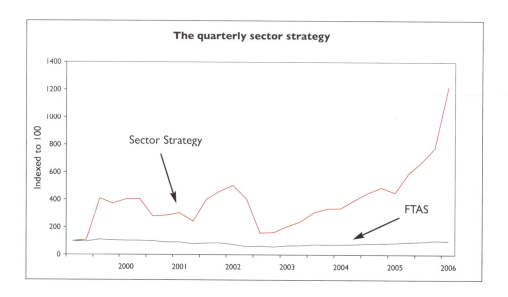

Over the 7 years the strategy would have grown £1000 into £12,190; while a £1000 investment in the FT All Share Index would have become just £1007.

## Mon

# 12

1994: Thieves stole one of the world's best-known paintings (Scream) from a gallery in the Norwegian capital, Oslo.

## Tues

# 13

1978: *Tomorrow's World* presenter, Anna Ford, was announced as ITN's first female newsreader.

## Wed

# 14

St. Valentine's Day
1989: Iranian Muslim leader Ayatollah Khomeini issued a death threat against British author Salman Rushdie and his publishers, over the book Satanic Verses.

## Thur

# 15

1882: The first cargo of frozen meat left New Zealand for Britain.

## Fri

# 16

1959: Fidel Castro became Cuba's youngest ever Prime Minister.

## Sat
# 17

1691: Thomas Neale was granted a British patent for American postal service.

## Sun
# 18

Chinese New Year
1900: Ajax soccer team was formed in Amsterdam.

---

Likely company announcements

### Interims

BHP Billiton plc
Diageo plc
Fiske plc
Hargreaves Services plc
Isotron plc
Jourdan plc
Macau Property Opportunities Fund Ltd
Northern Recruitment Group plc
Tristel plc
Ultrasis plc

### Finals

ARC International plc
Bradford & Bingley plc
Liberty International plc
Mariana Resources Ltd
Oxford Catalysts Group plc
Reed Elsevier plc
royalblue Group plc
St Modwen Properties plc
Work Group plc
Velti plc
Zetex plc

---

"If the world should blow itself up, the last audible voice would be that of an expert saying it can't be done."
— *Peter Ustinov*

# Correlation between UK and US markets

In general the UK stock market closely follows the movements of the US market. This can be seen on many days when the UK stock market will see large moves in the first half an hour or so, but then trade sideways waiting for the US market to open at 14h30.

The charts below show the correlation in weekly percentage moves between the S&P500 and FT All Share indices.

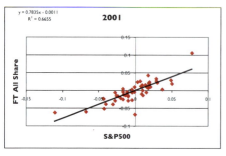

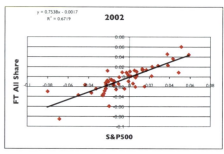

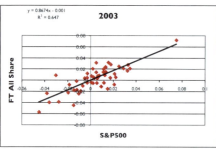

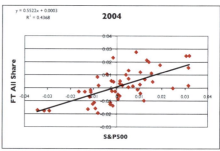

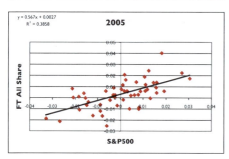

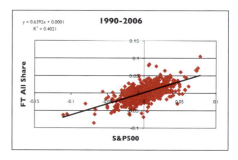

## Observations

1. The correlation of weekly movements changes significantly from year to year. In 2001 and 2002 the two markets were fairly closely correlated, with an R-Squared of 0.6 (R-Squared is a measure of how close the points are to the line of best fit). But in the three following years this correlation broke down, such that by 2005 the R-Squared had almost halved.

2. The final chart shows the overall correlation for the period 1990-2006, where the R-Squared is a low 0.4.

# FEBRUARY 2007

## Mon
- Hong Kong Stock Exchange closed
- New York Stock Exchange closed

# 19

1969: First test flight of Boeing 747 jumbo jet.

## Tues
- Hong Kong Stock Exchange closed

# 20

Shrove Tuesday
1986: The Soviets opened a new phase in space exploration with the launch of the world's biggest space station, Mir.

## Wed

# 21

Ash Wednesday
1991: George Bush threatened Iraq with land war.

## Thur

# 22

1997: A sheep named Dolly was cloned by scientists in Edinburgh.

## Fri

# 23

1743: Mayer Amschel Rothschild, founder of Europe's most prominent banking empire, was born.

## Sat
# 24

Rugby Union 6 Nations: Scotland v Italy : Ireland v England : France v Wales
1971: Commonwealth citizens lose their automatic right to remain in the UK, under the government's new Immigration Bill.

## Sun
# 25

The 79th Academy Awards will take place at the Kodak Theatre in Hollywood.
1972: Miners voted overwhelmingly in favour of a pay settlement, after a seven-week strike that seriously affected power supplies.

"If at first you don't succeed, failure may be your style."
– *Quentin Crisp*

---

Likely company announcements

### Interims

Amstrad plc
Antisoma plc
Brambles Industries plc
Compel Group plc
Galliford Try plc
Go-Ahead Group (The) plc
Haynes Publishing Group plc
Lincat Group plc
Macro 4 plc
PuriCore plc
Thorntons plc

### Finals

Allied Irish Banks plc
Anglo American plc
Associated British Ports Holdings plc
BAE SYSTEMS plc
Barclays plc
Cadbury Schweppes plc
Capita Group (The) plc
Centrica plc
Croda International plc
Davis Service Group (The) plc
Elementis plc
Hanson plc
Ladbrokes plc
McInerney Holdings plc
Millennium & Copthorne Hotels plc
Morgan Crucible Company (The) plc
Morgan Sindall plc
Rentokil Initial plc
Reuters Group plc
REXAM plc
Scarborough Minerals plc
Schroders plc
Scottish & Newcastle plc
SDL plc
Shire plc
Spirent Communications plc
Spring Group plc
Tomkins plc
Wimpey (George) plc

# March market

## Market performance in the month

March is another middling month for the market, ranking 7th of all months in performance. On average the market rises 0.6% this month (with a standard deviation of a fairly high 5.7).

The probability of a positive return in the month is 62%.

Historically, mid-cap stocks have performed marginally better than large cap stocks in March.

Historic performance of the market in March

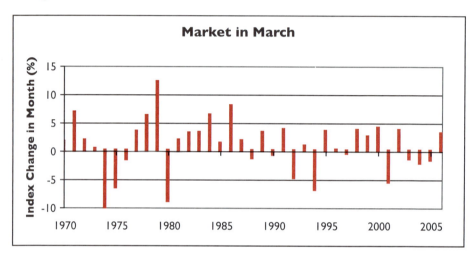

*Note*: In March 1974 the market fell 20.7%. As this distorts the chart, the Y-axis scale has been truncated at -10%.

## Company announcements

After September, March is the second busiest month for the announcement of company results. Over 300 finals and interims can be expected in the month.

Large companies reporting this month:

*   *Finals*: Aviva, British American Tobacco, Gallaher Group, HBOS, Kingfisher, Lloyds TSB Group, Prudential, Xstrata.

*   *Interims*: Wolseley

## What to look out for this month

*   The quarterly **FTSE100 Index review** should be implemented after market close 16 March (if any changes are made), with the announcement made about a week before this. (Don't forget: companies expelled from the Index often see their share price rise in the following weeks).
*   **9th weakest day** of the year: 12 Mar.
*   **3rd strongest week** of the year for the market: week 9; **6th weakest month** of the year: week 12; **7th weakest week** of the year: week 11.
*   **Triple witching** (derivatives contract expires) on 16 March.
*   The **MPC decision on interest rates** should be announced 12 noon on 7 March.
*   **Clocks go forward** one hour at 01h00 GMT, 25 March. Historically, the FTSE100 Index has risen slightly on the following Monday.

**Mon**

# 26

1987: The Church of England's General Synod voted by a huge majority, clearing the way for the ordination of women priests.

**Tues**

# 27

1953: The Simplified Spelling Bill — a proposal to simplify the English language - passed its second reading in parliament.

**Wed**

# 28

First edition of Henry Fielding's '*Tom Jones*' published.

**Thur**

# 1

St. David's Day
1966: The Chancellor of the Exchequer, James Callaghan, confirmed the "historic and momentous" decision to change over to decimal coinage in 5 years time.

**Fri**

# 2

1976: Walt Disney World welcomed its 50 millionth guest.

**Sat**
# 3

Total lunar eclipse (Through to the 4th)
1966: The BBC announced plans to begin broadcasting television programmes in colour from the following year.

**Sun**
# 4

1967: The first North Sea gas was pumped ashore at Easington, County Durham, by British Petroleum.

"If you want to know what God thinks of money, just look at the people he gave it to."
– Dorothy Parker

Likely company announcements

## Interims

Dechra Pharmaceuticals plc
FII Group plc
Freeport plc
Hays plc
London Finance & Investment Group
Mid-States plc
Morse plc
NXT plc
Pochin's plc
Ricardo plc
Trace Group plc
Wetherspoon (J D) plc

## Finals

Alliance & Leicester plc
Alliance UniChem plc
Arena Leisure plc
ARRIVA plc
Aviva plc
Bodycote International plc
British American Tobacco plc
Filtrona plc
Gallaher Group plc
Glanbia plc
HBOS plc
Henderson Group plc
Independent Media Distribution plc
InterContinental Hotels Group plc
Lloyds TSB Group plc
LogicaCMG plc
MFI Furniture Group plc
Michael Page International plc
Molins plc
Narborough Plantations plc
Old Mutual plc
Paddy Power plc
Pearson plc
Rotork plc
Royal Bank of Scotland Group (The)
Serco Group plc
SHL Group plc
St James's Place plc
Standard Chartered plc
Tarsus Group plc
Taylor Woodrow plc
TDG plc
Trinity Mirror plc
UK Coal plc
Ultra Electronics Holdings plc
United Business Media plc
William Hill plc
Wilson Bowden plc
WPP Group plc
Xstrata plc

# Market momentum (up) analysis

The table below displays the results of analysis on market momentum – the tendency of the market to increase in one period, having also risen in the previous period(s). Notes on the analysis-

1.  The index analysed was the FTSE All-Share. The number of observations to August 2006 (for each frequency) is indicated in column 0. For example, 9510 days to Aug 2006 (from Jan 1969) was the sample data for the "Daily" analysis.

2.  The first rows ("Total") of the columns display the number of consecutive periods that the index rose for that frequency. For example, the market rose 5036 days (out of the total 9510); 2860 times it rose on 2 consecutive days; and 269 times it rose 6 days in a row. The second rows ("% Total") express the first row as a percentage of the total sample. For example, the market rose 6 days in a row 2.8% of the whole period (9510 days).

3.  The rows "% 1 up" expresses the proportion of times that the market rose for n consecutive periods following the market rising for 1 period (expressed as a percentage of the number of times the market rose once). For example: after the market had risen for 1 day, the market rose for a second day in 56.8% of all cases; after the market had risen for 1 day, the market went on to rise 6 days consecutively in 5.3% of all cases.

4.  The subsequent rows display the tendency of the market to rise following n consecutive increases. For example: after the market has risen 4 days consecutively, the market rose for a 5th day in 55.6% of all cases; after the market had risen 3 years in a row, the market rose again the following year in 70.4% of all cases.

| Frequency | | 0 | 1 | 2 | 3 | 4 | 5 | 6 |
|---|---|---|---|---|---|---|---|---|
| Daily | Total | 9510 | 5036 | 2860 | 1591 | 885 | 492 | 269 |
| | % Total | | 53.0 | 30.1 | 16.7 | 9.3 | 5.2 | 2.8 |
| | % 1 up | | | 56.8 | 31.6 | 17.6 | 9.8 | 5.3 |
| | % 2 up | | | | 55.6 | 30.9 | 17.2 | 9.4 |
| | % 3 up | | | | | 55.6 | 30.9 | 16.9 |
| | % 4 up | | | | | | 55.6 | 30.4 |
| | % 5 up | | | | | | | 54.7 |
| Weekly | Total | 2170 | 1196 | 660 | 378 | 218 | 131 | 73 |
| | % Total | | 55.1 | 30.4 | 17.4 | 10.0 | 6.0 | 3.4 |
| | % 1 up | | | 55.2 | 31.6 | 18.2 | 11.0 | 6.1 |
| | % 2 up | | | | 57.3 | 33.0 | 19.8 | 11.1 |
| | % 3 up | | | | | 57.7 | 34.7 | 19.3 |
| | % 4 up | | | | | | 60.1 | 33.5 |
| | % 5 up | | | | | | | 55.7 |
| Monthly | Total | 727 | 448 | 285 | 181 | 118 | 79 | 52 |
| | % Total | | 61.6 | 39.2 | 24.9 | 16.2 | 10.9 | 7.2 |
| | % 1 up | | | 63.6 | 40.4 | 26.3 | 17.6 | 11.6 |
| | % 2 up | | | | 63.5 | 41.4 | 27.7 | 18.2 |
| | % 3 up | | | | | 65.2 | 43.6 | 28.7 |
| | % 4 up | | | | | | 66.9 | 44.1 |
| | % 5 up | | | | | | | 65.8 |
| Quarterly | Total | 425 | 252 | 148 | 86 | 56 | 36 | 24 |
| | % Total | | 59.3 | 34.8 | 20.2 | 13.2 | 8.5 | 5.6 |
| | % 1 up | | | 58.7 | 34.1 | 22.2 | 14.3 | 9.5 |
| | % 2 up | | | | 58.1 | 37.8 | 24.3 | 16.2 |
| | % 3 up | | | | | 65.1 | 41.9 | 27.9 |
| | % 4 up | | | | | | 64.3 | 42.9 |
| | % 5 up | | | | | | | 66.7 |
| Yearly | Total | 106 | 64 | 42 | 27 | 19 | 14 | 10 |
| | % Total | | 60.4 | 39.6 | 25.5 | 17.9 | 13.2 | 9.4 |
| | % 1 up | | | 65.6 | 42.2 | 29.7 | 21.9 | 15.6 |
| | % 2 up | | | | 64.3 | 45.2 | 33.3 | 23.8 |
| | % 3 up | | | | | 70.4 | 51.9 | 37.0 |
| | % 4 up | | | | | | 73.7 | 52.6 |
| | % 5 up | | | | | | | 71.4 |

The market would appear to display a degree of fractal behaviour, where its properties are similar whatever time-frame one looks at. Trends do seem to become more established the longer they last (i.e. the probability of the market rising in a year increases the longer the period of previous consecutive up years).

The market displays greater momentum for longer frequencies. For example, the market only rose 6 days consecutively 2.8% of the time, whereas it rose 6 years consecutively 9.5% of the time. In addition, the market rose for a 6th year (after 5 years of consecutive increases) 71.4% of the time, against just 55.0% for daily increases.

# March 2007

## Mon

# 5

1933: The day after becoming US President, Franklin Roosevelt declared a bank holiday - forcing the closure of banks and halted all financial transactions for four days.

## Tues

# 6

1899: Aspirin patented by Felix Hoffmann.

## Wed

• MPC meeting (anticipated) until 8th March

# 7

1854: Charles Miller patented the first US sewing machine to stitch buttonholes.

## Thur

# 8

1706: Vienna's Wiener Stadtbank established.

## Fri

# 9

1959: *Barbie*, the popular girls' doll, debuted - over 800 million sold.

## Sat

# 10

Rugby Union 6 Nations: Scotland v Ireland : Italy v Wales
1876: First telephone call made, from Alexander Graham Bell to Thomas Watson.

## Sun

# 11

Rugby Union 6 Nations: England v France, ICC Cricket World Cup Opening Ceremony
1996: EU Database Directive passed.

"I'm living so far beyond my income that we may almost be said to be living apart."
— *e e cummings*

---

Likely company announcements

### Interims

Centaur Media plc
Close Brothers Group plc
DX Services plc
ICM Computer Group plc
Mucklow (A & J) Group plc
Provalis plc
Redrow plc
Teesland plc
Town Centre Securities plc
Waterman Group plc

### Finals

4imprint Group plc
Acambis plc
Admiral Group plc
Aegis Group plc
Aggreko plc
Anglo Pacific Group plc
Ark Therapeutics Group plc
Avis Europe plc
Axis-Shield plc
Axon Group plc
Balfour Beatty plc
Benfield Group Ltd
Catlin Group Ltd
Corporate Services Group (The) plc
DMATEK Ltd
Drax Group plc
Gibbs and Dandy plc
Highway Insurance Holdings plc
HSBC Holdings plc
IMI plc
International Power plc
Irish Continental Group plc
Irish Life & Permanent plc
ITV plc
Jardine Lloyd Thompson Group plc
John Wood Group plc
Keller Group plc
Management Consulting Group plc
National Express Group plc
Premier Foods plc
Provident Financial plc
Rank Group (The) plc
Restaurant Group (The) plc
Royal & Sun Alliance Insurance Group
Savills plc
SIG plc
SOCO International plc
Travis Perkins plc
UMBRO plc
Vitec Group (The) plc

# Market momentum (down) analysis

The table on the previous page looked at market momentum for the market going up. The table below shows the results of analysis of market momentum when the market falls.

The structure of the table is similar to that on the previous page (where an explanation of the figures is given).

| Frequency | | 0 | 1 | 2 | 3 | 4 | 5 | 6 |
|---|---|---|---|---|---|---|---|---|
| Daily | Total | 9510 | 4458 | 2281 | 1150 | 561 | 269 | 129 |
| | % Total | | 46.9 | 24.0 | 12.1 | 5.9 | 2.8 | 1.4 |
| | % 1 down | | | 51.2 | 25.8 | 12.6 | 6.0 | 2.9 |
| | % 2 down | | | | 50.4 | 24.6 | 11.8 | 5.7 |
| | % 3 down | | | | | 48.8 | 23.4 | 11.2 |
| | % 4 down | | | | | | 48.0 | 23.0 |
| | % 5 down | | | | | | | 48.0 |
| Weekly | Total | 2170 | 971 | 433 | 210 | 107 | 53 | 29 |
| | % Total | | 44.7 | 20.0 | 9.7 | 4.9 | 2.4 | 1.3 |
| | % 1 down | | | 44.6 | 21.6 | 11.0 | 5.5 | 3.0 |
| | % 2 down | | | | 48.5 | 24.7 | 12.2 | 6.7 |
| | % 3 down | | | | | 51.0 | 25.2 | 13.8 |
| | % 4 down | | | | | | 49.5 | 27.1 |
| | % 5 down | | | | | | | 54.7 |
| Monthly | Total | 727 | 277 | 115 | 46 | 18 | 9 | 3 |
| | % Total | | 38.1 | 15.8 | 6.3 | 2.5 | 1.2 | 0.4 |
| | % 1 down | | | 41.5 | 16.6 | 6.5 | 3.2 | 1.1 |
| | % 2 down | | | | 40.0 | 15.7 | 7.8 | 2.6 |
| | % 3 down | | | | | 39.1 | 19.6 | 6.5 |
| | % 4 down | | | | | | 50.0 | 16.7 |
| | % 5 down | | | | | | | 33.3 |
| Quarterly | Total | 425 | 173 | 69 | 30 | 17 | 9 | 4 |
| | % Total | | 40.7 | 16.2 | 7.1 | 4.0 | 2.1 | 0.9 |
| | % 1 down | | | 39.9 | 17.3 | 9.8 | 5.2 | 2.3 |
| | % 2 down | | | | 43.5 | 24.6 | 13.0 | 5.8 |
| | % 3 down | | | | | 56.7 | 30.0 | 13.3 |
| | % 4 down | | | | | | 52.9 | 23.5 |
| | % 5 down | | | | | | | 44.4 |
| Yearly | Total | 106 | 42 | 20 | 8 | 2 | 0 | 0 |
| | % Total | | 39.6 | 18.9 | 7.5 | 1.9 | 0.0 | 0.0 |
| | % 1 down | | | 47.6 | 19.0 | 4.8 | 0.0 | 0.0 |
| | % 2 down | | | | 40.0 | 10.0 | 0.0 | 0.0 |
| | % 3 down | | | | | 25.0 | 0.0 | 0.0 |
| | % 4 down | | | | | | 0.0 | 0.0 |
| | % 5 down | | | | | | | 0.0 |

## Observations

1. Since 1969, the market has fallen 6 consecutive days on 129 occasions.

2. Since 1946 the market has only fallen 4 consecutive months on 18 occasions (2.5%). Random chance would suggest 6.25%.

3. Since 1900, the market has never fallen 5 consecutive years. The market has fallen for 3 consecutive years on 8 occasions, but having done so the market continued to fall for a 4th year only twice.

4. As with up markets (previous page), down markets appear to display a degree of fractal behaviour, where its properties are similar whatever time-frame one looks at.

5. Down markets display far less momentum tendency than that seen for up markets. For example, if the market rises for 3 consecutive months, there's a 65.2% probability that the market will continue to rise for a 4th month as well. However, if the market falls 3 consecutive months, there's only a 39.1% probability that the market will fall for a 4th month as well.

## Mon  *

# 12

1935: England established 30 mph speed limit for towns and villages.

## Tues

# 13

Horse Racing : Cheltenham Festival
1986: Microsoft has its initial public offering.

## Wed

# 14

1960: The British radio telescope at Jodrell Bank in Cheshire set a new space record, making contact with the American Pioneer V satellite at a distance of 407,000 miles.

## Thur

# 15

1906: Rolls Royce Ltd is registered.

## Fri

# 16

• Euronext.liffe stock options expiry
• Euronext.liffe UK USF expiry
• March Triple-Witching

1976: UK Prime Minister Harold Wilson resigns.

## Sat
# 17

Rugby Union 6 Nations: Italy v Ireland : France v Scotland : Wales v England
1845: The rubber band is invented.

## Sun
# 18

Mother's Day / Australian Grand Prix
1850: American Express founded.

"The only way not to think about money is to have a great deal of it."
– *Edith Wharton*

Likely company announcements

### Interims

Gondola Holdings plc
IAWS Group plc
Kier Group plc
Newcastle United plc
Northamber plc
Sinclair (William) Holdings plc
Smiths Group plc
Thor Mining plc
Wilmington Group plc

### Finals

888 Holdings plc
Alizyme plc
AMEC plc
Antofagasta plc
ArmorGroup International plc
BATM Advanced Communications Ltd
Bovis Homes Group plc
BPP Holdings plc
BRIT Insurance Holdings plc
Cairn Energy plc
Charter plc
Cookson Group plc
Costain Group plc
Countrywide plc
Dialight plc
Ennstone plc
Flying Brands Ltd
Foseco plc
French Connection Group plc
Grafton Group plc
Group 4 Securicor plc
Guinness Peat Group plc
Hiscox plc
Horizon Technology Group plc
Incisive Media plc
Informa plc
JKX Oil & Gas plc
Johnson Service Group plc
Laing (John) plc
Legal & General Group plc
Marshalls plc
McAlpine (Alfred) plc
Medical Solutions plc
Prudential plc
Psion plc
RPS Group plc
Shore Capital Group plc
SMG plc
UNITE Group plc

# The quarterly (weak) sector strategy

On the previous page we saw the performance of a strategy comprised of historically strong sectors through the calendar quarters. On this page we look at a strategy based on the quarterly weak sectors.

The weakest sectors in the respective quarters are: Technology Hardware & Equipment, Media, Nonlife Insurance, and Electricity.

The performance of these sectors, in their respective weak quarters, is shown in the table below.

| | Sector | 1999 | 2000 | 2001 | 2002 | 2003 | 2004 | 2005 | 2006 |
|---|---|---|---|---|---|---|---|---|---|
| 1st Quarter | Technology Hardware & Equipment | | -22.1 | -48.1 | -28.1 | 6.7 | -0.3 | -7.4 | 12.5 |
| 2nd Quarter | Media | | -8.7 | -8 | -22.8 | 24.1 | -1 | -4.8 | -3.9 |
| 3rd Quarter | Nonlife Insurance | -6.9 | 1.9 | -33.3 | -46.3 | -17.8 | -7.5 | 13.3 | |
| 4th Quarter | Electricity | -13.7 | 5.9 | -4.5 | 2 | 6.3 | 4.1 | -1.7 | |

This suggests a strategy which cycles a short trade through these four sectors throughout the year. In other words, the portfolio is short the Construction & Materials sector from 31 December to 31 March, it then closes the short and opens a new short in Leisure Goods to 31 June, then switches the short position to Mining to 30 September, then switches the short position to Technology Hardware & Equipment to 31 Dec, and then switches the short position back into Construction & Materials and starts the cycle again.

The chart below illustrates the performance of such a strategy for the period 3rd Qtr 1999 to 2nd Qtr 2006, with a comparison to the FT All Share Index.

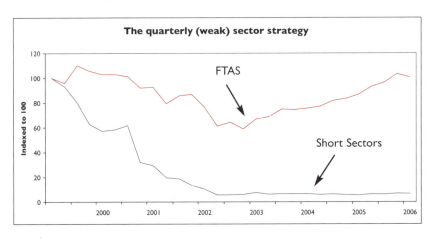

Over the 7 years the strategy would have ended with a value of 6.6 having started at an indexed 100 in 1999.

A composite strategy, with added zip, would combine the strategy here with that on the previous page. For example, in the first quarter the strategy would be long the Construction & Materials sector and short Technology Hardware & Equipment. The strategy for the whole year is shown in the table below.

| | Long this sector | Short this sector |
|---|---|---|
| 1st Quarter | Construction & Materials | Technology Hardware & Equipment |
| 2nd Quarter | Leisure Goods | Media |
| 3rd Quarter | Mining | Nonlife Insurance |
| 4th Quarter | Technology Hardware & Equipment | Electricity |

# MARCH 2007

## Mon
# 19

N. Ireland St. Patrick's Day
Partial solar eclipse
1831: The City Bank of New York became the site of the first bank robbery in US history – $245,000 was taken.

## Tues
# 20

• FOMC meeting (tentative) until 21st march

Vernal Equinox
1916: Albert Einstein published his theory of relativity.

## Wed
# 21

• Tokyo Stock Exchange closed

1963: Alcatraz Prison in San Francisco Bay closes down and transfers its last prisoners.

## Thur
# 22

1954: Closed since 1939, the London Bullion Market reopens.

## Fri ⬇
# 23

2006: Sony Computer Entertainment announced the end of production for the PlayStation.

## Sat
# 24

1972: The UK imposed direct rule over Northern Ireland.

## Sun
# 25

British Summer Time Begins
1996: The EU's Veterinarian Committee bans the export of British beef and its by-products as a result of BSE.

---

Likely company announcements

### Interims

Boustead plc
BNS Telecom Group plc
Cradley Group Holdings plc
Charlton Athletic plc
Herencia Resources plc
Loades plc
Palmaris Capital plc
Primary Health Properties plc
Sheffield United plc
Wolseley plc

### Finals

Abbot Group plc
AGA Foodservice Group plc
Asterand plc
Boustead plc
Capital & Regional plc
Chaucer Holdings plc
Collins Stewart Tullett plc
Derwent Valley Holdings plc
Dignity plc
Enterprise plc
Entertainment Rights plc
Evolution Group (The) plc
F&C Asset Management plc
Forth Ports plc
Friends Provident plc
Hardy Underwriting Group plc
Huntleigh Technology plc
Independent News & Media plc
Kesa Electricals plc
Kiln plc
Kingfisher plc
Lookers plc
Mallett plc
Menzies (John) plc
Morrison (Wm) Supermarkets plc
Next plc
Premier Oil plc
Prodesse Investment Ltd
ProStrakan Group plc
Regus Group plc
ROK plc
ServicePower Technologies plc
Slough Estates plc
Ted Baker plc
Trafficmaster plc
Weir Group plc
Wellington Underwriting plc

---

"Save a little money each month and at the end of the year you'll be surprised at how little you have."
– *Ernest Haskins*

# April market

## Market performance in the month

April is the star month of the year – the market is stronger in April than any other month. On average the market rises 2.8% (with a standard deviation of a relatively low 4.9).

The probability of a positive return in the month is a whopping 78%. From 1971, the market rose in April every year for 15 years – a recent record for any month. Although the number of years with negative returns in the month has been increasing lately.

In any one year the relative performance of large and mid-cap stocks can diverge significantly in this month, but overall mid-caps marginally out-perform large caps in this month.

## Six month effect

This is the last month in the six-month cycle (Nov-Apr) when stocks greatly outperform the May-Oct period. For investors impressed with this phenomenon, the end of April is the time to sell out, or reduce exposure to the market.

Historic performance of the market in April

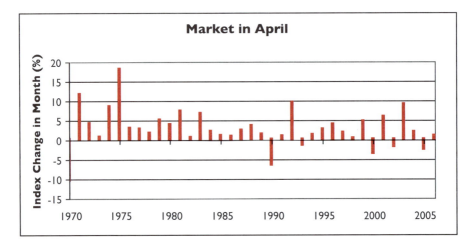

## Company announcements

Large companies reporting this month:

- *Finals*: Tesco.

- *Interims*: Associated British Foods, Imperial Tobacco Group.

## What to look out for this month

- Historic **strong sectors** in this second quarter are: Leisure Goods, Tobacco, and Personal Goods.

- Historic **weak sectors** in this second quarter are: Software & Computer Services, Technology Hardware & Equipment, and Media.

- **3rd weakest day** of the year: 8 Apr.

- **6th strongest week** in the year: week 17.

- The **MPC decision on interest rates** should be announced 12 noon on 4 April.

- **Holidays**: the LSE is closed 6th and 9th April.

# Mar/Apr 2007

## Mon
# 26

1996: The International Monetary Fund approves a $10.2 billion loan for Russia.

## Tues
# 27

1980: Silver Thursday market crash in the US.

## Wed
# 28

2006: At least 1 million union members, students and unemployed took to the streets in France, in protest at the government's proposed First Employment Contract law.

## Thur
# 29

1981: The first London marathon took place, with 6,700 participants taking part.

## Fri
# 30

1978: Saatchi & Saatchi got the job of revamping the Conservative Party image ahead of the General Election.

## Sat
# 31

1986: The Greater London Council was abolished.

## Sun
# 1

1999: A legally-binding minimum rate of pay was introduced in Britain for the first time.

"My problem lies in reconciling my gross habits with my net income."
– *Errol Flynn*

Likely company announcements

### Interims

ADVFN plc
Barratt Developments plc
Gleeson (M J) Group plc
IAF Group plc
Liberty plc
Marylebone Warwick Balfour Group plc
OEM plc
Plexus Holding plc
SCi Entertainment Group plc
Tenon Group plc
Tottenham Hotspur plc
White Young Green plc
Zyzygy plc

### Finals

Alexon Group plc
Alpha Airports Group plc
Barr (A G) plc
Berkeley Technology Ltd
Brixton plc
Burren Energy plc
Clarkson plc
Dana Petroleum plc
Delta plc
Development Securities plc
DRS Data & Research Services plc
GeneMedix plc
H.R.Owen plc
Hikma Pharmaceuticals plc
House of Fraser plc
Kazakhmys plc
Macfarlane Group plc
Metal Bulletin plc
MTL Instruments Group plc
North Midland Construction plc
Novae Group plc
Ottakar's plc
Parity Group plc
Pinewood Shepperton plc
Qualceram Shires plc
S & U plc
Simon Group plc
Sportech plc
Telspec plc
TT electronics plc
Tullow Oil plc
Vislink plc
Watermark Group plc
Woolworths Group plc

# Sector performance – second quarter

The table below shows the performance of sectors in the second quarter (31/3 – 30/6) of each year 2000-2006. The table is ranked by the final column – the average performance over the 7 years. For each year: the top 5 performing sectors are highlighted in red, the bottom 5 in grey.

| Sector | EPIC | 2000 | 2001 | 2002 | 2003 | 2004 | 2005 | 2006 | Average |
|---|---|---|---|---|---|---|---|---|---|
| Industrial Metals | NMX1750 | -5.4 | -2.8 | -2.3 | 1001.7 | -3.6 | -22.2 | 3.7 | 138.4 |
| Leisure Goods | NMX3740 | 8.3 | 6.2 | 9.4 | 26.6 | 0.7 | -7.5 | 57.1 | 14.4 |
| Tobacco | NMX3780 | 24.6 | 7.8 | 7.6 | 9.7 | 2.6 | 12.0 | -1.9 | 8.9 |
| Aerospace & Defence | NMX2710 | 15.1 | 7.6 | -1.6 | 24.1 | 10.4 | 10.6 | -10.3 | 8.0 |
| Personal Goods | NMX3760 | 24.1 | 14.1 | 1.8 | 7.3 | 15.4 | -2.0 | -6.9 | 7.7 |
| Industrial Engineering | NMX2750 | 8.1 | 14.8 | -10.2 | 23.1 | 5.2 | -2.3 | -0.7 | 5.4 |
| Beverages | NMX3530 | 16.5 | 10.4 | -4.1 | 2.1 | 6.3 | 10.5 | -4.2 | 5.4 |
| Nonlife Insurance | NMX8530 | 17.4 | 5.8 | -14.9 | 32.7 | -4.2 | 6.5 | -6.6 | 5.2 |
| Electricity | NMX7530 | 7.8 | 5.4 | -3.9 | 1.7 | 2.1 | 19.2 | 1.7 | 4.9 |
| Industrial Transportation | NMX2770 | 8.7 | -2.2 | -5.0 | 16.8 | 0.9 | 3.0 | 10.0 | 4.6 |
| Food & Drug Retailers | NMX5330 | 3.7 | 8.3 | -3.5 | 17.0 | 4.3 | -0.7 | 2.1 | 4.5 |
| Travel & Leisure | NMX5750 | -0.4 | 11.5 | -12.3 | 22.4 | 6.0 | 4.2 | -0.9 | 4.4 |
| Real Estate | NMX8730 | 9.1 | -0.1 | -1.0 | 17.4 | 3.4 | 6.5 | -5.1 | 4.3 |
| Pharmaceuticals & Biotechnology | NMX4570 | 10.3 | 5.4 | -16.9 | 11.2 | 1.8 | 10.8 | 4.2 | 3.8 |
| Oil & Gas | NMX0530 | 9.5 | 2.8 | -9.6 | 5.2 | 8.8 | 8.9 | -1.4 | 3.5 |
| Construction & Materials | NMX2350 | 6.6 | 8.8 | -6.5 | 21.2 | -2.8 | 4.5 | -8.2 | 3.4 |
| Automobiles & Parts | NMX3350 | 7.6 | -5.6 | -7.4 | 33.6 | 10.0 | 1.9 | -17.9 | 3.2 |
| Health Care Equip & Services | NMX4530 | 25.3 | 7.0 | -17.8 | 4.9 | 7.4 | 10.7 | -17.7 | 2.8 |
| General Retailers | NMX5370 | -0.2 | 0.9 | -12.7 | 26.1 | 9.7 | -3.6 | -0.5 | 2.8 |
| Food Producers | NMX3570 | 3.8 | 13.1 | 4.4 | -6.0 | 4.6 | 2.1 | -6.5 | 2.2 |
| Chemicals | NMX1350 | -4.0 | 4.5 | -3.9 | 13.5 | 3.2 | -0.5 | 0.8 | 1.9 |
| Banks | NMX8350 | -0.2 | 2.7 | -5.0 | 17.9 | -1.0 | 3.4 | -4.2 | 1.9 |
| General Financial | NMX8770 | 7.9 | 8.0 | -24.3 | 26.9 | -8.9 | 2.9 | -4.4 | 1.2 |
| Equity Investment Instruments | NMX8980 | 0.3 | 0.4 | -11.7 | 20.9 | -0.9 | 5.3 | -7.1 | 1.0 |
| Life Insurance | NMX8570 | 6.9 | 5.6 | -21.4 | 21.4 | 4.9 | -1.7 | -9.2 | 0.9 |
| Electronic & Electrical Equipment | NMX2730 | -4.6 | 1.6 | -26.3 | 51.2 | -1.1 | -14.5 | -7.3 | -0.1 |
| Mining | NMX1770 | 2.9 | 6.4 | -9.9 | 1.4 | -6.5 | 2.1 | 0.5 | -0.4 |
| Support Services | NMX2790 | 2.1 | -1.9 | -14.0 | 16.3 | -2.1 | 0.3 | -8.2 | -1.1 |
| Media | NMX5550 | -8.7 | -8.0 | -22.8 | 24.1 | -1.0 | -4.8 | -3.9 | -3.6 |
| Fixed Line Telecommunications | NMX6530 | -23.9 | -15.4 | -26.8 | 10.6 | -3.8 | 1.0 | 6.4 | -7.4 |
| Technology Hardware & Equip | NMX9570 | 3.2 | -26.1 | -44.6 | 36.1 | -0.9 | -13.2 | -6.4 | -7.4 |
| Software & Computer Services | NMX9530 | -32.6 | -14.3 | -37.9 | 47.4 | -6.7 | 5.4 | -14.4 | -7.6 |

## Observations

1. The general clustering of red highlights at the top of the table, and grey at the bottom, suggests that certain sectors consistently perform well (or badly) in this quarter.

2. The **strong sectors** in this quarter are: Leisure Goods, Tobacco, and Personal Goods.

3. The **weak sectors** in this quarter are: Software & Computer Services, Technology Hardware & Equipment, and Media.

# APRIL 2007

## Mon
# 2

1962: A new style of pedestrian crossing caused confusion among both drivers and pedestrians, following its launch in London.

## Tues
# 3

1954: Oxford won the 100th Boat Race.

## Wed
# 4

• MPC meeting (anticipated) until 5th April

1973: *The World Trade Center* in New York was officially dedicated.

## Thur
# 5

• Hong Kong Stock Exchange closed

Golf : The Masters, Augusta National, Georgia (5th-8th April)
1976: Eccentric American billionaire Howard Hughes died aged 70.

## Fri
# 6

• London Stock Exchange closed
• Hong Kong Stock Exchange closed
• New York Stock Exchange closed

Good Friday Bank Holiday (UK)
1980: *Post It Notes* are introduced.

## Sat
# 7

Oxford v Cambridge University Boat Race Horse Racing : Aintree Grand National
1999: The US claimed 'banana war' victory over Europe, after The World Trade Organisation ruled in favour of them in their long-running trade dispute.

## Sun  *
# 8

Malaysian Grand Prix
1986: Actor Clint Eastwood voted mayor of Californian town, Carmel.

"Money frees you from doing things you dislike. Since I dislike doing nearly everything, money is handy."
– *Groucho Marx*

---

**Likely company announcements**

### Interims

Air Partner plc
Ardent Group plc
Bellway plc
Charteris plc
COE Group plc
Egdon Resources plc
Manganese Bronze Holdings plc
Max Petroleum plc
Multi Group plc
Next Fifteen Communications Group plc

### Finals

Agcert International plc
Alea Group Holdings (Bermuda) Ltd
AutoLogic Holdings plc
Bloomsbury Publishing plc
Boot (Henry) plc
Chesnara plc
Gaskell plc
Havelock Europa plc
Headlam Group plc
Mayflower Corporation plc
Melrose Resources plc
MSB International plc
Resolution plc
Signet Group plc
Whatman plc

# Ten baggers

The term *ten bagger* was coined by Peter Lynch, the legendary manager of the Fidelity Magellan fund, in his classic book *One Up on Wall Street*. Ten-bagger comes from baseball, and Lynch used it to describe stocks that rise ten times in value.

The table below shows the UK stocks that rose ten times or more from July 1996 to July 2006.

UK ten baggers July 1996 – July 2006

| Company | EPIC | Price Increase(%) | P/E | Capital (£m) | Sector |
|---|---|---|---|---|---|
| Anglo Irish Bank Corporation PLC | ANGL | 3,049 | 16 | 5,514 | Banks |
| Numis Corporation PLC | NUM | 2,021 | 13 | 283 | General Financial |
| Tarsus Group PLC | TRS | 1,741 | 21 | 97 | Media |
| DTZ Holdings PLC | DTZ | 1,411 | 17 | 334 | Real Estate |
| Man Group PLC | EMG | 1,387 | 14 | 7,704 | General Financial |
| Clarke (T) PLC | CTO | 1,386 | 22 | 102 | Construction & Materials |
| Workspace Group PLC | WKP | 1,301 | 6 | 644 | Real Estate |
| Capita Group (The) PLC | CPI | 1,300 | 27 | 3,267 | Support Services |
| Savills PLC | SVS | 1,271 | 16 | 692 | Real Estate |
| Albemarle & Bond Holdings PLC | ABM | 1,212 | 23 | 91 | General Financial |
| Enterprise Inns PLC | ETI | 1,209 | 16 | 3,081 | Travel & Leisure |
| Bloomsbury Publishing PLC | BMY | 1,204 | 16 | 235 | Media |
| Kingspan Group PLC | KGP | 1,129 | 21 | 1,551 | Construction & Materials |
| McCarthy & Stone PLC | MCTY | 1,124 | 13 | 1,114 | Household Goods |
| Ben Bailey PLC | BBC | 1,096 | 6 | 51 | Household Goods |
| Grafton Group PLC | GFTU | 1,025 | 16 | 1,613 | Support Services |
| Amstrad PLC | AMT | 997 | 11 | 151 | Leisure Goods |
| ROK PLC | ROK | 917 | 13 | 161 | Construction & Materials |
| Goodwin PLC | GDWN | 904 | 18 | 45 | Industrial Engineering |

## Observations

1.  The table above does not include those companies that rose ten times in the interim, only to see their share prices fall back again. Of course, during the dot com boom, this included quite a few companies.

2.  Jim Slater's comment that "elephants don't gallop" would seem to hold true. Many of the above ten baggers are small companies - even after rising ten times in value. As Lynch says, "The very best way to make money in a market is in a small growth company that has been profitable for a couple of years and simply goes on growing."

3.  The sectors best represented in the list are not the exotic (e.g. mining) or those usually regarded as high growth (e.g. IT or telecoms), but the unglamorous construction, finance and real estate sectors. Again, an observation supported by Lynch who says, "If you stay half-alert, you can pick the spectacular performers right from your place of business or out of the neighbourhood shopping mall, and long before Wall Street discovers them."

# April 2007

**Mon**
- London Stock Exchange closed
- Hong Kong Stock Exchange closed

## 9

Easter Monday Bank Holiday (UK)
2003: Saddam statue topples with regime in Baghdad, Iraq.

**Tues**
## 10

1998: Northern Ireland peace deal reached.

**Wed**
## 11

1957: The island of Singapore is granted self-government from Britain, to come into effect the following year.

**Thur**
## 12

1961: The Soviet Union won the space race, by putting the first man into space - Major Yuri Alexeyevich Gagarin.

**Fri**
## 13

1997: Tiger Woods won his first major golfing trophy, The US Masters - at 21, he became the youngest player to do so.

**Sat**
## 14

1970: A critical explosion crippled the spacecraft, Apollo 13.

**Sun**
## 15

Bahrain Grand Prix
1755: Samuel Johnson's A Dictionary of the English Language published in London.

"If you can count your money, you don't have a billion dollars."
— J. Paul Getty

Likely company announcements

**Interims**

ADDleisure plc
Brinkley Mining plc
FishWorks plc
Formscan plc
St Ives plc
W H Smith plc

**Finals**

Anglo-Eastern Plantations plc
Ashley (Laura) Holdings plc
Austin Reed Group plc
Bioquell plc
Charles Taylor Consulting plc
CHE Hotel Group plc
Corin Group plc
I S Solutions plc
IFG Group plc
Moss Bros Group plc
Severfield-Rowen plc
UCM Group plc

# Daily volatility of the FTSE100 Index

*Volatility is an often used – and often misunderstood – term.*

The chart below shows the daily percentage performance of the FTSE100 Index from 1984 to 2006.

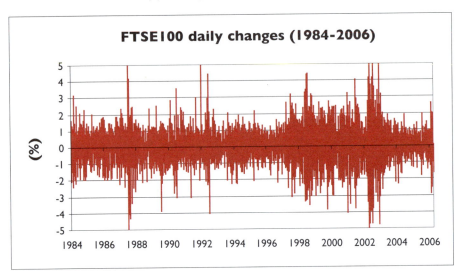

From 1984 to 2006 (a period comprising approximately 5630 trading days), the FTSE100 Index increased an average of 0.035% each day. This is equivalent to 2.1 FTSE100 points when the index is at the 6000 level.

However, as can be seen from the chart, the daily changes often diverged greatly from the average (and in fact the index changed by exactly 2.1 points on only 7 days in the past 22 years).

A measure of how much the actual daily changes diverged from the calculated mean (average) can be calculated. This measure is called the standard deviation. The interpretation of *standard deviation* is: 68% of all the data lie between two levels:

- the *lower* level given by the mean minus the standard deviation figure, and

- the *upper* level given by the mean plus the standard deviation figure.

In the case here, the standard deviation is calculated to be 1.023. This means that **68% of all daily changes in the FTSE100 lie between -0.982% (0.035-1.023) and 1.058% (0.035+1.023)**.

This analysis can be crudely checked by looking at the chart above, where it seems reasonable to accept that 68% of all daily changes were between -0.982% and 1.058%. When the index is at the level of 6000, this translates into saying that 68% of all daily changes are between down 58.9 points and up 63.5 points.

The interpretation of standard deviation can be extended to also say that 95% of all data lies within 2 standard deviations (i.e. the mean +/- 2 x standard deviation). In the case the FTSE100: 95% of all daily returns are between -2.005% (120 points) and 2.081% (124.9 points).

## Defining Volatility

Standard deviation is a statistical calculation that can be used to analyse the variability of many different types of data. In the financial markets, standard deviation is often used to calculate the *volatility* of prices.

Volatility is used to describe the likely variance of actual returns away from the historic mean. If a series of prices has a low volatility, then it is likely that returns will be close to the average. If the volatility is high, one can have less confidence that returns will be close to the historic average.

## Mon

# 16

1953: Queen Elizabeth II launched the Royal Yacht, *Britannia*.

## Tues

# 17

1969: 21-year old, Bernadette Devlin, became Britain's youngest-ever woman MP.

## Wed

# 18

1956: British Chancellor Harold Macmillan unveiled the premium bond scheme.

## Thur

# 19

1933: President Franklin Roosevelt announced that the US would be abandoning the gold standard.

## Fri

# 20

1972: Apollo 16 landed safely on the Moon, after an engine crisis.

## Sat

# 21

1948: 1st Polaroid camera is sold in US.

## Sun

# 22

Flora London Marathon
1990: The Big Number Change takes place in the UK, when dialling codes were updated.

"A large income is the best recipe for happiness I ever heard of."
– *Jane Austen, Mansfield Park*

Likely company announcements

**Interims**

Associated British Foods plc
Island Oil & Gas plc
Mediasurface plc
Telephone Maintenance Group plc

**Finals**

BNB Recruitment Solutions plcDragon Oil plc
Emerald Energy plc
Huntsworth plc
International Molybdenum plc
JJB Sports plc
Landround plc
PGI Group plc
Portmeirion Group plc
SkyePharma plc
Tesco plc

# Sinclair numbers – daily performance

The two tables below list the historic 10 best/worst days for the market.

For example, according to the analysis, historically the very best day of the whole year has been 28 December, when the market has risen on average 89% of all years. On this day the market has risen on average 0.4%, with a relatively low standard deviation (0.5).

Conversely, the very worst day of the year is 20 September (the market has only risen one in five years on this day).

The performance figures below are ranked by the Up(%) – the percentage of years that the market has historically risen on the day.

10 best performing days in the year

| Day | Up(%) | Avg Change(%) | StdDev |
|---|---|---|---|
| 28 Dec | 89 | 0.4 | 0.5 |
| 28 Jul | 87 | 0.4 | 0.4 |
| 16 Dec | 81 | 0.7 | 0.8 |
| 31 Oct | 81 | 0.6 | 0.6 |
| 29 Jul | 81 | 0.6 | 1.5 |
| 02 Aug | 81 | 0.6 | 0.9 |
| 24 Dec | 81 | 0.2 | 0.6 |
| 26 Jan | 80 | 0.5 | 0.8 |
| 27 Dec | 80 | 0.5 | 1.2 |
| 29 Dec | 80 | 0.3 | 1.2 |

10 worst performing days in the year

| Day | Up(%) | Avg Change(%) | StdDev |
|---|---|---|---|
| 08 Sep | 20 | -0.4 | 0.6 |
| 30 May | 21 | -0.4 | 1.3 |
| 08 Apr | 21 | -0.4 | 0.6 |
| 14 Apr | 21 | -0.3 | 0.9 |
| 25 Oct | 25 | -0.5 | 0.7 |
| 09 Sep | 25 | -0.4 | 0.5 |
| 10 Dec | 25 | -0.3 | 0.7 |
| 08 Jul | 25 | -0.2 | 0.8 |
| 12 Mar | 27 | -0.6 | 1.4 |
| 23 Jan | 27 | -0.4 | 0.8 |

Note: The above best days for the market are marked on the diary pages with a red star by the day of the week, and worst days are marked with a black star.

## Analysis of Up-Days

| | |
|---|---|
| Average Up(%) | 53 |
| Standard deviation | 13 |

On average, for any particular day, the market can be expected to rise 53% of the time.

The standard deviation is 13, which means that:

- days that have an Up(%) **over 66** (the average plus one standard deviation) can be considered strong days, and

- days that have an Up(%) **under 40** (the average minus one standard deviation) can be considered weak days.

## Mon
# 23

St. George's Day
1968: The UK produced its first decimalised coins - a 5p and a 10p coin.

## Tues
# 24

1913: The skyscraper *Woolworth Building* in New York City was opened.

## Wed
# 25

1961: Robert Noyce is granted a patent for an integrated circuit.

## Thur
# 26

1928: Madame Tussaud's waxworks exhibition opened in London.

## Fri
# 27

1992: Betty Boothroyd elected as the new Speaker of the House of Commons.

## Sat
# 28

2001: A Californian businessman became the first paying passenger to go into outer space.

## Sun
# 29

1974: President Richard Nixon announced the release of edited transcripts of White House tape recordings, related to the Watergate Scandal.

---

Likely company announcements

### Interims

Carr's Milling Industries plc
Carter & Carter Group plc
Clarkson Hill Group (The) plc
Clinton Cards plc
Fibernet Group plc
Imperial Tobacco Group plc
McCarthy & Stone plc
Mouchel Parkman plc
Smart (J) & Co (Contractors) plc

### Finals

Alexandra plc
Aminex plc
Atrium Underwriting plc
Camellia plc
Clinical Computing plc
Culver Holdings plc
Emblaze Ltd
European Motor Holdings plc
Fortune Oil plc
GAME Group (The) plc
Gresham Computing plc
Harvey Nash Group plc
Hitachi Capital (UK) plc
Instore plc
Kenmare Resources plc
Lambert Howarth Group plc
Pacific Media plc
Panther Securities plc
R.E.A. Holdings plc
Ross Group plc
South Wharf plc
Superscape Group plc
Vanco plc
Venture Production plc
Whitbread plc

---

"Do not be fooled into believing that because a man is rich he is necessarily smart. There is ample proof to the contrary."
– *Julius Rosenwald*

# May market

## Market performance in the month

This is the start of the under-performing half of the year. There are only three months where, since 1970, the market has an average return of below zero – this is one of them (the others are June and September). On average the market falls 0.6% in the month (with a relatively low standard deviation of 4.6).

The probability of a positive return in the month is below 50%, at 43%.

After a large fall in 2006, May is now challenging September to become the weakest month of the year. So, not a good month for investors.

However, the month *is* good for mid-cap stocks relative to large caps. On average the FTSE250 Index outperforms the FTSE100 Index by 0.6% in the month.

Historic performance of the market in May

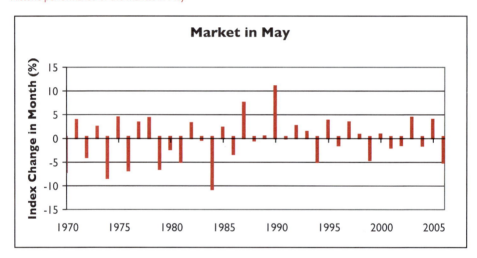

## Company announcements

Large companies reporting this month:

- Finals: BAA, BT Group, GUS, Land Securities Group, Marks & Spencer Group, National Grid, O2, SABMiller, Scottish & Southern Energy, Scottish Power, Vodafone Group.

- Interims: Compass Group.

## What to look out for this month

- Around the second week of May, the **annual changes to the MSCI UK Index** are announced. Companies joining the Index usually see their share price rise between the announcement date and implementation date (about two weeks later).

- **2nd weakest day** of the year for the market: 7 May.

- **4th weakest week** in the year: week 21.

- The **MPC decision on interest rates** should be announced 12 noon on 2 May.

- **Holidays**: the LSE is closed 7 and 28 May.

## Mon
# 30

1993: The World Wide Web was born at CERN.

## Tues
# 1

• Hong Kong Stock Exchange closed

1927: The first cooked meals on a scheduled flight are introduced, on an Imperial Airways flight from London to Paris.

## Wed
# 2

• MPC meeting (anticipated) until 3rd May

1997: The Labour Party's Tony Blair came to power, ending 18 years of Conservative rule.

## Thur
# 3

• Tokyo Stock Exchange closed

Parliamentary election in Scotland and an assembly election in Wales.
1955: Britain's first independent television station went on air, ending the BBC's 18-year monopoly.

## Fri
# 4

• Tokyo Stock Exchange closed

2000: Ken Livingstone was voted London mayor.

## Sat
# 5

1949: The Council of Europe is formed.

## Sun
# 6

Presidential election in France.
1840: The Penny Black postage stamp is valid for use in the UK and Ireland.

"Be rich to yourself and poor to your friends."
– *Juvenal (55 AD - 127 AD)*

---

Likely company announcements

### Interims

Aberdeen Asset Management plc
Debenhams plc
easyJet plc
Formation Group plc
Global Gaming Technologies plc
John Lewis of Hungerford plc
St James's Energy plc
Lonmin plc
Meriden Group plc
Numis Corporation plc
York Pharma plc

### Finals

Babcock International Group plc
Bisichi Mining plc
Blacks Leisure Group plc
Braemar Seascope Group plc
Braime (T F & J H) (Holdings) plc
Donegal Creameries plc
El Oro and Exploration Company plc
Eurotunnel plc
John David Group plc
London & Associated Properties plc
Matalan plc
Tex Holdings plc

# MSCI Index changes

When it comes to stock market indices, FTSE isn't the only player. Its great competitor is Morgan Stanley Capital International with their series of MSCI indices. Over $3 trillion of funds are believed to be benchmarked against MSCI's global indices.

MSCI index reviews are based on a combination of factors, including: the free float of a company's shares in issue, the average daily volume, market capitalisation and the existing representation of the company's industry group and home country in the MSCI indices. (Further information: www.msci.com).

## Profiting from the annual reviews

The MSCI full country index review occurs once a year in May. An announcement is usually made mid-May, and the index changes implemented at the end of May. Between these two dates lies the trading opportunity, as funds re-balance their portfolios.

On 10 May 2006, MSCI announced that nine stocks would be added to the MSCI United Kingdom Index. The performance between the announcement and implementation (31 May) is shown in the table below:

MSCI UK Index changes, May 2006

| Company | EPIC | 10 May 05 | 31 May 06 | Change (%) |
|---------|------|-----------|-----------|------------|
| Carphone Warehouse Group | CPW | 3.6075 | 3.24 | -10.2 |
| Charter | CHTR | 8.405 | 8.195 | -2.5 |
| Collins Stewart Tullett | CSTL | 7.94 | 7.18 | -9.6 |
| CSR (GB) | CSR | 14.79 | 14.48 | -2.1 |
| Investec plc | INVP | 32.39 | 28.7 | -11.4 |
| Michael Page | MPI | 4.02 | 3.955 | -1.6 |
| Partygaming | PRTY | 1.51 | 1.3 | -13.9 |
| Sportingbet | SBT | 4.265 | 4.2125 | -1.2 |
| Xstrata | XTA | 23.98 | 21.3 | -11.2 |
| FTSE100 | UKX | 6083.4 | 5723.8 | -5.9 |

## Failure

In previous years trading the MSCI index reviews has been a reliable strategy. However, the strategy would have failed in 2006. On average, the stocks decreased -7.1% in the two week period, compared with a decrease of -5.9% in the FTSE100 Index.

The cause for the failure was probably an unfortunate coincidence: that one day after the MSCI reviews were announced on 10 May, markets fell worldwide, resulting in a very weak market for the month of May. The nine stocks added to the MSCI review were candidates in the first place for their previous growth, but were therefore also likely to suffer most from any market correction.

So, 2006 was most likely an anomaly and the strategy will most probably be profitable in the future. But it does demonstrate that not even the most reliable of strategies are completely risk-free!

Source: "The UK Trader's Bible" by Dominic Connolly

## Mon
# 7

• London Stock Exchange closed

Bank Holiday (UK)
*2006: Rolling Stone magazine publishes its 1000th issue.*

## Tues
# 8

*2000: The Tate Modern, the world's largest modern art gallery, opened its doors to the media in London.*

## Wed
# 9

• FOMC meeting (tentative)

VE Day
*1901: Australia opens its first parliament in Melborne.*

## Thur
# 10

*1994: Nelson Mandela became South Africa's first black president.*

## Fri
# 11

*2000: The last performance of Cats in London's West End.*

## Sat
# 12

*2000: Ford confirmed that car production at its Dagenham plant was to end, after more than 70 years.*

## Sun
# 13

Spainish Grand Prix
*1912: The Royal Flying Corps (now the Royal Air Force) was established.*

"Lack of money is no obstacle. Lack of an idea is an obstacle."
*– Ken Hakuta*

---

Likely company announcements

### Interims

Anglo Irish Bank Corporation plc
BOC Group (The) plc
Dimension Data Holdings plc
Diploma plc
Fenner plc
Phytopharm plc
Sage Group (The) plc
Titon Holdings plc
United Drug plc

### Finals

3i Group plc
Brown (N) Group plc
C&C Group plc
Findel plc
Hemscott plc
JS Real Estate plc
Ormonde Mining plc
Pubs 'N' Bars plc
Sports Network Group plc
Tersus Energy plc

# Day of the the week performance

*Is the performance of the FTSE100 Index affected by the day of week?*

The table below shows the results of analysis on daily data for the FTSE100 Index since 1984 (comprising approximately 1150 weeks).

- Column B: number of weeks where the index increased on the day
- Column C: number of weeks where the index decreased on the day
- Column D: column B expressed as a percentage of the total
- Column E: average index change for the day

| Day | Up | Down | Up(%) | Avg Chng(%) |
|-----|-----|------|-------|-------------|
| (A) | (B) | (C) | (D) | (E) |
| Monday | 530 | 521 | 50.4 | -0.024 |
| Tuesday | 611 | 530 | 53.5 | 0.045 |
| Wednesday | 595 | 553 | 51.8 | 0.022 |
| Thursday | 596 | 552 | 51.9 | 0.035 |
| Friday | 627 | 498 | 55.7 | 0.089 |

The proportion of days where the index rose (column D) is displayed in the chart below.

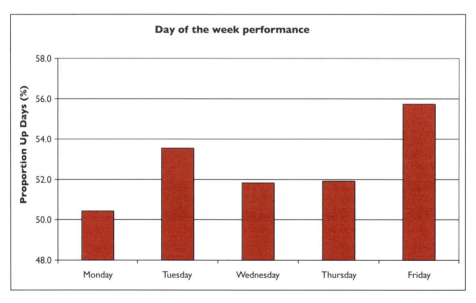

## Observations

1. The weakest day of the week can be quite clearly seen as Monday. The market is only up on 50% of Mondays and it is the only day with a negative average change.

2. The strongest day is clearly Friday: up 55% of all weeks, with an average increase of 0.089%.

3. The second strongest day is Tuesday, which can probably be explained as bounce-back effect after the weak Mondays.

# May 2007

## Mon
# 14

1889: The children's charity, NSPCC, was launched in London.

## Tues
# 15

2004: The largest known prime number (at the time of its discovery) was found by Josh Findley and the GIMPS collaborative effort.

## Wed
# 16

UEFA Cup Final to be held at Hampden Park, Glasgow
1965: Campbell Soup Company introduced *SpaghettiO*'s under its Franco-American brand.

## Thur
# 17

1955: Prime Minister Sir Anthony Eden presented the largest-scale election broadcast ever seen on television.

## Fri
# 18

1998: The United States Department of Justice and 20 US states filed an antitrust case against Microsoft.

## Sat
# 19

Rugby Union: Heineken Cup Final
1997: Labour announce that the sponsorship of sports events by tobacco firms was to be outlawed.

## Sun
# 20

1874: Levi Strauss and Jacob Davis receive a US patent for blue jeans, with copper rivets.

"It is pretty hard to tell what does bring happiness; poverty and wealth have both failed."
— *Kin Hubbard*

Likely company announcements

### Interims

Baggeridge Brick plc
Cardiff Property (The) plc
Compass Group plc
De Vere Group plc
Enodis plc
Enterprise Inns plc
Euromoney Institutional Investor plc
Holidaybreak plc
Howle Holdings plc
Jersey Electricity Company (The) Ltd
Jessops plc
RM plc
ScS Upholstery plc

### Finals

AVEVA Group plc
BAA plc
Big Yellow Group plc
Boots Group plc
BT Group plc
Castings plc
DCC plc
eircom Group plc
FirstGroup plc
Investec plc
Land Securities Group plc
Luminar plc
MICE Group plc
National Grid plc
Phoenix IT Group plc
Rensburg Sheppards plc
Robert Wiseman Dairies plc
SABMiller plc
Sainsbury (J) plc
Torotrak plc
VT Group plc

# The Friday-Monday strategy

On the previous page we saw that the strongest day of the week for the FTSE100 Index is historically Friday and the weakest day is Monday. This suggests a strategy: going long of the FTSE100 at the close on Thursdays, reversing the position at close on Friday (i.e. closing the long position and opening a short position), and then closing the short position at close on Monday.

The table below shows the results by year of applying the strategy every week since 1984.

| Year | Average Profit (%) | Profitable Trades (%) |
|------|------|------|
| 1984 | 0.123 | 47 |
| 1985 | 0.196 | 57 |
| 1986 | 0.269 | 66 |
| 1987 | 0.646 | 70 |
| 1988 | 0.311 | 61 |
| 1989 | 0.451 | 70 |
| 1990 | 0.153 | 57 |
| 1991 | -0.076 | 49 |
| 1992 | 0.204 | 47 |
| 1993 | -0.136 | 48 |
| 1994 | 0.020 | 52 |
| 1995 | 0.096 | 54 |
| 1996 | 0.143 | 64 |
| 1997 | -0.132 | 47 |
| 1998 | -0.368 | 37 |
| 1999 | -0.067 | 48 |
| 2000 | 0.336 | 57 |
| 2001 | -0.277 | 49 |
| 2002 | 0.353 | 55 |
| 2003 | 0.032 | 43 |
| 2004 | 0.112 | 50 |
| 2005 | 0.134 | 57 |
| 2006 | 0.177 | 54 |
| *average:* | 0.117 | 54 |

For example, if the strategy had been traded every week in 1984, the average profit per two-day trade (i.e. each week) would have been 0.123%, and for the whole year 47% of the weeks would have been profitable.

The average weekly profitability of the strategy since 1984 is shown in the chart below.

## Observations

1. Over the whole 23 year period, the average profit per week would have been 0.117%.

2. Over the 23 years, the strategy would have been profitable for 17 years and unprofitable for 6 years - although, only for two years (1998 and 2001) would the strategy have been significantly unprofitable.

3. During the period 1984-1990, the strategy was continuously profitable, then from 1991 to 2001 the profitability fluctuated from positive to negative. Since 2002 the strategy has been continuously profitable again.

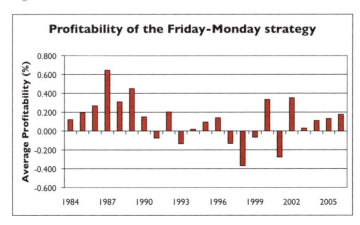

# May 2007

## Mon
### 21

1958: It was announced that an automated telephone connection (Subscriber Trunk Dialling) will be introduced in December, to make calls easier and cheaper.

## Tues
### 22

Senior PGA Golf Championship (until the 27th)
1936: Air Lingus is founded by the Irish government as the national airline for the Republic of Ireland.

## Wed
### 23

The UEFA Champions League 2006-07 season final will be held in the Olympic Stadium in Athens, Greece.
2003: The Euro exceeded its initial trading value, as it hit $1.18 for the first time since its introduction in 1999.

## Thur
### 24

• Hong Kong Stock Exchange closed

1976: The London to Washington DC Concorde service began.

## Fri
### 25

2006: Kenneth Lay and Jeff Skilling are convicted for their roles in the collapse of American energy company, Enron Corporation.

## Sat
### 26

The 2007 Isle of Man TT will take place, the event's 100th anniversary. (Through to June 8th)
1896: Charles Dow published the first edition of the Dow Jones Industrial Average.

## Sun
### 27

French Tennis Open begins / Monaco Grand Prix
1955: The Conservatives won the general election with a clear majority, ending a five-year political stalemate.

"Money can't buy happiness, but neither can poverty."
– Leo Rosten

---

Likely company announcements

### Interims

Arla Foods UK plc
Avon Rubber plc
Brewin Dolphin Holdings plc
Britvic plc
Cambridge Antibody Technology Group plc
Care UK plc
Chrysalis Group plc
Daily Mail and General Trust plc
Eurodis Electron plc
Ferraris Group plc
Innovation Group (The) plc
ITE Group plc
Mitchells & Butlers plc
Nord Anglia Education plc
Optos plc
Paragon Group of Companies (The) plc
Punch Taverns plc
Topps Tiles plc
Windsor plc

### Finals

Alterian plc
British Airways plc
British Land Co plc
BTG plc
Burberry Group plc
Business Post Group plc
Cable and Wireless plc
ClinPhone plc
Dairy Crest Group plc
De La Rue plc
EMAP plc
EMI Group plc
Great Portland Estates plc
GUS plc
Homeserve plc
Imagination Technologies Group plc
Invensys plc
Kelda Group plc
Kingston Communications (Hull) plc
Land of Leather Holdings plc
Liontrust Asset Management plc
London Stock Exchange plc
Marks & Spencer Group plc
MITIE Group plc
Mothercare plc
PayPoint plc
QXL ricardo plc
Scottish Power plc
Sondex plc
SSL International plc
Tate & Lyle plc
Viridian Group plc
Yell Group plc

# June market

## Market performance in the month

The weak month of May is followed by an almost equally weak June – this is traditionally a bad period for investors. June is the 3rd worst month in the year for the market. On average the market has fallen 0.9% in June (with a standard deviation of a relatively low 4.6).

The probability of a positive return in the month is a lowly 46%, although the market recently has been improving in the month – rising for the last 4 years.

Mid-cap stocks perform marginally better than large caps in June, but only to a small degree.

Summary: a quick glance at the chart below clearly demonstrates that this is not a good month for investors.

Historic performance of the market in June

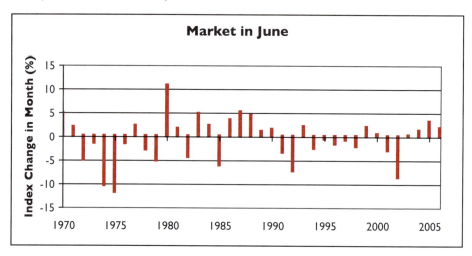

## Company announcements

Large companies reporting this month:

* Finals: United Utilities.

* Interims: Carnival.

## What to look out for this month

* The quarterly **FTSE100 Index review** should be implemented after market close 15 June (if any changes are made), with the announcement made about a week before this. (Don't forget: companies expelled from the Index often see their share price rise in the following weeks).

* **Triple witching** (derivatives contract expires) on 15 June.

* The **MPC decision on interest rates** should be announced 12 noon on 6 June.

* Celebrate **Tax Freedom Day** – when you stop working for the government and start working for yourself.

**Mon**
- London Stock Exchange closed
- New York Stock Exchange closed

# 28

Bank Holiday (UK)
1937: The Golden Gate Bridge in San Francisco, California was officially opened by President Franklin D. Roosevelt - who pushed a button in Washington DC.

**Tues**

# 29

1990: Boris Yeltsin was elected President of Russia.

**Wed**  *

# 30

1871: The Paris Commune fell.

**Thur**

# 31

2004: A foul-up during a routine software update at The Royal Bank of Canada led to a three-day misplacement of 10 million account balances.

**Fri**

# 1

1495: First written record of Scotch Whiskey appeared in the Exchequer Rolls of Scotland.

**Sat**
# 2

1953: Queen Elizabeth II was crowned at a coronation ceremony in Westminster Abbey, London.

**Sun**
# 3

1957: Noel Coward returned to Britain from the West Indies, amid criticism that he was living abroad to avoid paying income tax.

"Riches cover a multitude of woes."
– Menander (342 BC - 292 BC), Lady of Andros

---

Likely company announcements

## Interims

Abacus Group plc
API Group plc
Deep-Sea Leisure plc
Diablo Group plc
Food & Drink Group (The) plc
Innovata plc
Intec Telecom Systems plc
International Medical Devices plc
RWS Holdings plc
MedOil plc
Shaftesbury plc
Southern Cross Healthcare Group plc
Sumus plc

## Finals

AWG plc
Bank of Ireland (Governor & Co of)
BSS Group plc
Domestic & General Group plc
Electrocomponents plc
Expro International Group plc
Hornby plc
ICAP plc
Johnson Matthey plc
Man Group plc
Northern Foods plc
Pennon Group plc
Plasmon plc
Quintain Estates & Development plc
Scottish & Southern Energy plc
Shanks Group plc
Speedy Hire plc
TTP Communications plc
United Utilities plc
Vedanta Resources plc
Vodafone Group plc

# Performance focus on the FTSE All-Share Index

The FTSE All-Share is the aggregation of the FTSE100, FTSE250 and FTSE Small Cap indices. Effectively, all those LSE listed companies with a market capitalisation above the lower limit for inclusion in the FTSE Small Cap Index. The FTSE All-Share Index is the standard benchmark for measuring the performance of the broad UK market.

### Yearly data

| | |
|---|---|
| Data starts | 1693 (313 years) |
| Largest one year rise | 136.3% (1975) |
| Largest one year fall | -55.3% (1974 |
| Average annual change (Standard deviation) | 2.6% (15.7) |
| Number of times the index has risen 3 years in a row (last time) | 65 (2003-2005) |
| Number of times the index has risen 5 years in a row (last time) | 25 (1995-1999) |
| Number of times the index has risen 7 years in a row (last time) | 8 (1983-1989) |
| Most number of consecutive years risen | 13 (1977-1989) |
| Number of times the index has fallen 3 years in a row (last time) | 29 (2000-2002) |
| Number of times the index has fallen 4 years in a row (last time) | 11 (1900-1903) |
| Number of times the index has fallen 5 years in a row (last time) | 3 (1899-1903) |
| Number of times the index has fallen 6 years in a row | 0 |

### Monthly data

| | |
|---|---|
| Data starts | 1946 (726 months) |
| Largest one month rise | 52.7% (Jan 1975) |
| Largest one month fall | -26.6% (Oct 1987) |
| Average monthly change (Standard deviation) | 0.72% (5.2) |
| Number of times the index has risen 6 months in a row (last time) | 52 (Nov 05 – Apr 06) |
| Number of times the index has risen 8 months in a row (last time) | 16 (Dec 86 – Jul 87) |
| Number of times the index has risen 10 months in a row (last time) | 6 (Oct 86 – Jul 87) |
| Most number of consecutive months risen | 12 (Jun 53 – May 54) |
| Number of times the index has fallen 4 months in a row (last time) | 18 (Jun 02 – Sep 02) |
| Number of times the index has fallen 6 months in a row (last time) | 3 (Apr 02 – Sep 02) |
| Number of times the index has fallen 7 months in a row | 0 |

### Daily data

| | |
|---|---|
| Data starts | 2 Jan 1969 (9510 days) |
| Largest one day rise | 9.4% (24 Jan 75) |
| Largest one day fall | -11.2% (20 Oct 87) |
| Average daily change (Standard deviation) | 0.03% (1.02) |
| Number of times the index has risen 5 days in a row | 492 |
| Number of times the index has risen 8 days in a row (last time) | 84 (16 Dec 05 – 29 Dec 05) |
| Number of times the index has risen 10 days in a row (last time) | 26 (20 Dec 03 – 5 Jan 04) |
| Most number of consecutive days risen | 18 (19/12/86 – 16/01/87) |
| Number of times the index has fallen 5 days in a row | 267 |
| Number of times the index has fallen 8 days in a row (last time) | 23 (16 Jan 03 – 27 Jan 03) |
| Number of times the index has fallen 10 days in a row (last time) | 7 (14 Jan 03 – 27 Jan 03) |
| Most number of consecutive days fallen | 13 (6 Jun 74 – 24 Jun 74) |

# JUNE 2007

## Mon

# 4

1991: Defence Secretary Tom King confirmed that Britain was to reduce the amount it spends on the army by more than a quarter, over the next five years.

## Tues

# 5

1992: New figures showed the number of people having their water supplies cut off for failing to pay their bills had almost trebled in a year.

## Wed

# 6

• MPC meeting (anticipated) until 7th June

The 33rd G8 summit will take place in Heiligendamm, Germany. (Through to June 8th)
1975: British voters backed the UK's continued membership of the EEC by two-to-one in a nationwide referendum.

## Thur

# 7

1956: Sony Corporation unveiled the videocassette recorder (VCR).

## Fri

# 8

1824: Washing machine patented by Noah Cushing, of Quebec.

## Sat

# 9

1975: The first live transmission from the House of Commons was broadcast by BBC Radio and commercial stations.

## Sun

# 10

Canadian Grand Prix
2000: London's Millennium Bridge was closed for safety checks, after large crowds caused it to sway violently.

"No matter how rich you become, how famous or powerful, when you die the size of your funeral will still pretty much depend on the weather."
– Michael Pritchard

---

Likely company announcements

### Interims

Advanced Smartcard Technologies plc
Contemporary Enterprises plc
Dawson Holdings plc
Dewhurst plc
Future plc
Greencore Group plc
Internet Business Group plc
Renew Holdings plc
Theratase plc
Victrex plc

### Finals

AEA Technology plc
Caffyns plc
Carphone Warehouse Group (The) plc
Chapelthorpe plc
Charles Stanley Group plc
Chloride Group plc
Danka Business Systems plc
Dee Valley Group plc
Detica Group plc
e2v technologies plc
FKI plc
GB Group plc
Glotel plc
Halfords Group plc
Hampson Industries plc
Helical Bar plc
Intelek plc
Intermediate Capital Group plc
McKay Securities plc
Northumbrian Water Group plc
Penna Consulting plc
Protherics plc
QinetiQ Group plc
Queen's Walk Investment Ltd
RPC Group plc
Ryanair Holdings plc
Scapa Group plc
Severn Trent plc
Telecom plus plc
UMECO plc
Uniq plc
Vp plc
Wagon plc
Walker Crips Weddle Beck plc
Wincanton plc

# Performance focus on the FTSE100 Index

The FTSE100 Index comprises 100 of the top capitalised stocks listed on the LSE, and represents approximately 80% of the total market (by capitalisation). It is market capitalisation weighted, and the composition of the index is reviewed every three months. The index was first calculated on 3 January 1984 with a base value of 1000.

### Yearly data

| | |
|---|---|
| Data starts | 1970 (36 years) |
| Largest one year rise | 132.8% (1975) |
| Largest one year fall | -53.1% (1974) |
| Average annual change (Standard deviation) | 11.8% (28.7) |
| Number of times the index has risen 5 years in a row | 10 |
| Number of times the index has risen 10 years in a row | 4 |
| Most number of consecutive years risen | 13 (1977 – 1989) |
| Number of times the index has fallen 2 years in a row (last time) | 3 (2001 - 2002) |
| Number of times the index has fallen 3 years in a row (last time) | 1 (2000 – 2002) |

### Monthly data

| | |
|---|---|
| Data starts | Jan 1970 (438 months) |
| Largest one month rise | 46.8% (Jan 75) |
| Largest one month fall | -26.0% (Oct 87) |
| Average monthly change (Standard deviation) | 0.79% (5.97) |
| Number of times the index has risen 8 months in a row (last time) | 12 (Nov 82 – Jun 83) |
| Number of times the index has risen 10 months in a row (last time) | 5 (Sep 82 – Jun 83) |
| Number of times the index has risen 12 months in a row | 1 (Jul 82 – Jun 83) |
| Number of times the index has fallen 3 months in a row (last time) | 26 (Jul 02 – Sep 02) |
| Number of times the index has fallen 4 months in a row (last time) | 10 (Jun 02 – Sep 02) |
| Number of times the index has fallen 5 months in a row (last time) | 4 (May 02 – Sep 02) |
| Number of times the index has fallen 6 months in a row | 1 (Apr 02 – Sep 02) |

### Daily data

| | |
|---|---|
| Data starts | 2 Apr 1984 (5629 days) |
| Largest one day rise | 7.9% (21 Oct 87) |
| Largest one day fall | -12.2% (20 Oct 87) |
| Average daily change (Standard deviation) | 0.03% (1.02) |
| Number of times the index has risen 5 days in a row | 200 |
| Number of times the index has risen 8 days in a row (last time) | 19 (22 Dec 03 – 5 Jan 04) |
| Number of times the index has risen 11 days in a row (last time) | 2 (17 Dec 03 – 5 Jan 04) |
| Number of times the index has fallen 5 days in a row | 106 |
| Number of times the index has fallen 8 days in a row (last time) | 6 (16 Jan 03 – 27 Jan 03) |
| Number of times the index has fallen 11 days in a row | 1 (13 Jan 03 – 27 Jan 03) |

# JUNE 2007

## Mon
# 11

1987: Margaret Thatcher won a record third term as Britain's Prime Minister.

## Tues
# 12

1915: One of America's first families of industry and wealth grew a touch larger, with the birth of David Rockefeller.

## Wed
# 13

1825: Walter Hunt from New York took just 3 hours to design, sketch and patent the safety pin. He then sold the rights for $400, in order to pay a $15 debt.

## Thur
# 14

US Open Golf Tournament until 17th
1839: The first Henley Regatta took place on the Thames in London.

## Fri
# 15

- Euronext.liffe stock options expiry
- Euronext.liffe UK USF expiry
- June Triple-Witching

1924: The Ford Motor Company announced completion of their 10 millionth motor car.

## Sat
# 16

1903: Henry Ford formed his motor manufacturing company, with himself in the position of Chief Engineer and holding a quarter of the company shares.

## Sun
# 17

Father's Day / United States Grand Prix
1972: Five men were caught breaking into the offices of the Watergate complex in Washington DC, beginning one of the biggest political scandals in American history.

"It is better to have a permanent income than to be fascinating."
– Oscar Wilde, The Model Millionaire, 1912

---

Likely company announcements

### Interims

ATH Resources plc
Carnival plc
Compass Finance Group plc
Farley Group plc
First Choice Holidays plc
Glen Group plc
Grainger Trust plc
Helphire Group plc
MyTravel Group plc
Red Squared plc

### Finals

Carclo plc
Celsis International plc
Chamberlin & Hill plc
City of London Group plc
CML Microsystems plc
Fuller Smith & Turner plc
Hyder Consulting plc
IFX Group plc
Latchways plc
London Merchant Securities plc
Oxford Instruments plc
Patientline plc
Renovo Group plc
Triad Group plc
Volex Group plc
Waterford Wedgwood plc
Workspace Group plc

# Performance focus on the FTSE250 Index

Similar in construction to the FTSE100, except it comprises the next 250 highest capitalised stocks listed on the LSE after the top 100. The index is sometimes referred to as the index of mid-capitalised stocks, and comprises approximately 18% of the total market capitalisation.

### Yearly data

| | |
|---|---|
| Data starts | 1985 (21 years) |
| Largest one year rise | 34.3% (2003) |
| Largest one year fall | -27.3% (2002) |
| Average annual change (Standard deviation) | 11.0% (17.4) |
| Number of times the index has risen 3 years in a row | 8 |
| Number of times the index has risen 4 years in a row | 4 |
| Number of times the index has risen 6 years in a row | 1 |
| Number of times the index has fallen 2 years in a row (last time) | 1 (2001 – 2002) |
| Number of times the index has fallen 3 years in a row | 0 |

### Monthly data

| | |
|---|---|
| Data starts | Jan 86 (246 months) |
| Largest one month rise | 14.5% (Feb 91) |
| Largest one month fall | -28.7% (Oct 87) |
| Average monthly change (Standard deviation) | 0.91% (5.2) |
| Number of times the index has risen 5 months in a row (last time) | 27 (Dec 05 – Apr 06) |
| Number of times the index has risen 10 months in a row (last time) | 4 (Nov 92 – Aug 93) |
| Number of times the index has risen 12 months in a row | 1 (Sep 92 – Aug 93) |
| Number of times the index has fallen 3 months in a row (last time) | 15 (Mar 04 – May 04) |
| Number of times the index has fallen 4 months in a row (last time) | 4 (Apr 02 – Jul 02) |
| Number of times the index has fallen 5 months in a row | 0 |

### Daily data

| | |
|---|---|
| Data starts | 2 Jan 86 (5193 days) |
| Largest one day rise | 7.4% (10 Apr 92) |
| Largest one day fall | -11.3% (20 Oct 87) |
| Average daily change (Standard deviation) | 0.04% (0.79) |
| Number of times the index has risen 10 days in a row (last time) | 77 (20 May 05 – 3 Jun 2005) |
| Number of times the index has risen 15 days in a row (last time) | 18 (22 Feb 99 – 12 Mar 99) |
| Number of times the index has risen 20 days in a row (last time) | 2 (31 Jul 96 – 28 Aug 96) |
| Number of times the index has risen 21 days in a row | 0 |
| Number of times the index has fallen 5 days in a row | 169 |
| Number of times the index has fallen 8 days in a row (last time) | 19 (20 Jan 03 – 29 Jan 03) |
| Number of times the index has fallen 10 days in a row (last time) | 4 (11 Jun 98 – 24 Jun 98) |
| Number of times the index has fallen 12 days in a row | 0 |

# JUNE 2007

## Mon
# 18

1997: The National Trust won a National Lottery grant for £47,500 to restore Sir Paul McCartney's former council house in Allerton, Liverpool – where he composed the first Beatles' songs.

## Tues
# 19

• Hong Kong Stock Exchange closed

1997: Fast food chain McDonald's won a partial victory in its epic libel trial against two environmental campaigners.

## Wed
# 20

1995: Oil giant Shell caved in to international pressure and abandoned plans to dump the Brent Spar oil rig at sea.

## Thur
# 21

Longest Day
1991: The chairman of British Gas came under fire for accepting a pay rise ten times the rate of inflation.

## Fri
# 22

1994: The Daily Telegraph announced a reduction in price from 48p, to 30p. The Times was already selling at 30p.

## Sat
# 23

1994: A £78,000 rebate was sent by Thames Water to the Queen, after the company overestimated the bill for the Royal Mews.

## Sun
# 24

1989: Avon became the first big cosmetics firm to stop testing on animals - with the British Union for the Abolition of Vivisection declaring it a 'breakthrough'.

"Money is the opposite of the weather. Nobody talks about it, but everybody does something about it."
– Rebecca Johnson, in 'Vogue'

### Likely company announcements

**Interims**

Cagney plc
CareTech Holdings plc
Crest Nicholson plc
Electronic Data Processing plc
Griffin Group plc
GW Pharmaceuticals plc
InvestinMedia plc
Nasstar plc
Research Now plc
White Star Property Holdings plc

**Finals**

600 Group (The) plc
Acal plc
Atkins (W S) plc
BPB plc
British Energy Group plc
Cropper (James) plc
DSG International plc
Dyson Group plc
European Colour plc
Halma plc
Kewill Systems plc
Mountview Estates plc
Stewart & Wight plc
Thus Group plc
Tribal Group plc
Trifast plc
Victoria plc
Warner Estate Holdings plc

# July market

## Market performance in the month

Following May and June, July is another poor month for investors – capping the worst 3-month stretch for the market. On average the market increases 0.2% in July (with a standard deviation of a relatively low 4.2).

The probability of a positive return is 51%.

Over the longer term the performance of mid and large cap stocks is similar this month.

So, not a month to get excited by. A glance at the chart below shows the very unpredictable market in July.

Historic performance of the market in July

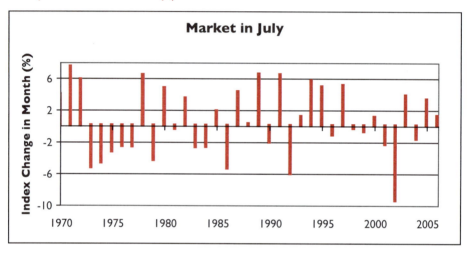

## Company announcements

Large companies reporting this month-

- *Interims:* AstraZeneca, BG Group, BP, British American Tobacco, Cadbury Schweppes, Centrica, GlaxoSmithKline, Legal & General Group, Lloyds TSB Group, Pearson, Prudential, Reckitt Benckiser, Reed Elsevier, Rolls-Royce Group, Royal Dutch Shell.

## What to look out for this month

- Historic **strong sectors** in this third quarter are: Mining, Personal Goods, and Leisure Goods.

- Historic **weak sectors** in this third quarter are: Nonlife Insurance, Media, and Travel & Leisure.

- **2nd strongest day of the year** for the market: 28 July; **5th strongest day** of the year for the market: 29 Jul; **7th weakest day** of the year for the market: 8 Jul.

- **4th strongest week** of the year: week 30; **2nd weakest week of the year** for the market: week 29.

- The **MPC decision on interest rates** should be announced 12 noon on 4 July.

## Mon

# 25

Lawn Tennis Championships at Wimbledon until the 8th July
1953: The first passenger flew commercially around the world in less than 100 hours.

## Tues

# 26

1498: The toothbrush was invented in China.

## Wed

# 27

• FOMC meeting (tentative) until 28th June

1967: The first cash dispenser in Britain became operational at a branch of Barclay's.

## Thur

# 28

1997: The government said that it was considering the return of free milk for school children, over 20 years after it was abolished by education minister Margaret Thatcher.

## Fri

# 29

1966: Barclays Bank introduced the first credit card in Britain.

## Sat

# 30

1995: At midnight local time, 5pm GMT, Hong Kong was returned to China after the colony's 156 years under British rule.

## Sun

# 1

French Grand Prix
1916: Coca Cola adopted their familiar contoured bottle to distinguish them from their competitors.

"Someday I want to be rich. Some people get so rich they lose all respect for humanity. That's how rich I want to be."
— Rita Rudner

Likely company announcements

### Interims

Beale plc
Chemring Group plc
Cosalt plc
Domino Printing Sciences plc
Medisys plc
Scarborough Minerals plc
Stanelco plc
Tadpole Technology plc
Nestor Healthcare Group plc
Ultraframe plc
World Trade Systems plc

### Finals

Abbeycrest plc
Ardana plc
Ashtead Group plc
Berkeley Group Holdings (The) plc
Carpetright plc
Creston plc
Goldshield Group plc
GoshawK Insurance Holdings plc
Highway Capital plc
Marchpole Holdings plc
Micro Focus International plc
MS International plc
Radstone Technology plc
RHM plc
Safeland plc
Smith (DS) plc
Stagecoach Group plc
Xansa plc

# Sector performance – third quarter

The table below shows the performance of sectors in the third quarter (30/6 – 30/9) of each year 1999-2005. The table is ranked by the final column – the average performance over the 7 years. For each year: the top 5 performing sectors are highlighted in red, the bottom 5 in grey.

| Sector | EPIC | 1999 | 2000 | 2001 | 2002 | 2003 | 2004 | 2005 | Average |
|---|---|---|---|---|---|---|---|---|---|
| Leisure Goods | NMX3740 | 60.3 | -16.5 | -1.4 | -11.7 | 17.0 | -7.3 | 2.5 | 6.1 |
| Mining | NMX1770 | 8.3 | 0.9 | -19.9 | -19.7 | 17.6 | 17.2 | 31.1 | 5.1 |
| Personal Goods | NMX3760 | 14.0 | 11.7 | -4.6 | 2.1 | 9.6 | -12.6 | 4.7 | 3.6 |
| Food & Drug Retailers | NMX5330 | 2.7 | 20.5 | -8.0 | -14.7 | 9.5 | -0.2 | -2.7 | 1.0 |
| Real Estate | NMX8730 | -4.2 | 8.3 | -10.2 | -17.2 | 6.0 | 5.5 | 6.2 | -0.8 |
| Tobacco | NMX3780 | -6.7 | 1.0 | 6.4 | -5.8 | -7.0 | -3.3 | 9.1 | -0.9 |
| Electricity | NMX7530 | -6.0 | -0.6 | -13.4 | -7.3 | -2.6 | 9.8 | 10.6 | -1.4 |
| Pharmaceuticals & Biotechnology | NMX4570 | -7.5 | 9.2 | -6.1 | -19.0 | 3.2 | 1.1 | 9.0 | -1.4 |
| Banks | NMX8350 | -6.4 | 17.3 | -12.2 | -24.2 | 0.4 | 5.7 | 1.4 | -2.6 |
| Health Care Equip & Services | NMX4530 | -5.1 | 9.5 | -1.9 | -8.1 | 11.8 | -12.5 | -11.8 | -2.6 |
| Technology Hardware & Equip | NMX9570 | 26.7 | 9.1 | -67.1 | -30.4 | 47.4 | -19.8 | 15.2 | -2.7 |
| Oil & Gas | NMX0530 | -3.1 | -3.7 | -7.1 | -22.3 | -3.4 | 6.5 | 12.7 | -2.9 |
| Beverages | NMX3530 | -4.8 | -2.3 | -10.5 | -8.5 | 3.6 | -5.1 | 6.3 | -3.0 |
| Food Producers | NMX3570 | -0.9 | -3.6 | -10.6 | -6.7 | 3.5 | -11.2 | 6.1 | -3.3 |
| General Financial | NMX8770 | -7.7 | 21.1 | -28.4 | -21.5 | 7.2 | -9.0 | 13.9 | -3.5 |
| Equity Investment Instruments | NMX8980 | -0.5 | 6.7 | -23.5 | -26.4 | 3.8 | 0.9 | 12.1 | -3.8 |
| Fixed Line Telecommunications | NMX6530 | 0.6 | -10.2 | -14.5 | -16.3 | -0.5 | 4.7 | 6.9 | -4.2 |
| Chemicals | NMX1350 | -0.3 | -11.1 | -17.0 | -21.5 | 9.1 | -3.7 | 14.8 | -4.2 |
| Construction & Materials | NMX2350 | -11.0 | -9.4 | -11.9 | -20.4 | 11.1 | 6.8 | 4.9 | -4.3 |
| Automobiles & Parts | NMX3350 | -8.0 | -20.4 | -0.5 | -16.9 | 14.1 | -14.3 | 12.9 | -4.7 |
| Industrial Transportation | NMX2770 | -5.3 | -1.0 | -22.6 | -20.4 | 5.7 | -2.7 | 7.6 | -5.5 |
| Support Services | NMX2790 | -4.5 | 7.5 | -15.0 | -29.5 | 7.9 | -8.6 | 2.5 | -5.7 |
| Life Insurance | NMX8570 | 2.2 | -5.0 | -17.5 | -33.8 | 10.5 | -1.2 | 2.9 | -6.0 |
| Aerospace & Defence | NMX2710 | -8.0 | -13.1 | -15.9 | -34.2 | 9.8 | 1.1 | 17.3 | -6.1 |
| Software & Computer Services | NMX9530 | 18.3 | 11.8 | -43.2 | -44.4 | 18.6 | -7.6 | 1.7 | -6.4 |
| General Retailers | NMX5370 | -15.2 | -9.9 | -10.7 | -13.6 | 3.0 | 0.5 | -4.0 | -7.1 |
| Industrial Metals | NMX1750 | -6.1 | -46.9 | -28.0 | -59.2 | 35.0 | 28.3 | 22.6 | -7.8 |
| Travel & Leisure | NMX5750 | -12.6 | -17.3 | -20.9 | -13.1 | 6.0 | 0.5 | 2.6 | -7.8 |
| Industrial Engineering | NMX2750 | -1.8 | -15.7 | -31.7 | -27.5 | 13.2 | -4.5 | 12.0 | -8.0 |
| Media | NMX5550 | -7.2 | -10.5 | -29.7 | -24.1 | 1.9 | -9.4 | 1.5 | -11.1 |
| Nonlife Insurance | NMX8530 | -6.9 | 1.9 | -33.3 | -46.3 | -17.8 | -7.5 | 13.3 | -13.8 |
| Electronic & Electrical Equip | NMX2730 | -8.1 | -24.9 | -61.1 | -31.2 | 24.2 | -18.7 | 22.6 | -13.9 |

## Observations

1. The general clustering of red highlights at the top of the table, and grey at the bottom, suggests that certain sectors consistently perform well (or badly) in this quarter. Although this characteristic is the weakest in the third quarter.

2. The **strong sectors** in this quarter are: Mining, Personal Goods, and Leisure Goods.

3. The **weak sectors** in this quarter are: Nonlife Insurance, Media, and Travel & Leisure.

## Mon
# 2

• Hong Kong Stock Exchange closed

1964: The Civil Rights Bill - one of the most important piece of legislation in American history - became law.

## Tues
# 3

1928: The world's first colour televsion transmission was made by John Logie Baird at his Baird studios in Covent Garden, London.

## Wed
# 4

• New York Stock Exchange closed
• MPC meeting (anticipated) until 5th July

Henley Royal Regatta until 8th July
1954: Fourteen years of food rationing in Britain was over as restrictions on the sale and purchase of meat (bacon in particular) were lifted.

## Thur
#  5

1994: Forbes magazine listed the Sainsbury family as the richest in Britain, with an estimated £4.4 billion.

## Fri
#  6

2005: It was announced that the 2012 Olympic Games will be held in London.

## Sat
# 7

Women's Final at Wimbledon and the 2007 Tour de France will take place; starting London.
1802: The first comic book was published in Hudson, New York. It was called 'The Wasp' and was created by Robert Rusticoat.

## Sun  *
# 8

Men's Final at Wimbledon / British Grand Prix
2005: The G8 summit in Gleneagles ended with a deal to boost aid for developing countries by $50 billion.

"Finance is the art of passing money from hand to hand until it finally disappears."
– *Robert W. Sarnoff*

### Likely company announcements

**Interims**

Alphameric plc
Porvair plc

**Finals**

Anglesey Mining plc
Birse Group plc
DTZ Holdings plc
Greene King plc
HMV Group plc
iSOFT Group plc
Jarvis plc
Northgate Information Solutions plc
Northgate plc
Photo-Me International plc
PlaneStation Group plc
Salvesen (Christian) plc
Total Systems plc
VEGA Group plc
Worthington Group plc

# FTSE100 v FTSE250 daily changes

The performance of the FTSE100 Index and the FTSE All-Share Index is very similar. This is not surprising as the FTSE100 stocks accounts for 82% of the capitalisation of All-Share Index – despite the latter comprising 680 stocks (being a composite index of the FTSE100, FTSE250, and FTSE Small Cap indices). However, the FTSE100 and mid-cap FTSE250 are mutually distinct indices; the analysis below looks at the difference in the daily performance of the two indices.

First, some stats.

|  | FTSE100 | FTSE250 |
|---|---|---|
| Overall performance 1985-2006(%) | +301.8 | +540.4 |
| Number of days the index increased | 2714 | 2935 |
| Number of days the index decreased | 2451 | 2234 |
| Average change (%) | +0. 0324 | +0. 0391 |
| STDEV | 1.0373 | 0.7903 |

The chart below shows the out-performance of the FTSE100 over the FTSE250 on a daily basis. For example, on 19 June 2006, the FTSE100 and FTSE250 indices increased 2.2% and 3.8% respectively, which is represented with a data point of -1.6 in the chart.

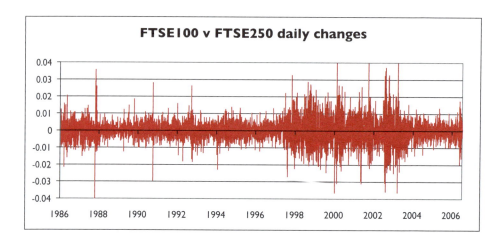

On the days when the FTSE100 rose, it out-performed the FTSE250 on average by 0.31%. On the days when the FTSE100 fell, it under-performed the FTSE250 on average by 0.35%.

## Observations

1.  Since 1985 the FTSE250 Index rose 57% of days, against just 52% of all days for the FTSE100.

2.  The FTSE250 is less volatile than the FTSE100 (as measured by the standard deviation of daily returns). This is despite the fact that smaller capitalised stocks are usually held to be more volatile than large cap stocks.

3.  From the above chart it can be seen that the divergence in daily performance between the two indices increased in the period 1998-2004. Recently, the relationship has returned to its longer-term norm.

# JULY 2007

## Mon
# 9

1991: The Post Office announced that it was to cut 2,000 jobs, despite pre-tax profits of around £153 million.

## Tues
# 10

1958: The first parking meter was installed in England.

## Wed
# 11

1859: The chimes of Big Ben were sounded for the first time.

## Thur
# 12

Battle of the Boyne (Orangemen's Day)
1960: The Ohio Art Co. introduced the first Etch-A Sketch for sale. Over 50 million units were sold in the following 25 years.

## Fri
# 13

1837: Queen Victoria became the first sovereign to move into Buckingham Palace, London.

## Sat
# 14

1995: 8 men were sentenced at Snaresbrook Crown Court for reprogramming mobile phones to make free calls to premium lines that had been set up in Pakistan - costing BT up to £25,000 a day.

## Sun
# 15

1912: British National Health Insurance Act went into effect.

"It has been said that the love of money is the root of all evil. The want of money is so quite as truly."
– Samuel Butler, Erewhon (1872)

Likely company announcements

### Interims

Interbulk Investments plc
IONA Technologies plc
IPSA Group plc
Kensington Group plc
OneClickHR plc
royalblue Group plc
St Modwen Properties plc
QA plc

### Finals

UMC Energy plc
THB Group plc
Swan (John) & Sons plc
Spice Holdings plc
Readybuy plc
Proventec plc
Personal Screening plc
Park Group plc
OneClickHR plc
Medal Entertainment & Media plc
Inter Link Foods plc
Homebuy Group plc
Henderson Morley plc
Halladale Group plc
GASOL plc
Fletcher King plc
Falkland Oil & Gas Ltd
Dipford Group plc
DA Group plc
Coral Products plc
Concateno plc
Bespak plc
Avocet Mining plc
Artisan (UK) plc
Anite Group plc
Abbey plc

# Sinclair numbers – weekly performance

The two tables below list the historic 10 best/worst weeks for the market.

The best week of the whole year – when the market has historically increased the most – is the 51st week, the week before Christmas. This week the market has increased on average 1.3%, with a relatively low standard deviation of 1.3. The proportion of years when the market has increased in the 51st week is 82%.

The week with the worst record is the 36th – the first or second week of September. In only about one year in four does the market increase in this week.

The performance figures below are ranked by the Up(%) – the percentage of years that the market has historically risen on the week.

### 10 best performing weeks in the year

| Week | Up(%) | Avg Change(%) | StdDev |
|------|-------|---------------|--------|
| 51 | 82 | 1.3 | 1.3 |
| 52 | 82 | 1 | 1.8 |
| 9 | 73 | 1 | 1.9 |
| 30 | 73 | 0.8 | 1.9 |
| 33 | 73 | 0.3 | 1.5 |
| 17 | 70 | 0.7 | 1.7 |
| 4 | 68 | 1 | 1.8 |
| 40 | 68 | 1 | 2.3 |
| 5 | 68 | 0.8 | 2 |
| 46 | 68 | 0.7 | 2.1 |

### 10 worst performing weeks in the year

| Week | Up(%) | Avg Change(%) | StdDev |
|------|-------|---------------|--------|
| 36 | 27 | -1.2 | 1.7 |
| 29 | 27 | -1 | 1.8 |
| 38 | 36 | -0.7 | 2.1 |
| 21 | 39 | -0.2 | 1.8 |
| 42 | 41 | -1.3 | 4.2 |
| 12 | 41 | -0.5 | 1.9 |
| 11 | 41 | 0.1 | 2.7 |
| 49 | 41 | 0.1 | 1.8 |
| 3 | 45 | -0.4 | 2 |
| 48 | 45 | -0.3 | 2.6 |

*Note:* The above best weeks for the market are marked on the diary pages with a red star at the top right hand of the page, and worst weeks are marked with a black star.

## Analysis of Up-Weeks

| | |
|------|----|
| Average Up(%) | 55 |
| Standard deviation | 12 |

On average, for any particular week, the market can be expected to rise 55% of the time.

The standard deviation is 12, which means that-:

- weeks that have an Up(%) over 67 (the average plus one standard deviation) can be considered strong weeks, and

- weeks that have an Up(%) under 43 (the average minus one standard deviation) can be considered weak weeks.

# JULY 2007

## Mon
• Tokyo Stock Exchange closed

# 16

1984: A jeroboam of Mouton Baron de Rothschild 1870 became the world's most expensive bottle of wine, when it was sold in Britain for over £26,500.

## Tues

# 17

1997: Tens of millions of e-mail messages failed to reach their destinations around the world, as the system crashed for the first time. Computer experts reported that the failure was unprecedented and may have cost businesses billions of dollars around the world.

## Wed

# 18

1990: A pilot scheme by Unigate, selling organically produced 'green top' milk in Torbay, Devon, proved so successful that the company was to expand the sales nationwide.

## Thur

# 19

Open Golf Championship Carnoustie until 22nd July
1994: Southampton Football Club were given the go-ahead to build a 25,000 all-seat stadium, next to the M27 motorway in Eastleigh.

## Fri

# 20

1993: Pub landlady Donna Swinburn from Sunderland, lifted a ban on smoking after takings fell by £14,000 in 4 months.

## Sat
# 21

1989: Comedian Ken Dodd was acquitted of trying to defraud the Inland Revenue. It took the jury 9 hours, 50 minutes to reach their verdict.

## Sun
# 22

German Grand Prix
1995: Lady Wilson, the widow of the former prime minister, Harold Wilson, had her pension reduced by almost a half - to £15,000.

"Money: There's nothing in the world so demoralizing as money."
— *Sophocles (496 BC - 406 BC), Antigone*

---

Likely company announcements

### Interims

Capita Group (The) plc
Electric Word plc
Flying Brands Ltd
Holders Technology plc
Huveaux plc
London Scottish Bank plc
MFI Furniture Group plc
Prestbury Holdings plc
Sperati (C.A.) (Special Agency) plc
Venue Solutions Holdings plc
Xpertise Group plc

### Finals

CityBlock plc
Daejan Holdings plc
European Home Retail plc
Greatland Gold plc
London Clubs International plc
Mayflower Corporation plc
NCC Group plc
Renold plc
Scott Wilson Group plc
Stanley Leisure plc
Syndicate Asset Management plc

# The worst days for the FTSE100

The 20 worst days in the history of the FTSE100 Index (i.e. since 1984) are listed in the table below.

| Date | FTSE100 Fall (%) |
|---|---|
| 20 Oct 1987 | -12.2 |
| 26 Oct 1987 | -6.2 |
| 19 Oct 1987 | -5.7 |
| 22 Oct 1987 | -5.7 |
| 15 Jul 2002 | -5.4 |
| 16 Oct 1987 | -5.4 |
| 22 Jul 2002 | -4.9 |
| 12 Mar 2003 | -4.8 |
| 01 Aug 2002 | -4.8 |
| 30 Sep 2002 | -4.7 |
| 19 Jul 2002 | -4.6 |
| 30 Nov 1987 | -4.3 |
| 11 Jul 2002 | -4.3 |
| 22 Mar 2001 | -4.1 |
| 05 Oct 1992 | -4.1 |
| 03 Nov 1987 | -4.0 |
| 18 Sep 2002 | -4.0 |
| 28 Aug 2002 | -3.9 |
| 16 Oct 1989 | -3.9 |
| 04 Jan 2000 | -3.9 |

The chart below plots:

1. The standard FTSE100 Index

2. How the index would have performed if the 10 worst days hadn't happened. In other words, if one had been able to get out of the market for just those 10 days.

3. As above, except the index minus the 20 worst days.

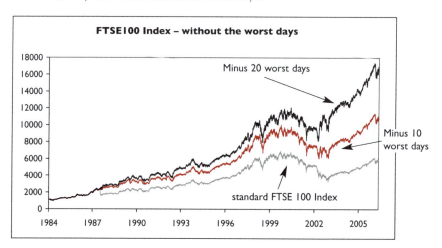

Without the 10 worst days, the FTSE100 Index would today be around 10,800, and without the 20 worst days the Index would be around 16,500. So, avoiding just the 10 worst days out of 5650 days, performance would have been doubled.

The lesson: avoid those few days when the market falls 4% or more. For information on how to do this, see page 246.

## Mon
# 23

1995: The Social Security Secretary was drawing up plans to restrict benefits to single mothers, in an attempt to cut his £90 million budget.

## Tues
# 24

1936: The Speaking Clock was introduced by the GPO.

## Wed
# 25

1994: The local council in Morecambe, Lancashire, invested £750,000 in a Noel Edmond's World of Crinkley Bottom theme park, in an attempt to reverse the seaside resort's popularity.

## Thur
# 26

1995: Bob Monkhouse was offering a reward of £10,000 for the return of 2 joke books stolen from the BBC television centre, which contained gags and scripts jotted down over 25 years.

## Fri
# 27

1900: The H.J.Heinz Company was incorporated.

## Sat
# 28

1995: A Japanese professor claimed a world record after calculating 'pi' to more than 3 billion decimal places.

## Sun
# 29

1976: Fire destroyed the famous pierhead at the end of the world's longest pier, in Southend - costing owners, Southend Council, more than £1m to repair.

"He had heard people speak contemptuously of money: he wondered if they had ever tried to do without it."
— W. Somerset Maugham, 'Of Human Bondage',

---

Likely company announcements

### Interims

Alliance & Leicester plc
Alliance UniChem plc
AMVESCAP plc
ARM Holdings plc
AstraZeneca plc
Autonomy Corporation plc
BG Group plc
Bradford & Bingley plc
British American Tobacco plc
Croda International plc
CSR plc
GlaxoSmithKline plc
Legal & General Group plc
Liberty International plc
Microgen plc
Northern Rock plc
Prudential plc
Rathbone Brothers plc
Reckitt Benckiser plc
Reed Elsevier plc
Reuters Group plc
Rolls-Royce Group plc
Royal Dutch Shell plc
Sanctuary Group (The) plc
Shire plc
Smith & Nephew plc
St James's Place plc
SThree plc
TDG plc
United Business Media plc
Wolfson Microelectronics plc
Zetex plc

### Finals

Associated British Engineering plc
Aston Villa plc
Berkeley Berry Birch plc
British Sky Broadcasting Group plc
Creightons plc
Games Workshop Group plc
Hidong Estate plc
IG Group Holdings plc
Misys plc
Network Technology plc
Oglesby & Butler Group plc
Renishaw plc
Universal Salvage plc

# August market

## Market performance in the month

The one strong month in the dismal period of May to October is August. This is the 5th best performing month of the year, with an average increase of 1.3% (with a standard deviation of 5.5).

The probability of a positive return in August is a good 67%. Although, there have been some nasty surprises, most recently with a 10.7% fall in August 1998. In the last four years, volatility has been very low in this month with very small absolute returns.

Over the longer term the performance of mid and large cap stocks is similar this month.

So, a quick respite for the market, after the poor months May-July, and just before September – the worst month of the year.

Historic performance of the market in August

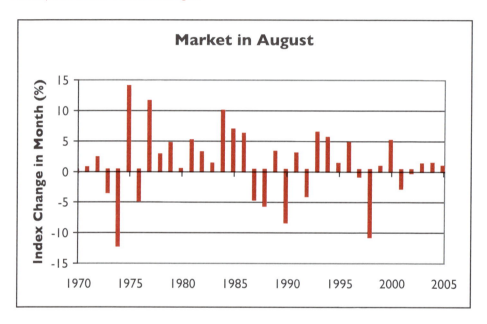

## Company announcements

Large companies reporting this month:

*   *Finals:* BHP Billiton, British Sky Broadcasting Group.

*   *Interims:* Anglo American, Aviva, Barclays, HBOS, HSBC Holdings, Rio Tinto, Royal Bank of Scotland Group, Standard Chartered, Unilever, WPP Group, Xstrata.

## What to look out for this month

*   The **MPC decision on interest rates** should be announced 12 noon on 8 August.

*   **6th strongest day** of the year for the market: 2 Aug.

*   **5th strongest week** of the year: week 33

*   **Holiday:** the LSE is closed 27 August.

# JUL/AUG 2007

### Mon
# 30

1898: Corn Flakes were invented by William Kellogg.

### Tues
# 31

1997: BT incurred anger announcing cuts of up to 5,000 jobs. The announcement came only days after the company revealed it had been making profits of £100 a second, over the previous 3 months.

### Wed
# 1

1941: The first Jeep was produced.

### Thur   *
# 2

1870: Tower Subway, the world's first underground tube railway, opened in London.

### Fri
# 3

1926: Britain installed its first taffic lights - at Piccadilly Circus in London.

### Sat
# 4

Skandia Cowes Week, until 11th August
1693: The date traditionally ascribed to Dom Perignon's invention of Champagne.

### Sun
# 5

Hungarian Grand Prix
1874: Japan launched its postal savings system, modelled on a similar system in England.

"If you don't risk anything you risk even more."
– Erica Jong

---

## Likely company announcements

### Interims

4imprint Group plc
Allied Irish Banks plc
Anglo American plc
ARC International plc
Cadbury Schweppes plc
Cookson Group plc
Elan Corporation plc
Elementis plc
GKN plc
Greggs plc
Hanson plc
HBOS plc
HSBC Holdings plc
Imperial Chemical Industries plc
Inmarsat plc
International Power plc
Jardine Lloyd Thompson Group plc
Laird Group (The) plc
Lloyds TSB Group plc
Mayflower Corporation plc
McAlpine (Alfred) plc
Millennium & Copthorne Hotels plc
Morgan Crucible Company (The) plc
Pearson plc
Quantica plc
Rio Tinto plc
Rotork plc
Royal Bank of Scotland Group (The) plc
Senior plc
Spring Group plc
Taylor Woodrow plc
Tomkins plc
Travis Perkins plc
Trinity Mirror plc
Ultra Electronics Holdings plc
Unilever plc
William Hill plc
Wimpey (George) plc
XP Power plc
Xstrata plc

### Finals

4Less Group (The) plc
Clinton Cards plc
Comland Commercial plc
Crucial Plan plc
Filtronic plc
Freeplay Energy plc
Hargreaves Services plc
ITM Power plc
Manpower Software plc
Multi Group plc
PZ Cussons plc

# MPC meetings and the FTSE100

The Bank Of England's Monetary Policy Committee meets once a month to set the official Bank rate. The table below displays the results of analysis of how the FTSE100 Index reacted in the days surrounding the 31 MPC announcements since January 2003. The table's columns are explained below:

(A): The date of the MPC interest announcement.

(B): The interest rate decision. A blank cell indicates the rate was maintained at the prevailing level.

(C): The change in the FTSE100 since the previous MPC meeting. (Positive moves are highlighted)

(D) – (F): The change in the FTSE100 on, respectively: the day preceding the announcement, the day of the MPC announcement, and the day after.

| MPC date | Decision | -MPC | MPC day -1 | MPC day | MPC day + 1 |
|---|---|---|---|---|---|
| (1) | (2) | (3) | (4) | (5) | (6) |
| 09 Jan 03 | | | -0.82 | 0.23 | 1.02 |
| 06 Feb 03 | -0.25 | -9.66 | 2.47 | -2.22 | 0.06 |
| 06 Mar 03 | | 0.73 | -1.70 | -0.23 | -1.79 |
| 10 Apr 03 | | 10.80 | -0.19 | -1.50 | 0.13 |
| 08 May 03 | | 5.21 | -0.34 | -1.60 | 1.03 |
| 05 Jun 03 | | 3.69 | 0.26 | -0.54 | 1.13 |
| 10 Jul 03 | -0.25 | -1.86 | -0.46 | -0.64 | 0.73 |
| 07 Aug 03 | | 1.55 | -1.23 | 0.62 | 1.27 |
| 04 Sep 03 | | 1.36 | 1.37 | -0.31 | 0.20 |
| 09 Oct 03 | | 0.35 | -0.08 | 1.06 | -0.07 |
| 06 Nov 03 | 0.25 | 0.45 | -0.62 | 0.48 | 1.22 |
| 09 Dec 03 | | -0.23 | -0.16 | 0.45 | -1.01 |
| 08 Jan 04 | | 3.92 | -0.71 | 0.47 | -0.62 |
| 05 Feb 04 | 0.25 | -1.69 | 0.18 | -0.32 | 0.42 |
| 04 Mar 04 | | 3.12 | -0.33 | 0.75 | -0.26 |
| 08 Apr 04 | | -1.63 | -0.09 | 0.47 | 0.58 |
| 06 May 04 | 0.25 | 0.70 | 0.49 | -1.17 | -0.39 |
| 10 Jun 04 | 0.25 | 0.14 | -0.34 | -0.08 | -0.05 |
| 08 Jul 04 | | -2.53 | -0.28 | 0.52 | 0.28 |
| 05 Aug 04 | 0.25 | 0.83 | -0.49 | 0.12 | -1.71 |
| 09 Sep 04 | | 5.25 | -0.16 | -0.45 | 0.15 |
| 07 Oct 04 | | 3.57 | -0.02 | -0.16 | 0.00 |
| 04 Nov 04 | | -0.12 | 0.54 | 0.21 | 0.24 |
| 09 Dec 04 | | -0.23 | -0.52 | -0.33 | 0.12 |
| 13 Jan 05 | | 2.66 | -0.73 | 0.35 | 0.43 |
| 10 Feb 05 | | 3.62 | -0.10 | 0.19 | 0.88 |
| 10 Mar 05 | | -0.66 | -0.30 | -0.68 | 0.40 |
| 07 Apr 05 | | -0.78 | 0.09 | 0.60 | 0.13 |
| 09 May 05 | | -1.63 | 0.34 | -0.17 | -0.36 |
| 09 Jun 05 | | 2.71 | -0.43 | 0.11 | 0.42 |
| 07 Jul 05 | | 3.17 | 0.76 | -1.36 | 1.43 |
| 04 Aug 05 | -0.25 | 1.82 | 0.09 | -0.32 | -0.02 |
| 08 Sep 05 | | 0.84 | 0.13 | -0.47 | 0.35 |
| 06 Oct 05 | | 2.52 | -1.21 | -1.02 | -0.19 |
| 10 Nov 05 | | 1.84 | -0.39 | -0.30 | 0.77 |
| 08 Dec 05 | | 1.35 | -0.18 | 0.04 | -0.25 |
| 12 Jan 06 | | 3.11 | 0.75 | 0.06 | -0.42 |
| 09 Feb 06 | | 0.63 | -0.38 | 1.46 | -0.77 |
| 09 Mar 06 | | 1.62 | -0.76 | 0.74 | 0.89 |
| 06 Apr 06 | | 1.64 | 0.66 | 0.03 | -0.32 |
| 04 May 06 | | 0.93 | -1.19 | 0.45 | 0.91 |
| 08 Jun 06 | | -6.93 | 0.64 | -2.51 | 1.66 |
| 06 Jul 06 | | 4.04 | -0.97 | 1.09 | -0.02 |
| 03 Aug 06 | 0.25 | -0.14 | 0.87 | -1.58 | 0.87 |

Continued on page 80

# AUGUST 2007

## Mon

# 6

Bank Holiday (Scotland)
PGA Golf Championship until 12th August
1997: Microsoft bought $150 million worth of shares of financially troubled Apple Computer.

## Tues

# 7

• FOMC meeting (tentative)

1944: IBM launched the first program-controlled calculator, the Automatic Sequence Controlled Calculator (best known as the Harvard Mark I).

## Wed

# 8

• MPC meeting (anticipated) until 9th August

1963: The Great Train Robbery took place, when a gang of 15 robbers stole £2.6 million worth of bank notes.

## Thur

# 9

1974: Richard Nixon became the first US President to resign from office. His Vice President, Gerald Ford, took his place.

## Fri

# 10

1977: The Queen visited Northern Ireland for the first time in 11 years, as part of her Silver Jubilee tour.

## Sat
# 11

1981: The IBM PC, an early personal computer, was introduced.

## Sun
# 12

2004: Sweden's nine millionth inhabitant was born.

"The safest way to double your money is to fold it over and put it in your pocket."
– *Kin Hubbard (1868 - 1930)*

Likely company announcements

### Interims

Aviva plc
Friends Provident plc
Management Consulting Group plc
Morgan Sindall plc
Pendragon plc
Peninsular & Oriental Steam Navigation Co
Premier Foods plc
Prodesse Investment Ltd
Readymix plc
Royal & Sun Alliance Insurance Group plc
Schroders plc
Scottish & Newcastle plc
Spirent Communications plc
Standard Chartered plc
Zotefoams plc

### Finals

Air Music & Media Group plc
Alpha Strategic plc
Aquarius Platinum Ltd
Bartercard plc
Chian Resources plc
County Contact Centres plc
Feedback plc
GoldStone Resources Ltd
GTL Resources plc
Herencia Resources plc
Hot Tuna (International) plc
Minster Pharmaceuticals plc
Nadlan plc
Northern Recruitment Group plc
NWF Group plc
Ragusa Capital plc

# MPC meetings and the FTSE100 (contd)

### Observations

From the table on page 78 the following observations can be made.

1. The most striking observation is that the Index fell 66% (29 of 44) of the days before the MPC announcement ("MPC Day"), and this was over a period when the market was generally rising. And on 11 of the 15 occasions that the market did rise on the day before MPC Day, the market fell the following day. This behaviour would seem to illustrate the maxim that markets dislike uncertainty: regardless almost of expectations and the prevailing economy, the market falls the day before an announcement and rises after the announcement has been made.

2. The situation reverses on the day following MPC Day, where the Index rises 64% of the time.

3. A strategy that went short of the FTSE100 at close 2 days before MPC Day, reversed to a long at close of MPC Day, and then closed the position at close of the day following MPC Day, would have made on average 0.51% every month.

The chart below plots the FTSE100 Index against the official Bank rate from January 2003.

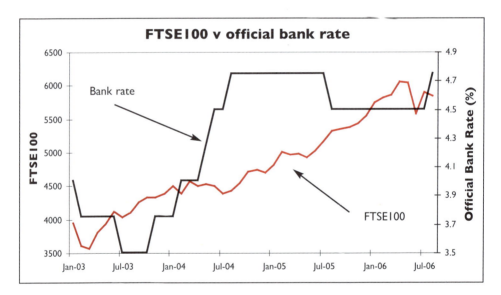

Reference: www.bankofengland.co.uk/monetarypolicy/

## Mon

# 13

1913: Stainless steel was invented by Harry Brearley.

## Tues

# 14

2004: Sales tax holiday in Massachusetts, US - all sales taxes were suspended on purchases of $2500 or less.

## Wed

# 15

1620: The *Mayflower* ship departed from Southampton.

## Thur

# 16

1977: Elvis Presley, whose singing and style revolutionised popular music in the 1950s, died.

## Fri

# 17

1998: US President, Bill Clinton, admits having an inappropriate relationship with former White House intern Monica Lewinsky.

## Sat

# 18

1989: Manchester United Football Club was sold for £20m - the biggest takeover deal up till then in the history of British football.

## Sun

# 19

1991: Soviet Union President, Mikhail Gorbachev, was overthrown by a coup.

---

Likely company announcements

### Interims

Balfour Beatty plc
Berkeley Technology Ltd
BP plc
BPP Holdings plc
Clarke (T) plc
Countrywide plc
Headlam Group plc
Mallett plc
Michael Page International plc
ROK plc
Weir Group plc
WPP Group plc

### Finals

Celtic plc
Ekay plc
Haynes Publishing Group plc
Maxima Holdings plc
Media Steps Group plc
Neptune Minerals plc
Original Investments plc
Poole Investments plc
Preston North End plc
Promethean plc
Speymill Deutsche Immobilien Company plc
Stagecoach Theatre Arts plc
Transport Systems plc

---

"Money is like a sixth sense without which you cannot make a complete use of the other five."
– W. Somerset Maugham (1874 - 1965), 'Of Human Bondage'

# FTSE100 Index – after large daily moves

*Analysis of the behaviour of the FTSE100 Index in the days following large moves.*

The table below shows the results of analysing the performance of the FTSE100 Index (1984-2006) in the days following large moves.

- The **Up** column shows the average performance of the FTSE100 Index in the 1, 2, 5, 10, and 20 days immediately following an exceptionally large increase in the index on one day. "Exceptionally large" is defined as a move more than 2 standard deviations over the mean – which in this case is calculated to be a move more than 2.081%.

- The **Down** column shows the average performance of the FTSE100 Index in the 1, 2, 5, 10, and 20 days immediately following an exceptionally large decrease in the index on one day. "Exceptionally large" is defined as a move more than 2 standard deviations below the mean – which in this case is calculated to be a move below -2.005%.

|  | Up | Down |
|---|---|---|
| 1 day after (%) | -0.07 | 0.07 |
| 2 days after (%) | -0.19 | 0.31 |
| 5 days after (%) | -0.45 | 0.44 |
| 10 days after (%) | -0.21 | 0.72 |
| 20 days after (%) | 0.18 | 1.57 |
| Number of days with large moves | 127 | 140 |

From the above table it can be seen that in 22 years there were 127 days with exceptionally large increases. On average, the FTSE100 Index falls -0.07% the day after a large market rise, and has fallen -0.45% from the close of the strong day after 5 days.

The average behaviour of the index in the days following these exceptionally strong days is shown in the chart on the right.

Immediately after a strong market rise, the index retreats to a low point 5 days after the event. On average, the index has recovered and is above the initial level by the 20th day.

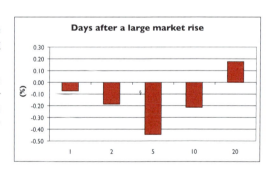

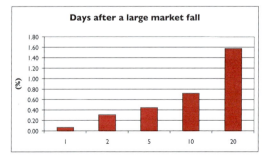

The chart on the left shows the average behaviour of the index in the days following an exceptional fall in the market.

Unlike the market rise, on average the index bounces back consistently in the days after a fall.

# AUGUST 2007

**Mon**

# 20

1862: America celebrated the birth of the eight-hour workday.

**Tues**

# 21

1911: The *Mona Lisa* was stolen by a Louvre employee.

**Wed**

# 22

1966: Britain's largest manufacturing company, Imperial Chemical Industries, announced 1000 redundancies at its nylon-fibre producing factories.

**Thur**

# 23

1617: The first one-way streets were established in London.

**Fri**

# 24

1995: Microsft's *Windows 95* computer operating system was released, with much fanfare.

**Sat**
# 25

1910: The Yellow Cab Company was founded in America.

**Sun**
# 26

Turkish Grand Prix
1994: A man was given the world's first battery-operated heart, in a pioneering operation in Britain.

"To win without risk is to triumph without glory."
– Pierre Corneille, 'The Cid,' 1636

Likely company announcements

## Interims

Barclays plc
Bodycote International plc
GeneMedix plc
Gibbs and Dandy plc
Henderson Group plc
Keller Group plc
Ladbrokes plc
Laing (John) plc
North Midland Construction plc
office2office plc
Persimmon plc
Raymarine plc
Rentokil Initial plc
REXAM plc
Slough Estates plc

## Finals

Bakery Services plc
Bella Media plc
BHP Billiton plc
Brambles Industries plc
Chaco Resources plc
Coolabi plc
EBTM plc
Fiske plc
Goodwin plc
Independent International Investment Research plc
Namibian Resources plc
Northacre plc
SiRViS IT plc
Stepquick plc
Tower Resources plc
Uranium Resources plc
White Nile Ltd

# September market

## Market performance in the month

September has the worst record of any month for the market. On average the market falls 1.4% in the month (with a standard deviation of 6.3). Further, the market only rises at all in September in 44% of years, and has fallen for 6 of the last 8 years.

As can be seen in the chart below, the upside is fairly limited for this month; but on the downside there is the potential for some large falls.

But, however bad the large caps are, the mid-cap cap stocks are even worse. On average the FTSE100 Index out-performs the FTSE250 Index by almost a full percentage point in September – making September the worst month for mid-cap stocks relative to large-cap.

In summary: a month to avoid.

Historic performance of the market in September

## Company announcements

September is the busiest month for company results – over 400 final and interim announcements can be expected. So, watch out for a deluge of news this month.

It's possible that the performance of the market and the high results activity are not unrelated. Investors will commonly reduce exposure and sell a stock over its reporting period – to avoid getting hit by nasty surprises. Such actions will help to depress the stock's share price. Therefore, it may be no surprise that the month with the greatest company reporting activity is also the month with the worst performance.

Large companies reporting this month:

*   *Finals*: Diageo, Wolseley.
*   *Interims*: BAE SYSTEMS, Gallaher Group, Kingfisher, Tesco.

## What to look out for this month

*   The quarterly **FTSE100 Index review** should be implemented after market close 21 September (if any changes are made), with the announcement made about a week before this. (Don't forget: companies expelled from the Index often see their share price rise in the following weeks).
*   **Weakest day** of the year for the market: 8 Sep; **6th weakest day** of the year for the market: 9 Sep.
*   **Weakest week** of the year for the market: week 36; **3rd weakest week** of the year for the market: week 38.
*   The **FTSE100 is particularly strong relative to the FTSE250** in this month.
*   **Triple witching** (derivatives contract expires) on 21 September.
*   The **MPC decision on interest rates** should be announced 12 noon on 5 September.

## Mon

• London Stock Exchange closed

# 27

Bank Holiday (UK except Scotland)
1859: Petroleum was discovered in Pennsylvania, US - the world's first successful oil well.

## Tues

# 28

1971: The dollar was allowed to float against the yen for the first time.

## Wed

# 29

1898: The Goodyear tyre company was founded - now, the third largest tyre and rubber company in the world.

## Thur

# 30

1913: The British economist, Richard Stone, is born. He was a Bank of Sweden prize winner, for developing an accounting model that could be used to track economic activities on a national and, later, an international scale.

## Fri

# 31

1959: British prime minister Harold Macmillan and American president Dwight Eisenhower gave a historic live television broadcast from Downing Street.

## Sat

# 1

1962: Channel Television was first transmitted to 54,000 households on the Channel Islands.

## Sun

# 2

1666: The Great Fire of London broke out and burnt for three days, destroying 10,000 buildings including St. Paul's Cathedral.

"Wealth is the slave of a wise man. The master of a fool."
– *Seneca (5 BC - 65 AD)*

Likely company announcements

### Interims

Agcert International plc
Alea Group Holdings (Bermuda) Ltd
AMEC plc
Ark Therapeutics Group plc
Avis Europe plc
Axis-Shield plc
BBA Group plc
Beazley Group plc
Bunzl plc
Clarkson plc
Corus Group plc
Costain Group plc
CRH plc
Filtrona plc
Fisher (James) & Sons plc
Glanbia plc
Hunting plc
Inch Kenneth Kajang Rubber plc
Johnston Press plc
Kerry Group plc
LogicaCMG plc
Melrose Resources plc
Metal Bulletin plc
Molins plc
Narborough Plantations plc
Paddy Power plc
Pinewood Shepperton plc
Queen's Walk Investment Ltd
Rank Group (The) plc
Rightmove plc
Serco Group plc
Signet Group plc
Vislink plc
Wellington Underwriting plc

### Finals

Diageo plc
DICOM Group plc
FII Group plc
Homestyle Group plc
London Finance & Investment Group plc
Mid-States plc
Morse plc
Rightmove plc
Wetherspoon (J D) plc

# FTSE100 reviews – companies joining the Index

The charts below show the share price of 12 companies that have joined the FTSE 100 Index since 2003. The time period for each chart is 6 months, starting from 3 months before the company joined the index. So it is possible to see the share price behaviour in the 3 months leading up to joining, and the 3 months after.

It can be seen that, in most cases, the share price rises immediately before the company joins the FTSE 100 Index. While immediately afterwards the price is usually flat or falls back again.

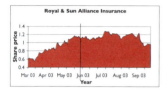

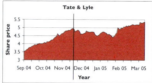
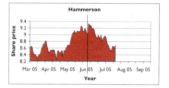

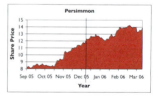

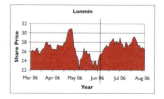

## Mon
### 3

• New York Stock Exchange closed

1954: The National Trust purchased Fair Isle in northern Scotland, famous for its bird sanctuary and knitted sweaters.

## Tues
### 4

1964: The Queen officially opened Europe's longest suspension bridge, linking Edinburgh to Perth across the River Forth.

## Wed
### 5

• MPC meeting (anticipated) until 6th September

1988: With $2 billion in federal aid, the Robert M. Bass Group agreed to buy the United States' largest bankrupt thrift, American Savings and Loan Association.

## Thur
### 6

2001: In the *US vs. Microsoft* legal case, the US Justice Department announced that it was no longer seeking to break-up the software maker and would instead be seeking a lesser antitrust penalty.

## Fri
### 7

1979: The Chrysler Motor Corporation asked the US government for $1 billion to avoid bankruptcy, after announcing that it was going to post record pre-tax losses for the year.

## Sat ★
### 8

2000: The fuel protests which had been crippling France, reached Britain. The protestors displayed their anger at Europe's highest fuel prices.

## Sun ★
### 9

Italian Grand Prix
1911: The first scheduled air mail service, from Hendon to Windsor, as part of the celebrations for the coronation of King George V.

"Business, you know, may bring money, but friendship hardly ever does."
– Jane Austen

---

Likely company announcements

### Interims

888 Holdings plc
Abbot Group plc
Acambis plc
Admiral Group plc
Aegis Group plc
AGA Foodservice Group plc
Anglo Pacific Group plc
Arena Leisure plc
ARRIVA plc
BATM Advanced Communications Ltd
Biotrace International plc
BRIT Insurance Holdings plc
British Polythene Industries plc
Cairn Energy plc
Catlin Group Ltd
Corporate Services Group (The) plc
Davis Service Group (The) plc
DMATEK Ltd
Evolution Group (The) plc
FBD Holdings plc
Gallaher Group plc
Hammerson plc
Highway Insurance Holdings plc
Horizon Technology Group plc
IMI plc
InterContinental Hotels Group plc
Irish Continental Group plc
ITV plc
John Wood Group plc
Kingspan Group plc
Lambert Howarth Group plc
Macfarlane Group plc
Menzies (John) plc
Robert Walters plc
Savills plc
Shore Capital Group plc
SMG plc
UK Coal plc
UMBRO plc
Vitec Group (The) plc
Wilson Bowden plc

### Finals

Alumasc Group plc
Dechra Pharmaceuticals plc
DX Services plc
Galliford Try plc
Go-Ahead Group (The) plc
Hays plc
McBride plc
Mucklow (A & J) Group plc
Pace Micro Technology plc
SurfControl plc
Teesland plc
Thorntons plc

# FTSE100 reviews – companies leaving the Index

The charts below show the share price of 12 companies that have exited the FTSE 100 Index since 2003. The time period for each chart is 6 months, starting from 3 months before the company joined the index. So it is possible to see the share price behaviour in the 3 months leading up to joining, and the 3 months after.

As can be clearly seen, a company's share price tends to decline leading up to the exit from the Index. But of more interest is the stronger observation that the share price tends to rise immediately after the exit (or, more strictly, after the announcement a week or two before implementation).

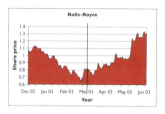
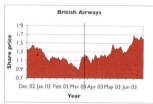
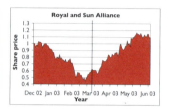

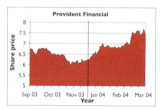

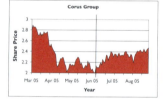

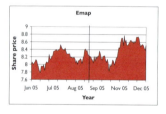
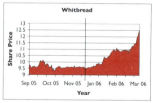
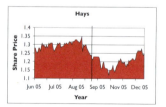

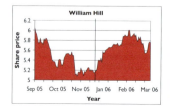

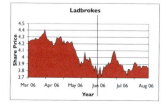

# September 2007

## Mon
# 10

1951: The UK began an economic boycott of Iran.

## Tues
# 11

Partial solar eclipse.
1980: The Marlborough diamond (worth £400,000) was stolen from a London jewellers.

## Wed
# 12

2005: Hong Kong Disneyland opened in Penny's Bay, Lantau Island, Hong Kong.

## Thur
# 13

1983: US mint strikes the first gold coin in 50 years (Olympic Eagle).

## Fri
# 14

2003: In a referendum, Sweden rejected adopting the Euro.

## Sat
# 15

1998: In America, WorldCom and MCI Communications finished their $37 billion landmark merger, forming MCI WorldCom - which was later renamed WorldCom and became the largest bankruptcy in US history.

## Sun
# 16

Belgium Grand Prix
1908: General Motors Corporation (GM) was founded.

"Money often costs too much."
– *Ralph Waldo Emerson*

---

Likely company announcements

### Interims

Aggreko plc
Antofagasta plc
Axon Group plc
BAE SYSTEMS plc
Bloomsbury Publishing plc
Bovis Homes Group plc
Centrica plc
Dignity plc
Drax Group plc
DRS Data & Research Services plc
El Oro and Exploration Company plc
Enterprise plc
Eurotunnel plc
F&C Asset Management plc
Foseco plc
French Connection Group plc
GoshawK Insurance Holdings plc
Grafton Group plc
Group 4 Securicor plc
Guinness Peat Group plc
Heywood Williams Group plc
Hill & Smith Holdings plc
Hiscox plc
Incisive Media plc
Kingfisher plc
Litho Supplies plc
Next plc
Old Mutual plc
OPD Group plc
Parkwood Holdings plc
PGI Group plc
Provident Financial plc
Randgold Resources Ltd
Regus Group plc
Retail Decisions plc
RPS Group plc
TT electronics plc
UNITE Group plc
UTV plc
Vanco plc
Whatman plc
Xaar plc

### Finals

Antisoma plc
Caffe Nero Group plc
Helphire Group plc
Isotron plc
Kier Group plc
Macro 4 plc
Redrow plc
Wilmington Group plc

# The greatest one day market rises

The table below shows the 20 greatest 1 day rises in the FTSE 100 Index since its launch in April 1984. The columns in the table are explained below.

1.  The highest Index value of the day.

2.  The closing Index value.

3.  The percentage rise from the previous day's close to the high of the day. (The table is ranked by this column.)

4.  The percentage move from the high of the day to the close.

5.  The percentage change in the close from the day to the following day.

6.  The percentage change in the close from the day to 5 days later.

7.  The percentage change in the close from the day to 30 days later.

| Date | High | Close | CI(D-1) - Hi(D) | Hi(D) - CI(D) | CI(D) - CI(D+1) | CI(D) - CI(D+5) | CI(D) - CI(D+30) |
|---|---|---|---|---|---|---|---|
| | (1) | (2) | (3) | (4) | (5) | (6) | (7) |
| 21 Oct 87 | 1983.1 | 1943.8 | 10.1 | -2.0 | -5.7 | -14.7 | -18.2 |
| 20 Sep 02 | 4064.1 | 3860.1 | 6.6 | -5.0 | -3.1 | 1.2 | 3.5 |
| 08 Oct 90 | 2283.7 | 2201.6 | 6.5 | -3.6 | -3.1 | -4.5 | -4.8 |
| 10 Apr 92 | 2587 | 2572.6 | 6.2 | -0.6 | 0.7 | 2.1 | 4.7 |
| 13 Mar 03 | 3489.1 | 3486.9 | 6.1 | -0.1 | 3.3 | 8.0 | 13.0 |
| 30 Oct 87 | 1773.8 | 1749.8 | 5.5 | -1.4 | -1.5 | -7.4 | -5.6 |
| 12 Nov 87 | 1723.6 | 1702.5 | 5.1 | -1.2 | -1.4 | -3.7 | 5.2 |
| 15 Oct 02 | 4130.3 | 4130.3 | 5.1 | 0.0 | -1.8 | -0.3 | -1.4 |
| 25 Jul 02 | 3965.9 | 3965.9 | 5.0 | 0.0 | 1.3 | 2.0 | 3.6 |
| 17 Mar 03 | 3774.3 | 3722.3 | 4.8 | -1.4 | 0.7 | 0.6 | 5.5 |
| 11 Oct 02 | 3953.4 | 3953.4 | 4.7 | 0.0 | -0.6 | 4.5 | 5.6 |
| 29 Jul 02 | 4202.7 | 4202.7 | 4.6 | 0.0 | -0.5 | -4.9 | -0.6 |
| 06 Oct 98 | 4863.7 | 4854 | 4.6 | -0.2 | 0.5 | 2.8 | 13.4 |
| 17 Sep 92 | 2487.7 | 2483.9 | 4.6 | 0.2 | 3.3 | 5.5 | 6.4 |
| 12 Oct 98 | 5043.4 | 5037.6 | 4.6 | -0.1 | -0.9 | 0.8 | 16.1 |
| 17 Jul 02 | 4200 | 4190.6 | 4.4 | -0.2 | 2.5 | -9.9 | 0.4 |
| 11 Nov 87 | 1640.3 | 1639.3 | 4.2 | -0.1 | 3.9 | 1.5 | 8.1 |
| 14 Sep 92 | 2470.4 | 2422.1 | 4.2 | -2.0 | -2.2 | 5.7 | 9.9 |
| 15 Aug 02 | 4345.7 | 4327.5 | 4.2 | -0.4 | 0.1 | 2.5 | -9.7 |
| 26 Sep 02 | 3850.6 | 3850.6 | 4.2 | 0.0 | 1.5 | 0.8 | 6.0 |
| Average: | | | 5.3 | -0.9 | -0.2 | -0.4 | 3.0 |

## Observations

1.  The average rise for the 20 greatest days is 5.3%. This contrasts with an average fall of 7.0% for the 20 greatest crashes over the same period. This observation is not surprising, confirming the sawtooth-like nature of market prices: that prices tend to rise steadily but fall abruptly.

2.  On 5 occasions the market closed at the high of the day. On average the market rebounded 0.9% off the high of the day to the close. This contrasts significantly with large market fall days, where the market on average rebounded a far greater percentage off the low.

3.  On average the market closed 0.2% down on the day following the large rise.

4.  But on average the market was 3.0% higher 30 days after the day of the large rise.

# September 2007

## Mon
## 17

• Tokyo Stock Exchange closed

2001: In the first day of trading after the September 11 attacks, stocks plummeted posting the biggest point drop in the history of the Dow Jones IA Index, closing down 684.81 points to 8920.70.

## Tues
## 18

• FOMC meeting (tentative)

1809: The Royal Opera House in London opened.

## Wed
## 19

1952: The US said they would prevent the film legend, Charlie Chaplin, from returning to his Hollywood home until he had been investigated by the Immigration Services.

## Thur
## 20

1946: The first Cannes Film Festival was held.

## Fri
## 21

• Euronext.liffe stock options expiry
• Euronext.liffe UK USF expiry
• September Triple-Witching

1931: With Americans still in the depths of the Depression, the feeling of insecurity grew more pronounced with the announcement that Great Britain had decided to abandon the gold standard.

## Sat
## 22

1955: Britain's first commercial television station, ITV, went on-air for the first time.

## Sun
## 23

Autumnal Equinox
1848: First commercial production of chewing gum, by John Curtis - on a stove at his home in Bangor, Maine in the United States and marketed as 'The State of Maine Pure Spruce Gum'.

"When it's a question of money, everybody is of the same religion."
– Voltaire

---

Likely company announcements

### Interims

Alizyme plc
ArmorGroup International plc
Ashley (Laura) Holdings plc
Asterand plc
AutoLogic Holdings plc
Biocompatibles International plc
Boot (Henry) plc
Burren Energy plc
Capital & Regional plc
Collins Stewart Tullett plc
Communisis plc
Development Securities plc
Ennstone plc
Gaskell plc
Gresham Computing plc
Hardy Underwriting Group plc
Independent Media Distribution plc
Independent News & Media plc
Kenmare Resources plc
Mapeley Ltd
Medical Solutions plc
Metalrax Group plc
Morrison (Wm) Supermarkets plc
Novae Group plc
Oakhill Group plc
Ottakar's plc
Oxford BioMedica plc
Petrofac Ltd
Premier Oil plc
Psion plc
Resolution plc
Restaurant Group (The) plc
Trafficmaster plc
UCM Group plc
Venture Production plc
Vernalis plc
Woolworths Group plc

### Finals

Amstrad plc
Compel Group plc
Gondola Holdings plc
Minerva plc
Northamber plc
NXT plc
Primary Health Properties plc
Regent Inns plc
Ricardo plc
Smiths Group plc
Trace Group plc

# The greatest one day market falls

The table below shows the 20 greatest 1 day falls in the FTSE 100 Index since launch in April 1984. The columns in the table are explained below.

1. The lowest Index value of the day.

2. The closing Index value.

3. The percentage fall from the previous day's close to the low of the day. (The table is ranked by this column.)

4. The percentage move from the low of the crash day to the close.

5. The percentage change in the close from the crash day to the following day.

6. The percentage change in the close from the crash day to 5 days later.

7. The percentage change in the close from the crash day to 30 days later.

| Date | Low | Close | Cl(D-1) - Lo(D) | Lo(D) - Cl(D) | Cl(D) - Cl(D+1) | Cl(D) - Cl(D+5) | Cl(D) - Cl(D+30) |
|------|-----|-------|-----------------|----------------|------------------|------------------|-------------------|
| | (1) | (2) | (3) | (4) | (5) | (6) | (7) |
| 20 Oct 87 | 1748.2 | 1801.6 | -14.8 | 3.1 | 7.9 | -5.5 | -12.4 |
| 22 Oct 87 | 1749.1 | 1833.2 | -10.0 | 4.8 | -2.1 | -8.2 | -13.4 |
| 28 Oct 97 | 4382.8 | 4755.4 | -9.5 | 8.5 | 2.4 | 3.0 | 8.9 |
| 16 Oct 89 | 2029.7 | 2146.5 | -9.1 | 5.8 | -0.5 | 2.0 | 3.6 |
| 26 Oct 87 | 1638.1 | 1684.1 | -8.8 | 2.8 | 1.1 | 2.4 | -5.1 |
| 19 Oct 87 | 1999.8 | 2052.3 | -8.1 | 2.6 | -12.2 | -17.9 | -23.0 |
| 12 Sep 01 | 4651.8 | 4882.1 | -7.6 | 5.0 | 1.3 | -3.3 | 5.8 |
| 21 Sep 01 | 4219.8 | 4433.7 | -7.4 | 5.1 | 4.1 | 10.6 | 15.7 |
| 28 Oct 87 | 1598 | 1658.4 | -6.2 | 3.8 | 1.4 | -3.0 | -1.2 |
| 30 Sep 02 | 3669.7 | 3721.8 | -6.1 | 1.4 | 2.0 | 1.6 | 7.9 |
| 24 Jul 02 | 3625.9 | 3777.1 | -6.0 | 4.2 | 5.0 | 12.4 | 6.2 |
| 15 Jul 02 | 3974.6 | 3994.5 | -5.9 | 0.5 | 0.7 | -2.5 | 11.4 |
| 16 Oct 87 | 2177.1 | 2177.1 | -5.4 | 0.0 | -5.7 | -17.5 | -24.1 |
| 04 Nov 87 | 1565.4 | 1608.1 | -5.4 | 2.7 | 1.9 | 1.9 | 5.1 |
| 12 Mar 03 | 3277.5 | 3287 | -5.1 | 0.3 | 6.1 | 14.6 | 17.7 |
| 22 Jul 02 | 3895.5 | 3895.5 | -4.9 | 0.0 | -1.0 | 7.9 | 3.4 |
| 30 Nov 87 | 1570 | 1579.9 | -4.9 | 0.6 | -0.1 | 1.2 | 10.3 |
| 28 Aug 98 | 5108.7 | 5249.4 | -4.8 | 2.8 | -1.5 | 1.9 | -4.0 |
| 19 Aug 91 | 2495.7 | 2540.5 | -4.8 | 1.8 | 0.6 | 3.1 | 4.1 |
| 01 Aug 02 | 4043.5 | 4044.5 | -4.8 | 0.0 | 0.8 | 4.8 | -0.9 |
| Average: | | | -7.0 | 2.8 | 0.6 | 0.5 | 0.8 |

## Observations

1. The 10 greatest falls all occurred in the months of September and October.

2. On only 3 occasions did the market close at the low of the day. On all other occasions the market rebounded, sometimes significantly, off the low of the day. The average rebound off the low was 2.8%. In general, the greater the fall, the greater the chance of a significant rebound off the low.

3. On average, the market rose 0.6% on the day following the crash.

4. On average the market was 0.8% higher 30 days after the falls. Generally, if the market was down 5 days after a crash, it would still be down 30 days after a crash.

# September 2007

## Mon
# 24

1948: The Honda Motor Company was founded.

## Tues
# 25

1926: Henry Ford announced the 8-hour, 5-day work week.

## Wed
# 26

• Hong Kong Stock Exchange closed

2000: Anti-globalisation protests in Prague turned violent, during the IMF and World Bank summits.

## Thur
# 27

1998: Google, the internet search engine, was founded.

## Fri
# 28

1959: The US satellite, Explorer VI, took the first video pictures of Earth.

## Sat
# 29

1829: London's reorganised police force, the Metropolitan Police, became the first official police department in the world.

## Sun
# 30

Chinese Grand Prix

1936: Pinewood Film Studios opened in Buckinghamshire, to provide Britian with a film studio to compete with America's Hollywood Studios in California.

"The entire essence of America is the hope to first make money -- then make money with money -- then make lots of money with lots of money."
*-- Paul Erdman*

---

Likely company announcements

### Interims

Alpha Airports Group plc
Aminex plc
Anglo-Eastern Plantations plc
Atrium Underwriting plc
Barr (A G) plc
Bioquell plc
Braime (T F & J H) (Holdings) plc
Camellia plc
Charles Taylor Consulting plc
Clinical Computing plc
CLS Holdings plc
Corin Group plc
Culver Holdings plc
Dana Petroleum plc
Donegal Creameries plc
Emerald Energy plc
Entertainment Rights plc
Fortune Oil plc
GAME Group (The) plc
H.R.Owen plc
Havelock Europa plc
House of Fraser plc
Huntsworth plc
IFG Group plc
Informa plc
Kesa Electricals plc
McInerney Holdings plc
Melrose plc
National Express Group plc
Ormonde Mining plc
Pacific Media plc
Parity Group plc
Ross Group plc
ServicePower Technologies plc
SkyePharma plc
SOCO International plc
South Wharf plc
Telspec plc

### Finals

Barratt Developments plc
Centaur Media plc
Close Brothers Group plc
IAWS Group plc
ICM Computer Group plc
Lincat Group plc
Newcastle United plc
Pochin's plc
SCi Entertainment Group plc
Sinclair (William) Holdings plc
Stavert Zigomala plc
White Young Green plc
Wolseley plc

# October market

## Market performance in the month

Despite its (deserved) reputation for large market falls, the long-term performance statistics for October are not as bad as one might think. On average the market rises 0.2% in the month (albeit with a relatively high standard deviation of 6.5).

The probability of a positive return in the month is a high 69% (second only to the best month, April). In fact, the FTSE100 Index has increased 12 years out of the last 14 in October. A record better than any other month.

After September, October is the second best month for the relative out-performance of large over mid-cap stocks.

October is 5th in the performance ranking of months, but there's no doubt that its figures are strongly influenced by the extraordinary 26.6% fall in October 1987. Without that (hopefully) freakish occurrence, the October market would be one of the better months in the year.

## Six month effect

A reminder to investors that the depressed six-month cycle (May-Oct) is ending this month, and now is the time – history suggests - to start thinking about increasing a portfolio's weighting to equities.

Historic performance of the market in October

## What to look out for this month

- Historic **strong sectors** in this fourth quarter are: Technology Hardware & Equipment, Electronic & Electrical Equipment, and Industrial Metals.
- Historic **weak sectors** in this fourth quarter are: Leisure Goods, Electricity and Oil & Gas.
- **4th strongest day** of the year for the market: 31 Oct; **5th weakest day** of the year for the market: 25 October.
- **8th strongest week** of the year for the market: week 40; **5th weakest week** of the year for the market: week 42.
- The **FTSE100 is particularly strong relative to the FTSE250** in this month.
- The **MPC decision on interest rates** should be announced 12 noon on 3 October.
- **Clocks go back** one hour at 01h00 GMT, 28 October. Historically, the FTSE100 Index has fallen slightly on the following Monday.

**Mon**    • Hong Kong Stock Exchange closed

## 1

1993: QVC, Britain's first home shopping channel on television, was launched.

**Tues**

## 2

1925: The first of London's now traditional red buses, with roofed-in upper decks, went into service after the lifting of restrictions that had prevented such buses being used in the capital city.

**Wed**    • MPC meeting (anticipated) until 4th October

## 3

1990: The official re-unification of East and West Germany, with Berlin named as its capital.

**Thur**

## 4

1976: British Rail began its new 125mph Intercity 'High Speed Train' (HST) service, between London and Bristol - which arrived three minutes early.

**Fri**

## 5

1947: The first televised White House address was given by US President Harry S. Truman.

**Sat**

## 6

2000: Yugoslav President, Slobodan Milosevic, resigned under mounting pressure after allegations of vote-rigging.

**Sun**

## 7

Japanese Grand Prix
1913: The Ford Motor Company started operation of the first assembly line - it could turn out a car in three hours.

"Money is like manure. You have to spread it around or it smells."
– J. Paul Getty

---

Likely company announcements

### Interims

Alexandra plc
Alexon Group plc
Austin Reed Group plc
John David Group plc
MSB International plc
MTL Instruments Group plc
S & U plc
Ted Baker plc
Tesco plc

### Finals

Charteris plc
Gleeson (M J) Group plc
Gourmet Holdings plc
James Halstead plc
Medical House (The) plc
Mercator Gold plc
Noble Investments (UK) plc
Petra Diamonds Ltd
Sinclair Pharma plc
Tottenham Hotspur plc
Tristel plc
Walker (Thomas) plc
Waterman Group plc

# Sector performance – fourth quarter

The table below shows the performance of sectors in the fourth quarter (30/9 – 31/12) of each year 1999-2005. The table is ranked by the final column – the average performance over the 7 years. For each year: the top 5 performing sectors are highlighted in red, the bottom 5 in grey.

| Sector | EPIC | 1999 | 2000 | 2001 | 2002 | 2003 | 2004 | 2005 | Average |
|---|---|---|---|---|---|---|---|---|---|
| Technology Hardware & Equipt | NMX9570 | 278.1 | -31.0 | 64.9 | -60.5 | 27.1 | 13.6 | 13.9 | 43.7 |
| Electronic & Electrical Equip | NMX2730 | 89.7 | -7.0 | 133.7 | -12.4 | -16.2 | 11.4 | 17.4 | 30.9 |
| Industrial Metals | NMX1750 | 33.3 | 37.6 | 64.6 | -20.4 | 48.1 | -1.0 | 14.6 | 25.3 |
| Software & Computer Services | NMX9530 | 93.2 | -37.1 | 26.0 | 29.4 | 2.3 | 10.1 | 10.3 | 19.2 |
| Mining | NMX1770 | 31.0 | 9.6 | 25.1 | 15.5 | 18.3 | -0.4 | 11.2 | 15.8 |
| Media | NMX5550 | 45.2 | -1.8 | 25.4 | 8.9 | 11.0 | 8.4 | 3.5 | 14.4 |
| Fixed Line Telecommunications | NMX6530 | 41.4 | -8.4 | 16.3 | 30.1 | 14.6 | 9.3 | -8.2 | 13.6 |
| Nonlife Insurance | NMX8530 | 2.9 | 25.7 | 17.4 | 22.3 | 2.9 | 2.9 | 17.0 | 13.0 |
| General Financial | NMX8770 | 19.6 | -3.0 | 28.5 | 5.3 | 4.0 | 19.4 | 10.2 | 12.0 |
| Life Insurance | NMX8570 | 14.2 | 12.9 | 3.5 | 21.3 | 7.7 | 11.3 | 9.8 | 11.5 |
| Chemicals | NMX1350 | -0.2 | 23.1 | 15.5 | 4.0 | 5.5 | 10.7 | 9.2 | 9.7 |
| Industrial Engineering | NMX2750 | 6.0 | 10.1 | 24.5 | -3.7 | 6.3 | 10.0 | 10.9 | 9.2 |
| Equity Investment Instruments | NMX8980 | 24.9 | -11.8 | 13.5 | 8.6 | 7.5 | 11.5 | 8.5 | 9.0 |
| Support Services | NMX2790 | 23.3 | 0.5 | 14.5 | 2.8 | 2.9 | 6.9 | 8.0 | 8.4 |
| Construction & Materials | NMX2350 | 3.3 | 19.1 | 12.3 | -5.6 | 6.5 | 8.2 | 13.7 | 8.2 |
| Banks | NMX8350 | 4.3 | 9.0 | 12.7 | 7.8 | 8.5 | 6.6 | 6.5 | 7.9 |
| Health Care Equip & Services | NMX4530 | 5.5 | -10.2 | 13.6 | -0.4 | 26.7 | 4.4 | 13.3 | 7.6 |
| Travel & Leisure | NMX5750 | 8.0 | -3.2 | 17.0 | -8.1 | 13.9 | 12.3 | 11.5 | 7.3 |
| General Retailers | NMX5370 | 1.0 | 10.8 | 20.3 | -1.2 | 2.7 | 1.4 | 14.1 | 7.0 |
| Real Estate | NMX8730 | -6.7 | 2.6 | -0.7 | 3.5 | 13.9 | 18.0 | 10.3 | 5.8 |
| Food Producers | NMX3570 | -13.6 | 26.1 | 7.5 | -2.0 | 4.1 | 15.0 | -1.0 | 5.2 |
| Beverages | NMX3530 | -12.5 | 21.4 | 8.8 | -11.5 | 14.1 | 10.7 | 1.5 | 4.6 |
| Food & Drug Retailers | NMX5330 | -5.3 | 8.0 | -0.9 | -3.2 | 8.2 | 11.2 | 7.6 | 3.7 |
| Industrial Transportation | NMX2770 | -7.8 | 3.2 | 0.6 | -0.2 | 6.5 | 12.9 | 9.6 | 3.5 |
| Personal Goods | NMX3760 | -23.0 | 11.6 | 2.2 | 0.8 | 4.2 | 15.8 | 11.3 | 3.3 |
| Tobacco | NMX3780 | -32.8 | 12.8 | 1.1 | -0.1 | 14.5 | 16.0 | 7.0 | 2.6 |
| Aerospace & Defence | NMX2710 | 2.7 | 6.5 | 2.0 | -11.9 | 1.6 | 3.4 | 11.5 | 2.3 |
| Oil & Gas | NMX0530 | 11.9 | -6.1 | -5.1 | 2.8 | 10.3 | -0.9 | -5.6 | 1.0 |
| Automobiles & Parts | NMX3350 | -1.9 | -2.1 | -3.5 | -14.2 | 7.2 | 15.9 | 4.2 | 0.8 |
| Pharmaceuticals & Biotechnology | NMX4570 | 8.3 | -6.4 | -6.9 | 2.3 | 4.0 | -3.5 | 3.7 | 0.2 |
| Electricity | NMX7530 | -13.7 | 5.9 | -4.5 | 2.0 | 6.3 | 4.1 | -1.7 | -0.2 |
| Leisure Goods | NMX3740 | 0.7 | | -8.3 | | 3.7 | -2.5 | -2.4 | -1.8 |

## Observations

1. The general clustering of red highlights at the top of the table, and grey at the bottom, suggests that certain sectors consistently perform well (or badly) in this quarter.

2. The strong sectors in this quarter are: Technology Hardware & Equipment, Electronic & Electrical Equipment, and Industrial Metals.

3. The weak sectors in this quarter are: Leisure Goods, Electricity and Oil & Gas.

# October 2007

**Mon**
# 8

• Tokyo Stock Exchange closed

2003: Film star Arnold Schwarzenegger was elected governor of California.

**Tues**
# 9

2002: After losing a massive amount of ground during the summer of 2002, the Dow Jones Industrial Average, closed at 7,286.27, its lowest level in five years. The NASDAQ also hit a six-year low, of 1,114.11.

**Wed**
# 10

1971: Sold, dismantled and moved to the US, the London Bridge reopened in Lake Havasu City, Arizona.

**Thur**
# 11

1982: The *Mary Rose*, flagship of King Henry VIII, rose to the surface after 437 years at the bottom of the Solent.

**Fri**
# 12

1999: The Day of Six Billion - the six billionth human in the world was born.

**Sat**
# 13

1988: The British Government fails to stop publication of the controversial book, Spycatcher, written by a former secret service agent.

**Sun**
# 14

Brazilian Grand Prix
1969: The UK introduced the fifty-pence coin - replacing the ten-shilling note, in anticipation of the decimalisation of the currency in 1971.

"Money, the root of all evil...but the cure for all sadness."
– *Mike Gill*

---

## Likely company announcements

### Interims

Ariana Resources plc
Brown (N) Group plc
C&C Group plc
Intermediate Capital Group plc
JJB Sports plc
Kazakhmys plc
Moss Bros Group plc
RDF Media Group plc
Rugby Estates plc
Watermark Group plc

### Finals

ADVFN plc
Air Partner plc
Associated British Foods plc
Cambrian Oil & Gas plc
Carter & Carter Group plc
Fairplace Consulting plc
Fibernet Group plc
Manganese Bronze Holdings plc
St Ives plc
Westmount Energy Ltd
W H Smith plc

# Winter v summer portfolios

*This is the strongest seasonality effect in the UK market, and therefore also the strangest anomaly.*

In last year's Almanac results were presented of the analysis comparing the performance of the FTSE100 Index in winter and summer. This analysis has been updated to include the latest data. First, a recap of the terms of the analysis.

The performance of the FTSE100 Index was studied from 1970 to 2005 for two periods each year-

- *Winter Period*: 1 Nov (from the previous year) to 30 Apr.

- *Summer Period*: 1 May to 31 Oct.

Two hypothetical portfolios were created, both with a starting capital of £1000-

- **Portfolio A**, only invested in the market in the Winter Period, and the rest of the year was in cash.

- **Portfolio B**, only invested in the market in the Summer Period, and the rest of the year was in cash.

The comparative performance of the two portfolios can be seen in the table below.

| Year | Portfolio A % Change (1 Nov - 30 Apr) | Value (£) | Portfolio B % Change (1 May - 31 Oct) | Value (£) |
|---|---|---|---|---|
|  |  | 1000 |  | 1000 |
| 1971 | 7.9 | 1079 | 6.1 | 1061 |
| 1972 | 29.7 | 1399 | -10.4 | 951 |
| 1973 | -2.7 | 1361 | -6.8 | 887 |
| 1974 | -31.1 | 938 | -33.7 | 588 |
| 1975 | 65.6 | 1553 | 7.4 | 631 |
| 1976 | 19.0 | 1849 | -33.8 | 418 |
| 1977 | 56.4 | 2892 | 16.8 | 488 |
| 1978 | -5.4 | 2737 | 3.8 | 507 |
| 1979 | 30.1 | 3560 | -15.1 | 430 |
| 1980 | 4.0 | 3702 | 24.0 | 534 |
| 1981 | 5.1 | 3891 | -12.3 | 468 |
| 1982 | 13.7 | 4424 | 14.2 | 535 |
| 1983 | 17.2 | 5185 | -2.6 | 521 |
| 1984 | 22.7 | 6359 | 1.1 | 527 |
| 1985 | 12.2 | 7133 | 6.7 | 562 |
| 1986 | 20.6 | 8600 | -1.7 | 552 |
| 1987 | 25.6 | 10805 | -14.7 | 471 |
| 1988 | 3.0 | 11129 | 2.8 | 484 |
| 1989 | 14.3 | 12724 | 1.2 | 490 |
| 1990 | -1.8 | 12491 | -2.5 | 478 |
| 1991 | 21.3 | 15147 | 3.2 | 493 |
| 1992 | 3.4 | 15667 | 0.2 | 494 |
| 1993 | 5.8 | 16579 | 12.7 | 556 |
| 1994 | -1.4 | 16341 | -0.9 | 552 |
| 1995 | 3.9 | 16970 | 9.7 | 605 |
| 1996 | 8.2 | 18359 | 4.2 | 631 |
| 1997 | 11.5 | 20467 | 9.2 | 688 |
| 1998 | 22.4 | 25057 | -8.3 | 631 |
| 1999 | 20.5 | 30188 | -4.5 | 603 |
| 2000 | 1.1 | 30534 | 1.8 | 613 |
| 2001 | -7.3 | 28298 | -15.5 | 518 |
| 2002 | 2.5 | 29005 | -21.8 | 405 |
| 2003 | -2.8 | 28189 | 9.2 | 443 |
| 2004 | 4.7 | 29518 | 3.0 | 456 |
| 2005 | 3.8 | 30,651 | 10.7 | 505 |

## Observations

1.  In 2005, the Winter Portfolio (Nov 2004 – Apr 2005) unusually under-performed the summer portfolio (May 2005 – Oct 2005).

2.  From the start in 1970, Portfolio A has now increased in value to **£30,651**, while Portfolio B has fallen in value to **£505**.

3.  In only 6 of the last 33 years, has the Summer Portfolio significantly out-performed the Winter Portfolio. (See chart below).

4.  The magnitude of the difference is decreasing – the 1970s saw some huge differences.

Yearly performance difference between Portfolios A and B

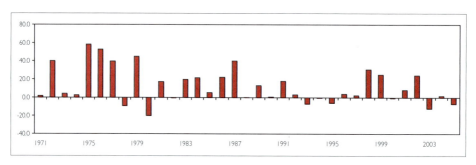

## Mon
# 15

1995: Saddam Hussein gained 99.96% of votes in Iraq's presidential elections.

## Tues
# 16

1923: The Walt Disney Company was founded by Walt Disney and his brother, Roy Disney.

## Wed
# 17

1931: Al Capone convicted of income tax evasion.

## Thur
# 18

1960: *The News Chronicle* and *Daily Mail* merged and *The London Evening Star* merged with the *Evening News*.

## Fri
# 19

• Hong Kong Stock Exchange closed

1987: Black Monday - the Dow Jones Industrial Average fell by 22%.

## Sat
# 20

1971: The Nepal stock exchange collapsed.

## Sun
# 21

1982: Gerry Adams and Martin McGuinness made history, as they became the first members of Sinn Fein to be elected to the Ulster Assembly.

"A feast is made for laughter, and wine maketh merry: but money answereth all things."
– Bible Ecclesiastes (ch. X, v. 19)

---

### Likely company announcements

### Interims

AfriOre Ltd
Bisichi Mining plc
Block Shield Corporation plc
CHE Hotel Group plc
Collins and Hayes Group plc
Harvey Nash Group plc
Instore plc
LiDCO Group plc
Low & Bonar plc
QXL ricardo plc
Superscape Group plc
Thomson Intermedia plc

### Finals

Accuma Group plc
Actif Group plc
All IPO plc
Bellway plc
BowLeven plc
FishWorks plc
Freeport plc
Hamsard Group plc
Karelian Diamond Resources plc
Mouchel Parkman plc
Offshore Hydrocarbon Mapping plc
On-Line plc
Provalis plc
Third Advance Value Realisation
Company (UK) Ltd
Victoria Oil & Gas plc

# Winter v summer portfolios (FTSE250)

*On the previous page we saw the dramatic difference between the performance of the FTSE100 Index in the winter and the summer. But perhaps this is just a large company phenomenon?*

To test whether the 6-month effect also applies to mid-cap stocks, the same analysis was applied to the FTSE250 Index. The results are shown in the table below.

| Year | Portfolio A % Change (1 Nov - 30 Apr) | Value (£) | Portfolio B % Change (1 May - 31 Oct) | Value (£) |
|---|---|---|---|---|
| 1986 | | 1000 | | 1000 |
| 1987 | 26.7 | 1267 | -11.5 | 885 |
| 1988 | 9.8 | 1391 | 6.8 | 945 |
| 1989 | 9.7 | 1526 | -3.5 | 912 |
| 1990 | -6.7 | 1424 | -9.8 | 822 |
| 1991 | 21.0 | 1724 | 2.4 | 842 |
| 1992 | 6.6 | 1838 | -7.0 | 783 |
| 1993 | 24.2 | 2284 | 12.6 | 882 |
| 1994 | 7.2 | 2447 | -7.0 | 820 |
| 1995 | 0.4 | 2457 | 10.3 | 905 |
| 1996 | 16.9 | 2871 | -2.8 | 879 |
| 1997 | 1.7 | 2921 | 3.2 | 907 |
| 1998 | 20.8 | 3530 | -14.2 | 778 |
| 1999 | 21.6 | 4291 | -3.9 | 748 |
| 2000 | 10.2 | 4728 | 7.0 | 800 |
| 2001 | -3.3 | 4571 | -16.3 | 670 |
| 2002 | 14.1 | 5218 | -27.9 | 483 |
| 2003 | -0.6 | 5184 | 30.4 | 630 |
| 2004 | 8.5 | 5624 | 1.8 | 642 |
| 2005 | 6.4 | 5987 | 14.6 | 735 |

## Observations

1.  The value of the £1000 Winter Portfolio had increased to £5987 by 2005, whereas the Summer Portfolio had fallen to £735.

2.  The results are not quite as dramatic as those for the FTSE100 Index, but this analysis is over a shorter time period. However, the greater performance of mid-cap stocks in the winter period over the summer can still clearly be seen.

3.  In only 3 of the last 18 years has the Summer Portfolio significantly out-performed the Winter Portfolio. (See chart below).

Yearly performance difference between Portfolios A and B

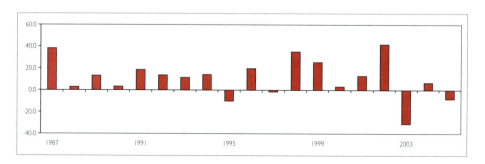

# October 2007

## Mon
# 22

1938: Chester Carlson invented the photocopier.

## Tues
# 23

2001: iPod released in USA.

## Wed
# 24

1929: "Black Thursday" stock market crash on the New York Stock Exchange, beginning The Wall Street Crash of 1929.

## Thur   *
# 25

2004: Cuba's President, Fidel Castro, announced that transactions using the US dollar would be banned by 8 November 2004.

## Fri
# 26

2004: AT&T Wireless was officially acquired by Cingular Wireless.

## Sat
# 27

1904: The first New York Subway line opens. The system became the biggest in the USA and one of the biggest in the world.

## Sun
# 28

British Summer Time Ends
1914: The single largest one-day decline in terms of percentage by the Dow Jones Industrial Average was recorded, in stock market history.

"Money cannot buy health, but I'd settle for a diamond-studded wheelchair."
— *Dorothy Parker*

---

**Likely company announcements**

### Interims

Alterian plc
Azman plc
Blacks Leisure Group plc
Boots Group plc
Cordillera Resources plc
European Motor Holdings plc
Hitachi Capital (UK) plc
International Ferro Metals
London & Associated Properties plc
LHP Investments plc
Motive Television plc
R.E.A. Holdings plc
Whitbread plc

### Finals

BWA Group plc
Egdon Resources plc
European Convergence Property Company plc
Formation Group plc
Hill Station plc
IAF Group plc
Innobox plc
Jubilee Platinum plc
Marylebone Warwick Balfour Group plc
MultiMedia Television plc
OEM plc
Premier Management Holdings plc
Rambler Metals and Mining plc
Scott Tod plc
SRS Technology Group plc
The Parkmead Group plc
Voss Net plc

# November market

## Market performance in the month

While market performance this month is nothing special – it is 6th in the ranking of months – November is worthy of note as being the first month in the six-month cycle (Nov-Apr) of strong market returns. In other words, investors should be increasing exposure to the market this month.

On average the market rises 0.6% this month (with a standard deviation of a high 6.0).

The probability of a positive return for the month is a good 67%. As can be seen from the chart below, apart from the occasional very bad years, the risk-return is favourable. In fact, the FTSE100 Index has only had one significant fall in a November in the past 13 years.

Over the longer term the performance of mid and large cap stocks is similar this month.

Historic performance of the market in November

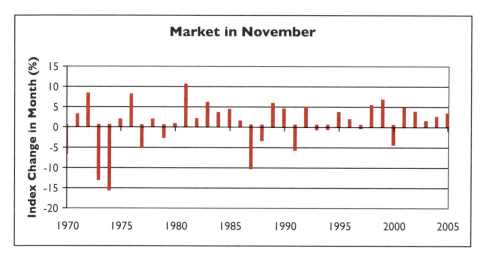

## Company announcements

Large companies reporting this month:

*   *Finals*: Associated British Foods, Compass Group, Imperial Tobacco Group.

*   *Interims*: BAA, BT Group, GUS, Land Securities Group, Marks & Spencer Group, National Grid, O2, SABMiller, Scottish & Southern Energy, Scottish Power, United Utilities, Vodafone Group.

## What to look out for this month

*   The **MPC decision on interest rates** should be announced 12 noon on 7 November.

*   **10th strongest week** of the year: week 46; **10th weakest week** of the year: week 48.

# Oct/Nov 2007

## Mon
# 29

1929: The New York Stock Exchange crashed, in what was called the "Crash of 29" or "Black Tuesday" - ending the bull market of the 1920s and beginning the Great Depression.

## Tues
# 30

• FOMC meeting (tentative) until 31st October

1988: Philip Morris bought Kraft Foods for US$13.1 billion.

## Wed  *
# 31

Halloween
2003: A bankruptcy court approved MCI's reorganisation plans, essentially clearing the telecommunications company to exit bankruptcy.

## Thur
# 1

All Saint's Day
1993: The Maastricht Treaty took effect, formally establishing the European Union.

## Fri
# 2

1904: *The Daily Mirror* began publishing.

## Sat
# 3

1817: The Bank of Montreal, Canada's oldest chartered bank, opened in Montreal, Quebec.

## Sun
# 4

1994: The first conference that focused exclusively on the subject of the commercial potential of the World Wide Web was held in San Fransisco.

"Money will not buy happiness, but it will let you be unhappy in nice places."
— *Anonymous*

---

Likely company announcements

### Interims

African Consolidated Resources plc
BAA plc
Angus & Ross plc
Carphone Warehouse Group (The) plc
Danka Business Systems plc
London Stock Exchange plc
Matalan plc
PSG Solutions plc
Tate & Lyle plc
Theo Fennell plc
TTP Communications plc
UMECO plc

### Finals

Arc Fund Management Holdings plc
Armour Group plc
Asia Energy plc
Brinkley Mining plc
Cambrian Mining plc
Catalyst New Opportunities plc
Character Group (The) plc
Debenhams plc
Europa Oil & Gas (Holdings) plc
Global Gaming Technologies plc
Healthcare Communications Group plc
Imperial Tobacco Group plc
ISIS Medical Technology plc
Lok'n Store Group plc
McCarthy & Stone plc
MG Capital plc
Netb2b2 plc
Phytopharm plc
Smart (J) & Co (Contractors) plc
Transvision Resources plc

# The 6-month strategy

On page 98 analysis showed the great out-performance of the market between November to April over the six-month period for the rest of the year.

This behaviour suggests a strategy of holding shares in the market from November to April, and in May selling the share portfolio and holding cash from May to October. The chart below illustrates the performance of such a portfolio (buying the FTSE Index), compared to a constant portfolio of the FTSE100 stocks.

Starting in 1971 with £100, the constant portfolio would have a value of £1,229 by mid 2006, compared to the £2,842 value of the 6-Month Strategy.

*Note:* The analysis does not take into account the transaction costs of buying and selling the portfolio every 6 months, but neither does it account for the interest earned on the cash for 6 months of every year which would help to defray the costs.

The reasons for the 6-month effect are not known for sure, although there are a number of theories. One such theory concerns the effect on investors of the lengthening and shortening of days through the seasons. If this is the case, then it suggests that such an effect may also

occur in Australia – albeit reversed in timing. And analysis on data from 1970 does show that the Australian market (in Sterling terms) tends to out-perform the UK market from May to October.

A variation on the above strategy would therefore be: go long of the UK market from November to April, then switch the whole portfolio into the Australian market from May to October.

The chart to the left illustrates the cumulative performance of this 6-Month Strategy (Australian Variant), compared to the ordinary 6-Month Strategy (described above) and the FTSE100 Index.

On the same basis as the analysis above, this new adjusted strategy would have grown £100 in 1971 to £4,708 by mid 2006.

# November 2007

## Mon
## 5

Guy Fawkes Night
1935: Parker Brothers released one of the best-selling commercial board games, Monopoly.

## Tues
## 6

2001: Belgian national airline, Sabena, is declared bankrupt.

## Wed
## 7

• MPC meeting (anticipated) until 8th November

2000: Hillary Clinton, wife of an incumbent US president, made history when she won a New York Senate seat.

## Thur
## 8

1793: The French Revolutionary government in Paris opened the Louvre to the public as a museum.

## Fri
## 9

1998: In the largest civil settlement in US history, brokerage houses were ordered to pay US$1.03 billion to cheated NASDAQ investors, to compensate for their price-fixing.

## Sat
## 10

1997: WorldCom and MCI Communications announced a $37 billion merger - the largest in US history at the time.

## Sun
## 11

Remembrance Day
1954: Thousands of elderly people took part in a rally in London, calling for an increase in their pensions.

"Money speaks sense in a language all nations understand."
— *Aphra Behn*

---

Likely company announcements

### Interims

3i Group plc
AVEVA Group plc
BPB plc
Braemar Seascope Group plc
British Airways plc
BT Group plc
BTG plc
Cable and Wireless plc
Celsis International plc
Charles Stanley Group plc
DCC plc
Electrocomponents plc
Hornby plc
Invensys plc
Liontrust Asset Management plc
Marks & Spencer Group plc
Penna Consulting plc
Robert Wiseman Dairies plc
Ryanair Holdings plc
SABMiller plc
Shanks Group plc
Volex Group plc
Wincanton plc
Yell Group plc

### Finals

Caplay plc
Careforce Group plc
Connaught plc
Felix Group plc
Fenner plc
Ferraris Group plc
Fulcrum Pharma plc
IDMoS plc
Impax Group plc
Infoscreen Networks plc
Next Fifteen Communications Group plc
Platinum Mining Corporation of India plc
Punch Taverns plc
Pursuit Dynamics plc
VTR plc
World Careers Network plc

# Sinclair numbers – monthly performance

The table below ranks the 12 months by their historic performance since 1970.

The best month of the whole year – when the market has historically increased the most – is April. This month the market has increased on average 2.8%, with a standard deviation of 4.9. The proportion of years when the market has increased in April is 78%.

The month with the worst record is May. On average the market falls 0.6% in this month, and only rises 43% of years.

The performance figures were ranked by the P-Factor. (The Sinclair analysis that produced these numbers is explained in the introduction).

Ranking of monthly performance

| Month | Up(%) | Avg Change (%) | StdDev(%) |
|---|---|---|---|
| April | 78 | 2.8 | 4.9 |
| January | 69 | 2.7 | 9.1 |
| December | 69 | 2.2 | 4.7 |
| October | 69 | 0.2 | 6.5 |
| August | 67 | 1.3 | 5.5 |
| November | 67 | 0.6 | 6.0 |
| March | 62 | 0.6 | 5.7 |
| February | 54 | 1.5 | 6.2 |
| July | 51 | 0.2 | 4.2 |
| June | 46 | -0.9 | 4.6 |
| September | 44 | -1.4 | 6.3 |
| May | 43 | -0.6 | 4.6 |

The variation in performance between the months is statistically significant.

## Six month effect

The chart below shows the average monthly performance of the FTSE100 Index.

The strength of the market in the period November to April can be clearly seen in the chart – which gives rise to the Six month effect.

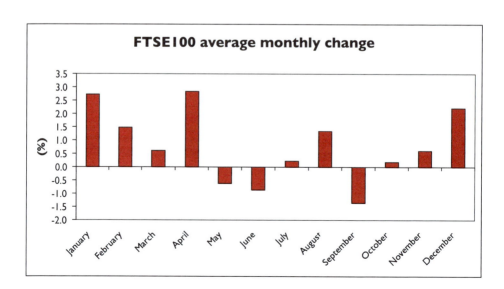

# November 2007

**Mon**

## 12

1946: A branch of the Exchange National Bank in Chicago, Illinois, opened the first ten drive-up teller windows.

**Tues**

## 13

1990: The first known World Wide Web page was written.

**Wed**

## 14

1972: The Dow Jones Industrial Average closed above 1,000 (1,003.16) for the first time.

**Thur**

## 15

2001: Microsoft released the *Xbox* in North America - the company's first video game console.

**Fri**

## 16

1973: US President, Richard Nixon, signed the Trans-Alaska Pipeline Authorisation Act into law, authorising the construction of the Alaska pipeline.

**Sat**
## 17

2004: In America, Kmart Corp. announced it was buying Sears, Roebuck and Co. for $11 billion and naming the newly merged company, Sears Holdings Corporation.

**Sun**
## 18

1996: A fire occurred in the Channel Tunnel just six months after it was officially opened.

"Those who have some means think that the most important thing in the world is love. The poor know that it is money."
– *Gerald Brenan*

Likely company announcements

### Interims

600 Group (The) plc
Babcock International Group plc
Bank of Ireland (Governor & Co of)
Big Yellow Group plc
Burberry Group plc
Business Post Group plc
Chloride Group plc
eircom Group plc
EMAP plc
Glotel plc
GUS plc
Helical Bar plc
Investec plc
Kewill Systems plc
Land Securities Group plc
Latchways plc
Luminar plc
Man Group plc
Marchpole Holdings plc
Mothercare plc
National Grid plc
Northern Foods plc
QinetiQ Group plc
Rensburg Sheppards plc
Sainsbury (J) plc
Scottish & Southern Energy plc
Scottish Power plc
Uniq plc
Vedanta Resources plc
Vodafone Group plc
VT Group plc

### Finals

Charlton Athletic plc
Chrysalis Group plc
Dimension Data Holdings plc
Diploma plc
easyJet plc
Euromoney Institutional Investor plc
European Diamonds plc
Lonmin plc
Mecom Group plc
PipeHawk plc
Sheffield United plc

# Share performance in December

## Stocks that like December

The 15 companies in the table below have all risen nine times in the last ten years in the month of December. (The table shows the percentage price change for the stock in the month of December for that year. For example, the share price of CRH increased 1.2% in December 1996.)

| Company | 1996 | 1997 | 1998 | 1999 | 2000 | 2001 | 2002 | 2003 | 2004 | 2005 |
|---|---|---|---|---|---|---|---|---|---|---|
| Anite Group PLC | 1.4 | 14.6 | -13.0 | 51.4 | 4.0 | 26.3 | 10.6 | 2.5 | 6.6 | 13.3 |
| Atkins (W S) PLC | 4.5 | 5.5 | -5.4 | 15.8 | 2.3 | 11.9 | 9.4 | 6.5 | 1.4 | 0.3 |
| CRH PLC | 1.2 | 4.1 | 12.1 | 7.5 | 18.1 | 8.8 | -20.0 | 4.2 | 3.4 | 10.4 |
| Daily Mail and General Trust PLC | 2.5 | 12.7 | 2.8 | 19.1 | 3.7 | 1.3 | -11.6 | 6.8 | 3.0 | 5.0 |
| Diageo PLC | 2.8 | 4.2 | 0.7 | -12.3 | 2.5 | 4.7 | 0.8 | 1.4 | 1.5 | 0.9 |
| Headlam Group PLC | 0.5 | 8.8 | -7.5 | 12.6 | 2.6 | 7.0 | -14.8 | 2.1 | 5.2 | 6.0 |
| Hiscox PLC | -2.1 | 6.0 | 8.2 | 0.4 | 0.7 | 3.0 | 13.7 | 0.9 | 4.7 | 6.7 |
| Kingfisher PLC | -2.7 | 3.9 | 12.5 | 18.7 | 8.2 | 0.3 | 0.3 | 1.0 | 7.6 | 5.4 |
| Kingspan Group PLC | 1.0 | 0.9 | 16.8 | 24.9 | 28.1 | 1.0 | -11.9 | 5.2 | 7.8 | 3.7 |
| McKay Securities PLC | 0.7 | 7.7 | 3.2 | 2.0 | 6.5 | 1.4 | -6.3 | 6.7 | 6.7 | 2.1 |
| Richmond Foods PLC | 1.0 | 6.8 | 4.2 | 11.2 | 2.4 | 18.7 | -1.2 | 0.9 | 18.3 | 15.6 |
| Savills PLC | 5.8 | 2.3 | 4.9 | 12.2 | 1.4 | 17.3 | 2.9 | 12.5 | 24.9 | 9.3 |
| Slough Estates PLC | 6.3 | -0.9 | 0.4 | 1.3 | 5.4 | 2.0 | 0.1 | 4.3 | 13.9 | 9.6 |
| Wagon PLC | 0.2 | 14.4 | 22.6 | 7.3 | 5.0 | 14.6 | -23.7 | 4.1 | 6.1 | 6.5 |
| Young & Co's Brewery PLC | 1.2 | 1.1 | -2.0 | 0.6 | 8.0 | 1.1 | 5.2 | 1.4 | 1.9 | 4.8 |
| Average | 1.6 | 6.1 | 5.0 | 11.5 | 6.6 | 8.0 | -3.1 | 4.0 | 7.5 | 6.6 |
| FTSE All-Share | 1.4 | 5.3 | 1.8 | 5.0 | 1.3 | 0.4 | -5.5 | 2.8 | 2.8 | 3.9 |

Only one listed company, Savills, has risen in December in all ten of the years from 1996 to 2005. One year, 2002, accounted for the one bad year for seven of the stocks.

On average the best performing company in December has been Anite Group (average December increase of +11.8%), followed by Savills (+9.4%), Richmond Foods (+7.8%) and then Kingspan Group (+7.8%).

## Stocks that don't like December

The 15 companies in the table below have all fallen eight times in the last ten years in the month of December.

| Company | 1996 | 1997 | 1998 | 1999 | 2000 | 2001 | 2002 | 2003 | 2004 | 2005 |
|---|---|---|---|---|---|---|---|---|---|---|
| Abbeycrest PLC | -6.3 | -2.1 | -5.6 | -5.5 | -3.0 | 13.2 | -29.7 | 11.1 | -7.0 | -11.8 |
| Abbot Group PLC | 11.8 | -1.8 | -4.5 | -9.6 | -1.5 | -13.8 | -2.5 | -13.1 | -0.6 | 1.2 |
| Character Group (The) PLC | -7.0 | 23.1 | -10.0 | -12.0 | -40.7 | -18.7 | -22.3 | -11.9 | -14.7 | 16.5 |
| CHE Hotel Group PLC | -1.6 | -4.0 | -2.4 | -3.6 | -11.0 | | -2.8 | 5.1 | -1.2 | -5.6 |
| Fulmar PLC | -5.3 | -1.9 | -16.4 | -7.4 | -2.0 | 11.9 | 8.3 | -1.3 | -1.2 | -4.2 |
| Innovata PLC | -4.9 | -38.4 | 30.4 | 26.2 | -2.3 | -6.1 | -6.5 | -2.4 | -6.9 | -3.0 |
| Instore PLC | -10.3 | -1.5 | -1.3 | -10.1 | -26.4 | -20.5 | -9.9 | -10.0 | 3.3 | 4.8 |
| Menzies (John) PLC | -5.0 | -0.8 | -5.3 | 1.8 | -6.8 | -0.8 | -4.4 | -1.6 | 13.4 | -4.4 |
| Nichols PLC | -3.8 | -5.0 | -8.9 | -3.0 | 6.5 | -9.4 | -3.1 | -3.3 | -5.3 | 3.1 |
| Pace Micro Technology PLC | -3.4 | -9.8 | 6.3 | 15.6 | -9.0 | -14.2 | -7.0 | -0.9 | -26.4 | -7.2 |
| Park Group PLC | -6.8 | 8.0 | -10.3 | -21.4 | -10.9 | -17.4 | -2.1 | -7.8 | 3.3 | -25.0 |
| Reflec PLC | -8.6 | -50.7 | | -7.4 | -2.9 | | -9.8 | -14.6 | -3.3 | -5.6 |
| Renold PLC | -2.1 | -3.3 | -0.3 | -9.8 | -3.6 | -19.5 | 15.4 | -5.4 | 0.7 | -4.0 |
| SR Pharma PLC | 5.5 | -1.1 | -1.9 | -11.3 | 28.2 | -3.4 | -9.8 | -4.4 | -11.7 | -17.1 |
| Vernalis PLC | -2.1 | -14.8 | -16.7 | -0.8 | -21.4 | -5.7 | -8.8 | -11.4 | 2.3 | -3.9 |
| Average | -3.3 | -6.9 | -3.4 | -3.9 | -7.1 | -8.0 | -6.3 | -4.8 | -3.7 | -4.4 |
| FTSE All-Share | 1.4 | 5.3 | 1.8 | 5.0 | 1.3 | 0.4 | -5.5 | 2.8 | 2.8 | 3.9 |

Of the 15 companies above just one, Vernalis, has fallen in nine of the previous ten years in December.

On average, the worst performing stocks have been: Reflec (average December decrease of -12.9%), Character Group (-9.8%), Park Group (-9.0%), Vernalis (-8.3%).

## Mon
# 19

1994: Britain's first national lottery draw shown live on a flagship BBC1 show.

## Tues
# 20

1993: The US Senate Ethics Committee issued a stern censure of California senator, Alan Cranston, for his dealings with savings-and-loan executive, Charles Keating - fallout from the Savings and Loans scandal.

## Wed
# 21

1995: The Dow Jones Industrial Average closed above 5,000 (5,023.55) for the first time.

## Thur
# 22

• New York Stock Exchange closed

1990: Margaret Thatcher resigned as Prime Minister, after her cabinet refused to back her in a second round of leadership elections.

## Fri
# 23

• Tokyo Stock Exchange closed

1954: For the first time, the Dow Jones Industrial Average closed above the peak it reached just before the 1929 crash.

## Sat
# 24

1998: America Online (AOL) announced it would acquire Netscape Communications, in a stock-for-stock transaction worth US$4.2 billion.

## Sun
# 25

1994: Sony founder, Akio Morita, announced he would be stepping down as CEO of the company.

"No man's credit is as good as his money."
– *Edgar Watson Howe*

---

Likely company announcements

### Interims

Abbeycrest plc
British Land Co plc
Castings plc
ClinPhone plc
CML Microsystems plc
Cranswick plc
Cropper (James) plc
EMI Group plc
European Colour plc
GCap Media plc
Great Portland Estates plc
Halfords Group plc
ICAP plc
Imagination Technologies Group plc
Intelek plc
Johnson Matthey plc
Land of Leather Holdings plc
MICE Group plc
Oxford Instruments plc
PayPoint plc
Phoenix IT Group plc
Radstone Technology plc
Scapa Group plc
Speedy Hire plc
SSL International plc
Telent plc
Thus Group plc
Tribal Group plc
Trifast plc
Victoria plc
Viridian Group plc
Walker Crips Weddle Beck plc
Workspace Group plc

### Finals

Abacus Group plc
Anglo Irish Bank Corporation plc
BOC Group (The) plc
Care UK plc
Carr's Milling Industries plc
Daily Mail and General Trust plc
Enodis plc
Enterprise Inns plc
Greencore Group plc
Innovation Group (The) plc
Nord Anglia Education plc
Paragon Group of Companies (The) plc
RM plc
ScS Upholstery plc
United Drug plc

# December market

## Market performance in the month

This is the month to throw all the chips on to equities! December-January is the strongest two-month period of the year – with the market increasing an average 4.8% over the two months.

December itself is the 3rd strongest month of the year (behind April and January), with an average increase of 2.2% (with a standard deviation of a relatively low 4.7).

The probability of positive returns in December is a high 69%. The chart below shows that the market has had only one significant fall in a December since 1981.

Over the longer term the performance of mid and large cap stocks is similar this month.

In summary: this is a great month for investors.

Historic performance of the market in December

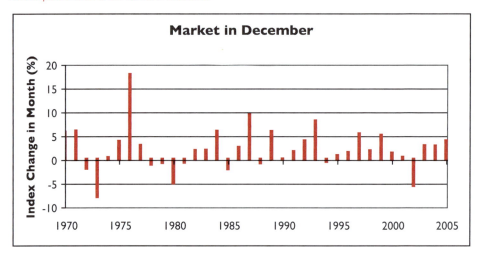

## Company announcements

Large companies reporting this month:

*   *Finals*: Carnival.

## What to look out for this month

*   The quarterly **FTSE100 Index review** should be implemented after market close 21 December (if any changes are made), with the announcement made about a week before this. (Don't forget: companies expelled from the Index often see their share price rise in the following weeks).

*   **Strongest day** of the year for the market: 28 Dec; **3rd strongest day** of the year for the market: 16 Dec; **6th strongest day** of the year for the market: 24 Dec; **7th weakest day** of the year for the market: 10 Dec.

*   **Strongest week** of the year for the market: week 51; **2nd strongest week** of the year for the market: week 52; **7th weakest week** of the year: week 49.

*   **Triple witching** (derivatives contract expires) on 21 December.

*   The **MPC decision on interest rates** should be announced 12 noon on 5 December.

*   **Holidays:** the LSE is closed 25 and 26 December.

## Mon
# 26

1992: It was announced that the Queen was to become the first British monarch since the 1930s to pay income tax.

## Tues
# 27

1967: The French President, Charles de Gaulle, said he would veto Britain's application to join the Common Market for a second time.

## Wed
# 28

1990: Margaret Thatcher formally tendered her resignation to the Queen and left Downing Street for the last time.

## Thur
# 29

1975: The name "Micro-soft" (short for "microcomputer software") was first used in a letter from Bill Gates to Paul Allen.

## Fri
# 30

St. Andrew's Day
1998: Deutsche Bank announced a $10 billion deal to buy Bankers Trust, thus creating the largest financial institution in the world.

## Sat
# 1

1998: Exxon announced a US$73.7 billion deal to buy Mobil, thus creating Exxon-Mobil, the largest company on the planet.

## Sun
# 2

1995: Nick Leeson was sentenced for financial dealings which contributed to the fall of Britain's oldest merchant bank.

Likely company announcements

### Interims

Atkins (W S) plc
AWG plc
BSS Group plc
Caffyns plc
Chapelthorpe plc
Dairy Crest Group plc
De La Rue plc
Dee Valley Group plc
Detica Group plc
Domestic & General Group plc
Dyson Group plc
Expro International Group plc
FKI plc
Fuller Smith & Turner plc
GB Group plc
Goldshield Group plc
Hampson Industries plc
Highway Capital plc
Homeserve plc
IFX Group plc
Jarvis plc
Kelda Group plc
Kingston Communications (Hull) plc
London Merchant Securities plc
Micro Focus International plc
MITIE Group plc
MS International plc
Patientline plc
RPC Group plc
Torotrak plc
United Utilities plc
Vp plc
Wagon plc
Xansa plc

### Finals

Eurodis Electron plc
Arla Foods UK plc
Avon Rubber plc
Brewin Dolphin Holdings plc
Cambridge Antibody Technology Group plc
Cardiff Property (The) plc
Compass Group plc
Dawson Holdings plc
De Vere Group plc
Future plc
Holidaybreak plc
Jessops plc
Mitchells & Butlers plc
Optos plc
Sage Group (The) plc
Southern Cross Healthcare Group plc
Topps Tiles plc
World Trade Systems plc

"Money, it turned out, was exactly like sex, you thought of nothing else if you didn't have it and thought of other things if you did."
– James Baldwin

# Bounceback stocks 1

In the US there is a famous stock market phenomenon called the S&P 500 Dog Effect. This holds that stocks that have fallen strongly in the 3 years to 30 September, bounce back strongly in the following 3 months (or, alternatively, the following 12 months).

*Does this work for the UK market as well?*

The table below shows the results of analysis to test the Bounceback Effect in the UK market for the last two years. Instead of using 30 September, the performance of the 10 worst stocks for the whole year (Jan-Dec) was compared with their performance in the following January and January-March periods.

The columns in the table are:

1.  Percentage performance of the stock the previous year.

2.  Percentage performance of the stock in January the next year.

3.  Percentage performance of the stock in the January-March period the next year.

The universe of stocks examined was the FTSE350.

Bounceback Effect for FTSE350 Dog Stocks for 2004 and 2005

| Company | 2004 | Jan | Jan-Mar | Company | 2005 | Jan | Jan-Mar |
|---|---|---|---|---|---|---|---|
| COLT Telecom | -50.4 | 20.7 | 5.9 | MFI Furniture Group PLC | -35.5 | -16.9 | 34.4 |
| MyTravel Group | -44.8 | 9.2 | -2.5 | GCap Media PLC | -33.9 | -12.2 | -20.0 |
| Avis Europe | -43.4 | -6.0 | 19.1 | Spirent Communications PLC | -32.9 | 4.0 | -9.1 |
| Computacenter | -38.1 | 8.2 | 2.1 | HMV Group PLC | -30.5 | 2.1 | -3.9 |
| easyJet | -35.9 | 17.2 | 14.9 | F&C Asset Management PLC | -27.9 | 19.6 | 28.9 |
| Compass Group | -35.2 | -2.1 | -1.9 | Topps Tiles PLC | -23.5 | 6.5 | 10.8 |
| Jardine Lloyd Thompson | -29.5 | -0.3 | 3.0 | Kingfisher PLC | -23.4 | 0.1 | 1.4 |
| AstraZeneca | -29.5 | 5.3 | 10.4 | Travis Perkins PLC | -19.2 | 5.5 | 18.7 |
| Premier Farnell | -27.0 | 2.3 | -0.7 | Provident Financial PLC | -18.5 | -2.3 | 28.9 |
| JJB Sports | -24.9 | 21.5 | 18.8 | Matalan PLC | -17.4 | -4.8 | 5.3 |
| average: | | 7.6 | 6.9 | average: | | 0.2 | 9.5 |

## Observations

1   The Bounceback Effect worked well in the last two years. The 10 worst stocks in 2004 bounced back, on average, 6.9% in the first three months of 2005 period, and the 10 worst stocks in 2005 bounced back, on average, 9.5% in the first three months of 2006.

2   For the 2005 Dogs, the Bounceback Effect was seen mainly in the Jan-Mar period. In some years, the bounceback happens quickly, and if a strong performance is seen in January then there is usually little to gain in holding the strategy open to March (as was the case for the 2004 Dogs).

*Note*

There is some evidence to suggest that the Bounceback Effect works far better in bull, rather than bear, markets. A filter may therefore be to only apply the strategy when the FTSE350 Index has increased in the year.

[The analysis is continued on the following page.]

# December 2007

## Mon
# 3

1992: The Greek oil tanker, Aegean Sea, runs aground in a storm carrying 80,000 tones of crude oil, spilling much of its cargo.

## Tues
# 4

1791: The first issue of *The Observer*, the world's first Sunday newspaper, was published.

## Wed
• MPC meeting (anticipated) until 6th December
# 5

1766: The world-famous auction house, Christie's, was founded by James Christies.

## Thur
# 6

1994: The Queen gave the go-ahead for oil drilling to take place in the grounds of Windsor Castle.

## Fri
# 7

1732: The Royal Opera House opened in Covent Garden, London.

## Sat
# 8

1983: House of Lords members voted in favour of allowing live television broadcasts from its chamber.

## Sun
# 9

1957: The Post Master General kicked off a campaign urging the public to send their Christmas cards in good time.

"Money can't buy happiness, but it does quiet the nerves."
-- *Anonymous*

---

Likely company announcements

### Interims

Acal plc
AEA Technology plc
Anite Group plc
Carclo plc
Coral Products plc
Creston plc
European Home Retail plc
Greene King plc
Halma plc
iSOFT Group plc
Northumbrian Water Group plc
Pennon Group plc
Protherics plc
Quintain Estates & Development plc
Salvesen (Christian) plc
Severn Trent plc
Smith (DS) plc
Stagecoach Group plc
Universal Salvage plc
Warner Estate Holdings plc

### Finals

Aberdeen Asset Management plc
API Group plc
First Choice Holidays plc
Grainger Trust plc
Intec Telecom Systems plc
ITE Group plc
Shaftesbury plc
Titon Holdings plc
Ultraframe plc
Victrex plc
Wolverhampton & Dudley Breweries plc

# Bounceback stocks 2

On the previous page it was seen that the Bounceback Effect worked for 2004 and 2005 FTSE350 Dog Stocks. On this page the tables below show the results of analysis to see if the effect is as strong for large and small caps equally.

(For an explanation of the table columns see the previous page.)

## Bounceback Effect for FTSE100 Dog Stocks for 2004 and 2005

| Company | 2004 | Jan | Jan-Mar | Company | 2005 | Jan | Jan-Mar |
|---|---|---|---|---|---|---|---|
| Compass Group | -35.2 | -2.1 | -1.9 | Kingfisher PLC | -23.4 | 0.1 | 1.4 |
| AstraZeneca | -29.5 | 5.3 | 10.4 | British Sky Broadcasting Group PLC | -11.7 | -2.1 | 8.4 |
| Rentokil Initial | -22.2 | 2.9 | 9.6 | Vodafone Group PLC | -11.2 | -6.0 | -2.4 |
| AMVESCAP | -20.9 | 8.5 | 4.1 | Compass Group PLC | -10.5 | 0.6 | 3.9 |
| BSkyB | -20.1 | 0.5 | 3.3 | Alliance Boots PLC | -7.7 | 5.1 | 13.7 |
| Sainsbury | -13.5 | 4.6 | 6.9 | Next PLC | -7.0 | 12.9 | 8.6 |
| Royal & Sun Alliance | -12.2 | 10.6 | 1.3 | Morrison (Wm) Supermarkets PLC | -6.5 | -3.4 | -0.6 |
| Cable and Wireless | -10.7 | 3.1 | 8.4 | Royal Bank of Scotland Group (The) PLC | 0.2 | -0.9 | 8.0 |
| Morrison Supermarkets | -8.4 | -2.7 | -5.3 | Smith & Nephew PLC | 0.5 | 4.2 | -3.5 |
| Boots Group | -5.1 | 1.7 | -4.9 | Liberty International PLC | 1.0 | 7.6 | 20.9 |
| average: | | 3.2 | 3.2 | average: | | 1.8 | 5.8 |

## Bounceback Effect for FTSE Small Cap Dog Stocks for 2004 and 2005

| Company | 2004 | Jan | Jan-Mar | Company | 2005 | Jan | Jan-Mar |
|---|---|---|---|---|---|---|---|
| Ultraframe | -74.4 | -26.1 | -8.9 | Jarvis PLC | -89.9 | -6.5 | -8.7 |
| Tribal Group | -56.5 | -7.6 | -2.1 | Games Workshop Group PLC | -58.1 | -13.7 | -22.3 |
| Wolfson Microelect. | -54.8 | 6.9 | 4.8 | Zetex PLC | -51.4 | 25 | 53.7 |
| Eurotunnel | -54.7 | 1.5 | -11.8 | Alea Group Holdings (Bermuda) Ltd | -46.8 | -42.1 | -34.1 |
| Thus Group | -52.1 | 8.6 | -3.4 | Business Post Group PLC | -46.2 | 6.9 | 4 |
| BTG | -51.4 | 11.0 | 19.9 | Uniq PLC | -43.6 | 13.9 | 13 |
| Filtronic | -49.0 | 14.3 | 17.7 | Jessops PLC | -39.8 | 6.7 | 22.4 |
| Telecom plus | -44.0 | 11.9 | -15.7 | Telecom plus PLC | -39.3 | 12.8 | 2.2 |
| Danka Business Sys | -38.5 | -6.7 | -48.0 | Alba PLC | -37.1 | 23.4 | -39.6 |
| TTP Communications | -38.5 | -6.5 | -16.8 | Moss Bros Group PLC | -36.7 | 21.1 | 4.7 |
| average: | | 0.7 | -6.4 | average: | | 4.8 | -0.5 |

## Observations

1.  It can be seen that the Bounceback Effect was not as strong for the FTSE100 and FTSE Small Cap Dog Stocks, as it was for the FTSE350 Dog Stocks. Although the returns were still decent – except for the 2004 Small Cap Dogs.

2.  With the Small Cap Dogs, the table above would suggest that it might be wise to eliminate the worst performing Dog from the Bounceback portfolio, on the grounds that the very worst performing small cap stock is likely to be in serious trouble – as was the case for both Ultraframe and Jarvis.

3.  There is some evidence that the Effect works very well for FTSE Fledgling stocks. However, there is a danger that stocks that have fallen so much to qualify as Dog Stocks will go bankrupt. So Fledgling Dog Stocks would have to be considered high risk.

# December 2007

## Mon
# 10

1901: The first Nobel Prizes were awarded.

## Tues
# 11

• FOMC meeting (tentative)

1946: The United Nations International Children's Emergency Fund (UNICEF) was established.

## Wed
# 12

1927: Robert Noyce was born - nicknamed "the Mayor of Silicon Valley".

## Thur
# 13

1978: The Susan B. Anthony dollar entered circulation, depicting the women's suffrage campaigner.

## Fri
# 14

1959: The *Motown* record label was founded in Detroit, Michigan, by Berry Gordy.

## Sat
# 15

2002: The digital radio station BBC7 was launched by comedian, Paul Merton, during a simulcast with BBC Radio 4.

## Sun *
# 16

1977: The Queen unveiled the new underground link from central London to Heathrow - the first from a capital city to its major airport.

"Don't stay in bed, unless you can make money in bed."
– *George Burns*

Likely company announcements

**Interims**

Alba plc
Ardana plc
Ashtead Group plc
Berkeley Group Holdings (The) plc
Birse Group plc
British Energy Group plc
Carpetright plc
London Clubs International plc
McKay Securities plc
Renold plc
Renovo Group plc
RHM plc
Safeland plc
Sondex plc
Stewart & Wight plc
Telecom plus plc
VEGA Group plc
Waterford Wedgwood plc
Worthington Group plc

**Finals**

Baggeridge Brick plc
Electronic Data Processing plc
Jersey Electricity Company (The) Ltd
Medisys plc
MyTravel Group plc
Sperati (C.A.) (Special Agency) plc
Theratase plc
Treatt plc
Windsor plc

# Be a John, but buy Michael

The results of complex analysis on the first names of the three major officers in all the FTSE100 companies is shown in the table below.

The lesson seems to be: if you want to run a FTSE100 company, think of changing your name to John. 17 Chairmen and 7 CEOs of FTSE100 companies have the first name John. The second most popular name is David.

| First Name | Chairman | CEO | CFO | Total |
|------------|----------|-----|-----|-------|
| John | 17 | 7 | 6 | 30 |
| David | 3 | 3 | 8 | 14 |
| Philip | 2 | 5 | 4 | 11 |
| Michael | 4 | 4 | 3 | 11 |
| Andrew | 0 | 3 | 7 | 10 |
| Paul | 1 | 4 | 3 | 8 |
| Richard | 2 | 3 | 3 | 8 |
| Robert | 6 | 0 | 2 | 8 |
| Richard | 2 | 3 | 3 | 8 |
| Peter | 5 | 0 | 2 | 7 |
| Martin | 2 | 2 | 3 | 7 |
| Mark | 0 | 1 | 4 | 5 |
| Simon | 1 | 1 | 3 | 5 |
| Stephen | 0 | 2 | 3 | 5 |

It's interesting to note how first names differ between the three roles. Apart from John, Robert and Peter are popular names for Chairmen, Philip is popular with CEOs, and David and Andrew are common for Chief Financial Officers. What does this tell us? Probably not very much.

The charts below, however, may give some guidance for investors.

The first chart plots the performance of a portfolio comprised of those FTSE100 companies whose CEO's first name is Michael.

The second chart is similar, except the CEO's name is Philip. The result: Michael out-performs Philip by a wide margin. Recommendation: buy Michael, sell Philip.

# December 2007

## Mon
# 17

1976: Saudi Arabia and the United Arab Emirates rejected Opec's recommended 15% oil price increase and chose to impose a lower price rise.

## Tues
# 18

1950: The Christmas edition of the Radio Times returned after an industrial dispute, in time for the festive season.

## Wed
# 19

1984: A historic agreement was signed, stating that the British colony of Hong Kong is to be returned to China in 1997.

## Thur
# 20

1979: More than five million council house tenants in Britain were given the right to buy their home.

## Fri
# 21

- Euronext.liffe stock options expiry
- Euronext.liffe UK USF expiry
- December Triple-Witching

1913: Arthur Wynne's "word-cross", the first crossword puzzle, was published in the New York World.

## Sat
# 22

1882: The first Christmas tree lights were created by Thomas Edison.

## Sun
# 23

1964: The government announced that Dr Richard Beeching, who instigated major and controversial changes to the rail network, would quit.

"Many wealthy people are little more than janitors of their possessions."
– *Frank Lloyd Wright*

---

Likely company announcements

### Interims

Anglesey Mining plc
Associated British Engineering plc
City of London Group plc
Creightons plc
Jasmin plc
Network Technology plc
Northgate Information Solutions plc
Oglesby & Butler Group plc
Park Group plc
Total Systems plc
Triad Group plc

### Finals

African Diamonds plc
Caledonian Trust plc
CamAxys Group plc
Coal International plc
COE Group plc
Cradley Group Holdings plc
EiRx Therapeutics plc
Elite Strategies plc
European Nickel plc
Glen Group plc
India Star Energy plc
Leeds Group plc
Niche Group (The) plc
Probus Estates plc
Qonnectis plc
Renewable Energy Holdings plc
Rheochem plc
Tecteon plc
Wichford plc

# The long term

The chart below plots the FT All Share Index from 1946 to the present day. Notes:

1. The straight line is a line of best fit calculated by regression analysis.

2. The Y-scale is logarithmic, which presents percentage (rather than absolute) changes better over long periods, and so is more suitable for long-term share charts.

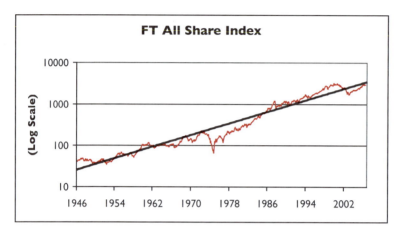

Douglas Adams thought that the answer to the universe was 42. However, a far more useful number (or, strictly, equation) is-

$$y = 24.668e^{0.0067x}$$

This is the equation of the line of best fit in the chart above. The equation allows us to make forecasts for the FT All Share Index. It is, in effect, the Holy Grail – the key to the stock market.

## Forecasts

The table below shows forecasts for the FT All Share and FTSE100 indices calculated using the equation.

| Date | FTAS Forecast | FTSE Forecast | Inc(%) |
|------|---------------|---------------|--------|
| Dec-2012 | 5,390 | 10,607 | +80 |
| Dec-2017 | 8,057 | 15,855 | +169 |
| Dec-2022 | 12,044 | 23,701 | +302 |
| Dec-2027 | 18,003 | 35,428 | +501 |
| Dec-2057 | 200,849 | 395,243 | +6,606 |

- For December 2012 (approximately 5 years forward), the equation (based on the market trend since 1946) estimates that the FTSE100 will be at 10,600 – a modest 80% above the current level.

- Looking forward 10 years, to 2017, the forecast is for a FTSE100 level of 15,855 (+169% above the current level).

- And in 50 year's time (well, why not) the FTSE100 is forecast to be 395,243 (+6,606%).

Now's the time to place those 50-year spread bets.

Definition of statistics:
*The science of producing unreliable facts from reliable figures.*
Evan Esar

# December 2007

## Mon   ★

# 24

Christmas Eve
1988: North Sea oil production was dealt another blow just five months when the Piper Alpha disaster, after a giant floating storage vessel, the Medora, broke free of its moorings in gale-force winds.

## Tues

# 25

- London Stock Exchange closed
- Hong Kong Stock Exchange closed
- Tokyo Stock Exchange closed
- New York Stock Exchange closed

Christmas Day Bank Holiday
1991: Mikhail Gorbachev, leader of the Soviet Union for almost seven years, stepped down from office.

## Wed

# 26

- London Stock Exchange closed
- Hong Kong Stock Exchange closed

Boxing Day Bank Holiday
1982: For the first time, *TIME* magazine's Man of the Year was given to a non-human - the personal computer.

## Thur   ★

# 27

1831: Charles Darwin embarked on his journey aboard the *HMS Beagle*, where he would formulate the theory of evolution.

## Fri   ★

# 28

2003: The British Government announced plans to tighten airline security, by allowing armed guards on some British flights to the USA.

## Sat  ★

# 29

1891: Thomas Edison patented the radio.

## Sun

# 30

1996: Proposed budget cuts by Benjamin Netanyahu sparked protests from 250,000 workers - who shut down services across Israel.

"Black holes are where God divided by zero."
– Steven Wrigh

---

### Likely company announcements

**Interims**

Berkeley Berry Birch plc
Energy Technique plc
Global Marine Energy plc
Hidong Estate plc
Kuju plc
Legendary Investments plc
Real Affinity plc
Seven Arts Pictures plc
Solid State plc
Trading New Homes plc
Wilshaw plc

**Finals**

# Share performance in January

## Stocks that like January

The 24 companies in the table below have all risen nine times in the last ten years in the month of January. (The table shows the percentage price change for the stock in the month of January for that year. For example, the share price of Abbey increased 1.1% in January 1997.)

| Company | 1997 | 1998 | 1999 | 2000 | 2001 | 2002 | 2003 | 2004 | 2005 | 2006 |
|---|---|---|---|---|---|---|---|---|---|---|
| Abbey PLC | 1.1 | 15.4 | 15.0 | 16.8 | 33.3 | -0.2 | 3.0 | 13.8 | 5.2 | 0.4 |
| Anite Group PLC | 42.5 | 21.3 | 2.5 | 30.3 | 21.4 | -0.3 | 12.8 | 7.4 | 2.2 | 10.7 |
| Barr (A G) PLC | 22.6 | 18.6 | 5.9 | 1.0 | 10.4 | 1.5 | -1.1 | 3.6 | 5.5 | 0.3 |
| Biotrace International PLC | 52.8 | 5.1 | 0.6 | 56.7 | 6.5 | -3.6 | 10.1 | 6.5 | 12.7 | 22.7 |
| BPP Holdings PLC | 6.5 | 14.8 | 6.1 | 10.8 | 7.6 | 3.1 | 1.6 | 6.3 | 1.4 | -1.3 |
| Christie Group PLC | 15.1 | 1.2 | 10.0 | 3.8 | 3.3 | 4.7 | 11.5 | 18.1 | 18.3 | 18.2 |
| Dee Valley Group PLC | 0.6 | 0.6 | 6.6 | 0.6 | -0.6 | 1.8 | 0.5 | 5.8 | 19.6 | 1.5 |
| DICOM Group PLC | 7.7 | -4.4 | 50.9 | 46.3 | 24.5 | 3.2 | 1.2 | 9.7 | 8.6 | 7.5 |
| Dragon Oil PLC | 26.8 | 1.3 | 17.4 |  | 20.3 | 1.0 | 9.5 | 24.0 | 20.4 | 14.4 |
| Elan Corporation PLC | 23.4 | 6.5 | 0.9 | 6.0 | 8.7 | -37.4 | 96.2 | 29.9 | 4.9 | 11.5 |
| Grafton Group PLC | 7.2 | 3.8 | 7.7 | 6.7 | 23.6 | 7.0 | -5.3 | 6.1 | 19.6 | 7.6 |
| Gresham Computing PLC | 17.1 | 63.0 | 37.4 | 11.4 | 7.1 | 1.9 | -20.0 | 20.2 | 6.0 | 18.8 |
| Hay (Norman) PLC | 12.2 | 1.4 | 4.6 | -9.3 | 4.3 | 11.1 | 17.1 | 10.9 | 11.2 | 7.9 |
| Helphire Group PLC |  | 19.9 | 1.3 | 4.3 | 4.1 | 6.5 | 3.1 | 9.3 | 4.1 | 4.0 |
| Irish Continental Group PLC | 13.3 | 22.1 | 14.7 | 17.7 | 33.3 | 23.8 | -1.1 | 13.8 | 6.4 | 4.6 |
| Kingspan Group PLC | 6.1 | 18.1 | -11.3 | 1.7 | 16.6 | 3.9 | 13.5 | 9.3 | 4.1 | 4.5 |
| McCarthy & Stone PLC | 19.3 | 2.2 | 2.8 | 6.7 | -2.8 | 2.5 | 0.5 | 6.8 | 3.8 | 8.0 |
| McInerney Holdings PLC | 61.5 | 29.5 | 6.7 | -2.8 | 1.4 | 28.1 | 8.5 | 7.0 | 5.1 | 1.5 |
| Morgan Sindall PLC | 12.9 | 13.9 | 0.5 | 8.7 | 12.4 | 5.8 | 11.4 | 7.8 | 9.3 | 17.2 |
| RM PLC | 18.1 | 22.3 | 33.0 | 3.8 | 5.7 | -3.2 | 2.2 | 9.4 | 5.8 | 15.3 |
| Rugby Estates PLC | 12.7 | 5.7 | 6.0 | 8.9 | 7.7 | 2.0 | -3.2 | 3.5 | 0.2 | 4.9 |
| S & U PLC | 1.8 | 6.9 | -3.0 | 3.2 | 3.7 | 3.1 | 11.0 | 5.0 | 8.3 | 7.5 |
| Serco Group PLC | 1.5 | 24.2 | 6.6 | 15.7 | 6.9 | 1.6 | -7.5 | 6.4 | 3.6 | 0.1 |
| Vardy (Reg) PLC | 18.8 | -0.2 | 28.1 | 26.3 | 20.5 | 10.7 | 5.9 | 16.0 | 3.4 | 3.1 |
| Average | 17.1 | 13.3 | 10.1 | 11.9 | 11.7 | 3.6 | 7.3 | 10.5 | 7.8 | 8.0 |
| FTSE All-Share | 3.7 | 5.2 | 0.8 | -8.2 | 1.5 | -1.1 | -9.1 | -0.9 | 1.3 | 2.9 |

Only two listed companies, Christie Group and Morgan Sindall, have risen in January in all ten of the years from 1997 to 2006.

On average the best performing companies in January have been: Biotrace International (average January increase of +17%), Gresham Computing(+16.3%), DICOM Group(+15.5%), Anite Group(+15.1%), and Elan Corporation (+15.1%).

## Stocks that don't like January

The 12 companies in the table below have all fallen eight times in the last ten years in the month of January.

| Company | 1997 | 1998 | 1999 | 2000 | 2001 | 2002 | 2003 | 2004 | 2005 | 2006 |
|---|---|---|---|---|---|---|---|---|---|---|
| Associated British Foods PLC | -1.2 | 14.2 | -6.3 | -5.9 | -2.7 | -5.6 | -12.6 | -3.6 | -3.5 | -1.7 |
| Beale PLC | 12.7 | -0.3 | -5.4 | -3.9 |  | -0.4 | -8.2 | -12.6 | -12.2 | -8.8 |
| BTG PLC | -0.6 | 13.4 | -11.4 | -2.0 | -4.8 | -15.2 | -9.7 | -7.6 | 11.0 | -4.4 |
| Cadbury Schweppes PLC | -4.6 | 16.5 | -5.9 | -7.6 | -5.4 | -2.5 | -14.5 | -2.0 | -2.0 | 0.5 |
| Diageo PLC | -4.8 | -1.9 | -1.8 | -8.1 | -12.3 | 5.0 | -8.0 | -2.0 | -2.6 | -0.7 |
| GlaxoSmithKline PLC | 5.4 | 14.1 | -1.6 | -9.4 | -5.0 | -2.0 | -4.0 | -7.8 | -3.8 | -2.1 |
| Kelda Group PLC | 4.0 | -2.6 | -10.8 | -25.7 | -10.0 | -2.0 | -5.2 | -6.6 | -4.7 | 1.2 |
| Morrison (Wm) Supermarkets PLC | -7.3 | 12.9 | 10.2 | -4.1 | -1.6 | -3.3 | -26.6 | -1.7 | -2.7 | -3.4 |
| Renold PLC | 1.0 | -9.0 | -7.2 | -7.4 | 12.3 | -11.2 | -16.3 | -1.9 | -20.1 | -0.8 |
| Sainsbury (J) PLC | -16.9 | -2.4 | -11.3 | -2.6 | -9.1 | 7.1 | -15.6 | -10.6 | 4.6 | -4.5 |
| Smith & Nephew PLC | -0.7 | -1.1 | -2.1 | -12.4 | -0.6 | -5.5 | -9.1 | 2.1 | -2.6 | 4.2 |
| Tottenham Hotspur PLC | 0.6 | -7.3 | -2.7 | -0.8 | -5.8 | -0.6 | -14.6 | -17.9 | -4.5 | -17.1 |
| Average | -1.0 | 3.9 | -4.7 | -7.5 | -4.1 | -3.0 | -12.0 | -6.0 | -3.6 | -3.1 |
| FTSE All-Share | 3.7 | 5.2 | 0.8 | -8.2 | 1.5 | -1.1 | -9.1 | -0.9 | 1.3 | 2.9 |

Of the 12 companies above, three, Associated British Foods, Diageo, and Tottenham Hotspur, have fallen nine times in the past ten years.

On average, the worst performing stocks in January have been: Tottenham Hotspur(average January decrease of -7.1%), Kelda Group (-6.2%), J Sainsbury(-6.1%), and Renold (-6.1%).

# Dec 2007/Jan 2008

## Mon

# 31

New Year's Day Bank Holiday
1999: Boris Yeltsin resigned as Russian president and said Prime Minister Vladimir Putin would take over immediately.

## Tues

# 1

1772: The first traveller's cheques were issued in London.

## Wed

# 2

1882: Standard Oil was organised as a trust, because of anti-monopoly laws.

## Thur

# 3

1977: Apple Computer Inc. was incorporated.

## Fri

# 4

1865: The New York Stock Exchange (NYSE) opened its first permanent headquarters at 10-12 Broad, near Wall Street in New York City.

## Sat
# 5

1914: In America, the Ford Motor Company announced an eight-hour workday and a minimum wage of $5 for a day's labour.

## Sun
# 6

1930: The first diesel engine automobile trip was completed, between Indiana and New York City.

"Be nice to people on your way up because you meet them on your way down."
– Jimmy Durant

Likely company announcements

**Interims**

AdEPT Telecom plc
Chariot (UK) plc
Cohort plc
Empire Interactive plc
Games Workshop Group plc

**Finals**

# 3.

# Reference pages

# Contents

- Basic information

# UK stock exchanges

There used to be many different regional stock exchanges in the UK. However, over the years, these closed and one exchange, the London Stock Exchange, became the dominant exchange in the land. However, it is not the only exchange in the UK, and in recent years several new, small exchanges have opened.

## London Stock Exchange

### UKLA Official List (Main Market)

The Stock Exchange started life in the coffee houses of 17th Century London. By mid-2004, about 2,400 companies were quoted on the Main Market of the London Stock Exchange known as the *UKLA Official List*.

Joining is a two-stage process of having the company's securities admitted:

* to the **Official List** by the UK Listing Authority (now part of the FSA); and also

* to **trading** by the Exchange.

Stocks can have their quote suspended for a number of reasons, including breaking of the Listing Rules (such as failing to report financial results, or failing to file accounts on time), or pending an announcement clarifying the company's financial position. Generally a company must finalise its annual results within 120 days (4 months) after the period to which it relates.

www.fsa.gov.uk/ukla/officialList.do

## AIM

AIM opened in 1995 and is run by the London Stock Exchange. In mid-2006, about 1,500 companies were members of AIM. It can be attractive for a new company to list on AIM, rather than the Main Market, as the entry criteria are less rigorous. For example, there is no rule stipulating a minimum issue of shares to the public, or minimum market value for the company. Once a company has been on AIM for 2 years it can request admittance to the Main Market.

www.londonstockexchange.com/aim

## OFEX

PLUS Markets operates an equity market that trades more than 800 small and mid-cap stocks. Plus Markets' platform the Plus service, now incorporates the 151 companies that were formerly quoted on Ofex, several hundred small and mid-cap companies quoted on the LSE and six AIM companies (due to be extended). Ofex was originally created in October 1995 and permitted LSE member firms to enter into matched bargains off-exchange in unquoted securities. Ofex itself floated on the AIM market in 2003, but in November 2004 shareholders backed a rescue plan that involved a refinancing and change of name to Plus Markets.

The Plus service is based on a competing market model (quote-driven system) in direct contrast to the LSE's drive towards electronic trading. There are currently four market makers in Ofex stocks: Hoodless Brennan, KBC Peel Hunt, Teather & Greenwood and Winterflood Securities. These four market makers, in addition to Cenkos Securities, also make markets in the other listed stocks on Plus.

www.plusmarketsgroup.com and
www.unquoted.co.uk

Reference

## ShareMark

Founded in June 2000, ShareMark is an internet-based facility for dealing in shares through regular auctions in around 10 companies and run by Aylesbury-based stockbroker, The Share Centre and its parent company, Share plc. ShareMark allows dealings in shares also listed on AIM and OFEX. Listing costs are around £5,000 per year.

www.sharemark.co.uk

## 535X

A new matched-bargain platform for unlisted PLCs, which takes its name from an old Stock Exchange rule that permitted off-Exchange trading. Currently 14 companies have signed up. The market runs through 535X's website and allows FSA registered brokers to post bids and offers.

www.535x.com

## J P Jenkins Ltd

J P Jenkins Limited is a UK stockbroker that is authorised and regulated by the Financial Services Authority, and is a member of the London Stock Exchange and APCIMS.

It specialises in matching trades in the shares of certain unlisted securities, featured on its website. It deals with other UK stockbrokers and does not provide a service directly to the general public.

Shareholders wishing to buy or sell unlisted shares can leave an order with J P Jenkins Limited via their stockbroker.

www.jpjenkins.co.uk

Source: 'The UK Trader's Bible', by Dominic Connolly (Harriman House)

# EPIC, TIDM, SEDOL, CIN and ISIN codes

This page describes the common codes associated with securities.

## EPIC

Some time ago the London Stock Exchange devised a system of code names for listed companies. These codes provide a short and unambiguous way to reference stocks.

For example, the code for Marks & Spencer is MKS. This code, MKS, is easier to use than wondering whether one should call the company Marks & Spencer, Marks and Spencer or Marks & Spencer plc.

These codes were called EPIC codes, after the name of the Stock Exchange's central computer prior to 1996. Codes are standardised now as comprising 3 characters (e.g. NMS), with a fourth character indicating a secondary stock (e.g. NMSW, for New Media Spark warrants). Although some securities (e.g. Boots, Barclays) still have 4 characters, from when that was the standard with the old system.

## TIDM

You will today search the website of the London Stock Exchange in vain for any mention of EPIC codes. That's because after the introduction of the Sequence trading platform, EPIC codes were renamed Tradable Instrument Display Mnemonics (TIDMs), or Mnemonics for short. So, strictly, we should now be calling them TIDMs or Mnemonics – but almost everyone still refers to them as EPIC codes.

### References for EPICs/TIDMs

London Stock Exchange: www.londonstockexchange-rns.com

Yahoo! Finance: uk.finance.yahoo.co.uk

## SEDOL

SEDOL stands for Stock Exchange Daily Official List Number, and are 7 digit security identifiers assigned by the London Stock Exchange. They are only assigned to UK-listed securities.

## CIN

CIN stands for CUSIP International Number, where CUSIP is the Committee on Uniform Securities Identification Procedures. CIN codes are the international extension of CUSIP codes used for Canadian and US securities. The codes are 10-character: the first character is always a letter, which represents the country of issue; the next 6 characters are numbers which represent the issuer; followed by 2 digits representing the security; the final digit is the check digit.

## ISIN

ISIN stands for International Securities Identification Number, and are 12 digit alphanumeric identifiers assigned by the International Standards Organisation (ISO) in order to provide standardisation of international securities. The first two letters represent the country code; the next 9 characters usually use some other code, such as CUSIP in the United States or SEDOL in Great Britain with leading spaces padded with 0. The final digit is the check digit.

### References

Corporate information: www.corporateinformation.com/defext.asp

A good description of international security codes and company suffixes (e.g. 'plc' in the UK).

# Trade codes

| Code | Trade Type | Description |
|------|-----------|-------------|
| AI | Automated Input | If reporting that a member firm has disabled its automated input facility in response to a request from the Exchange. |
| AT | Automatic Trade | An automatic trade generated by the SETS system through the order book. |
| | Average Price | The transaction was effected at a price based on a volume weighted average price over a given period. |
| | Bargain Conditions Apply | Certain conditions were agreed between the 2 participants at the time of trading. |
| K | Block Trade | The transaction was reported using the block trade facility, which is ≥75 times the NMS for a security with an NMS of 2,000 shares or ≥50 times the NMS for a security with an NMS of 1,000 shares. |
| B | Broker to Broker | The transaction was between two member firms where neither firm is registered as a market maker in the security in question and neither is a designated fund manager. Brokers may also apply this indicator when buying or selling domestic equity market securities through a broker, which is not a member firm. |
| CT | Contra Trade | The trade was reported for a transaction previously automatically executed through the order book. |
| | Correction | This covers any corrections made to trade reports. |
| X | Cross | The transaction was effected as an agency cross or a riskless principle trade between 2 member firms at the same price and on the same terms. |
| | Currency Conversion | The trade was executed in one currency but converted for trade reporting. |
| EU | Euro Automated Trades | |
| ER | Euro Trades | |
| L | Late Reported Trade | Late trades, as the name implies, are trades that are reported to the Stock Exchange some time after the trade has been executed. There can be a number of reasons for this. If a trade is executed that is six times the Normal Market Size then the market makers, for stocks traded on the full list, do not have to report the trade for 1 hour after the trade was executed. Once reported, this would show as a Late Trade. A trade would also show as being late if the bargain had to be amended for any reason, like an alteration to the settlement date. Once the bargain was amended, the amended bargain would show up as a late trade. |
| LC | Late Trade Correction | A correction submitted more than 3 days after the trade date, or where deferred publication is permitted at any time after the trade report was submitted to the Exchange reporting system. |
| M | Market Maker to Market Maker | The transaction was between 2 market makers registered in the security in question. This may also include those executed through an inter-dealer broker or a public display system. |
| N | Non-Protected Portfolio | A non-protected portfolio transaction or a fully disclosed portfolio transaction. Normally a transaction of a number of stocks dealt with by 1 market maker at an agreed discount to the market price. |
| NR | Non-Risk Trade | These trades are the same as Ordinary Trades but specifically for SEATS based segments only (i.e. SEQ1, AIM, SEAT). |
| NM | Not to Mark | A transaction where the Exchange has granted permission for non-publication. |
| O | Ordinary Trade | A standard trade made through the Market Makers and dealt at normal settlement date. (System will delay if over 6 times NMS.) |
| | Overnight Trade | The transaction was reported after 17h15 and before 07h15 the following day. |
| PC | Post Contra | Used when reporting a Contra Trade when the contra date is not the trade date. |
| P | Protected Portfolio | A protected portfolio transaction or a trade resulting from a worked principal agreement for a portfolio transaction. Like a non-protected portfolio, but the price dealt at can be amended if the market maker manages to make a profit. |
| PA | Protection Applied | Protected transaction at the time that protection is applied. |

| RC | Regulatory Conformance | This is a test segment for which no trade reports will be disseminated. |
|---|---|---|
| RO | Result of Exercising Option | A transaction reported as a result of exercising a traditional option or a negotiated option. |
| | Result of Stock Swap | The transaction was reported as a result of a stock swap or stock switch (1 report is required for each line of stock swapped or switched). |
| RT | Risk Trade | The transaction was reported by a Market Maker registered in either a SEATS security, an AIM security or a covered warrant market security. |
| R | Riskless Principal | A riskless principal transaction with 2 non members, where the 2 transactions are executed at different prices or on different terms (this requires 2 separate trade reports). This happens often on a trade where commission is not charged. Instead of paying commission, the client will pay extra for their shares. |
| ST | SEAQ Trade | This is used for the single uncrossing trade, detailing the total executed volume and uncrossing price as a result of a SEAQ auction |
| T | Single Protected Trade | The trade was reported as a result of a single protected transaction. A protected transaction occurs when a large order is going through the market. The buyer (or seller) may wish to keep the order anonymous from the rest of the market as the size of the order could greatly alter the price of the stock. With a protected transaction, the dealer will put the trade through in small quantities rather than in one go. The entire transaction is reported once the deal is completed. The London Stock Exchange is notified at the start and at the end of the transaction. However, the market as a whole isn't told until the end, thus the order is protected. |
| SW | Stock Swap | Transactions comprised in a stock swap or stock switch (one report is required for each line of stock swapped or switched). |
| TS | Test Security | If using a test security to test trade reporting. |
| UT | Uncrossing Trade | This is used for the single uncrossing trade, detailing the total executed volume and uncrossing price as a result of a SETS auction. |
| VW | Volume Weighted Average Price | A transaction that was effected at a price based on a volume weighted average price over a given period. |
| WN | Worked Principal | The Exchange is notified that a member firm has entered into a worked principal agreement for a single security. |
| PN | Worked Principal Portfolio Notification | A Member firm has agreed to take on a worked principal agreement for a portfolio transaction. |
| WT | Worked Principal Trade | The reported trade was from a worked principle agreement for a single security. |

**Source:** ADVFN, London Stock Exchange

# Daily timetable of the UK trading day

The table displays the basic structure of the UK trading day, with some comments from a trader.

| 07.00 | Regulatory News Services open |
|---|---|
| | The period before the market opens at 08.00 is the most important hour of the day. By the time the opening auction begins at 07.50 traders will have a clear idea at what price any particular major stock should be opening at. |
| | Scheduled announcements are normally in the Regulatory News. Having a good idea of what companies are reporting for the forthcoming week is essential. Quite a few banks, brokers and websites provide comprehensive forward diaries. |
| | As well as checking the movement of the major stock indices overnight, check the early show for the futures contracts on the main indices, as well as any US company results that were released after hours. Unlike the UK, in the US it is common for companies to release results after the markets close. |
| 07.50-08.00 | Pre-market auction |
| | There are fewer opportunities in the opening auction than the closing auction, partly because there are lower volumes in the opening auction. It is safer to trade against an 'at-market' order, than against several orders from several other participants that appear to be at the wrong price — almost certainly they have seen something that you haven't. |
| | Despite representing only a small proportion of the total day's volume, the opening uncrossing trade will often be (or very close to) the high or low trade of the day for that stock. |
| 08.00 | UK market and FTSE 100 Index Futures open |
| | By 08.00 as the UK market opens you should be fully prepared for the day's trading. |
| 08.00-16.30 | Continuous trading |
| | Trading is continuous until 16.30. During the day there is a calendar of key economic figures to look out for, as well as both ad-hoc and scheduled announcements. Some company-scheduled trading figures come out at midday, particularly companies that are dual-quoted, such as Reckitt Benckiser and Carnival. |
| | US index futures should be monitored throughout the day as well as other influential continental indices such as Germany's DAX Index. |
| | Traders will often concentrate on watching the high volatility shares as these provide the most trading opportunities, although many will add 'guest' stocks to their watch list and go to where the day's action is and join 'event' traders. Such stocks are often high beta, liquid stocks and will include companies such as Reuters, Amvescap (which correlates closely with the US indices and is one of the most popular UK trading stocks), Vodafone and Cable and Wireless. Stocks to watch during the day include the biggest movers on the day (both risers and fallers), those experiencing high volume and constant gainers (popular with momentum players). |
| 14.30 | US markets open |
| | The US markets usually open at 14.30 UK time, although at certain times of the year, due to daylight saving, it may be an hour earlier or later. As the futures contracts on the US markets trade throughout morning trading in the UK, traders will always have a good idea where the US markets are due to open, subject to the release of economic figures at 13.30 UK time. |
| 16.30-16.35 | Post-market auction |
| | There can often be opportunities in the closing auction, particularly on the last business day of the month or when there are index constituent changes. The general strategy is to take the other side of a large 'at-market' order that is forcing the uncrossing price away from the day's trading range, in the anticipation that the stock will revert to the previous ('normal') level the following day. |
| 17.30 | FTSE 100 Index Futures close |
| 18.30 | Regulatory News Services close |
| | A number of key announcements can come out after the market close and although most newspapers will pick up any significant stories, it is worth scanning through the day's late announcements before the start of trading the following day. |

Source: '*The UK Trader's Bible*', by Dominic Connolly (Harriman House)

# Tax Freedom Day

*How much time do you spend working for the government and how much for yourself?*

After all the deductions made for tax and national insurance it may seem that little is left of your salary. It all goes to the government! But what is the actual tax burden?

One way of looking at this is to imagine that all tax and deductions were paid at the beginning of the year, instead of a slug every month. A date could then be calculated at which point one has finished paying the taxes and after which one starts working for oneself. The Adam Smith Institute calculates this date every year for the UK and calls it Tax Freedom Day. The chart below shows the progression of Tax Freedom Day since 1963. In 2006, Tax Freedom Day was on the 3rd June.

Tax Freedom Day

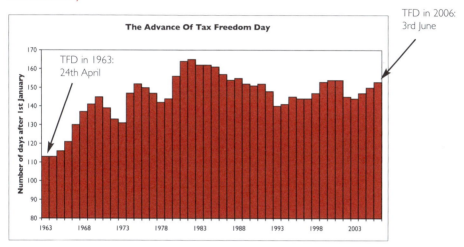

In the early 60s, Tax Freedom Day came in April. Unfortunately, those days have not been seen again. Throughout the 60s and 70s the day came later in the year, reaching, at its worst, 15 June in 1982. Over the following decade, Tax Freedom Day retreated slightly, back to 22 May in 1994; but since then has been advancing again.

But before we feel too sorry for ourselves, have some pity for poor tax payers in France – where Tax Freedom Day is 16 July (edging towards Christmas).

| Country | TFD | Days confiscated by the state |
|---|---|---|
| Ireland | 10 May | 129 |
| Switzerland | 15 May | 134 |
| Spain | 22 May | 141 |
| Slovakia | 27 May | 146 |
| Poland | 07 Jun | 157 |
| UK | 17 Jun | 167 |
| Germany | 17 Jun | 167 |
| Italy | 27 Jun | 177 |
| France | 16 Jul | 196 |
| Average in EU | 23 Jun | 173 |
| Average in OECD | 31 May | 150 |

**Source**: Adam Smith Institute (www.adamsmith.org)

# Exchanges, associations and regulatory bodies

## List of organisations

535X (UK) Ltd

Accounting Standards Board (ASB)

Accounts Commission for Scotland

Alternative Investment Management Association (AIMA)

Association of Private Client Investment Managers and Stockbrokers (APCIMS)

Association of Accounting Technicians

Association of British Insurers

Association of Chartered Certified Accountants (ACCA)

Association of Corporate Treasurers (ACT)

Association of Investment Trust Companies (AITC)

Association of Solicitor Investment Managers (ASIM)

Bank of England

British Bankers Association (BBA)

Building Societies Association (BSA)

Building Societies Commission

Cabinet Office

Chartered Institute of Bankers

Chartered Institute of Taxation (CIOT)

Chartered Insurance Institute

Competition Commission

Compliance Institute

Compliance Register

Confederation of British Industry

CRESTCo Ltd

Department of Trade and Industry

Euronext.liffe

Financial Ombudsman Service (FOS)

Financial Reporting Review Panel (FRRP)

Financial Services Authority (FSA)

Financial Supervision Commission (Isle of Man)

FTSE

Futures and Options Association (FOA)

General Council of the Bar, The

Guernsey Financial Services Commission

HM Treasury

Inland Revenue

Institute of Chartered Accountants in England and Wales

Institute of Chartered Accountants of Scotland (ICAS)

Institute of Chartered Secretaries and Administrators (ICSA)

International Petroleum Exchange (IPE)

International Swaps & Derivatives Association (ISDA)

Investment Management Association (IMA)

Investment Management Regulatory Organisation (IMRO)

Investors Compensation Scheme

LCH.Clearnet

London International Insurance and Reinsurance Market Association

London Stock Exchange, The

National Audit Office

OFEX

Office of Fair Trading

Panel on Takeovers and Mergers (POTAM)

Pensions Management Institute

Personal Investment Authority

ProShare (UK) Ltd

Securities and Futures Authority

Securities Institute

Sharemark

Society of Pension Consultants

# Organisation contact details

## 535X (UK) Ltd

4 - 10 Barttelot Road
Horsham
RH12 1DQ
Tel: 0870 744 5920
Email: info@535X.co.uk
Web: www.535x.com

## Accounting Standards Board (ASB)

5th floor, Aldwych House
71-91 Aldwych
London
WC2B 4HN
Tel: 020 7492 2300
Fax: 020 7492 2301
Web: www.frc.org.uk/asb/

## Accounts Commission for Scotland

110 George Street
Edinburgh
EH2 4LH
Tel: 0131 477 1234
Fax: 0131 477 4567
Email: info@audit-scot.gov.uk
Web: www.audit-scotland.gov.uk/accounts

## Alternative Investment Management Association Ltd (AIMA)

Meadows House
20-22 Queen Street
Mayfair
London
W1J 5PR
Tel: 020 7659 9920
Fax: 020 7659 9921
Email: info@aima.org
Web: www.aima.org

## Association of Private Client Investment Managers and Stockbrokers (APCIMS)

114 Middlesex Street
London
E1 7JH
Tel: 020 7247 7080
Fax: 020 7377 0939
Email: info@apcims.co.uk
Web: www.apcims.co.uk

## Association of Accounting Technicians

154 Clerkenwell Road
London
EC1R 5AD
Tel: 020 7415 7500
Fax: 020 7837 6970
Email: aat@aat.org.uk
Web: www.aat.org.uk

## Association of British Insurers

51 Gresham Street
London
EC2V 7HQ
Tel: 020 7600 3333
Fax: 020 7696 8999
Email: info@abi.org.uk
Web: www.abi.org.uk

## Association of Chartered Certified Accountants (ACCA)

29 Lincoln's Inn Fields
London
WC2A 3EE
Tel: 020 7059 5000
Fax: 020 7059 5050
Email: info@accaglobal.com
Web: www.accaglobal.com

## Association of Corporate Treasurers (ACT)

Ocean House
10-12 Little Trinity Lane
London
EC4V 2DJ
Tel: 020 7213 9728
Fax: 020 7248 2591
Email: enquiries@treasurers.co.uk
Web: www.treasurers.org

## Association of Investment Trust Companies (AITC)

9th floor
24 Chiswell Street
London
EC1Y 4YY
Tel: 020 7282 5555
Fax: 020 7282 5556
Email: enquiries@aitc.co.uk
Web: www.aitc.co.uk

### Association of Solicitor Investment Managers (ASIM)

Riverside House
River Lawn Road
Tonbridge
Kent
TN9 1EP
Tel: 01732 783 548
Fax: 01732 362 626
Email: admin@asim.org.uk
Web: www.asim.org.uk

### Bank of England

Threadneedle Street
London
EC2R 8AH
Tel: 020 7601 4878
Fax: 020 7601 5460
Email: enquiries@bankofengland.co.uk
Web: www.bankofengland.co.uk

### British Bankers' Association (BBA)

Pinners Hall
105-108 Old Broad Street
London
EC2N 1EX
Tel: 020 7216 8810
Fax: 020 7216 8811
Email: info@bba.org.uk
Web: www.bba.org.uk

### British Insurance Brokers' Association (BIBA)

14 Bevis Marks
London
EC3A 7NT
Tel: 0870 950 1790
Fax: 020 7626 9676
Email: enquiries@biba.org.uk
Web: www.biba.org.uk

### Building Societies Association (BSA)

3 Savile Row
London
W1S 3BP
Tel: 020 7437 0655
Fax: 020 7734 6416
Email: information@bsa.org.uk
Web: www.bsa.org.uk

### Building Societies Commission

12th Floor
25 The North Colonnade
Canary Wharf
London
E14 5HS
Tel: 020 7066 0708
Fax: 020 7676 9763

### Cabinet Office

70 Whitehall
London
SW1A 2AS
Tel: 020 7276 1234
Web: www.cabinetoffice.gov.uk

### Chartered Institute of Taxation (CIOT)

12 Upper Belgrave Street
London
SW1X 8BB
Tel: 020 7235 9381
Fax: 020 7235 2562
Email: post@tax.org.uk
Web: www.tax.org.uk

### Chartered Insurance Institute (CII)

42- 48 High Road
South Woodford
London
E18 2JP
Tel: 020 8989 8464
Fax: 020 8530 3052
Email: customer.serv@cii.co.uk
Web: www.cii.co.uk

## Competition Commission

Victoria House
Southampton Row
London
WC1B 4AD
Tel: 020 7271 0100
Fax: 020 7271 0367
Email: info@cc.gsi.gov.uk
Web:
www.competition-commission.org.uk

## Compliance Institute

107 Barkby Road
Leicester
LE4 9LG
Tel: 01162 461 316
Fax: 01162 742 239
Email: hlacey.compinst@btconnect.com
Web: www.complianceinstitute.co.uk

## Compliance Register

Enterprise House
PO Box 843
Greenleys
Milton Keynes
MK12 6YZ
Tel: 01908 322 450
Fax: 01908 220 213
Email: compliance.register@btinternet.com
Web: www.compliance-register.com

## Confederation of British Industry (CBI)

Centre Point Tower
103 New Oxford Street
London
WC1A 1DU
Tel: 020 7240 1578
Web: www.cbi.org.uk

## CRESTCo Ltd

33 Cannon Street
London
EC4M 5SB
Tel: 020 7849 0000
Fax: 020 7849 0130
Email: info@crestco.co.uk
Web: www.crestco.co.uk

## Department of Trade and Industry

1 Victoria Street
London
SW1H 0ET
Tel: 020 7215 5000
Fax: 020 7215 0105
Email: dti.enquiries@dti.gsi.gov.uk
Web: www.dti.gov.uk

## Euronext.liffe

Cannon Bridge House
1 Cousin Lane
London
EC4R 3XX
Tel: 020 7623 0444
Fax: 020 7588 3624
Web: www.liffe.com

## Financial Ombudsman Service

South Quay Plaza
183 Marsh Wall
London
E14 9SR
Tel: 020 7964 1000
Fax: 020 7964 1001
Email:
complaint.info@financial-ombudsman.org.uk
Web: www.financial-ombudsman.org.uk

## Financial Reporting Review Panel (FRRP)

5th floor, Aldwych House
71-91 Aldwych
London
WC2B 4HN
Tel: 020 7492 2300
Fax: 020 7492 2479
Email: c.page@frc-frrp.org.uk
Web: www.frc.org.uk/frrp

## Financial Services Authority (FSA)

25 The North Colonnade
Canary Wharf
London
E14 5HS
Tel: 020 7066 1000
Fax: 020 7066 1099
Email: consumerhelp@fsa.gov.uk
Web: www.fsa.gov.uk

## Financial Services Compensation Scheme (FSCS)

7th Floor
Lloyds Chambers
Portsoken Street
London
E1 8BN
Tel: 020 7892 7300
Fax: 020 7892 7301
Email: enquiries@fscs.org.uk
Web: www.fscs.org.uk

## Financial Supervision Commission (Isle of Man)

PO Box 58
Finch Hill House
Douglas
Isle of Man
IM99 1DT
Tel: 01624 689 300
Fax: 01624 689 399
Web: www.gov.im/fsc

## FTSE

12th Floor
10 Upper Bank Street
Canary Wharf
London
E14 5NP
Tel: 020 7866 1800
Fax: 020 7866 1804
Email: info@ftse.com
Web: www.ftse.com

## Futures and Options Association (FOA)

2nd Floor
36-38 Botolph Lane
London
EC3R 8DE
Tel: 020 7929 0081
Fax: 020 7621 0223
Email: info@foa.co.uk
Web: www.foa.co.uk

## General Council of the Bar

289-293 High Holborn
London
WC1V 7HZ
Tel: 020 7242 0082
Fax: 020 7831 9217
Web: www.barcouncil.org.uk

## Guernsey Financial Services Commission (GFSC)

La Plaiderie Chambers
La Plaiderie
St Peter Port
Guernsey
GY1 3HQ
Tel: 01481 712 706/801
Fax: 01481 712 010
Email: info@gfsc.gg
Web: www.gfsc.gg

## HM Treasury

1 Horse Guards Road
London
SW1A 2HQ
Tel: 020 7270 4558
Fax: 020 7270 4861
Email:
public.enquiries@hm-treasury.gsi.gov.uk
Web: www.hm-treasury.gov.uk

## HM Revenue and Customs

North West Wing
Bush House
Aldwych
London
WC2B 4PP
Tel: 020 7438 64205
Fax: 020 7438 7541
Web: www.hmrc.gov.uk

## Institute of Chartered Accountants in England and Wales, The

Chartered Accountants' Hall
PO Box 433
London
EC2P 2BJ
Tel: 020 7920 8100
Fax: 020 7920 0547
Web: www.icaew.co.uk

## Institute of Chartered Accountants of Scotland (ICAS)

CA House
21 Haymarket Yards
Edinburgh
EH12 5BH
Tel: 0131 347 0100
Fax: 0131 347 0105
Email: enquiries@icas.org.uk
Web: www.icas.org.uk

## Institute of Chartered Secretaries and Administrators (ICSA)

16 Park Crescent
London
W1B 1AH
Tel: 020 7580 4741
Fax: 020 7323 1132
Email: info@icsa.co.uk
Web: www.icsa.org.uk

## Institute of Financial Services

96th Floor
100 Cannon Street
London
EC4N 6EU
Tel: 020 7444 7111
Fax: 020 7444 7115
Email: customerservices@ifslearning.com
Web: www.ifslearning.com/institute/index.cfm

## International Swaps & Derivatives Association (ISDA)

1 New Change
London
EC4M 9QQ
Tel: 020 7330 3550
Fax: 020 7330 3555
Email: isdaeurope@isda.org
Web: www.isda.org

## International Underwriting Association of London (IUA)

London Underwriting Centre
3 Minster Court
Mincing Lane
London
EC3R 7DD
Tel: 020 7617 4444
Fax: 020 7617 4440
Email: info@iua.co.uk
Web: www.iua.co.uk

## Investment Management Association (IMA)

65 Kingsway
London
WC2B 6TD
Tel: 020 7831 0898
Fax: 020 7831 9975
Email: ima@investmentuk.org
Web: www.investmentuk.org

## LCH.Clearnet Ltd (formerly London Clearing House)

Aldgate House
33 Aldgate High Street
London
EC3N 1EA
Tel: 020 7426 7000
Fax: 020 7426 7001
Email: webmaster@lch.com
Web: www.lchclearnet.com

## London Stock Exchange, The

10 Paternoster Square
London
EC4M 7LS
Tel: 020 7797 1000
Fax: 020 7334 8949
Web: www.londonstockexchange.com

## National Audit Office

157-197 Buckingham Palace Road
Victoria
London
SW1W 9SP
Tel: 020 7798 7000
Fax: 020 7798 7070
Email: enquiries@nao.gsi.gov.uk
Web: www.nao.org.uk

## OFEX

Standon House
21 Mansell Street
London
E1 8AA
Tel: 020 7553 2000
Fax: 020 7553 2004
Email: enquiries@ofex.com
Web: www.ofex.com

### Office of Fair Trading

Fleetbank House
2-6 Salisbury Square
London
EC4Y 8JX
Tel: 020 7211 8993
Fax: 020 7211 8961
Email: enquiries@oft.gsi.gov.uk
Web: www.oft.gov.uk

### Panel on Takeovers and Mergers (POTAM)

10 Paternoster Square
London
EC4M 7DY
Tel: 020 7382 9026
Fax: 020 7236 7005
Web: www.thetakeoverpanel.org.uk

### Pensions Management Institute (PMI)

PMI House
4-10 Artillery Lane
London
E1 7LS
Tel: 020 7247 1452
Fax: 020 7375 0603
Email: enquiries@pensions-pmi.org.uk
Web: www.pensions-pmi.org.uk

### ifs ProShare (UK) Ltd

6th floor
100 Cannon Street
London
EC4N 6EU
Tel: 020 7444 7101
Fax: 020 7444 7115
Web: www.ifsproshare.org

### Quoted Companies Alliance (QCA)

6 Kinghorn Street
London
EC1A 7HW
Tel: 020 7600 3745
fax: 020 7600 8288
Email: mail@qcanet.co.uk
Web: www.qcanet.co.uk

### Securities and Investment Institute

Centurion House
24 Monument Street
London
EC3R 8AQ
Tel: 020 7645 0600
Fax: 020 7645 0601
Email: info@sii.org.uk
Web: www.securities-institute.org.uk

### Sharemark

The Share Centre
Oxford House
Oxford Road
Aylesbury
Buckinghamshire
HP21 8SZ
Tel: 01296 439 432
Fax: 01296 414 330
Email: info@sharemark.co.uk
Web: www.sharemark.co.uk

### Society of Pension Consultants (SPC)

St Bartholomew House
92 Fleet Street
London
EC4Y 1DG
Tel: 020 7353 1688
Fax: 020 7353 9296
Web: www.spc.uk.com

- Market indices and performance

# Stock indices – UK

### FT Ordinary Share Index (FT 30)

The FT 30 Index was first calculated in 1935 by the *Financial Times* newspaper. The Index started at a base level of 100, and calculated from a subjective collection of 30 major companies – which in the early years were concentrated in the industrial and retailing sectors.

For a long time the Index was the best known performance measure of the UK stock market. But the Index became less representative of the whole market, and also the Index was price-weighted (like the DJIA), and not market capitalisation weighted. Although the Index was calculated every hour, the increasing sophistication of the market needed an index calculated every minute and so the FT 30 has been usurped by the FTSE 100.

### FTSE 100

Today, the FTSE 100 Index (sometimes called the 'footsie') is the most well known index tracking the performance of the UK market. The Index comprises 100 of the top capitalised stocks listed on the London Stock Exchange, and represents approximately 80% of the total market (by capitalisation). It is market capitalisation weighted, and the composition of the Index is reviewed every 3 months. The FTSE 100 is commonly used as the basis for investment funds and derivatives. The Index was first calculated on 3rd January 1984 with a base value of 1000.

The FTSE 100 Index, and all the FTSE indices, are calculated by FTSE International – a joint venture between the *Financial Times* newspaper and the London Stock Exchange.

### FTSE 250

Similar in construction to the FTSE 100, except it comprises the next 250 highest capitalised stocks listed on the London Stock Exchange after the top 100. The Index is sometimes referred to as the index of 'mid-capitalised' stocks, and comprises approximately 18% of the total market capitalisation.

### FTSE 350

Similar in construction to the FTSE 100, but including all the companies from the FTSE 100 and FTSE 250 Indices.

### FTSE Small Cap

Comprised of companies with a market capitalisation below the FTSE 250, but above a fixed limit. This lower limit is reviewed every December. In December 2003 the lower limit was set to approximately £56 million. Consequently the FTSE Small Cap Index does not have a fixed number of constituents. In mid-2004, there were approximately 338 companies in the Index, which represented about 2% of the total market by capitalisation.

### FTSE All-Share

The FTSE All-Share is the aggregation of the FTSE 100, FTSE 250 and FTSE Small Cap Indices. Effectively all those London Stock Exchange listed companies with a market capitalisation above the lower limit for inclusion in the FTSE Small Cap Index. In mid-2004, there were approximately 688 companies in the Index. The FTSE All-Share Index is the standard benchmark for measuring the performance of the broad UK market.

## FTSE Fledgling

This index comprises the smallest companies that do not meet the minimum size requirement of the FTSE Small Cap Index.

## FTSE TMT

Reflects the performance of companies in the Technology, Media and Telecommunications sectors.

## FTSE techMARK All-Share

An index of all companies included in the London Stock Exchange's techMARK sector.

## FTSE techMARK 100

The top 100 companies of the FTSE techMARK All-Share, under £4 billion by full market capitalisation.

# Stock indices – international

### Dow Jones Industrial Average Index (DJIA)

The DJIA is the oldest continuing stock index of the US market, and is now the most famous stock index in the world. Created in 1896, it originally comprised 12 stocks, but over the years the Index expanded and today it includes 30 stocks. The Index is weighted by price, which is unusual for a stock index. It is calculated simply by summing the prices of the 30 stocks and dividing by the divisor. Originally the divisor was 30, but this has been adjusted periodically to reflect capital changes such as stock splits, and is currently about 0.2. This means that companies with high stock prices have the greatest influence in the Index – not those with large market values. Only one company remains in the Index from the beginning: General Electric.

### Standard & Poor's 500 (S&P 500)

This is the main benchmark index for the performance of the US market. The Index is weighted by market value, and constituents are chosen based upon their market size, liquidity, and sector. The Index was created in 1957, although values for it have been back-calculated several decades.

### Nasdaq 100

This Index tracks the performance of the 100 largest stocks listed on the NASDAQ exchange. The Index is calculated using a modified capitalisation weighting method ('modified' so that large companies like Microsoft don't overwhelm the Index). NASDAQ companies tend to be smaller and younger than those listed on the NYSE, and although there is no attempt to select technology stocks, it is regarded as the tech stock index. The Index can be traded as there is an ETF associated with it (the most actively traded ETF in the US). The ETF has the symbol QQQ, and is sometimes referred to as the 'Qs' or 'Qubes'.

### Nikkei 225

The Nikkei 225 Index is owned by the Nihon Keizai Shimbun ('Nikkei') newspaper. It was first calculated in 1949 (when it was known as the Nikkei-Dow Index) and is the most widely watched stock index in Japan. It is a price-weighted index of 225 top-rated Japanese companies listed in the First Section of the Tokyo Stock Exchange. The calculation method is therefore similar to that of the Dow Jones Industrial Average (upon which it was modelled).

### TOPIX

The TOPIX Index is calculated by the Tokyo Stock Exchange. Unlike the Nikkei 255, TOPIX is a market capitalisation weighted index. The Index is calculated from all members of the First Section of the Tokyo SE, which is about 1,500 companies. For these reasons, TOPIX is preferred over the Nikkei 225 as a benchmark for Japanese equity portfolios.

### Hang Seng

The Hang Seng Index was first calculated in 1964. Today it has 33 constituents representing some 70% of the total Hong Kong market by capitalisation.

### CAC 40

The CAC 40 Index is the main benchmark for Euronext Paris (what used to be the Paris Bourse). The index contains 40 stocks selected from among the top 100 by market capitalization and the most active stocks listed on Euronext Paris. The base value was 1,000 at 31 December 1987.

### DAX

The DAX 30 Index is published by the Frankfurt Stock Exchange, and is the main real-time German share index. It contains 30 stocks from the leading German stock markets. The DAX is a total return index (which is uncommon), whereby it measures not only the price appreciation of its constituents but also the return provided by the dividends paid.

# Company profile of the FTSE100 Index

| No. | Name | EPIC | Turnover (£m) | Profit Margin (£m) | Profit (%) | Capital (£m) | Weighting (%) | Cumulative Weighting (%) |
|---|---|---|---|---|---|---|---|---|
| 1 | BP PLC | BP. | 152,235 | 18,638 | 10.6 | 122,664 | 8.8 | 8.8 |
| 2 | HSBC Holdings PLC | HSBA | 0 | 12,187 | | 110,848 | 7.9 | 16.7 |
| 3 | GlaxoSmithKline PLC | GSK | 21,660 | 6,732 | 31.2 | 83,296 | 6.0 | 22.7 |
| 4 | Vodafone Group PLC | VOD | 36,616 | -19,301 | 20.6 | 67,858 | 4.9 | 27.5 |
| 5 | Royal Bank of Scotland Group (The) PLC | RBS | 0 | 7,936 | | 55,619 | 4.0 | 31.5 |
| 6 | Royal Dutch Shell PLC | RDSB | 178,290 | 25,727 | 11.8 | 53,808 | 3.9 | 35.4 |
| 7 | AstraZeneca PLC | AZN | 13,921 | 3,875 | 27.5 | 50,258 | 3.6 | 39.0 |
| 8 | Barclays PLC | BARC | 0 | 5,280 | | 41,800 | 3.0 | 42.0 |
| 9 | HBOS PLC | HBOS | 0 | 4,808 | | 36,933 | 2.6 | 44.6 |
| 10 | Anglo American PLC | AAL | 17,110 | 3,027 | 18.7 | 35,168 | 2.5 | 47.1 |
| 11 | British American Tobacco PLC | BATS | 9,325 | 2,588 | 28.7 | 29,688 | 2.1 | 49.3 |
| 12 | Lloyds TSB Group PLC | LLOY | 0 | 3,820 | | 28,799 | 2.1 | 51.3 |
| 13 | Tesco PLC | TSCO | 39,588 | 2,226 | 5.29 | 28,756 | 2.1 | 53.4 |
| 14 | Rio Tinto PLC | RIO | 11,064 | 4,250 | 34.7 | 28,387 | 2.0 | 55.4 |
| 15 | Diageo PLC | DGE | 9,036 | 1,822 | 21.6 | 25,940 | 1.9 | 57.3 |
| 16 | BG Group PLC | BG. | 5,612 | 2,509 | 38.1 | 24,964 | 1.8 | 59.0 |
| 17 | BHP Billiton PLC | BLT | 16,502 | 4,875 | 28.4 | 24,224 | 1.7 | 60.8 |
| 18 | BT Group PLC | BT.A | 19,514 | 2,040 | 13.5 | 20,756 | 1.5 | 62.3 |
| 19 | Aviva PLC | AV. | 0 | 3,450 | | 17,342 | 1.2 | 63.5 |
| 20 | Standard Chartered PLC | STAN | 0 | 1,558 | | 17,263 | 1.2 | 64.7 |
| 21 | National Grid PLC | NG. | 9,361 | 4,461 | 28.5 | 16,869 | 1.2 | 66.0 |
| 22 | Unilever PLC | ULVR | 27,460 | 3,285 | 13.8 | 15,774 | 1.1 | 67.1 |
| 23 | Reckitt Benckiser PLC | RB. | 4,179 | 876 | 20.1 | 15,600 | 1.1 | 68.2 |
| 24 | SABMiller PLC | SAB | 8,807 | 1,411 | 17 | 15,308 | 1.1 | 69.3 |
| 25 | Xstrata PLC | XTA | 4,679 | 1,433 | 30.7 | 14,620 | 1.0 | 70.3 |
| 26 | Prudential PLC | PRU | 0 | 2,148 | | 13,474 | 1.0 | 71.3 |
| 27 | Imperial Tobacco Group PLC | IMT | 3,149 | 862 | 41.3 | 12,022 | 0.9 | 72.2 |
| 28 | Cadbury Schweppes PLC | CBRY | 7,157 | 940 | 16.2 | 11,100 | 0.8 | 73.0 |
| 29 | BAE SYSTEMS PLC | BA. | 11,130 | 677 | 6.06 | 11,001 | 0.8 | 73.7 |
| 30 | Scottish & Southern Energy PLC | SSE | 10,145 | 897 | 8.06 | 10,573 | 0.8 | 74.5 |
| 31 | Centrica PLC | CNA | 13,448 | 1,812 | 10.9 | 10,564 | 0.8 | 75.3 |
| 32 | Marks & Spencer Group PLC | MKS | 8,026 | 749 | 10.7 | 9,692 | 0.7 | 76.0 |
| 33 | British Sky Broadcasting Group PLC | BSY | 4,148 | 798 | | 9,687 | 0.7 | 76.6 |
| 34 | Scottish Power PLC | SPW | 7,945 | 1,876 | 21.4 | 9,027 | 0.6 | 77.3 |
| 35 | Land Securities Group PLC | LAND | 1,829 | 2,359 | 117 | 9,020 | 0.6 | 77.9 |
| 36 | Old Mutual PLC | OML | 0 | 1,606 | | 8,657 | 0.6 | 78.6 |
| 37 | GUS PLC | GUS | 7,915 | 793 | 9.98 | 8,560 | 0.6 | 79.2 |
| 38 | BOC Group (The) PLC | BOC | 3,755 | 594 | 11.6 | 8,276 | 0.6 | 79.8 |
| 39 | Legal & General Group PLC | LGEN | 0 | 1,586 | | 8,132 | 0.6 | 80.3 |
| 40 | Man Group PLC | EMG | 2,010 | 711 | 34.7 | 7,679 | 0.5 | 80.9 |
| 41 | WPP Group PLC | WPP | 26,674 | 592 | 2.61 | 7,590 | 0.5 | 81.4 |
| 42 | Rolls-Royce Group PLC | RR. | 6,603 | 477 | 12 | 7,475 | 0.5 | 82.0 |
| 43 | Alliance Boots PLC | AB. | 5,471 | 1,810 | 5.61 | 7,416 | 0.5 | 82.5 |
| 44 | British Land Co PLC | BLND | 690 | 1,590 | 267 | 7,061 | 0.5 | 83.0 |
| 45 | Reed Elsevier PLC | REL | 2,733 | 241 | 11.5 | 6,872 | 0.5 | 83.5 |
| 46 | Associated British Foods PLC | ABF | 5,622 | 479 | 9.87 | 6,666 | 0.5 | 84.0 |
| 47 | Wolseley PLC | WOS | 11,258 | 648 | 6.3 | 6,529 | 0.5 | 84.5 |
| 48 | Sainsbury (J) PLC | SBRY | 16,061 | 104 | 1.42 | 6,057 | 0.4 | 84.9 |
| 49 | Pearson PLC | PSON | 4,123 | 767 | 10.6 | 5,978 | 0.4 | 85.3 |
| 50 | Gallaher Group PLC | GLH | 8,214 | 516 | 7.56 | 5,871 | 0.4 | 85.7 |
| 51 | Morrison (Wm) Supermarkets PLC | MRW | 12,115 | -313 | -0.358 | 5,832 | 0.4 | 86.1 |
| 52 | United Utilities PLC | UU. | 2,562 | 422 | 29.4 | 5,796 | 0.4 | 86.6 |
| 53 | Kazakhmys PLC | KAZ | 1,510 | 493 | 33 | 5,731 | 0.4 | 87.0 |
| 54 | Kingfisher PLC | KGF | 8,010 | 232 | 7.13 | 5,464 | 0.4 | 87.4 |
| 55 | Compass Group PLC | CPG | 12,704 | 171 | 5.51 | 5,431 | 0.4 | 87.8 |
| 56 | Reuters Group PLC | RTR | 2,875 | 327 | 2.96 | 5,004 | 0.4 | 88.1 |
| 57 | Scottish & Newcastle PLC | SCTN | 3,260 | 245 | 8.28 | 4,977 | 0.4 | 88.5 |
| 58 | Smiths Group PLC | SMIN | 3,017 | 310 | 14 | 4,976 | 0.4 | 88.8 |
| 59 | Hanson PLC | HNS | 3,740 | 423 | 11.6 | 4,666 | 0.3 | 89.2 |
| 60 | Northern Rock PLC | NRK | 0 | 494 | | 4,659 | 0.3 | 89.5 |
| 61 | Alliance & Leicester PLC | AL. | 0 | 547 | | 4,538 | 0.3 | 89.8 |

| No. | Name | EPIC | Turnover Margin (£m) | Profit (£m) | Profit (%) | Capital (£m) | Weighting (%) | Cumulative Weighting (%) |
|---|---|---|---|---|---|---|---|---|
| 62 | International Power PLC | IPR | 1,933 | 419 | 18.4 | 4,510 | 0.3 | 90.1 |
| 63 | PartyGaming PLC | PRTY | 568 | 189 | 34 | 4,490 | 0.3 | 90.5 |
| 64 | British Airways PLC | BAY | 8,515 | 620 | 8.7 | 4,410 | 0.3 | 90.8 |
| 65 | Severn Trent PLC | SVT | 2,295 | 266 | 20.9 | 4,395 | 0.3 | 91.1 |
| 66 | 3i Group PLC | III | 0 | 0 | | 4,337 | 0.3 | 91.4 |
| 67 | Carnival PLC | CCL | 6,402 | 1,345 | 23.8 | 4,334 | 0.3 | 91.7 |
| 68 | Shire PLC | SHP | 930 | -83 | 23.5 | 4,286 | 0.3 | 92.0 |
| 69 | Imperial Chemical Industries PLC | ICI | 5,812 | 500 | 10.8 | 4,276 | 0.3 | 92.3 |
| 70 | British Energy Group PLC | BGY | 2,593 | 599 | | 4,209 | 0.3 | 92.6 |
| 71 | AMVESCAP PLC | AVZ | 1,674 | 209 | 18.1 | 4,184 | 0.3 | 92.9 |
| 72 | Antofagasta PLC | ANTO | 1,421 | 893 | 63.2 | 4,165 | 0.3 | 93.2 |
| 73 | Smith & Nephew PLC | SN. | 1,407 | 240 | 19.1 | 4,150 | 0.3 | 93.5 |
| 74 | ITV PLC | ITV | 2,177 | 311 | 15 | 4,150 | 0.3 | 93.8 |
| 75 | Yell Group PLC | YELL | 1,621 | 317 | 28.2 | 3,968 | 0.3 | 94.1 |
| 76 | Royal & Sun Alliance Insurance Group PLC | RSA | 0 | 865 | | 3,953 | 0.3 | 94.4 |
| 77 | Lonmin PLC | LMI | 637 | 182 | 30.9 | 3,840 | 0.3 | 94.7 |
| 78 | Next PLC | NXT | 3,106 | 449 | 14.9 | 3,811 | 0.3 | 94.9 |
| 79 | Friends Provident PLC | FP. | 0 | 149 | | 3,770 | 0.3 | 95.2 |
| 80 | Liberty International PLC | LII | 434 | 527 | 196 | 3,756 | 0.3 | 95.5 |
| 81 | Drax Group PLC | DRX | 929 | 264 | 13.9 | 3,709 | 0.3 | 95.7 |
| 82 | Persimmon PLC | PSN | 2,286 | 495 | 23 | 3,701 | 0.3 | 96.0 |
| 83 | Vedanta Resources PLC | VED | 2,130 | 538 | 25.5 | 3,611 | 0.3 | 96.3 |
| 84 | DSG International PLC | DSGI | 7,403 | 303 | | 3,599 | 0.3 | 96.5 |
| 85 | Hammerson PLC | HMSO | 249 | 699 | 71.8 | 3,573 | 0.3 | 96.8 |
| 86 | Corus Group PLC | CS. | 10,140 | 580 | 7.12 | 3,490 | 0.2 | 97.0 |
| 87 | Tate & Lyle PLC | TATE | 3,720 | 42 | 8.68 | 3,363 | 0.2 | 97.3 |
| 88 | Cairn Energy PLC | CNE | 153 | 59 | 21.2 | 3,336 | 0.2 | 97.5 |
| 89 | Capita Group (The) PLC | CPI | 1,436 | 153 | 13 | 3,251 | 0.2 | 97.7 |
| 90 | InterContinental Hotels Group PLC | IHG | 1,910 | 595 | 15.3 | 3,109 | 0.2 | 98.0 |
| 91 | Slough Estates PLC | SLOU | 405 | 582 | 191 | 3,095 | 0.2 | 98.2 |
| 92 | Enterprise Inns PLC | ETI | 920 | 304 | 57 | 3,077 | 0.2 | 98.4 |
| 93 | ICAP PLC | IAP | 919 | 193 | 20.3 | 2,983 | 0.2 | 98.6 |
| 94 | Rentokil Initial PLC | RTO | 2,403 | 213 | 5.33 | 2,974 | 0.2 | 98.8 |
| 95 | Kelda Group PLC | KEL | 884 | 248 | 39.3 | 2,941 | 0.2 | 99.0 |
| 96 | Sage Group (The) PLC | SGE | 777 | 205 | 27.3 | 2,872 | 0.2 | 99.2 |
| 97 | Brambles Industries PLC | BI. | 2,275 | 210 | 12.4 | 2,821 | 0.2 | 99.4 |
| 98 | REXAM PLC | REX | 3,237 | 331 | 12.6 | 2,803 | 0.2 | 99.6 |
| 99 | Johnson Matthey PLC | JMAT | 4,756 | 214 | 4.93 | 2,760 | 0.2 | 99.8 |
| 100 | Schroders PLC | SDR | 808 | 251 | 26.5 | 2,160 | 0.2 | 100.0 |

## Notes to the table

1. Turnover figures are not given for financial companies.

2. The weighting column expresses a company's market capitalisation as a percentage of the total capitalisation of all companies in the FTSE 100 Index. The table is ranked (in descending order) by this column.

3. The final column is the Cumulative Weighting.

4. Figures accurate as of August 2006.

## Observations

- The 5 largest companies in the FTSE 100 Index account for almost one third (31.5%) of total capitalisation. (This is less than in 2005, when they accounted for 35.7% of the total index.)

- The 12 largest companies in the index account for just over half of total capitalisation. (In 2005, it was the 10 largest companies.)

- The 22 smallest companies in the index account for only roughly 5% of total capitalisation. In other words, the individual movements of these 22 companies has very little impact on the value of the index.

- The aggregate capitalisation of all 100 companies in the Index is £1,397bn. (When the index started in 1984, the aggregate capitalisation was £100 billion).

# Sector profile of the FTSE100 and FTSE250 Indices

The table below displays the sector weightings in the FTSE100 and FTSE250 Indices.

| Sector | FTSE 100 | | FTSE 250 | |
|---|---|---|---|---|
| | Cap. Weighting (%) | Companies | Cap. Weighting (%) | Companies |
| Banks | 21.6 | 8 | 1.1 | 1 |
| Oil & Gas Producers | 14.4 | 4 | 3.2 | 7 |
| Pharmaceuticals & Biotechnology | 10.0 | 3 | 0.3 | 1 |
| Mining | 8.8 | 8 | 0.6 | 2 |
| Mobile Telecommunications | 4.1 | 1 | 0.6 | 1 |
| Life Insurance | 3.7 | 5 | 1.4 | 2 |
| Beverages | 3.6 | 3 | 0.2 | 1 |
| Tobacco | 3.5 | 3 | 0.0 | 0 |
| Media | 3.2 | 7 | 5.9 | 11 |
| Food & Drug Retailers | 3.0 | 3 | 0.2 | 2 |
| Gas; Water & Multiutilities | 3.0 | 5 | 1.9 | 3 |
| General Retailers | 2.8 | 6 | 7.0 | 18 |
| Food Producers | 2.7 | 4 | 1.1 | 4 |
| Electricity | 2.3 | 5 | 0.5 | 1 |
| Real Estate | 1.9 | 5 | 5.8 | 20 |
| Travel & Leisure | 1.8 | 6 | 12.5 | 25 |
| Aerospace & Defense | 1.7 | 3 | 2.3 | 5 |
| General Financial | 1.6 | 5 | 6.6 | 15 |
| Fixed Line Telecommunications | 1.4 | 1 | 1.5 | 2 |
| Household Goods | 1.4 | 2 | 6.2 | 12 |
| Support Services | 1.1 | 4 | 10.9 | 30 |
| Chemicals | 1.1 | 3 | 0.4 | 2 |
| Construction & Materials | 0.3 | 1 | 1.5 | 5 |
| Health Care Equipment & Services | 0.3 | 1 | 0.4 | 2 |
| Nonlife Insurance | 0.3 | 1 | 3.0 | 8 |
| Industrial Metals | 0.3 | 1 | 0.0 | 0 |
| Software & Computer Services | 0.2 | 1 | 2.2 | 7 |
| General Industrials | 0.2 | 1 | 1.6 | 3 |
| Automobiles & Parts | 0.0 | 0 | 0.8 | 1 |
| Electronic & Electrical Equipment | 0.0 | 0 | 2.0 | 6 |
| Equity Investment Instruments | 0.0 | 0 | 9.7 | 30 |
| Industrial Engineering | 0.0 | 0 | 2.8 | 8 |
| Industrial Transportation | 0.0 | 0 | 1.3 | 4 |
| Oil Equipment; Services & Distribution | 0.0 | 0 | 1.6 | 5 |
| Personal Goods | 0.0 | 0 | 1.4 | 3 |
| Technology Hardware & Equipment | 0.0 | 0 | 1.6 | 4 |

*Note*: Figures as of August 2006.

## Observations

1. The top 4 FTSE 100 sectors (Banks, Oil & Gas Producers, Pharmaceuticals & Biotechnology and Mining) account for 55% of the total Index capitalisation.

2. Despite the 'new economy' cheerleaders of recent years, the FTSE 100 Index hasn't yet been taken over by TMT stocks. Even the (very old economy) mining sector has been growing and is now the 4th largest in the Index.

3. In 1935 the FT30 Index was dominated by engineering and machinery companies. Today, the sector isn't represented at all in the FTSE 100 Index.

4. It can be seen that the sector profiles of the FTSE 100 and 250 indices are completely different. The only two sectors with a reasonably high weighting in both indices are Oil & Gas and Media. While the three big FTSE250 sectors (Travel & Leisure, Support Services, Equity Investment Instruments) have a very light presence in the FTSE 100.

# FTSE100 quarterly reviews

A table of companies entering and exiting the FTSE100 Index since January 2001, as a result of the quarterly reviews.

| Company | In | Out |
|---|---|---|
| Alliance UniChem | Sep 02 | |
| ARM Holdings | | Jun 02 |
| Autonomy Corporation | | Mar 01 |
| BPB | Jun 04 | |
| Bradford & Bingley | | Sep 04 |
| Brambles Industries | | Dec 02 |
| British Airways | Dec 02, Dec 03 | Sep 02, Mar 03 |
| British Land Co | Sep 01 | |
| Bunzl | Jun 02 | Jun 05 |
| Cable & Wireless | Mar 03 | Dec 02, Jun 06 |
| Cairn Energy | Sep 04, Sep 05 | Mar 05 |
| Canary Wharf | | Apr 03 |
| Capita Group | Jun 04 | Jun 03 |
| Carlton Communications | | Sep 01 |
| Celltech Group | | Mar 02 |
| CMG | | Sep 01 |
| Colt Telecom Group | | Sep 01 |
| Corus Group | Mar 02 | Dec 02, Jun 05 |
| Daily Mail & General Trust | | Jun 06 |
| Drax Group | Jun 06 | |
| Electrocomponents | | Jun 02 |
| Emap | Oct 02 | Sep 05 |
| EMI Group | | Sep 02 |
| Energis | | Sep 01 |
| Enterprise Inns | Mar 04 | |
| Enterprise Oil | Sep 01 | |
| Exel | | Mar 01 |
| Foreign & Colonial Investment Trust | Mar 03 | Mar 04 |
| Friends Provident | Sep 01 | |
| GKN | | Dec 01 |
| Hammerson | | |
| Hays | Dec 03 | Jun 03, Sep 05 |
| Innogy Holdings | Sep 01 | |
| InterContinental Hotels Group (demerger of Six Continents) | Apr 03 | |
| International Power | Mar 05 | Sep 02 |
| Invensys | | Mar 03 |
| Johnson Matthey | Jun 02 | |
| Kazakhmys | Dec 05 | |
| Kelda | Mar 03 | Sep 03 |
| Ladbrokes | | Jun 06 |
| Lattice (following merger between National Grid and Lattice) | | Oct 02 |
| Liberty International | Dec 02 | |
| Logica | | Jun 02 |
| Lonmin | Jun 06 | |
| MAN GROUP | Sep 01 | |
| Marconi | | Sep 01 |
| Misys | | Sep 01 |
| Mitchells & Butlers (demerger of Six Continents) | Apr 03 | Dec 03 |
| Northern Rock | Sep 01 | |
| P & O Princess Cruises | Dec 01 | |
| PartyGaming | Sep 05 | |
| Persimmon | Dec 05 | |
| Provident Financial | Mar 03 | Dec 03 |
| Rexam | Sep 02 | |
| Rolls-Royce | Jun 03 | Mar 03 |
| Royal & Sun Alliance | Jun 03 | Mar 03 |
| Scottish and Newcastle | Mar 01 | |
| Sema | Mar 01 | |
| Severn Trent | Sep 01 | |
| Spirent | | Sep 01 |
| Tate & Lyle | Dec 04 | |
| Telewest Communications | | Sep 01 |
| Tomkins | Sep 02 | Dec 04 |
| Vedanta Resources | Jun 06 | |
| Whitbread | Dec 02 | Dec 05 |
| William Hill | | Dec 05 |
| Wolseley | Sep 01 | |
| Xstrata | Jun 02 | |
| Yell Group | Sep 03 | |

Source: FTSE International

# Top tens

On the following few pages are tables with the top 10 companies ranked according to various criteria:

## Top 10 table contents

1. 10 **largest investment trusts** by market capitalisation

2. 10 **largest companies** by market capitalisation

3. 10 companies with largest **average volume** of shares traded

4. **5-year share performance** 30/06/2001-30/06/2006 [FTSE 350]

5. 10 companies with highest **turnover**

6. 10 companies with greatest **turnover growth** in 5 years to 2006 [FTSE 350]

7. 10 companies with highest **turnover/capitalisation** ratio [FTSE 350]

8. 10 companies with highest **profits**

9. 10 companies with greatest **profit growth** in the 5 years to 2006 [FTSE 350]

10. 10 companies with highest **profit/turnover margins** [FTSE 350]

11. 10 companies with highest **EPS growth** in the 5 years to 2006 [FTSE 350]

12. 10 companies with highest **dividend growth** in the 5 years to 2006 [FTSE 350]

13. 10 companies with largest **market capitalisation** [AIM]

14. 10 companies with largest **profits** [AIM]

15. **5-year share performance** 30/06/2001-30/06/2006 [AIM]

Notes:

•  Unless otherwise stated, the universe of shares considered is all listed shares.

•  The tables were compiled on 17th August 2006, so all figures are the latest to that date.

### Table 1: 10 largest investment trusts by capitalisation

| No. | Company | EPIC | Capital (£m) |
|-----|---------|------|--------------|
| 1 | Alliance Trust | ATST | 2,325 |
| 2 | Foreign & Colonial Investment Trust | FRCL | 1,967 |
| 3 | RIT Capital Partners | RCP | 1,477 |
| 4 | Templeton Emerging Markets Inv Tr | TEM | 1,449 |
| 5 | Scottish Mortgage Investment Trust | SMT | 1,347 |
| 6 | JP Morgan Fleming Mercantile Investment Trust | JFM | 1,281 |
| 7 | Caledonia Investments | CLDN | 1,255 |
| 8 | Witan Investment Trust | WTAN | 1,084 |
| 9 | SVG Capital | SVI | 1,023 |
| 10 | F&C Commercial Property Trust Ltd | FCPT | 992 |

## Size, volume and performance

### Table 2: 10 largest companies by market capitalisation

| No. | Company | EPIC | Capital (£m) |
|---|---|---|---|
| 1 | BP | BP. | 120,216 |
| 2 | HSBC Holdings | HSBA | 109,987 |
| 3 | GlaxoSmithKline | GSK | 84,963 |
| 4 | Vodafone Group | VOD | 57,924 |
| 5 | Royal Bank of Scotland Group (The) | RBS | 56,131 |
| 6 | Royal Dutch Shell | RDSB | 53,449 |
| 7 | AstraZeneca | AZN | 51,228 |
| 8 | Barclays | BARC | 42,157 |
| 9 | HBOS | HBOS | 37,958 |
| 10 | Anglo American | AAL | 36,018 |

### Table 3: 10 companies with largest average volume of shares traded

| No. | Company | EPIC | 200 day Volume Average |
|---|---|---|---|
| 1 | Vodafone Group | VOD | 433m |
| 2 | BP | BP. | 87.5m |
| 3 | BT Group | BT.A | 56.2m |
| 4 | Tesco | TSCO | 52.5m |
| 5 | Legal & General Group | LGEN | 42.5m |
| 6 | Old Mutual | OML | 42.0m |
| 7 | ITV | ITV | 41.9m |
| 8 | PartyGaming | PRTY | 41.6m |
| 9 | HSBC Holdings | HSBA | 40.2m |
| 10 | Cable and Wireless | CW. | 39.7m |

### Table 4: 5-year share performance 30/06/2001 – 30/06/2006 [FTSE 350]

| No. | Company | EPIC | 5-yr change (%) |
|---|---|---|---|
| 1 | JKX Oil & Gas | JKX | 2,416.1 |
| 2 | SCi Entertainment Group | SEG | 1,088.5 |
| 3 | SOCO International | SIA | 994.4 |
| 4 | Cairn Energy | CNE | 539.4 |
| 5 | Pendragon | PDG | 508.8 |
| 6 | Inchcape | INCH | 493.7 |
| 7 | Savills | SVS | 457.4 |
| 8 | Dana Petroleum | DNX | 426.3 |
| 9 | Helphire Group | HHR | 412.0 |
| 10 | Kensington Group | KGN | 396.4 |

## Turnover

### Table 5: 10 companies with highest turnover

| No. | Company | EPIC | Turnover (£m) |
|---|---|---|---|
| 1 | Royal Dutch Shell | RDSB | 178,290 |
| 2 | BP | BP. | 152,235 |
| 3 | Tesco | TSCO | 39,588 |
| 4 | Vodafone Group | VOD | 36,616 |
| 5 | Unilever | ULVR | 27,460 |
| 6 | WPP Group | WPP | 26,674 |
| 7 | GlaxoSmithKline | GSK | 21,660 |
| 8 | BT Group | BT.A | 19,514 |
| 9 | Anglo American | AAL | 17,110 |
| 10 | BHP Billiton | BLT | 16,502 |

**Table 6: 10 companies with greatest turnover growth in 5 years to 2006 [FTSE 350]**

| No. | Company | EPIC | Turnover 5 years' growth % |
|---|---|---|---|
| 1 | Xstrata | XTA | 1000+ |
| 2 | Collins Stewart Tullett | CSTL | 1000+ |
| 3 | Tullow Oil | TLW | 1000+ |
| 4 | Venture Production | VPC | 1000+ |
| 5 | Wolfson Microelectronics | WLF | 1000+ |
| 6 | Big Yellow Group | BYG | 904 |
| 7 | Gallaher Group | GLH | 691 |
| 8 | Burren Energy | BUR | 502 |
| 9 | Gyrus Group | GYG | 463 |
| 10 | Dana Petroleum | DNX | 455 |

**Table 7: 10 companies with highest turnover/capitalisation ratio [FTSE 350]**

| No. | Company | EPIC | Turnover / Cap |
|---|---|---|---|
| 1 | Computacenter | CCC | 5.8 |
| 2 | Ladbrokes | LAD | 5.5 |
| 3 | Woolworths Group | WLW | 5.5 |
| 4 | AMEC | AMEC | 5.4 |
| 5 | Pendragon | PDG | 4.9 |
| 6 | William Hill | WMH | 4.8 |
| 7 | Wincanton | WIN | 4.7 |
| 8 | Northern Foods | NFDS | 3.6 |
| 9 | WPP Group | WPP | 3.4 |
| 10 | Interserve | IRV | 3.3 |

## Profits

**Table 8: 10 companies with highest profits**

| No. | Company | EPIC | Profit (£m) |
|---|---|---|---|
| 1 | Royal Dutch Shell | RDSB | 25,727 |
| 2 | BP | BP. | 18,638 |
| 3 | HSBC Holdings | HSBA | 12,187 |
| 4 | Royal Bank of Scotland Group (The) | RBS | 7,936 |
| 5 | GlaxoSmithKline | GSK | 6,732 |
| 6 | Barclays | BARC | 5,280 |
| 7 | BHP Billiton | BLT | 4,875 |
| 8 | HBOS | HBOS | 4,808 |
| 9 | National Grid | NG. | 4,461 |
| 10 | Rio Tinto | RIO | 4,250 |

**Table 9: 10 companies with greatest profit growth in the 5 years to 2006 [FTSE 350]**

| No. | Company | EPIC | 5 years' Profit Growth% |
|---|---|---|---|
| 1 | British Land Co | BLND | 1000+ |
| 2 | Xstrata | XTA | 1000+ |
| 3 | Royal & Sun Alliance Insurance Group | RSA | 1000+ |
| 4 | Stanley Leisure | SLY | 1000+ |
| 5 | Tullow Oil | TLW | 1000+ |
| 6 | William Hill | WMH | 1000+ |
| 7 | Derwent Valley Holdings | DWV | 1000+ |
| 8 | Dana Petroleum | DNX | 1000+ |
| 9 | Intertek Group | ITRK | 1000+ |
| 10 | Hiscox | HSX | 1000+ |

## Table 10: 10 companies with highest profit/turnover margins [FTSE 350]

| No. | Company | EPIC | Profit as % of Turnover |
|---|---|---|---|
| 1 | SOCO International | SIA | 83.9 |
| 2 | Evolution Group | EVG | 73.2 |
| 3 | Slough Estates | SLOU | 62.0 |
| 4 | Antofagasta | ANTO | 60.9 |
| 5 | Hammerson | HMSO | 57.9 |
| 6 | Burren Energy | BUR | 55.7 |
| 7 | Brixton | BXTN | 54.3 |
| 8 | Great Portland Estates | GPOR | 50.0 |
| 9 | McCarthy & Stone | MCTY | 46.6 |
| 10 | Derwent Valley Holdings | DWV | 45.7 |

## EPS and dividends

## Table 11: 10 companies with highest EPS growth in the 5 years to 2006 [FTSE 350]

| No. | Company | EPIC | Most recent EPS 5 years' Growth % |
|---|---|---|---|
| 1 | Great Portland Estates | GPOR | 1000+ |
| 2 | Derwent Valley Holdings | DWV | 1000+ |
| 3 | Workspace Group | WKP | 1000+ |
| 4 | British Land Co | BLND | 1000+ |
| 5 | Stanley Leisure | SLY | 1000+ |
| 6 | Burren Energy | BUR | 1000+ |
| 7 | Tullow Oil | TLW | 1000+ |
| 8 | William Hill | WMH | 1000+ |
| 9 | Kensington Group | KGN | 1000+ |
| 10 | Caledonia Investments | CLDN | 949 |

## Table 12: 10 companies with highest dividend growth in the 5 years to 2006 [FTSE 350]

| No. | Company | EPIC | Dividend 5 years' Growth % |
|---|---|---|---|
| 1 | Topps Tiles | TPT | 997 |
| 2 | Helphire Group | HHR | 812 |
| 3 | Sage Group (The) | SGE | 639 |
| 4 | Collins Stewart Tullett | CSTL | 586 |
| 5 | Bradford & Bingley | BB. | 383 |
| 6 | Aquarius Platinum Ltd | AQP | 365 |
| 7 | Vodafone Group | VOD | 334 |
| 8 | Enterprise Inns | ETI | 325 |
| 9 | Capita Group (The) | CPI | 324 |
| 10 | Fidelity European Values | FEV | 317 |

### Table 13: 10 companies with largest market capitalisation [AIM]

| No. | Company | EPIC | Capital (£m) |
|-----|---------|------|--------------|
| 1 | EP&F Capital PLC | ECA | 1,353.3 |
| 2 | Sibir Energy PLC | SBE | 1,335.9 |
| 3 | Sportingbet PLC | SBT | 1,075.4 |
| 4 | Peter Hambro Mining PLC | POG | 1,058.3 |
| 5 | New Star Asset Management Group PLC | NSAM | 1,048.3 |
| 6 | Nikanor PLC | NKR | 844.8 |
| 7 | Monsoon PLC | MSN | 712.5 |
| 8 | Central African Mining & Exploration Company PLC | CFM | 536.5 |
| 9 | Playtech Ltd | PTEC | 501.3 |
| 10 | NETeller PLC | NLR | 486.9 |

### Table 14: 10 companies with largest profits [AIM]

| No. | Company | EPIC | Profit (£m) |
|-----|---------|------|-------------|
| 1 | NETeller PLC | NLR | 56.8 |
| 2 | Monsoon PLC | MSN | 53.5 |
| 3 | Abbey PLC | ABBY | 47.1 |
| 4 | Sportingbet PLC | SBT | 40.8 |
| 5 | Numis Corporation PLC | NUM | 39.9 |
| 6 | RAB Capital PLC | RAB | 25.6 |
| 7 | Wogen PLC | WGN | 23.2 |
| 8 | New Star Asset Management Group PLC | NSAM | 19.6 |
| 9 | Hardys & Hansons PLC | HDYS | 18.3 |
| 10 | Fayrewood PLC | FWY | 18.3 |

### Table 15: 5-year share performance 31/12/1999 – 31/12/2004 [AIM]

| No. | Company | EPIC | 5-yr share price (%) |
|-----|---------|------|----------------------|
| 1 | Griffin Mining | GFM | 1,271 |
| 2 | First Quantum Minerals LD | FQM | 1,194 |
| 3 | Northern Petroleum PLC | NOP | 1,051 |
| 4 | Avocet Mining PLC | AVM | 944 |
| 5 | E Wood Holdings PLC | EWD | 810 |
| 6 | Cape PLC | CIU | 753 |
| 7 | Tolent PLC | TLT | 693 |
| 8 | Stanley Gibbons Group (The) Ltd | SGI | 650 |
| 9 | Internet Business Group PLC | IBG | 605 |
| 10 | Numis Corporation PLC | NUM | 570 |

# Comparative performance of UK indices

## Year end closing values of UK indices

| Name | 1995 | 1996 | 1997 | 1998 | 1999 | 2000 | 2001 | 2002 | 2003 | 2004 | 2005 |
|------|------|------|------|------|------|------|------|------|------|------|------|
| FTSE 100 | 3689.3 | 4118.5 | 5135.5 | 5879.4 | 6665.9 | 6222.5 | 5217.4 | 3940.4 | 4476.9 | 4814.3 | 5618.8 |
| FTSE 250 | 4021.3 | 4490.4 | 4787.6 | 4851.0 | 6432.1 | 6547.5 | 5939.1 | 4319.3 | 5802.3 | 6936.8 | 8794.3 |
| FTSE All-Share | 1802.6 | 2013.7 | 2411.0 | 2673.2 | 3141.3 | 2983.8 | 2523.9 | 1893.7 | 2207.4 | 2410.8 | 2847.0 |
| FTSE AIM | | 1042.9 | 989.9 | 801.5 | 1920.1 | 1437.8 | 897.8 | 602.9 | 835.4 | 1005.6 | 1046.1 |
| FTSE Fledgling | 1106.4 | 1219.9 | 1262.7 | 1152.5 | 2153.8 | 2266.2 | 2054.7 | 1676.6 | 2624.2 | 3170.4 | 3748.8 |
| FTSE Small Cap | 1941.6 | 2183.1 | 2313.3 | 2082.8 | 3098.4 | 3183.3 | 2579.1 | 1820.6 | 2475.1 | 2758.1 | 3305.5 |
| FTSE TechMARK 100 | | | | | | 2564.1 | 1472.7 | 648.8 | 1015.0 | 1196.4 | 1431.7 |
| FTSE4Good UK 50 | | | | | | | 4662.2 | 3480.6 | 3918.6 | 4199.5 | 4802.2 |

## Annual percentage performance

| Name | 1995 | 1996 | 1997 | 1998 | 1999 | 2000 | 2001 | 2002 | 2003 | 2004 | 2005 |
|------|------|------|------|------|------|------|------|------|------|------|------|
| FFTSE 100 | 20.3 | 11.6 | 24.7 | 14.5 | 13.4 | -6.7 | -16.2 | -24.5 | 13.6 | 7.5 | 16.7 |
| FTSE 250 | 14.8 | 11.7 | 6.6 | 1.3 | 32.6 | 1.8 | -9.3 | -27.3 | 34.3 | 19.6 | 26.8 |
| FTSE All-Share | 18.5 | 11.7 | 19.7 | 10.9 | 17.5 | -5.0 | -15.4 | -25.0 | 16.6 | 9.2 | 18.1 |
| FTSE AIM | | | -5.1 | -19.0 | 139.6 | -25.1 | -37.6 | -32.8 | 38.6 | 20.4 | 4.0 |
| FTSE Fledgling | | 10.3 | 3.5 | -8.7 | 86.9 | 5.2 | -9.3 | -18.4 | 56.5 | 20.8 | 18.2 |
| FTSE Small Cap | 11.2 | 12.4 | 6.0 | -10.0 | 48.8 | 2.7 | -19.0 | -29.4 | 35.9 | 11.4 | 19.8 |
| FTSE TechMARK 100 | | | | | | | -42.6 | -55.9 | 56.4 | 17.9 | 19.7 |
| FTSE4Good UK 50 | | | | | | | | -25.3 | 12.6 | 7.2 | 14.4 |

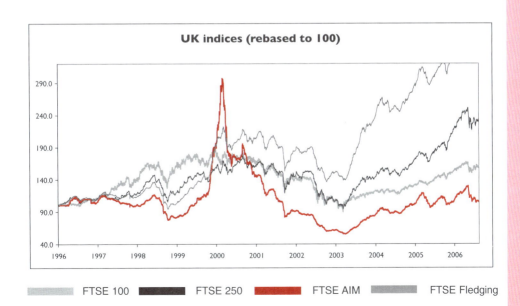

# Comparative performance of international indices

## Year end closing values of international indices

| Index | 1997 | 1998 | 1999 | 2000 | 2001 | 2002 | 2003 | 2004 | 2005 |
|---|---|---|---|---|---|---|---|---|---|
| CAC 40 | 2998.91 | 3942.66 | 5958.32 | 5926.42 | 4624.58 | 3063.91 | 3529.18 | 3821.16 | 4715.2 |
| DAX (Xetra) | 4224.3 | 5006.57 | 6958.14 | 6433.61 | 5160.1 | 2892.63 | 3965.16 | 4256.08 | 5458.6 |
| Dow Jones IA | 7908.25 | 9181.43 | 11497.13 | 10788 | 10021.5 | 8341.63 | 10453.92 | 10783 | 10717.5 |
| FTSE 100 | 5135.5 | 5882.6 | 6930.2 | 6222.5 | 5217.4 | 3940.4 | 4476.9 | 4814.3 | 5618.8 |
| Hang Seng | 10722.75 | 10048.5 | 16962 | 15095.5 | 11397.25 | 9321.25 | 12576 | 14230.25 | 14876.5 |
| Nasdaq Comp. | 1570.35 | 2192.69 | 4069.31 | 2470.5 | 1950.4 | 1335.51 | 2003.37 | 2175.44 | 2205.3 |
| Nikkei 225 | 15258.75 | 13842.25 | 18934.25 | 13785.75 | 10542.5 | 8579 | 10676.75 | 11488.75 | 16428.3 |
| S&P 500 | 970.43 | 1229.23 | 1469.25 | 1320.28 | 1148.08 | 879.82 | 1111.92 | 1211.92 | 1254.4 |

## Annual percentage performance

| Index | 1997 | 1998 | 1999 | 2000 | 2001 | 2002 | 2003 | 2004 | 2005 |
|---|---|---|---|---|---|---|---|---|---|
| CAC 40 | 29.5 | 31.5 | 51.1 | -0.5 | -22.0 | -33.7 | 15.2 | 8.3 | 23.4 |
| DAX (Xetra) | 46.7 | 18.5 | 39.0 | -7.5 | -19.8 | -43.9 | 37.1 | 7.3 | 28.3 |
| Dow Jones IA | 22.6 | 16.1 | 25.2 | -6.2 | -7.1 | -16.8 | 25.3 | 3.1 | -0.6 |
| FTSE 100 | 24.7 | 14.5 | 17.8 | -10.2 | -16.2 | -24.5 | 13.6 | 7.5 | 16.7 |
| Hang Seng | -20.3 | -6.3 | 68.8 | -11.0 | -24.5 | -18.2 | 34.9 | 13.2 | 4.5 |
| Nasdaq Comp. | 21.6 | 39.6 | 85.6 | -39.3 | -21.1 | -31.5 | 50.0 | 8.6 | 1.4 |
| Nikkei 225 | -21.2 | -9.3 | 36.8 | -27.2 | -23.5 | -18.6 | 24.5 | 7.6 | 43.0 |
| S&P 500 | 31.0 | 26.7 | 19.5 | -10.1 | -13.0 | -23.4 | 26.4 | 9.0 | 3.5 |

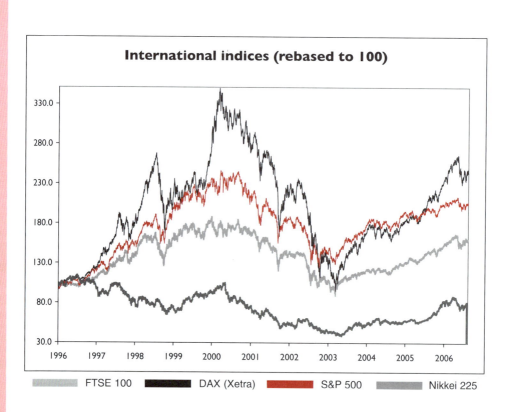

International indices (rebased to 100)

FTSE 100   DAX (Xetra)   S&P 500   Nikkei 225

# Sector annual performance

## Sector performance 2000-2005 (percentage change YoY)

The table below shows the performance of the market sectors in the years 2000-2005. The three best (worst) performing sectors in each year are highlighted in red (grey).

| Index | Code | 2000 | 2001 | 2002 | 2003 | 2004 | 2005 |
|---|---|---|---|---|---|---|---|
| Aerospace & Defence | NMX2710 | -5.8 | -15.4 | -36.8 | 23.3 | 31.9 | 54.3 |
| Automobiles & Parts | NMX3350 | -34.4 | -8.9 | -16.0 | 44.4 | 9.1 | 25.0 |
| Banks | NMX8350 | 14.0 | -3.1 | -22.1 | 17.8 | 6.8 | 7.3 |
| Beverages | NMX3530 | 29.1 | 3.1 | -11.8 | 8.6 | 12.4 | 19.7 |
| Chemicals | NMX1350 | 2.5 | -11.6 | -15.9 | -1.4 | 14.3 | 32.1 |
| Construction & Materials | NMX2350 | 4.6 | 10.0 | -19.4 | 45.8 | 22.6 | 35.1 |
| Electricity | NMX7530 | 14.0 | -15.9 | -4.1 | 3.5 | 21.0 | 33.4 |
| Electronic & Electrical Equipment | NMX2730 | -11.2 | -26.5 | -57.4 | -30.8 | -5.3 | 35.7 |
| Equity Investment Instruments | NMX8980 | -2.1 | -21.9 | -28.3 | 20.7 | 12.1 | 30.8 |
| Fixed Line Telecommunications | NMX6530 | -38.3 | -35.9 | -38.9 | 22.2 | 4.9 | -1.1 |
| Food & Drug Retailers | NMX5330 | 34.0 | -6.4 | -20.8 | 26.2 | 12.1 | 3.8 |
| Food Producers | NMX3570 | 22.6 | -0.9 | -0.8 | -5.2 | 10.7 | 12.1 |
| Gas Water & Multiutilities | NMX7570 | | | | | 24.8 | 13.9 |
| General Financial | NMX8770 | 28.5 | -18.9 | -37.5 | 28.2 | 7.3 | 25.9 |
| General Retailers | NMX5370 | -14.2 | 16.5 | -19.4 | 21.9 | 14.2 | 3.3 |
| Health Care Equipment & Services | NMX4530 | 15.4 | 10.3 | -19.3 | 29.6 | 5.8 | 4.0 |
| Industrial Engineering | NMX2750 | -18.9 | -9.7 | -29.0 | 37.1 | 14.4 | 27.6 |
| Industrial Metals | NMX1750 | -56.2 | 2.1 | -62.2 | 639.9 | 68.3 | 16.8 |
| Industrial Transportation | NMX2770 | -10.6 | -31.9 | -15.5 | 23.6 | 15.3 | 25.7 |
| Leisure Goods | NMX3740 | -9.6 | -3.9 | 3.7 | 70.9 | 13.4 | -12.8 |
| Life Insurance | NMX8570 | -0.3 | -25.4 | -41.1 | 7.4 | 17.9 | 17.1 |
| Media | NMX5550 | -0.1 | -35.4 | -32.5 | 15.7 | 4.9 | 6.0 |
| Mining | NMX1770 | -16.6 | 15.7 | -7.7 | 33.5 | 8.6 | 63.0 |
| Nonlife Insurance | NMX8530 | 33.4 | -33.2 | -56.4 | -9.0 | -5.4 | 44.6 |
| Oil & Gas | NMX0530 | -6.1 | -4.9 | -16.8 | 4.9 | 12.5 | 25.6 |
| Personal Goods | NMX3760 | 58.8 | 8.5 | 20.9 | 5.5 | 24.2 | 20.9 |
| Pharmaceuticals & Biotechnology | NMX4570 | 16.5 | -9.9 | -31.2 | 12.9 | -12.1 | 28.7 |
| Real Estate | NMX8730 | 17.2 | -9.1 | -4.6 | 25.6 | 40.8 | 17.3 |
| Software & Computer Services | NMX9530 | -48.2 | -56.3 | -61.1 | 42.9 | -6.1 | 16.7 |
| Support Services | NMX2790 | 0.2 | -17.1 | -40.0 | 12.1 | -0.9 | 17.5 |
| Technology Hardware & Equipment | NMX9570 | -39.5 | -79.2 | -89.1 | 172.2 | -9.9 | 5.5 |
| Tobacco | NMX3780 | 45.8 | 16.8 | 20.5 | 12.1 | 23.4 | 31.0 |
| Travel & Leisure | NMX5750 | -17.2 | 2.5 | -24.7 | 46.9 | 29.8 | 18.5 |
| FTSE All-Share | ASX | -8.0 | -15.4 | -25.0 | 16.6 | 9.2 | 18.1 |

# Sector sensitivities to economic variables

The numbers in the table below show the response of sectors (in percentage change) to a 1% (or percentage point in the case of index-linked yields and short rates) rise in 8 economic variables.

| Sector | All-share | House prices | Short rate | Index-linked yield | Retail sales | Manu-facturing output | £ Index | Oil Price |
|---|---|---|---|---|---|---|---|---|
| Mining | 0.42 | 0.04 | -4.33 | 3.22 | 1.40 | 0.96 | -0.48 | 0.23 |
| Oil & gas | 0.85 | -0.55 | 1.07 | -4.02 | 1.26 | 2.68 | 0.87 | 0.09 |
| Chemicals | 0.71 | -0.62 | -2.38 | 0.31 | -0.57 | 0.14 | 0.24 | -0.01 |
| Construction | 0.61 | 0.28 | -3.54 | -11.97 | 2.64 | 0.45 | 0.28 | -0.07 |
| Forestry & paper | 0.40 | 0.09 | 0.77 | 11.06 | -0.04 | 0.65 | 0.18 | 0.17 |
| Aerospace & defence | 1.20 | -0.88 | 0.47 | -14.87 | 0.81 | 3.11 | 0.74 | -0.19 |
| Electronics | 1.49 | -0.83 | -0.47 | -21.73 | -1.16 | 4.77 | 0.44 | 0.51 |
| Eng. & machinery | 1.00 | -0.76 | -2.86 | -6.01 | -0.75 | 1.03 | 0.04 | -0.06 |
| Autos | 1.14 | -0.68 | -1.52 | -16.63 | -0.01 | 2.52 | -0.15 | -0.04 |
| Household goods | 0.21 | 0.11 | -5.41 | 2.62 | -0.61 | -1.84 | -0.96 | -0.07 |
| Beverages | 0.31 | -0.63 | -0.88 | 5.02 | -1.28 | -2.17 | 0.35 | -0.20 |
| Food producers | 0.35 | -0.40 | -0.15 | -7.39 | 0.42 | -0.71 | 0.16 | -0.26 |
| Healthcare | 0.60 | -0.61 | -1.65 | -5.25 | -0.70 | -0.25 | 0.15 | -0.08 |
| Personal care | 0.12 | 0.01 | 0.62 | 4.97 | 0.47 | -2.15 | 0.44 | -0.21 |
| Pharmaceuticals | 0.99 | -1.48 | 2.28 | 0.11 | -4.53 | -0.61 | 0.62 | -0.20 |
| Tobacco | 0.04 | -0.37 | -4.00 | -15.86 | -0.23 | -2.75 | -1.31 | -0.35 |
| General retailers | 0.54 | -0.67 | -4.11 | -3.98 | -1.10 | -1.42 | -0.09 | -0.20 |
| Leisure | 0.85 | -0.33 | -0.60 | -8.94 | 0.18 | 1.44 | 0.19 | -0.07 |
| Media | 1.33 | -0.97 | -1.02 | -15.93 | -1.32 | 4.32 | 0.07 | 0.17 |
| Support services | 1.27 | -1.02 | 0.58 | -15.95 | -0.91 | 2.32 | 0.66 | -0.14 |
| Transport | 0.96 | -0.98 | -2.64 | -17.67 | -1.64 | 1.05 | 0.10 | -0.23 |
| Food retailers | 0.42 | -0.88 | 1.26 | -1.11 | -1.39 | 0.05 | 0.11 | -0.15 |
| Telecoms | 1.57 | -0.90 | -1.44 | -42.66 | -4.69 | 2.03 | 0.48 | -0.03 |
| Utilities | 0.75 | -1.07 | -0.88 | -13.27 | -1.40 | 0.58 | 0.37 | -0.26 |
| Banks | 1.26 | 1.20 | -2.60 | -18.72 | 0.29 | 1.77 | 0.45 | -0.20 |
| Insurance | 1.28 | -1.29 | 1.03 | -17.82 | -0.97 | 2.61 | 0.45 | -0.19 |
| Life assurance | 1.44 | -1.65 | 0.91 | -19.31 | -2.45 | 2.10 | 0.54 | -0.19 |
| Investment co.s | 1.16 | -0.79 | -1.53 | -14.54 | -0.88 | 2.88 | 0.11 | 0.05 |
| Real estate | 0.92 | 0.16 | -1.38 | -19.20 | 3.79 | 2.08 | 0.98 | -0.13 |
| Speciality finance | 1.56 | -1.13 | -0.61 | -25.21 | -0.07 | 3.91 | 0.41 | -0.13 |
| IT hardware | 2.99 | 1.17 | 9.75 | -39.60 | 1.11 | 12.26 | 3.51 | 1.98 |
| Software | 2.33 | -0.71 | 4.67 | -34.85 | -1.33 | 6.82 | 2.13 | 0.38 |

*Note*: Sensitivities are calculated from annual changes between 1990 and 2003.

High and low values are highlighted in each column with green and grey respectively.

By reading across the table, you can see the states in which each sector pays off well or badly. And, by reading down the table you can see which sectors do well or badly in different states.

For example:

- Construction stocks do relatively badly when the market rises (23rd out of 32 sectors, with a beta below 1), but they do well in states where retail sales rise (2nd of all sectors).

- Tech stocks do well in states where: the stock market is rising, or index-linked gilt yields are falling, or manufacturing output is rising or where short-term interest rates are rising.

The figures in the table show that, for the average sector, three-fifths of their variation in annual returns can be explained by just 8 macroeconomic variables. This suggests that stock picking has little use, as macroeconomic events are the most important influence upon the average sector. There's much more to equity investing than judgement about individual companies.

Source: *Investors Chronicle*

# Shares, interest rates, sterling and gold since WWII

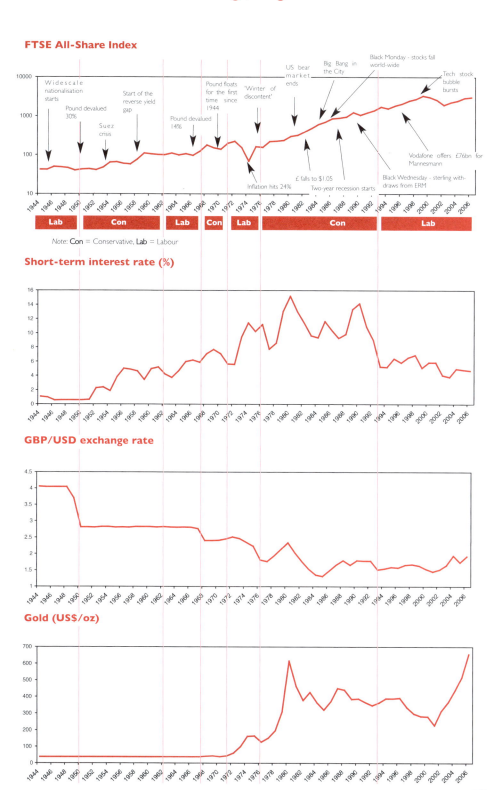

## FTSE All-Share Index

Widescale nationalisation starts

Pound devalued 30%

Suez crisis

Start of the reverse yield gap

Pound devalued 14%

Pound floats for the first time since 1944

'Winter of discontent'

US bear market ends

Big Bang in the City

Black Monday - stocks fall world-wide

Tech stock bubble bursts

Inflation hits 24%

£ falls to $1.05

Two-year recession starts

Vodafone offers £76bn for Mannesmann

Black Wednesday - sterling withdraws from ERM

| Lab | Con | Lab | Con | Lab | Con | Lab |

*Note:* **Con** = Conservative, **Lab** = Labour

## Short-term interest rate (%)

## GBP/USD exchange rate

## Gold (US$/oz)

161

# Sinclair numbers – daily performance

| Day | Up(%) | Avg Change(%) | StdDev | Day | Up(%) | Avg Change(%) | StdDev |
|---|---|---|---|---|---|---|---|
| 02 Jan | 54 | 0.1 | 0.8 | 25 Feb | 69 | 0.3 | 1.1 |
| 03 Jan | 62 | 0.2 | 1.1 | 26 Feb | 50 | 0.0 | 0.7 |
| 04 Jan | 60 | 0.2 | 1.3 | 27 Feb | 56 | 0.1 | 0.6 |
| 05 Jan | 40 | 0.0 | 1.0 | 28 Feb | 50 | -0.1 | 1.1 |
| 06 Jan | 56 | 0.3 | 0.9 | 01 Mar | 69 | 0.3 | 1.1 |
| 07 Jan | 38 | -0.1 | 0.9 | 02 Mar | 53 | 0.2 | 0.7 |
| 08 Jan | 44 | -0.1 | 0.7 | 03 Mar | 56 | 0.3 | 0.5 |
| 09 Jan | 47 | 0.0 | 1.0 | 04 Mar | 69 | 0.4 | 0.9 |
| 10 Jan | 38 | -0.2 | 0.8 | 05 Mar | 57 | 0.1 | 1.0 |
| 11 Jan | 27 | -0.4 | 0.7 | 06 Mar | 56 | 0.4 | 0.8 |
| 12 Jan | 40 | -0.4 | 0. | 07 Mar | 44 | -0.2 | 0.8 |
| 13 Jan | 44 | -0.1 | 0.9 | 08 Mar | 56 | 0.0 | 0.7 |
| 14 Jan | 63 | 0.1 | 1.1 | 09 Mar | 40 | -0.1 | 0.8 |
| 15 Jan | 69 | 0.5 | 1.0 | 10 Mar | 75 | 0.2 | 0.7 |
| 16 Jan | 63 | 0.3 | 0.9 | 11 Mar | 50 | -0.3 | 1.1 |
| 17 Jan | 63 | 0.3 | 0.9 | 12 Mar | 27 | -0.6 | 1.4 |
| 18 Jan | 53 | 0.1 | 1.2 | 13 Mar | 44 | 0.2 | 1.7 |
| 19 Jan | 33 | -0.2 | 0.8 | 14 Mar | 75 | 0.7 | 1.1 |
| 20 Jan | 38 | -0.3 | 0.7 | 15 Mar | 56 | 0.1 | 0.8 |
| 21 Jan | 44 | -0.2 | 0.6 | 16 Mar | 40 | -0.1 | 1.1 |
| 22 Jan | 56 | -0.1 | 1.2 | 17 Mar | 56 | 0.1 | 1.1 |
| 23 Jan | 27 | -0.4 | 0.8 | 18 Mar | 50 | 0.0 | 0.8 |
| 24 Jan | 56 | 0.2 | 0.6 | 19 Mar | 67 | 0.2 | 0.8 |
| 25 Jan | 47 | -0.1 | 0.8 | 20 Mar | 50 | 0.2 | 1.0 |
| 26 Jan | 80 | 0.5 | 0.8 | 21 Mar | 38 | 0.0 | 1.0 |
| 27 Jan | 63 | 0.4 | 1.3 | 22 Mar | 44 | -0.5 | 1.2 |
| 28 Jan | 63 | 0.2 | 0.8 | 23 Mar | 27 | -0.1 | 0.8 |
| 29 Jan | 31 | -0.3 | 0.7 | 24 Mar | 47 | -0.3 | 1.4 |
| 30 Jan | 69 | 0.6 | 1.1 | 25 Mar | 40 | -0.1 | 0.9 |
| 31 Jan | 69 | 0.3 | 0.8 | 26 Mar | 60 | 0.3 | 1.0 |
| 01 Feb | 53 | 0.3 | 0.8 | 27 Mar | 53 | 0.0 | 1.1 |
| 02 Feb | 73 | 0.4 | 0.8 | 28 Mar | 38 | -0.3 | 0.8 |
| 03 Feb | 50 | 0.2 | 1.1 | 29 Mar | 50 | 0.2 | 0.8 |
| 04 Feb | 44 | -0.3 | 0.9 | 30 Mar | 47 | -0.3 | 1.0 |
| 05 Feb | 44 | 0.0 | 1.1 | 31 Mar | 36 | -0.2 | 1.0 |
| 06 Feb | 56 | -0.2 | 0.9 | 01 Apr | 67 | 0.2 | 1.0 |
| 07 Feb | 56 | 0.2 | 1.0 | 02 Apr | 57 | 0.4 | 0.8 |
| 08 Feb | 53 | 0.1 | 1.1 | 03 Apr | 47 | -0.2 | 1.0 |
| 09 Feb | 47 | 0.0 | 0.8 | 04 Apr | 57 | 0.2 | 0.7 |
| 10 Feb | 38 | -0.2 | 0.7 | 05 Apr | 71 | 0.3 | 0.7 |
| 11 Feb | 56 | 0.5 | 1.0 | 06 Apr | 63 | 0.2 | 0.7 |
| 12 Feb | 40 | -0.3 | 0.9 | 07 Apr | 50 | 0.4 | 1.0 |
| 13 Feb | 69 | 0.2 | 0.6 | 08 Apr | 21 | -0.4 | 0.6 |
| 14 Feb | 50 | 0.0 | 0.8 | 09 Apr | 64 | 0.2 | 0.7 |
| 15 Feb | 67 | 0.2 | 0.6 | 10 Apr | 56 | 0.5 | 1.7 |
| 16 Feb | 47 | 0.2 | 1.1 | 11 Apr | 41 | -0.2 | 0.9 |
| 17 Feb | 75 | 0.6 | 0.7 | 12 Apr | 53 | 0.1 | 0.6 |
| 18 Feb | 44 | 0.0 | 0.7 | 13 Apr | 67 | 0.2 | 0.6 |
| 19 Feb | 31 | -0.3 | 0.8 | 14 Apr | 21 | -0.3 | 0.9 |
| 20 Feb | 47 | -0.1 | 0.9 | 15 Apr | 63 | 0.3 | 0.9 |
| 21 Feb | 50 | 0.1 | 0.8 | 16 Apr | 50 | -0.2 | 1.0 |
| 22 Feb | 47 | -0.1 | 0.7 | 17 Apr | 62 | 0.0 | 1.1 |
| 23 Feb | 47 | -0.1 | 1.0 | 18 Apr | 56 | 0.2 | 0.9 |
| 24 Feb | 44 | -0.1 | 1.0 | 19 Apr | 63 | 0.2 | 0.8 |
|  |  |  |  | 20 Apr | 54 | -0.2 | 1.0 |

| Day | Up(%) | Avg Change(%) | StdDev | Day | Up(%) | Avg Change(%) | StdDev |
|---|---|---|---|---|---|---|---|
| 21 Apr | 50 | 0.0 | 0.5 | 18 Jun | 38 | -0.3 | 0.7 |
| 22 Apr | 50 | 0.1 | 0.8 | 19 Jun | 47 | -0.2 | 0.8 |
| 23 Apr | 38 | -0.3 | 0.8 | 20 Jun | 41 | -0.3 | 0.8 |
| 24 Apr | 50 | -0.1 | 0.8 | 21 Jun | 59 | 0.0 | 0.6 |
| 25 Apr | 53 | 0.0 | 0.6 | 22 Jun | 56 | -0.1 | 0.7 |
| 26 Apr | 65 | 0.2 | 0.7 | 23 Jun | 38 | -0.2 | 0.7 |
| 27 Apr | 53 | -0.1 | 1.1 | 24 Jun | 38 | -0.4 | 0.8 |
| 28 Apr | 56 | 0.3 | 1.0 | 25 Jun | 63 | 0.2 | 0.8 |
| 29 Apr | 44 | 0.1 | 0.7 | 26 Jun | 47 | -0.4 | 0.9 |
| 30 Apr | 63 | 0.2 | 0.6 | 27 Jun | 53 | 0.0 | 0.8 |
| 01 May | 57 | 0.1 | 0.8 | 28 Jun | 65 | 0.1 | 0.9 |
| 02 May | 77 | 0.5 | 0.7 | 29 Jun | 50 | 0.0 | 0.9 |
| 03 May | 50 | -0.4 | 1.1 | 30 Jun | 56 | -0.1 | 0.8 |
| 04 May | 62 | 0.3 | 0.8 | 01 Jul | 69 | 0.5 | 1.2 |
| 05 May | 54 | 0.0 | 0.8 | 02 Jul | 63 | 0.1 | 1.0 |
| 06 May | 73 | 0.3 | 0.8 | 03 Jul | 59 | 0.2 | 1.3 |
| 07 May | 31 | -0.4 | 0.7 | 04 Jul | 53 | 0.3 | 0.8 |
| 08 May | 50 | 0.1 | 1.0 | 05 Jul | 41 | 0.1 | 1.1 |
| 09 May | 47 | 0.0 | 0.7 | 06 Jul | 56 | 0.0 | 0.8 |
| 10 May | 35 | -0.1 | 0.9 | 07 Jul | 56 | 0.3 | 0.9 |
| 11 May | 56 | 0.2 | 1.2 | 08 Jul | 25 | -0.2 | 0.8 |
| 12 May | 56 | -0.1 | 0.9 | 09 Jul | 50 | -0.1 | 0.7 |
| 13 May | 63 | 0.3 | 0.8 | 10 Jul | 41 | -0.3 | 0.8 |
| 14 May | 31 | -0.4 | 1.3 | 11 Jul | 59 | -0.1 | 1.4 |
| 15 May | 53 | 0.2 | 0.9 | 12 Jul | 29 | -0.2 | 0.6 |
| 16 May | 47 | 0.1 | 0.6 | 13 Jul | 63 | 0.1 | 0.8 |
| 17 May | 53 | -0.1 | 1.3 | 14 Jul | 63 | 0.3 | 1.0 |
| 18 May | 50 | 0.0 | 0.7 | 15 Jul | 50 | -0.1 | 1.6 |
| 19 May | 50 | -0.2 | 1.3 | 16 Jul | 56 | 0.2 | 0.8 |
| 20 May | 63 | 0.1 | 0.8 | 17 Jul | 69 | 0.2 | 1.3 |
| 21 May | 63 | 0.1 | 0.5 | 18 Jul | 38 | -0.2 | 1.0 |
| 22 May | 53 | -0.1 | 1.0 | 19 Jul | 44 | -0.4 | 1.2 |
| 23 May | 47 | 0.0 | 1.0 | 20 Jul | 47 | -0.2 | 0.8 |
| 24 May | 35 | -0.2 | 0.8 | 21 Jul | 33 | -0.4 | 0.7 |
| 25 May | 46 | -0.1 | 1.0 | 22 Jul | 38 | -0.7 | 1.5 |
| 26 May | 46 | 0.1 | 0.6 | 23 Jul | 56 | -0.1 | 0.9 |
| 27 May | 31 | -0.3 | 0.7 | 24 Jul | 44 | -0.5 | 0.9 |
| 28 May | 54 | 0.2 | 0.7 | 25 Jul | 50 | 0.2 | 1.3 |
| 29 May | 67 | 0.3 | 0.8 | 26 Jul | 50 | 0.1 | 0.7 |
| 30 May | 21 | -0.4 | 1.3 | 27 Jul | 53 | 0.1 | 1.0 |
| 31 May | 50 | 0.0 | 0.6 | 28 Jul | 87 | 0.4 | 0.4 |
| 01 Jun | 69 | 0.5 | 1.0 | 29 Jul | 81 | 0.6 | 1.5 |
| 02 Jun | 67 | 0.4 | 0.9 | 30 Jul | 56 | 0.2 | 0.7 |
| 03 Jun | 60 | 0.2 | 0.5 | 31 Jul | 50 | 0.2 | 0.8 |
| 04 Jun | 60 | 0.2 | 0.9 | 01 Aug | 69 | -0.1 | 1.4 |
| 05 Jun | 53 | 0.1 | 0.8 | 02 Aug | 81 | 0.6 | 0.9 |
| 06 Jun | 59 | 0.1 | 0.8 | 03 Aug | 47 | -0.1 | 0.9 |
| 07 Jun | 47 | -0.1 | 0.8 | 04 Aug | 33 | -0.2 | 0.6 |
| 08 Jun | 50 | 0.0 | 0.9 | 05 Aug | 56 | -0.2 | 1.0 |
| 09 Jun | 44 | 0.1 | 0.8 | 06 Aug | 38 | -0.3 | 1.5 |
| 10 Jun | 50 | 0.0 | 0.6 | 07 Aug | 69 | 0.2 | 0.9 |
| 11 Jun | 50 | -0.1 | 1.0 | 08 Aug | 63 | 0.2 | 1.0 |
| 12 Jun | 41 | -0.2 | 0.9 | 09 Aug | 50 | 0.0 | 0.8 |
| 13 Jun | 41 | -0.3 | 0.8 | 10 Aug | 40 | -0.2 | 1.1 |
| 14 Jun | 35 | -0.2 | 1.1 | 11 Aug | 47 | -0.1 | 1.0 |
| 15 Jun | 44 | 0.0 | 0.8 | 12 Aug | 69 | 0.2 | 0.9 |
| 16 Jun | 69 | 0.2 | 0.5 | 13 Aug | 56 | 0.1 | 0.8 |
| 17 Jun | 63 | 0.3 | 0.9 | 14 Aug | 75 | 0.3 | 1.0 |

| Day | Up(%) | Avg Change(%) | StdDev |
|---|---|---|---|
| 15 Aug | 63 | 0.1 * | 1.3 |
| 16 Aug | 56 | 0.1 | 0.7 |
| 17 Aug | 60 | -0.1 | 0.9 |
| 18 Aug | 60 | 0.3 | 1.1 |
| 19 Aug | 50 | 0.0 | 1.2 |
| 20 Aug | 50 | 0.0 | 0.7 |
| 21 Aug | 63 | 0.1 | 1.2 |
| 22 Aug | 50 | 0.0 | 0.7 |
| 23 Aug | 44 | 0.0 | 0.9 |
| 24 Aug | 73 | 0.2 | 0.9 |
| 25 Aug | 75 | 0.2 | 1.0 |
| 26 Aug | 55 | -0.1 | 0.8 |
| 27 Aug | 54 | 0.1 | 1.1 |
| 28 Aug | 46 | -0.4 | 1.4 |
| 29 Aug | 38 | -0.1 | 0.9 |
| 30 Aug | 69 | 0.1 | 0.8 |
| 31 Aug | 58 | -0.1 | 0.8 |
| 01 Sep | 67 | 0.3 | 1.0 |
| 02 Sep | 53 | 0.2 | 0.8 |
| 03 Sep | 56 | 0.0 | 1.5 |
| 04 Sep | 56 | 0.0 | 0.7 |
| 05 Sep | 63 | 0.0 | 0.5 |
| 06 Sep | 63 | 0.0 | 1.1 |
| 07 Sep | 53 | 0.1 | 1.2 |
| 08 Sep | 20 | -0.4 | 0.6 |
| 09 Sep | 25 | -0.4 | 0.5 |
| 10 Sep | 44 | -0.3 | 1.2 |
| 11 Sep | 27 | -0.2 | 0.7 |
| 12 Sep | 38 | -0.4 | 1.1 |
| 13 Sep | 44 | -0.1 | 0.8 |
| 14 Sep | 53 | -0.1 | 1.5 |
| 15 Sep | 53 | -0.1 | 1.0 |
| 16 Sep | 63 | 0.0 | 0.9 |
| 17 Sep | 56 | 0.4 | 1.6 |
| 18 Sep | 44 | -0.2 | 1.5 |
| 19 Sep | 50 | -0.2 | 0.9 |
| 20 Sep | 44 | -0.4 | 1.3 |
| 21 Sep | 33 | -0.4 | 1.0 |
| 22 Sep | 60 | 0.2 | 0.9 |
| 23 Sep | 38 | -0.2 | 1.1 |
| 24 Sep | 38 | -0.1 | 1.4 |
| 25 Sep | 44 | -0.1 | 1.1 |
| 26 Sep | 50 | 0.4 | 1.4 |
| 27 Sep | 75 | 0.5 | 0.8 |
| 28 Sep | 53 | 0.2 | 1.2 |
| 29 Sep | 60 | 0.0 | 0.7 |
| 30 Sep | 50 | -0.2 | 1.3 |
| 01 Oct | 75 | 0.4 | 1.5 |
| 02 Oct | 50 | 0.1 | 1.3 |
| 03 Oct | 56 | 0.2 | 0.9 |
| 04 Oct | 63 | 0.3 | 0.9 |
| 05 Oct | 67 | -0.1 | 1.7 |
| 06 Oct | 53 | 0.4 | 1.3 |
| 07 Oct | 50 | 0.1 | 0.7 |
| 08 Oct | 50 | 0.0 | 1.1 |
| 09 Oct | 38 | -0.3 | 1.3 |
| 10 Oct | 38 | 0.0 | 1.0 |
| 11 Oct | 60 | 0.3 | 1.4 |

| Day | Up(%) | Avg Change(%) | StdDev |
|---|---|---|---|
| 12 Oct | 40 | 0.2 | 1.4 |
| 13 Oct | 60 | 0.4 | 0.9 |
| 14 Oct | 38 | -0.2 | 0.7 |
| 15 Oct | 56 | 0.2 | 1.5 |
| 16 Oct | 44 | -0.7 | 1.8 |
| 17 Oct | 69 | 0.3 | 1.1 |
| 18 Oct | 50 | -0.1 | 0.9 |
| 19 Oct | 47 | -0.3 | 1.9 |
| 20 Oct | 53 | -0.6 | 3.3 |
| 21 Oct | 56 | 0.4 | 2.0 |
| 22 Oct | 44 | -0.4 | 1.6 |
| 23 Oct | 50 | -0.3 | 1.4 |
| 24 Oct | 44 | 0.0 | 1.1 |
| 25 Oct | 25 | -0.5 | 0.7 |
| 26 Oct | 40 | -0.4 | 1.8 |
| 27 Oct | 60 | 0.0 | 1.2 |
| 28 Oct | 69 | 0.1 | 1.2 |
| 29 Oct | 50 | 0.1 | 1.5 |
| 30 Oct | 75 | 0.6 | 1.4 |
| 31 Oct | 81 | 0.6 | 0.6 |
| 01 Nov | 56 | 0.0 | 0.6 |
| 02 Nov | 53 | 0.1 | 0.9 |
| 03 Nov | 60 | 0.1 | 1.3 |
| 04 Nov | 31 | 0.1 | 1.3 |
| 05 Nov | 69 | 0.1 | 1.1 |
| 06 Nov | 56 | 0.0 | 0.6 |
| 07 Nov | 50 | -0.2 | 0.8 |
| 08 Nov | 69 | 0.2 | 0.7 |
| 09 Nov | 47 | -0.3 | 1.0 |
| 10 Nov | 60 | 0.1 | 0.5 |
| 11 Nov | 56 | 0.2 | 1.3 |
| 12 Nov | 63 | 0.4 | 1.3 |
| 13 Nov | 44 | -0.2 | 1.1 |
| 14 Nov | 56 | 0.2 | 0.7 |
| 15 Nov | 63 | 0.2 | 0.7 |
| 16 Nov | 73 | 0.3 | 0.5 |
| 17 Nov | 47 | 0.1 | 1.0 |
| 18 Nov | 63 | 0.0 | 0.6 |
| 19 Nov | 38 | -0.2 | 1.0 |
| 20 Nov | 50 | 0.1 | 1.0 |
| 21 Nov | 63 | 0.4 | 0.8 |
| 22 Nov | 50 | -0.2 | 1.0 |
| 23 Nov | 60 | 0.4 | 1.1 |
| 24 Nov | 60 | 0.2 | 0.9 |
| 25 Nov | 50 | -0.2 | 1.0 |
| 26 Nov | 63 | 0.2 | 0.9 |
| 27 Nov | 63 | 0.2 | 0.7 |
| 28 Nov | 38 | -0.3 | 0.8 |
| 29 Nov | 69 | 0.1 | 0.5 |
| 30 Nov | 47 | -0.4 | 1.4 |
| 01 Dec | 64 | 0.2 | 1.4 |
| 02 Dec | 38 | -0.2 | 0.7 |
| 03 Dec | 56 | 0.1 | 0.8 |
| 04 Dec | 31 | -0.1 | 0.8 |
| 05 Dec | 50 | 0.3 | 0.9 |
| 06 Dec | 44 | -0.1 | 0.8 |
| 07 Dec | 36 | -0.1 | 0.7 |
| 08 Dec | 67 | 0.3 | 0.7 |

| Day | Up(%) | Avg Change(%) | StdDev |
|---|---|---|---|
| 09 Dec | 44 | 0.0 | 0.9 |
| 10 Dec | 25 | -0.3 | 0.7 |
| 11 Dec | 31 | -0.2 | 1.1 |
| 12 Dec | 50 | -0.1 | 0.7 |
| 13 Dec | 69 | 0.1 | 0.7 |
| 14 Dec | 47 | -0.1 | 0.7 |
| 15 Dec | 53 | 0.0 | 0.8 |
| 16 Dec | 81 | 0.7 | 0.8 |
| 17 Dec | 50 | 0.1 | 0.8 |
| 18 Dec | 69 | 0.2 | 0.9 |
| 19 Dec | 63 | 0.0 | 0.9 |
| 20 Dec | 63 | 0.0 | 0.9 |
| 21 Dec | 60 | 0.4 | 0.9 |
| 22 Dec | 67 | 0.3 | 0.5 |
| 23 Dec | 75 | 0.4 | 0.6 |
| 24 Dec | 81 | 0.2 | 0.6 |
| 27 Dec | 80 | 0.5 | 1.2 |
| 28 Dec | 89 | 0.4 | 0.5 |
| 29 Dec | 80 | 0.3 | 1.2 |
| 30 Dec | 63 | 0.3 | 0.9 |
| 31 Dec | 57 | 0.1 | 1.2 |

# Sinclair numbers – weekly performance

| Week | Up(%) | Avg Change(%) | StdDev |
|------|-------|---------------|--------|
| 1 | 45 | 0.1 | 2.4 |
| 2 | 45 | 0.1 | 2 |
| 3 | 45 | -0.4 | 2 |
| 4 | 68 | 1 | 1.8 |
| 5 | 68 | 0.8 | 2 |
| 6 | 52 | 0.1 | 1.4 |
| 7 | 59 | 0.6 | 1.6 |
| 8 | 50 | 0 | 1.8 |
| 9 | 73 | 1 | 1.9 |
| 10 | 55 | 0.2 | 1.5 |
| 11 | 41 | 0.1 | 2.7 |
| 12 | 41 | -0.5 | 1.9 |
| 13 | 45 | 0.2 | 2.2 |
| 14 | 57 | 0.7 | 2.1 |
| 15 | 61 | 0.1 | 1.9 |
| 16 | 52 | 0.1 | 1.5 |
| 17 | 70 | 0.7 | 1.7 |
| 18 | 52 | 0 | 2.1 |
| 19 | 61 | 0.1 | 1.6 |
| 20 | 48 | -0.2 | 2.2 |
| 21 | 39 | -0.2 | 1.8 |
| 22 | 65 | 0.8 | 2 |
| 23 | 48 | -0.3 | 2.2 |
| 24 | 52 | -0.2 | 1.6 |
| 25 | 52 | -0.4 | 1.7 |
| 26 | 48 | 0.4 | 1.6 |
| 27 | 52 | -0.2 | 2.6 |
| 28 | 52 | 0.4 | 2.1 |
| 29 | 27 | -1 | 1.8 |
| 30 | 73 | 0.8 | 1.9 |
| 31 | 64 | 0.3 | 2.5 |
| 32 | 59 | 0.2 | 2.1 |
| 33 | 73 | 0.3 | 1.5 |
| 34 | 64 | 0 | 2.4 |
| 35 | 50 | 0.4 | 1.9 |
| 36 | 27 | -1.2 | 1.7 |
| 37 | 45 | -0.2 | 2.9 |
| 38 | 36 | -0.7 | 2.1 |
| 39 | 55 | 0.6 | 2.9 |
| 40 | 68 | 1 | 2.3 |
| 41 | 59 | 0 | 3 |
| 42 | 41 | -1.3 | 4.2 |
| 43 | 55 | 0.5 | 2.3 |
| 44 | 64 | 0.2 | 2.4 |
| 45 | 64 | 0.5 | 1.3 |
| 46 | 68 | 0.7 | 2.1 |
| 47 | 64 | 0.3 | 1.8 |
| 48 | 45 | -0.3 | 2.6 |
| 49 | 41 | 0.1 | 1.8 |
| 50 | 64 | 0.3 | 1.9 |
| 51 | 82 | 1.3 | 1.3 |
| 52 | 82 | 1 | 1.8 |

# 4.

# Company Directory

# Company Directory

This section contains a comprehensive directory of all companies listed on the London Stock Exchange and members of AIM. The Directory is in 3 parts:

1. Companies with a full listing on the London Stock Exchange [795]

2. Listed investment trusts [465]

3. Members of AIM [1,335]

(Figures in square brackets indicate the number of companies.)

## Description of columns

For each company, the following information is given:

- Company name
- EPIC

  The 3- or 4-character code assigned by the London Stock Exchange.

- Sector
- Index

  Indication if the company is a component of 1 of 4 distinct indices (characterised by market capitalisation):

  > 100 – FTSE 100 Index
  >
  > Mid 250 – FTSE 250 Index
  >
  > S-Cap – FTSE Small Cap Index
  >
  > Fledge – FTSE Fledgling Index

- Capital (£m)

  Market capitalisation (£ million).

- NMS

  Normal market size (thousand shares).

- 200D Avg Vol

  The 200-day average trading volume (shares). In other words, the average daily trading volume calculated from the previous 200 days.

- AGM

  The forecast date of the next Annual General Meeting. This date is estimated from the previous year. Since the Directory was compiled in August 2006, some forecast AGMs will occur towards the end of 2006, but the date can be used for an approximate forecast for 200. Because these dates are estimated, the exact date should be confirmed closer to the time. There are many week-ahead financial diaries available on the internet (a good one can be found at www.digitallook.com).

- **Year End** Company financial year end.
- **URL** Company's website.

- Companies with a full listing on the London Stock Exchange

Listed Companies

| Company Name | EPIC | Sector | Index | Capital (£m) | NMS | 200D Avg Vol | AGM | Year End | URL |
|---|---|---|---|---|---|---|---|---|---|
| 3i Group PLC | III | General Financial | 100 | 4337.2 | 50 | 3.57m | 12/07/06 | 31/03 | www.3igroup.com |
| 4imprint Group PLC | FOUR | Support Services | Fledge | 88.0 | 2 | 21.5m | 18/04/06 | 31/12 | www.4imprint.com |
| 600 Group (The) PLC | SIXH | Industrial Engineering | Fledge | 28.4 | 3 | 104k | 07/09/05 | 01/04 | www.600group.com |
| 888 Holdings PLC | 888 | Travel & Leisure | Mid 250 | 528.4 | 50 | 2.35m | 10/05/06 | 31/12 | www.888holdingsplc.com |
| Abacus Group PLC | ABU | Electronic & Electrical Equipment | Fledge | 119.4 | 5 | 507k | 27/01/06 | 30/09 | www.abacus-group.co.uk |
| Abbeycrest PLC | ACR | Personal Goods | Fledge | 4.3 | 2 | 46.2k | 20/07/05 | 28/02 | www.abbeycrest.co.uk |
| Abbot Group PLC | ABG | Oil Equipment; Services & Dist | Mid 250 | 636.7 | 15 | 1.30m | 24/05/06 | 31/12 | www.abbotgroup.com |
| Aberdeen Asset Management PLC | ADN | General Financial | Mid 250 | 961.1 | 100 | 7.15m | 20/01/06 | 30/09 | www.aberdeen-asset.com |
| Acal PLC | ACL | Electronic & Electrical Equipment | S-Cap | 92.9 | 1 | 30.7k | 20/07/05 | 31/03 | www.acalplc.co.uk |
| Acambis PLC | ACM | Pharmaceuticals & Biotechnology | S-Cap | 139.6 | 10 | 581k | 23/06/06 | 31/12 | www.acambis.com |
| Admiral Group PLC | ADM | Nonlife Insurance | Mid 250 | 1729.0 | 15 | 1.14m | 18/05/06 | 31/12 | www.admiralgroup.co.uk |
| AEA Technology PLC | AAT | Support Services | S-Cap | 122.7 | 5 | 200k | 27/07/06 | 31/03 | www.aeat.co.uk |
| Aegis Group PLC | AGS | Media | Mid 250 | 1393.6 | 150 | 7.62m | 14/06/06 | 31/12 | www.aegisplc.com |
| AGA Foodservice Group PLC | AGA | Household Goods | Mid 250 | 469.7 | 10 | 597k | 05/05/05 | 31/12 | www.agafoodservice.com |
| Agcert International PLC | AGC | Support Services | S-Cap | 280.1 | 5 | 540k | | 31/12 | www.agcert.com |
| Aggreko PLC | AGK | Support Services | Mid 250 | 737.0 | 25 | 1.50m | 26/04/06 | 31/12 | www.aggreko.com |
| Air Partner PLC | AIP | Travel & Leisure | Fledge | 62.8 | 0.5 | 8.55k | 23/11/05 | 31/07 | www.airpartner.com |
| Alba PLC | ABA | Leisure Goods | S-Cap | 109.6 | 5 | 273k | 22/09/05 | 31/03 | www.albaplc.com |
| Alea Group Holdings (Bermuda) Ltd | ALEA | Nonlife Insurance | S-Cap | 142.5 | 15 | 645k | 29/06/06 | 31/12 | www.aleagroup.com |
| Alexandra PLC | AXD | Personal Goods | Fledge | 54.0 | 0.5 | 36.5k | 27/06/06 | 31/01 | www.alexandra.co.uk |
| Alexon Group PLC | AXN | General Retailers | S-Cap | 70.3 | 5 | 239k | 25/05/06 | 28/01 | www.alexon.co.uk |
| Alizyme PLC | AZM | Pharmaceuticals & Biotechnology | S-Cap | 176.8 | 15 | 1.13m | 27/06/06 | 31/12 | www.alizyme.com |
| Alliance & Leicester PLC | AL. | Banks | 100 | 4538.0 | 25 | 2.98m | 03/05/05 | 31/12 | www.alliance-leicester.co.uk |
| Alliance Boots PLC | AB. | General Retailers | 100 | 7416.1 | 100 | 6.75m | 20/07/06 | 31/03 | www.boots-plc.com |
| Allied Irish Banks PLC | ALBK | Banks | Mid 250 | 12313.2 | 50 | 2.97m | 26/04/06 | 31/12 | www.aibgroup.com |
| Alpha Airports Group PLC | AAP | Industrial Transportation | S-Cap | 112.5 | 10 | 382k | 02/06/06 | 31/01 | www.alpha-group.com |
| Alphameric PLC | ALM | Software & Computer Services | S-Cap | 83.5 | 5 | 330k | 30/03/06 | 30/11 | www.alphameric.com |
| Alterian PLC | ALN | Software & Computer Services | Fledge | 43.2 | 1 | 145k | 25/07/06 | 31/03 | www.alterian.com |
| Alumasc Group PLC | ALU | Construction & Materials | Fledge | 51.7 | 5 | 25.2k | 20/10/05 | 30/06 | www.alumasc.co.uk |
| AMEC PLC | AMEC | Support Services | Mid 250 | 940.0 | 50 | 3.50m | 17/05/06 | 31/12 | www.amec.com |
| Aminex PLC | AEX | Oil & Gas Producers | | 47.0 | 2 | 823k | 21/06/06 | 31/12 | www.aminex-plc.com |
| Amlin PLC | AML | Nonlife Insurance | Mid 250 | 1290.1 | 25 | 2.72m | 25/05/06 | 31/12 | www.amlin.com |
| Amlin PLC | AMLR | Nonlife Insurance | Mid 250 | | | | 25/05/06 | 31/12 | www.amlin.com |
| Amstrad PLC | AMT | Leisure Goods | S-Cap | 146.1 | 3 | 200k | 24/11/05 | 30/06 | www.amstrad.com |
| AMVESCAP PLC | AVZ | General Financial | 100 | 4183.8 | 100 | 9.12m | 27/04/06 | 31/12 | www.amvescap.com |
| Anglesey Mining PLC | AYM | Mining | Fledge | 17.4 | 5 | 196k | 27/09/05 | 31/03 | www.angleseymining.co.uk |
| Anglo American PLC | AAL | Mining | 100 | 35168.3 | 75 | 9.23m | 25/04/06 | 31/12 | www.angloamerican.co.uk |
| Anglo Irish Bank Corporation PLC | ANGL | Banks | | 5637.0 | 25 | 3.43m | 27/01/06 | 30/09 | www.angloirishbank.com |
| Anglo Pacific Group PLC | APF | Mining | S-Cap | 134.9 | 5 | 156k | 26/04/06 | 31/12 | www.anglopacificgroup.com |
| Anglo-Eastern Plantations PLC | AEP | Food Producers | S-Cap | 122.9 | 1 | 36.6k | 26/05/06 | 31/12 | www.angloeastern.co.uk |
| Anite Group PLC | AIE | Software & Computer Services | S-Cap | 250.3 | 50 | 1.38m | 04/10/05 | 30/04 | www.anite.com |
| Antisoma PLC | ASM | Pharmaceuticals & Biotechnology | Fledge | 53.5 | 15 | 1.09m | 09/12/05 | 30/06 | www.antisoma.com |
| Antofagasta PLC | ANTO | Mining | 100 | 4165.2 | 10 | 6.40m | 14/06/06 | 31/12 | www.antofagasta.co.uk |
| API Group PLC | API | Support Services | Fledge | 28.1 | 2 | 43.6k | 01/02/06 | 30/09 | www.apigroup.co.uk |

**Company Directory**

## Listed Companies

| Company Name | EPIC | Sector | Index | Capital (£m) | NMS | 200D Avg Vol | AGM | Year End | URL |
|---|---|---|---|---|---|---|---|---|---|
| Aquarius Platinum Ltd | AQP | Mining | Mid 250 | 758.3 | 5 | 600k | 30/11/05 | 30/06 | www.aquariusplatinum.com |
| ARC International PLC | ARK | Technology Hardware & Equipment | Fledge | 44.5 | 10 | 414k | 25/04/06 | 31/12 | www.arc.com |
| Ardana PLC | ARA | Pharmaceuticals & Biotechnology | Fledge | 69.7 | 2 | 97.2k | 07/09/05 | 31/03 | www.ardana.co.uk |
| Arena Leisure PLC | ARE | Travel & Leisure | S-Cap | 143.9 | 10 | 445k | 08/05/06 | 31/12 | www.arenaleisureplc.com |
| Ark Therapeutics Group PLC | AKT | Pharmaceuticals & Biotechnology | S-Cap | 124.3 | 10 | 630k | 28/04/05 | 31/12 | www.arktherapeutics.com |
| Arla Foods UK PLC | ARU | Food Producers | S-Cap | 278.2 | 15 | 632k | 24/01/06 | 30/09 | www.arlafoodsuk.com |
| ARM Holdings PLC | ARM | Technology Hardware & Equipment | Mid 250 | 1584.7 | 200 | 15.0m | 25/04/06 | 31/12 | www.arm.com |
| ArmorGroup International PLC | ARG | Support Services | Fledge | 32.5 | 5 | 192k | 26/05/06 | 31/12 | www.armorgroup.com |
| ARRIVA PLC | ARI | Travel & Leisure | Mid 250 | 1115.6 | 25 | 1.71m | 19/04/06 | 31/12 | www.arriva.co.uk |
| Ashley (Laura) Holdings PLC | ALY | General Retailers | S-Cap | 198.5 | 5 | 374k | 16/06/06 | 28/01 | www.lauraashley.com |
| Ashtead Group PLC | AHT | Support Services | Mid 250 | 666.6 | 50 | 5.84m | 20/09/05 | 30/04 | www.ashtead-group.com |
| Associated British Engineering PLC | ASBE | Industrial Engineering | Fledge | 0.6 | 0.5 | 95.7 | 11/10/05 | 31/03 | www.abf.co.uk |
| Associated British Foods PLC | ABF | Food Producers | 100 | 6665.9 | 50 | 2.75m | 09/12/05 | 17/09 | www.abports.co.uk |
| Associated British Ports Holdings PLC | ABP | Industrial Transportation | Mid 250 | 2746.6 | 25 | 3.71m | 26/04/06 | 31/12 | www.asterand.com |
| Asterand PLC | ATD | Pharmaceuticals & Biotechnology | Fledge | 6.5 | 2 | 64.7k | 31/07/06 | 31/12 | www.avfc.co.uk |
| Aston Villa PLC | ASV | Travel & Leisure | Fledge | 57.4 | 0.5 | 2.83k | 14/10/05 | 31/05 | www.astrazeneca.com |
| AstraZeneca PLC | AZN | Pharmaceuticals & Biotechnology | 100 | 50258.3 | 100 | 8.42m | 27/04/06 | 31/12 | www.atkinsglobal.com |
| Atkins (W S) PLC | ATK | Support Services | Mid 250 | 875.8 | 10 | 554k | 07/09/05 | 31/03 | www.atrium-uw.com |
| Atrium Underwriting PLC | AUW | Nonlife Insurance | S-Cap | 104.3 | 5 | 63.8k | 30/06/06 | 31/12 | www.austinreedgroup.co.uk |
| Austin Reed Group PLC | ARD | General Retailers | Fledge | 40.3 | 0.5 | 20.9k | 13/06/06 | 31/01 | www.autologic.co.uk |
| AutoLogic Holdings PLC | ALG | General Retailers | Fledge | 36.2 | 5 | 338k | 29/06/06 | 31/12 | www.autonomy.com |
| Autonomy Corporation PLC | AU. | Software & Computer Services | Mid 250 | 717.9 | 15 | 1.27m | 07/06/06 | 31/12 | www.aveva.com |
| AVEVA Group PLC | AVV | Software & Computer Services | S-Cap | 220.4 | 1 | 150k | 14/07/06 | 31/03 | www.avis-europe.com |
| Avis Europe PLC | AVE | Travel & Leisure | Mid 250 | 616.8 | 50 | 2.12m | 25/05/06 | 31/12 | www.aviva.com |
| Aviva PLC | AV. | Life Insurance | 100 | 17342.0 | 150 | 12.0m | 24/04/06 | 31/12 | www.avon-rubber.com |
| Avon Rubber PLC | AVON | Automobiles & Parts | Fledge | 54.4 | 2 | 83.5k | 19/01/06 | 30/09 | www.awg.com |
| AWG PLC | AWG | Gas; Water & Multiutilities | Mid 250 | 1748.9 | 15 | 986k | 26/07/06 | 31/03 | www.axis-shield.com |
| Axis-Shield PLC | ASD | Pharmaceuticals & Biotechnology | S-Cap | 167.4 | 2 | 152k | 12/05/05 | 31/12 | www.axonglobal.com |
| Axon Group PLC | AXO | Software & Computer Services | S-Cap | 221.0 | 2 | 104k | 26/05/06 | 31/12 | www.baa.com |
| BAA PLC | BAA | Industrial Transportation | 100 | 10109.5 | 100 | 17.4m | 14/07/06 | 31/03 | www.babcock.co.uk |
| Babcock International Group PLC | BAB | Support Services | Mid 250 | 692.3 | 25 | 1.50m | 14/07/06 | 31/03 | www.baesystems.com |
| BAE SYSTEMS PLC | BA. | Aerospace & Defense | 100 | 11000.8 | 200 | 25.9m | 04/05/06 | 31/12 | www.baggeridge.co.uk |
| Baggeridge Brick PLC | BGBK | Construction & Materials | Fledge | 68.6 | 2 | 36.5k | 14/02/06 | 30/09 | www.balfourbeatty.com |
| Balfour Beatty PLC | BBY | Construction & Materials | Mid 250 | 1483.3 | 50 | 2.42m | 11/05/06 | 31/12 | www.bankofireland.ie |
| Bank of Ireland (Governor & Co of) | BKIR | Banks | | 9503.5 | 50 | 3.39m | 21/07/06 | 31/03 | www.barclays.com |
| Barclays PLC | BARC | Banks | 100 | 41799.8 | 200 | 36.9m | 27/04/06 | 31/12 | www.agbarr.co.uk |
| Barr (A G) PLC | BAG | Beverages | S-Cap | 210.7 | 0.5 | 11.4k | 22/05/06 | 28/01 | www.barratthomes.co.uk |
| Barratt Developments PLC | BDEV | Household Goods | Mid 250 | 2275.9 | 25 | 2.13m | 17/11/05 | 30/06 | www.batm.com |
| BATM Advanced Communications Ltd | BVC | Technology Hardware & Equipment | S-Cap | 97.2 | 25 | 1.08m | 06/07/06 | 31/12 | www.bbagroup.com |
| BBA Group PLC | BBA | Industrial Transportation | Mid 250 | 1253.1 | 50 | 4.19m | 28/04/05 | 31/12 | www.beales.co.uk |
| Beale PLC | BAE | General Retailers | Fledge | 13.9 | 0.5 | 12.0k | 21/03/06 | 29/10 | www.beazley.com |
| Beazley Group PLC | BEZ | Nonlife Insurance | S-Cap | 383.4 | 15 | 602k | 20/06/05 | 31/12 | www.bede.com |
| Bede PLC | BED | Technology Hardware & Equipment | Fledge | 6.4 | 15 | 208k | 18/05/06 | 31/12 | www.bellway.co.uk |
| Bellway PLC | BWY | Household Goods | Mid 250 | 1336.0 | 10 | 658k | 13/01/06 | 31/07 | |

Source: Hemscott (Hemscott.com)

# Listed Companies

| Company Name | EPIC | Sector | Index | Capital (£m) | NMS | 200D Avg Vol | AGM | Year End | URL |
|---|---|---|---|---|---|---|---|---|---|
| Ben Bailey PLC | BBC | Household Goods | Fledge | 49.9 | 1 | 30.8k | 28/04/06 | 31/12 | www.ben-bailey.co.uk |
| Benfield Group Ltd | BFD | Nonlife Insurance | Mid 250 | 840.5 | 25 | 1.23m | 26/04/06 | 31/12 | www.benfieldgroup.com |
| Berkeley Berry Birch PLC | BBB | General Financial | | 4.6 | 3 | 3.57k | 30/11/05 | 31/03 | www.bbb.co.uk |
| Berkeley Group Holdings (The) PLC | BKG | Household Goods | Mid 250 | 1466.8 | 10 | 656k | 01/09/05 | 30/04 | www.berkeleygroup.co.uk |
| Berkeley Technology Ltd | BEK | General Financial | Fledge | 4.2 | 0.5 | 13.4k | 10/08/05 | 31/12 | |
| Bespak PLC | BPK | Health Care Equipment & Services | S-Cap | 170.4 | 0.5 | 70.9k | 08/09/05 | 30/04 | www.bespak.com |
| BG Group PLC | BG. | Oil & Gas Producers | 100 | 24963.5 | 150 | 16.5m | | 31/12 | www.bg-group.com |
| BHP Billiton PLC | BLT | Mining | 100 | 24223.8 | 200 | 19.6m | 20/10/05 | 30/06 | www.bhpbilliton.com |
| Big Yellow Group PLC | BYG | Real Estate | Mid 250 | 487.4 | 5 | 496k | 06/07/06 | 31/03 | www.bigyellow.co.uk |
| Biocompatibles International PLC | BII | Health Care Equipment & Services | S-Cap | 64.3 | 3 | 95.7k | 22/06/06 | 31/12 | www.biocompatibles.com |
| Bioquell PLC | BQE | Health Care Equipment & Services | Fledge | 40.7 | 0.5 | 31.9k | 18/05/06 | 31/12 | www.bioquellplc.com |
| Biotrace International PLC | BOI | Health Care Equipment & Services | Fledge | 34.7 | 2 | 91.4k | 11/05/06 | 31/12 | www.biotrace.com |
| Birse Group PLC | BIE | Construction & Materials | | 31.7 | 5 | 258k | 15/09/05 | 30/04 | www.birse.co.uk |
| Bisichi Mining PLC | BISI | Mining | Fledge | 24.3 | 0.5 | 12.6k | 29/06/06 | 31/12 | www.bisichi.co.uk |
| Blacks Leisure Group PLC | BSLA | General Retailers | S-Cap | 194.1 | 5 | 284k | 19/07/06 | 28/02 | www.blacksleisure.co.uk |
| Bloomsbury Publishing PLC | BMY | Media | S-Cap | 228.2 | 3 | 161k | 29/06/06 | 31/12 | www.bloomsbury.com |
| BOC Group (The) PLC | BOC | Chemicals | 100 | 8275.8 | 75 | 6.60m | 27/01/06 | 30/09 | www.boc.com |
| Bodycote International PLC | BOY | Industrial Engineering | Mid 250 | 736.2 | 25 | 2.14m | 23/05/06 | 31/12 | www.bodycote.com |
| Boot (Henry) PLC | BHY | Construction & Materials | | 213.0 | 0.5 | 6.96k | 19/05/06 | 31/12 | www.henryboot.co.uk |
| Boustead PLC | BOU | Construction & Materials | Fledge | 1.4 | 0.5 | 978k | 26/10/05 | 31/03 | |
| Bovis Homes Group PLC | BVS | Household Goods | Mid 250 | 954.7 | 25 | 88.0m | 05/05/06 | 31/12 | www.bovishomesgroup.plc.uk |
| BP PLC | BP. | Oil & Gas Producers | 100 | 122664.3 | 200 | 6.59m | 20/04/06 | 31/12 | www.bp.com |
| BPB PLC | BPB | Construction & Materials | | 3881.5 | 75 | 84.4k | 20/07/05 | 31/03 | www.bpb.com |
| BPP Holdings PLC | BPP | Support Services | S-Cap | 214.3 | 3 | 20.04m | | 31/12 | www.bpp.com |
| Bradford & Bingley PLC | BB. | Banks | Mid 250 | 2783.5 | 75 | 4.46m | 25/04/06 | 31/12 | www.bbg.co.uk |
| Braemar Seascope Group PLC | BMS | Industrial Transportation | S-Cap | 80.3 | 0.5 | 21.5m | 21/06/06 | 28/02 | www.braemarseascope.com |
| Braime (T F & J H) (Holdings) PLC | BMT | Industrial Engineering | Fledge | 1.0 | 0.5 | 720 | 26/05/06 | 31/12 | www.pressings-u-net.com |
| Braime (T F & J H) (Holdings) PLC | BMTO | Industrial Engineering | Fledge | | | 10 | 26/05/06 | 31/12 | www.pressings-u-net.com |
| Brambles Industries PLC | BI. | Support Services | 100 | 2821.1 | 75 | 6.85m | 25/10/05 | 30/06 | www.brambles.com |
| Brammer PLC | BRAM | Support Services | S-Cap | 107.6 | 3 | 141k | 25/05/06 | 31/12 | www.brammer.biz |
| Brewin Dolphin Holdings PLC | BRW | General Financial | S-Cap | 324.2 | 10 | 292k | 28/02/06 | 30/09 | www.brewindolphin.co.uk |
| BRIT Insurance Holdings PLC | BRE | Nonlife Insurance | Mid 250 | 890.8 | 50 | 1.78m | 25/04/06 | 31/12 | www.britinsurance.com |
| BRIT Insurance Holdings PLC | BREU | Nonlife Insurance | Mid 250 | | | 8.00k | 25/04/06 | 31/12 | www.britinsurance.com |
| British Airways PLC | BAY | Travel & Leisure | 100 | 4410.4 | 200 | 16.3m | 18/07/06 | 31/03 | www.bashares.com |
| British American Tobacco PLC | BATS | Tobacco | 100 | 29688.4 | 100 | 8.14m | 28/04/05 | 31/12 | www.bat.com |
| British Energy Group PLC | BGY | Electricity | 100 | 4209.4 | 75 | 7.34m | 15/09/05 | 31/03 | www.british-energy.com |
| British Land Co PLC | BLND | Real Estate | 100 | 7060.9 | 50 | 3.77m | 14/07/06 | 31/03 | www.britishland.com |
| British Polythene Industries PLC | BPI | General Industrials | S-Cap | 115.8 | 1 | 89.8k | 12/05/05 | 31/12 | www.bpipoly.com |
| British Sky Broadcasting Group PLC | BSY | Media | 100 | 9687.0 | 200 | 17.3m | 04/11/05 | 30/06 | www.sky.com |
| Britvic PLC | BVIC | Beverages | Mid 250 | 452.7 | 50 | | 15/02/06 | 02/10 | www.britvic.com |
| Brixton PLC | BXTN | Real Estate | Mid 250 | 1389.2 | 25 | 1.08m | 10/05/06 | 31/12 | www.brixton.plc.uk |
| Brown (N) Group PLC | BWNG | General Retailers | Mid 250 | 638.8 | 10 | 744k | 18/07/06 | 25/02 | www.nbrown.co.uk |
| BSS Group PLC | BTSM | Support Services | Mid 250 | 396.4 | 5 | 320k | 27/07/06 | 31/03 | ww6.investorrelations.co.uk/bss |
| BT Group PLC | BT.A | Fixed Line Telecommunications | 100 | 20755.8 | 200 | 55.5m | 12/07/06 | 31/03 | www.btplc.com |

Source: Hemscott (Hemscott.com)

## Listed Companies

| Company Name | EPIC | Sector | Index | Capital (£m) | NMS | 200D Avg Vol | AGM | Year End | URL |
|---|---|---|---|---|---|---|---|---|---|
| BT Group PLC | BT.N | Fixed Line Telecommunications | 100 | 180.0 | 10 | 783k | 12/07/06 | 31/03 | www.btplc.com |
| BTG PLC | BGC | Pharmaceuticals & Biotechnology | S-Cap | 2148.2 | 25 | 1.94m | 26/07/06 | 31/03 | www.btgplc.com |
| Bunzl PLC | BNZL | Support Services | Mid 250 | 2087.9 | 75 | 5.50m | 18/05/05 | 31/12 | www.bunzl.com |
| Burberry Group PLC | BRBY | Personal Goods | Mid 250 | 1265.2 | 15 | 1.27m | 14/07/06 | 31/03 | www.burberry.com |
| Burren Energy PLC | BUR | Oil & Gas Producers | Mid 250 | 239.9 | 15 | 167k | 24/05/06 | 31/12 | www.burren.co.uk |
| Business Post Group PLC | BPG | Industrial Transportation | S-Cap | | 5 | | 11/07/06 | 31/03 | www.businesspost.biz |
| C&C Group PLC | CCR | Beverages | Mid 250 | 1912.6 | 15 | 1.92m | 07/07/06 | 28/02 | www.candgroupplc.com |
| Cable and Wireless PLC | CW. | Fixed Line Telecommunications | 100 | 2837.5 | 200 | 40.4m | 21/07/06 | 31/03 | www.cw.com |
| Cadbury Schweppes PLC | CBRY | Food Producers | 100 | 11100.3 | 200 | 14.0m | 18/05/06 | 01/01 | www.cadburyschweppes.com |
| Caffe Nero Group PLC | CFN | Travel & Leisure | S-Cap | 142.8 | 5 | 261k | 08/11/05 | 31/05 | www.caffenero.com |
| Caffyns PLC | CFYN | General Retailers | Fledge | 27.0 | 0.5 | 1.22k | 27/07/06 | 31/03 | www.caffyns.co.uk |
| Cairn Energy PLC | CNE | Oil & Gas Producers | 100 | 3336.4 | 15 | 1.53m | 20/04/06 | 31/12 | www.cairn-energy.plc.uk |
| Camellia PLC | CAM | General Financial | S-Cap | 207.5 | 75 | 547 | 08/06/06 | 31/12 | www.camellia.plc.uk |
| Capita Group (The) PLC | CPI | Support Services | 100 | 3250.7 | 5 | 4.65m | 25/04/06 | 31/12 | www.capita.co.uk |
| Capital & Regional PLC | CAL | Real Estate | Mid 250 | 719.2 | 0.5 | 318k | 05/06/06 | 30/12 | www.capreg.com |
| Carclo PLC | CAR | Chemicals | Fledge | 41.6 | 2 | 100k | 01/09/05 | 31/03 | www.carclo-plc.com |
| Cardiff Property (The) PLC | CDFF | Real Estate | Fledge | 17.1 | 25 | 710 | 12/01/06 | 30/09 | www.cardiff-property.com |
| Care UK PLC | CUK | Health Care Equipment & Services | S-Cap | 232.7 | 25 | 101k | 02/02/06 | 30/09 | www.careuk.com |
| Carillion PLC | CLLN | Construction & Materials | Mid 250 | 845.0 | 3 | 1.63m | 10/05/06 | 31/12 | www.carillionplc.com |
| Carnival PLC | CCL | Travel & Leisure | 100 | 4333.8 | 50 | 2.38m | 13/04/06 | 30/11 | www.carnivalplc.com |
| Carpetright PLC | CPR | General Retailers | Mid 250 | 818.4 | 0.5 | 213k | 16/08/05 | 29/04 | www.carpetright.plc.uk |
| Carphone Warehouse Group (The) PLC | CPW | General Retailers | Mid 250 | 2380.5 | 2 | 6.82m | 27/07/06 | 01/04 | www.cpwplc.com |
| Carr's Milling Industries PLC | CRM | Food Producers | Fledge | 38.7 | 1 | 11.4k | 09/01/06 | 03/09 | www.carrs-milling.com |
| Carter & Carter Group PLC | CART | Support Services | S-Cap | 252.8 | 15 | 117k | 28/11/05 | 31/07 | www.carter-and-carter.com |
| Castings PLC | CGS | Industrial Engineering | S-Cap | 115.0 | 50 | 38.6k | 16/08/05 | 31/03 | www.castings.plc.uk |
| Catlin Group Ltd | CGL | Nonlife Insurance | Mid 250 | 722.0 | 1 | 726k | 06/06/06 | 31/12 | www.catlin.com |
| Cattles PLC | CTT | General Financial | Mid 250 | 1093.7 | 10 | 2.56m | 05/05/05 | 31/12 | www.cattles.co.uk |
| Celsis International PLC | CEL | Health Care Equipment & Services | Fledge | 35.6 | 200 | 65.8k | 26/07/06 | 31/03 | www.celsis.com |
| Centaur Media PLC | CAU | Media | S-Cap | 179.6 | 0.5 | 335k | 08/12/05 | 30/06 | www.centaur.com |
| Centrica PLC | CNA | Gas; Water & Multiutilities | 100 | 10563.9 | 10 | 24.3m | 19/05/06 | 31/12 | www.centrica.com |
| Chamberlin & Hill PLC | CMH | Industrial Engineering | Fledge | 15.6 | 0.5 | 18.5k | 28/07/06 | 31/03 | www.chamberlin.co.uk |
| Chapelthorpe PLC | CPL | Personal Goods | Fledge | 22.4 | 2 | 318k | 21/07/06 | 31/03 | www.chapelthorpe.com |
| Charles Stanley Group PLC | CAY | General Financial | S-Cap | 144.6 | 15 | 30.7k | 18/07/06 | 31/03 | www.charlesstanleyplc.co.uk |
| Charles Taylor Consulting PLC | CTR | General Financial | S-Cap | 161.6 | 15 | 91.9k | 05/05/06 | 31/12 | www.charlestaylorconsulting.com |
| Charter PLC | CHTR | Industrial Engineering | Mid 250 | 1283.9 | 2 | 1.38m | 27/06/06 | 31/12 | www.charterplc.com |
| Chaucer Holdings PLC | CHU | Nonlife Insurance | S-Cap | 194.9 | 10 | 1.30m | 25/05/06 | 31/12 | www.chaucerplc.com |
| CHE Hotel Group PLC | CEU | Travel & Leisure | Fledge | 34.4 | 10 | 154k | 29/06/06 | 31/12 | www.choicehotelseurope.com |
| Chemring Group PLC | CHG | Aerospace & Defense | S-Cap | 425.4 | 15 | 137k | 23/06/06 | 31/10 | www.chemring.co.uk |
| Chesnara PLC | CSN | Life Insurance | S-Cap | 183.6 | 15 | 21.7m | 26/04/05 | 31/12 | www.chesnara.co.uk |
| Chime Communications PLC | CHW | Media | Fledge | 93.9 | 0.5 | 693k | 07/06/06 | 31/12 | www.chime.plc.uk |
| Chloride Group PLC | CHLD | Electronic & Electrical Equipment | S-Cap | 272.0 | 2 | 657k | 25/07/06 | 31/03 | www.chloridegroup.com |
| Chrysalis Group PLC | CHS | Media | S-Cap | 193.9 | 15 | 497k | 09/02/06 | 31/08 | www.chrysalis.com |
| City of London Group PLC | CIN | Media | Fledge | 5.9 | 0.5 | 3.49k | 03/08/06 | 31/03 | www.cityoflondongroup.com |
| Clarke (T) PLC | CTO | Construction & Materials | S-Cap | 101.7 | 2 | 80.1k | 06/05/05 | 31/12 | www.tclarke.com |

## Listed Companies

| Company Name | EPIC | Sector | Index | Capital (£m) | NMS | 200D Avg Vol | AGM | Year End | URL |
|---|---|---|---|---|---|---|---|---|---|
| Clarkson PLC | CKN | Industrial Transportation | S-Cap | 154.8 | 2 | 38.9k | 24/05/06 | 31/12 | www.clarksons.com |
| Clinical Computing PLC | CLC | Software & Computer Services | Fledge | 2.5 | 2 | 87.4k | 08/06/05 | 31/12 | www.ccl.com |
| ClinPhone PLC | CNP | Software & Computer Services | | 120.4 | 5 | | | | www.clinphone.com |
| Clinton Cards PLC | CC. | General Retailers | S-Cap | 99.3 | 15 | 941k | 31/05/05 | 30/01 | www.clintoncards.co.uk |
| Close Brothers Group PLC | CBG | General Financial | Mid 250 | 1279.0 | 10 | 834k | 27/10/05 | 31/07 | www.closebrothers.co.uk |
| CLS Holdings PLC | CLI | Real Estate | Mid 250 | 462.7 | 2 | 133k | 10/05/05 | 31/12 | www.clsholdings.com |
| CML Microsystems PLC | CML | Technology Hardware & Equipment | Fledge | 31.0 | 0.5 | 19.7k | 02/08/06 | 31/03 | www.cmlmicroplc.com |
| Cobham PLC | COB | Aerospace & Defense | Mid 250 | 1783.9 | 75 | 4.70m | 07/06/06 | 31/12 | www.cobham.com |
| Collins Stewart Tullett PLC | CSTL | General Financial | Mid 250 | 1621.2 | 25 | 1.92m | 08/06/06 | 31/12 | www.cstplc.com |
| COLT Telecom Group SA | COLT | Fixed Line Telecommunications | Mid 250 | 843.3 | 50 | 1.73m | | | www.colt.net |
| Communisis PLC | CMS | Support Services | S-Cap | 83.7 | 5 | 547k | 21/04/06 | 31/12 | www.communisis.com |
| Compass Group PLC | CPG | Travel & Leisure | 100 | 5430.6 | 200 | 19.3m | 10/02/06 | 30/09 | www.compass-group.com |
| Compel Group PLC | CGR | Software & Computer Services | Fledge | 26.1 | 1 | 61.4k | 01/11/05 | 30/06 | www.compel.co.uk |
| Computacenter PLC | CCC | Software & Computer Services | Mid 250 | 369.4 | 25 | 1.27m | 28/04/05 | 31/12 | www.computacenter.com |
| Cookson Group PLC | CKSN | General Industrials | Mid 250 | 1007.9 | 25 | 2.56m | 25/05/06 | 31/12 | www.cooksongroup.co.uk |
| Coral Products PLC | CRU | General Industrials | Fledge | 2.6 | 0.5 | 18.2k | 23/09/05 | 30/04 | www.coralproducts.com |
| Corin Group PLC | CRG | Health Care Equipment & Services | S-Cap | 92.0 | 2 | 122k | 05/06/06 | 31/12 | www.coringroup.com |
| Corporate Services Group (The) PLC | CSV | Support Services | S-Cap | 86.6 | 50 | 3.28m | 09/06/06 | 31/12 | www.csg-group.com |
| Corus Group PLC | CS. | Industrial Metals | 100 | 3490.1 | 200 | 16.0m | 16/06/05 | 31/12 | www.corusgroup.com |
| Cosalt PLC | CSLT | General Industrials | Fledge | 41.1 | 0.5 | 30.3k | 28/03/06 | 30/10 | www.cosalt.plc.uk |
| Costain Group PLC | COST | Construction & Materials | S-Cap | 177.7 | 10 | 661k | 28/04/05 | 31/12 | www.costain.com |
| Countrywide PLC | CWD | Real Estate | Mid 250 | 707.0 | 25 | 2.57m | 27/04/05 | 31/12 | www.countrywideplc.co.uk |
| Cranswick PLC | CWK | Food Producers | S-Cap | 326.1 | 1 | 86.1k | 31/07/06 | 31/03 | www.cranswick.co.uk |
| Creightons PLC | CRL | Personal Goods | Fledge | 2.6 | 2 | 48.3k | 19/12/05 | 31/03 | www.creightons.com |
| Crest Nicholson PLC | CRST | Household Goods | Mid 250 | 1029.3 | 10 | 864k | 07/04/06 | 31/10 | www.crestnicholson.com |
| Creston PLC | CRE | Media | Fledge | 93.7 | 2 | 78.1k | 03/08/06 | 31/03 | www.creston.com |
| CRH PLC | CRH | Construction & Materials | | 9461.4 | 25 | 1.43m | 04/05/05 | 31/12 | www.crh.com |
| Croda International PLC | CRDA | Chemicals | Mid 250 | 537.0 | 10 | 673k | 26/04/06 | 31/12 | www.croda.com |
| Cropper (James) PLC | CRPR | Forestry & Paper | Fledge | 12.8 | 0.5 | 7.37k | 03/08/06 | 01/04 | www.cropper.com |
| CSR PLC | CSR | Technology Hardware & Equipment | Mid 250 | 1381.1 | 25 | 2.36m | 02/05/06 | 30/12 | www.csr.com |
| Culver Holdings PLC | CVE | Nonlife Insurance | Fledge | 0.3 | | 53.9 | 29/07/05 | 31/12 | www.culver-holdings.com |
| Daejan Holdings PLC | DJAN | Real Estate | Mid 250 | 682.4 | 0.5 | 8.37k | 23/09/05 | 31/03 | www.daejanholdings.com |
| Daily Mail and General Trust PLC | DMGT | Media | Mid 250 | 2139.9 | 50 | 2.39m | 08/02/06 | 02/10 | www.dmgt.co.uk |
| Daily Mail and General Trust PLC | DMGO | Media | Mid 250 | | | 1.79k | 08/02/06 | 02/10 | www.dmgt.co.uk |
| Dairy Crest Group PLC | DCG | Food Producers | Mid 250 | 667.9 | 10 | 574k | 20/07/06 | 31/03 | www.dairycrest.co.uk |
| Dana Petroleum PLC | DNX | Oil & Gas Producers | Mid 250 | 1154.2 | 5 | 973k | 31/07/06 | 31/12 | www.dana-petroleum.com |
| Danka Business Systems PLC | DNK | Technology Hardware & Equipment | Fledge | 38.5 | 10 | 255k | 09/11/05 | 31/03 | www.danka.com |
| Datamonitor PLC | DTM | Media | S-Cap | 285.5 | 1 | 250k | 25/04/06 | 31/12 | www.datamonitor.com |
| Davis Service Group (The) PLC | DVSG | Support Services | Mid 250 | 813.5 | 10 | 654k | 25/04/06 | 31/12 | www.dsgplc.co.uk |
| Dawson Holdings PLC | DWN | Support Services | S-Cap | 64.9 | 5 | 139k | 23/01/06 | 01/10 | www.dawson.co.uk |
| DCC PLC | DCC | Support Services | | 1015.4 | 1 | 112k | 10/07/06 | 31/03 | www.dcc.ie |
| De La Rue PLC | DLAR | Support Services | Mid 250 | 876.6 | 10 | 789k | 27/07/06 | 25/03 | www.delarue.com |
| De Vere Group PLC | DVR | Travel & Leisure | Mid 250 | 730.1 | 10 | 918k | 10/02/06 | 31/12 | www.deveregroupplc.co.uk |
| Debenhams PLC | DEB | General Retailers | Mid 250 | 4032.9 | 50 | 3.43m | | 25/09 | www.debenhams.com |

Source: Hemscott (Hemscott.com)

# Listed Companies

## Company Directory

| Company Name | EPIC | Sector | Index | Capital (£m) | NMS | 200D Avg Vol | AGM | Year End | URL |
|---|---|---|---|---|---|---|---|---|---|
| Dechra Pharmaceuticals PLC | DPH | Pharmaceuticals & Biotechnology | S-Cap | 119.4 | 3 | 88.8k | 19/10/05 | 30/06 | www.dechra.com |
| Dee Valley Group PLC | DVW | Gas; Water & Multiutilities | Fledge | 46.7 | 0.5 | 2.04k | 27/07/06 | 31/03 | www.deevalleygroup.com |
| Dee Valley Group PLC | DVWA | Gas; Water & Multiutilities | Fledge | | | 108 | 27/07/06 | 31/03 | www.deevalleygroup.com |
| Delta PLC | DLTA | Chemicals | S-Cap | 198.7 | 5 | 640k | 28/04/06 | 31/12 | www.deltaplc.com |
| Derwent Valley Holdings PLC | DWV | Real Estate | Mid 250 | 909.5 | 3 | 221k | 23/05/06 | 31/12 | www.derwentvalley.co.uk |
| Detica Group PLC | DCA | Software & Computer Services | S-Cap | 328.6 | 1 | 211k | 20/07/06 | 31/03 | www.detica.com |
| Development Securities PLC | DSC | Real Estate | S-Cap | 210.0 | 2 | 84.1k | 11/05/06 | 31/12 | www.developmentsecurities.com |
| Devro PLC | DVO | Food Producers | S-Cap | 178.3 | 10 | 342k | 05/05/05 | 31/12 | www.devro.plc.uk |
| Diageo PLC | DGE | Beverages | 100 | 25939.6 | 200 | 17.1m | 18/10/05 | 30/06 | www.diageo.com |
| Dialight PLC | DIA | Electronic & Electrical Equipment | S-Cap | 76.0 | 1 | 62.7k | 09/05/06 | 31/12 | www.dialight.com |
| DICOM Group PLC | DCM | Software & Computer Services | S-Cap | 186.9 | 3 | 258k | 08/11/05 | 30/06 | www.dicomgroup.com |
| Dignity PLC | DTY | General Retailers | S-Cap | 361.9 | 3 | 232k | 08/06/06 | 30/12 | www.dignityfuneralsplc.co.uk |
| Dimension Data Holdings PLC | DDT | Software & Computer Services | Mid 250 | 521.9 | 75 | 4.40m | 19/01/06 | 30/09 | www.dimensiondata.com |
| Diploma PLC | DPLM | Support Services | S-Cap | 160.0 | 2 | 52.4k | 11/01/06 | 30/09 | www.diplomaplc.com |
| DMATEK Ltd | DTK | Technology Hardware & Equipment | Fledge | 27.0 | 1 | 28.0k | 26/06/06 | 31/12 | www.dmatek.com |
| Domestic & General Group PLC | DGG | Nonlife Insurance | S-Cap | 358.4 | 3 | 149k | 28/07/06 | 31/03 | www.dgplc.com |
| Domino Printing Sciences PLC | DNO | Industrial Engineering | S-Cap | 304.0 | 10 | 326k | 16/03/06 | 31/10 | www.domino-printing.com |
| Dragon Oil PLC | DGO | Oil & Gas Producers | S-Cap | 944.7 | 25 | 1.23m | 20/06/06 | 31/12 | www.dragonoil.com |
| Drax Group PLC | DRX | Electricity | 100 | 3708.5 | | | 12/05/06 | 31/12 | www.draxgroup.plc.uk |
| DRS Data & Research Services PLC | DRS | Software & Computer Services | Fledge | 10.8 | 0.5 | 17.0k | 16/05/05 | 31/12 | www.drs.co.uk |
| DSG International PLC | DSGI | General Retailers | 100 | 3599.2 | 200 | 22.1m | 07/09/05 | 30/04 | www.dsgiplc.com |
| DTZ Holdings PLC | DTZ | Real Estate | S-Cap | 339.0 | 2 | 203k | 13/09/05 | 30/04 | www.dtz.com |
| DX Services PLC | DXS | Industrial Transportation | S-Cap | 348.3 | 15 | 974k | 11/11/05 | 30/06 | www.thedx.co.uk |
| Dyson Group PLC | DYS | Chemicals | S-Cap | 65.7 | 2 | 94.3k | 26/08/05 | 31/03 | www.dyson-group.com |
| e2v technologies PLC | E2V | Electronic & Electrical Equipment | S-Cap | 176.3 | 2 | 149k | 08/09/05 | 31/03 | www.e2v.com |
| easyJet PLC | EZJ | Travel & Leisure | Mid 250 | 1729.6 | 75 | 5.27m | 22/02/06 | 30/09 | www.easyjet.com |
| eircom Group PLC | EIR | Fixed Line Telecommunications | | 1589.8 | 100 | 8.49m | 26/07/06 | 31/03 | www.eircom.ie |
| Elan Corporation PLC | ELA | Pharmaceuticals & Biotechnology | | 3368.3 | 3.5 | 312k | 26/05/06 | 31/12 | www.elan.com |
| Electrocomponents PLC | ECM | Support Services | Mid 250 | 994.6 | 75 | 3.38m | 14/07/06 | 31/03 | www.electrocomponents.com |
| Electronic Data Processing PLC | EDP | Software & Computer Services | Fledge | 15.1 | 0.5 | 9.24k | 03/03/05 | 30/09 | www.edp.fastfreenet.com |
| Elementis PLC | ELM | Chemicals | S-Cap | 382.2 | 25 | 2.35m | 28/04/05 | 31/12 | www.elementis.com |
| Elementis PLC | ELMB | Chemicals | S-Cap | | | 49.7k | 28/04/05 | 31/12 | www.elementis.com |
| EMAP PLC | EMA | Media | Mid 250 | 1779.8 | 50 | 2.79m | 13/07/06 | 31/03 | www.emap.com |
| Emblaze Ltd | BLZ | Software & Computer Services | S-Cap | 210.3 | 5 | 551k | 08/08/05 | 31/12 | www.emblaze.com |
| Emerald Energy PLC | EEN | Oil & Gas Producers | S-Cap | 127.9 | 3 | 303k | 26/05/06 | 31/12 | www.emeraldenergy.com |
| EMI Group PLC | EMI | Media | Mid 250 | 1982.8 | 150 | 14.2m | 13/07/06 | 31/03 | www.emigroup.com |
| Ennstone PLC | ENN | Construction & Materials | S-Cap | 172.0 | 15 | 1.52m | 18/05/06 | 31/12 | www.ennstone.co.uk |
| Enodis PLC | ENO | Industrial Engineering | Mid 250 | 727.7 | 50 | 5.31m | 16/02/06 | 01/10 | www.enodis.com |
| Enterprise Inns PLC | ETI | Travel & Leisure | 100 | 3076.5 | 50 | 3.59m | 19/01/06 | 30/09 | www.enterpriseinns.com |
| Enterprise PLC | ETR | Support Services | S-Cap | 347.3 | 3 | 316k | 04/05/05 | 31/12 | www.enterprise.plc.uk |
| Entertainment Rights PLC | ERT | Media | S-Cap | 135.5 | 25 | 846k | 25/05/06 | 31/12 | www.entertainmentrights.com |
| Erinaceous Group PLC | ERG | Support Services | S-Cap | 288.3 | 5 | 516k | 26/04/06 | 31/12 | www.erinaceous.com |
| Eurodis Electron PLC | ELH | Electronic & Electrical Equipment | | 9.9 | 75 | | 30/01/06 | 31/05 | www.eurodis.com |
| Euromoney Institutional Investor PLC | ERM | Media | S-Cap | 389.9 | 2 | 67.6k | 25/01/06 | 30/09 | www.euromoneyplc.com |

Source: Hemscott (Hemscott.com)

| Company Name | EPIC | Sector | Index | Capital (£m) | NMS | 200D Avg Vol | AGM | Year End | URL |
|---|---|---|---|---|---|---|---|---|---|
| European Colour PLC | EUC | Chemicals | | 3.0 | 1 | 30.2k | 21/07/05 | 31/03 | www.ecplc.com |
| European Home Retail PLC | EHR | Food & Drug Retailers | Fledge | 8.4 | 2 | 25.5k | 28/09/05 | 28/04 | www.europeanhomeretail.com |
| European Motor Holdings PLC | EMH | General Retailers | S-Cap | 214.7 | 1 | 130k | 23/06/06 | 28/02 | www.emhplc.com |
| Eurotunnel PLC | ETL | Industrial Transportation | | 636.5 | 15 | 356k | 17/06/05 | 31/12 | www.eurotunnel.com |
| Evolution Group (The) PLC | EVG | General Financial | S-Cap | 297.3 | 25 | 1.89m | 25/05/06 | 31/12 | www.evgplc.com |
| Expro International Group PLC | EXR | Oil Equipment; Services & Dist | Mid 250 | 540.8 | 10 | 414k | 06/07/06 | 31/03 | www.exprogroup.com |
| F&C Asset Management PLC | FCAM | General Financial | Mid 250 | 927.0 | 50 | 1.03m | 16/05/06 | 31/12 | www.fandc.com |
| Fenner PLC | FENR | Industrial Engineering | S-Cap | 318.6 | 10 | 502k | 11/01/06 | 31/08 | www.fenner.com |
| Fenner PLC | FEND | Industrial Engineering | | | | | 11/01/06 | 31/08 | www.fenner.com |
| Ferraris Group PLC | FER | Health Care Equipment & Services | Fledge | 19.5 | 2 | 137k | 18/01/06 | 31/08 | www.ferraris.co.uk |
| Fibernet Group PLC | FIB | Fixed Line Telecommunications | Fledge | 32.6 | 10 | 193k | 21/12/05 | 31/08 | www.fibernet.co.uk |
| FII Group PLC | FII | Personal Goods | | 1.6 | 1 | | 16/01/06 | 31/05 | www.fiigroupplc.com |
| Filtrona PLC | FLTR | Support Services | Mid 250 | 598.8 | 50 | 1.21m | 26/04/06 | 31/12 | www.filtrona.com |
| Filtronic PLC | FTC | Technology Hardware & Equipment | S-Cap | 138.1 | 25 | 476k | 30/09/05 | 31/05 | www.filtronic.com |
| Findel PLC | FDL | General Retailers | Mid 250 | 450.4 | 3 | 302k | 03/07/06 | 31/03 | www.findel.co.uk |
| First Choice Holidays PLC | FCD | Travel & Leisure | Mid 250 | 1148.3 | 50 | 4.60m | 23/03/06 | 31/10 | www.firstchoiceholidaysplc.com |
| FirstGroup PLC | FGP | Travel & Leisure | Mid 250 | 1766.4 | 50 | 2.52m | 13/07/06 | 31/03 | www.firstgroup.com |
| Fisher (James) & Sons PLC | FSJ | Industrial Transportation | S-Cap | 211.9 | 1 | 42.2k | 29/04/05 | 31/12 | www.james-fisher.co.uk |
| FKI PLC | FKI | Industrial Engineering | Mid 250 | 552.7 | 100 | 6.19m | 01/08/06 | 31/03 | www.fki.co.uk |
| Fletcher King PLC | FLK | Real Estate | Fledge | 5.2 | 0.5 | 9.60k | 23/09/05 | 30/04 | www.fletcherking.co.uk |
| Flying Brands Ltd | FBDU | General Retailers | Fledge | 58.1 | 2 | 84.1k | 12/04/05 | 30/12 | www.flyingbrands.com |
| Forth Ports PLC | FPT | Industrial Transportation | Mid 250 | 804.7 | 3 | 214k | 03/05/06 | 31/12 | www.forthports.co.uk |
| Fortune Oil PLC | FTO | Oil & Gas Producers | S-Cap | 107.4 | 25 | 1.62m | 21/06/06 | 31/12 | www.fortuneoil.co.uk |
| Foseco PLC | FOSE | Industrial Engineering | S-Cap | 271.1 | 15 | 737k | 17/05/05 | 31/12 | www.foseco.com |
| Freeport PLC | FPR | Real Estate | S-Cap | 152.6 | 2 | 167k | 30/11/05 | 25/06 | www.freeportplc.com |
| French Connection Group PLC | FCCN | General Retailers | S-Cap | 163.9 | 15 | 287k | 10/05/06 | 31/01 | www.frenchconnection.com |
| Friends Provident PLC | FP. | Life Insurance | 100 | 3770.2 | 150 | 13.4m | 25/05/06 | 31/12 | www.friendsprovident.com |
| Fuller Smith & Turner PLC | FSTA | Travel & Leisure | S-Cap | 295.0 | 0.5 | 16.2k | 26/07/06 | 01/04 | www.fullers.co.uk |
| Future PLC | FUTR | Media | S-Cap | 124.1 | 25 | 1.33m | 25/01/06 | 30/09 | www.futureplc.com |
| Fyffes PLC | FFY | Food Producers | | 336.4 | 1 | 1.73m | 30/05/06 | 31/12 | www.fyffes.com |
| Gallaher Group PLC | GLH | Tobacco | 100 | 5871.4 | 50 | 4.52m | 10/05/06 | 31/12 | www.gallaher-group.com |
| Galliford Try PLC | GFRD | Construction & Materials | S-Cap | 319.7 | 10 | 589k | 28/10/05 | 30/06 | www.gallifordtry.plc.uk |
| GAME Group (The) PLC | GMG | General Retailers | S-Cap | 277.5 | 50 | 1.48m | 06/07/06 | 31/01 | www.gamegroup.plc.uk |
| Games Workshop Group PLC | GAW | Leisure Goods | S-Cap | 111.9 | 5 | 93.7k | 15/09/05 | 28/05 | www.games-workshop.com |
| Gaskell PLC | GKLL | Household Goods | | 0.6 | 2 | | 29/05/06 | 31/12 | www.gaskell.co.uk |
| GB Group PLC | GBG | Software & Computer Services | Fledge | 28.5 | 10 | 279k | 12/07/06 | 31/03 | www.gb.co.uk |
| GCap Media PLC | GCAP | Media | Mid 250 | 307.9 | 15 | 1.19m | 24/07/06 | 31/03 | www.gcapmedia.com |
| GeneMedix PLC | GMX | Pharmaceuticals & Biotechnology | Fledge | 13.9 | 1 | 39.3k | 31/07/06 | 30/11 | www.genemedix.com |
| Gibbs and Dandy PLC | GDYA | Support Services | Fledge | 37.4 | 0.5 | 12.6k | 25/04/06 | 31/12 | www.gibbsanddandy.com |
| Gibbs and Dandy PLC | GDYO | Support Services | Fledge | | | 7.52k | 25/04/06 | 31/12 | www.gibbsanddandy.com |
| GKN PLC | GKN | Automobiles & Parts | Mid 250 | 2086.0 | 75 | 5.96m | 12/05/06 | 31/12 | www.gkn.com |
| Glanbia PLC | GLB | Food Producers | | 432.7 | 0.5 | 91.2k | 16/05/06 | 31/12 | www.glanbia.com |
| GlaxoSmithKline PLC | GSK | Pharmaceuticals & Biotechnology | 100 | 83295.9 | 200 | 19.4m | 17/05/06 | 31/12 | www.gsk.com |
| Gleeson (M J) Group PLC | GLE | Construction & Materials | S-Cap | 200.6 | 1 | 51.2k | 11/01/06 | 30/06 | www.mjgleeson.com |

Source: Hemscott (Hemscott.com)

## Listed Companies

| Company Name | EPIC | Sector | Index | Capital (£m) | NMS | 200D Avg Vol | AGM | Year End | URL |
|---|---|---|---|---|---|---|---|---|---|
| Glotel PLC | GLO | Support Services | Fledge | 29.9 | 1 | 46.2k | 12/09/05 | 31/03 | www.glotel.com |
| Go-Ahead Group (The) PLC | GOG | Travel & Leisure | Mid 250 | 876.0 | 5 | 328k | 27/10/05 | 02/07 | www.go-ahead.com |
| Goldshield Group PLC | GSD | Pharmaceuticals & Biotechnology | S-Cap | 99.7 | 2 | 25.2k | 27/07/05 | 31/03 | www.goldshieldplc.com |
| Gondola Holdings PLC | GND | Travel & Leisure | Mid 250 | 437.7 | 5 | | | | |
| Goodwin PLC | GDWN | Industrial Engineering | Fledge | 45.4 | 0.5 | 1.58k | 02/11/05 | 30/04 | www.goodwin.co.uk |
| GoshawK Insurance Holdings PLC | GOS | Nonlife Insurance | Fledge | 10.4 | 25 | 796k | 11/07/05 | 31/12 | www.goshawk.co.uk |
| Grafton Group PLC | GFTU | Support Services | | 1651.6 | 3 | 596k | 09/05/05 | 31/12 | www.graftonplc.com |
| Grainger Trust PLC | GRI | Real Estate | Mid 250 | 669.9 | 5 | 293k | 02/03/06 | 30/09 | www.graingertrust.co.uk |
| Great Portland Estates PLC | GPOR | Real Estate | Mid 250 | 870.1 | 15 | 741k | 06/07/06 | 31/03 | www.gpe.co.uk |
| Greencore Group PLC | GNC | Food Producers | | 556.7 | 2 | 21.6m | 09/02/06 | 30/09 | www.greencore.com |
| Greene King PLC | GNK | Travel & Leisure | Mid 250 | 1261.4 | 10 | 792k | 02/09/05 | 30/04 | www.greeneking.co.uk |
| Greggs PLC | GRG | Food & Drug Retailers | Mid 250 | 479.1 | 1 | 55.5k | 17/05/05 | 31/12 | www.greggs.co.uk |
| Gresham Computing PLC | GHT | Software & Computer Services | Fledge | 53.3 | 5 | 245k | 01/07/06 | 31/12 | www.gresham-computing.com |
| Group 4 Securicor PLC | GFS | Support Services | Mid 250 | 2107.3 | 100 | 6.50m | 29/06/06 | 31/12 | www.group4securicor.com |
| Guinness Peat Group PLC | GPG | General Financial | | 1050.2 | 2 | 23.4k | 13/06/06 | 31/12 | www.gpgplc.com |
| GUS PLC | GUS | General Retailers | 100 | 8560.1 | 50 | 7.40m | 19/07/06 | 31/03 | www.gusplc.com |
| Gyrus Group PLC | GYG | Health Care Equipment & Services | Mid 250 | 500.9 | 15 | 848k | 02/05/06 | 31/12 | www.gyrusgroup.com |
| H.R.Owen PLC | HRO | General Retailers | Fledge | 29.9 | 0.5 | 13.4k | 24/05/06 | 31/12 | www.hrowen.co.uk |
| Halfords Group PLC | HFD | General Retailers | Mid 250 | 682.3 | 25 | 1.74m | 02/08/06 | 31/03 | www.halfordscompany.com |
| Halma PLC | HLMA | Electronic & Electrical Equipment | Mid 250 | 703.5 | 25 | 1.80m | 02/08/06 | 01/04 | www.halma.com |
| Hammerson PLC | HMSO | Real Estate | 100 | 3572.8 | 25 | 1.84m | 05/05/05 | 31/12 | www.hammerson.co.uk |
| Hampson Industries PLC | HAMP | Aerospace & Defense | S-Cap | 136.0 | 10 | 210k | 30/08/05 | 31/03 | www.hampsongroup.com |
| Hanson PLC | HNS | Construction & Materials | 100 | 4665.7 | 75 | 4.71m | 26/04/06 | 31/12 | www.hanson.biz |
| Hardy Underwriting Group PLC | HDU | Nonlife Insurance | S-Cap | 71.9 | 2 | 96.9k | 07/06/06 | 31/12 | www.hardygroup.co.uk |
| Harvey Nash Group PLC | HVN | Support Services | Fledge | 41.5 | 3 | 183k | 30/06/06 | 31/01 | www.harveynash.com |
| Havelock Europa PLC | HVE | Household Goods | Fledge | 49.8 | 0.5 | 81.4k | 27/06/06 | 31/12 | www.havelockeuropa.com |
| Haynes Publishing Group PLC | HYNS | Media | Fledge | 26.8 | 0.5 | 5.44k | 13/10/05 | 31/05 | www.haynes.co.uk |
| Hays PLC | HAS | Support Services | Mid 250 | 1920.4 | 200 | 14.4m | 03/11/05 | 30/06 | www.haysplc.co.uk |
| HBOS PLC | HBOS | Banks | 100 | 36932.9 | 200 | 18.9m | 25/04/06 | 31/12 | www.hbosplc.com |
| Headlam Group PLC | HEAD | Household Goods | Mid 250 | 426.2 | 5 | 254k | 01/06/06 | 31/12 | www.headlam.com |
| Helical Bar PLC | HLCL | Real Estate | S-Cap | 381.3 | 5 | 159k | 20/07/06 | 31/03 | www.helical.co.uk |
| Helphire Group PLC | HHR | General Financial | Mid 250 | 490.5 | 5 | 631k | 08/09/05 | 31/03 | www.helphire.co.uk |
| Henderson Global Property Cos Ltd | HGPC | Real Estate | | 38.4 | 2 | | | | |
| Henderson Group PLC | HGI | General Financial | Mid 250 | 906.9 | 100 | 4.94m | 11/05/06 | 31/12 | www.henderson.com |
| Heywood Williams Group PLC | HYWD | Construction & Materials | S-Cap | 58.4 | 5 | 140k | 05/05/05 | 31/12 | www.heywoodwilliams.com |
| Hidong Estate PLC | HID | Food Producers | Fledge | 1.5 | | 86.8 | 30/09/05 | 31/03 | |
| Highway Capital PLC | HWC | General Financial | Fledge | 1.4 | 0.5 | 783 | 07/09/05 | 28/02 | www.sf2.co.uk |
| Highway Insurance Holdings PLC | HWY | Nonlife Insurance | S-Cap | 138.9 | 15 | 837k | 12/05/05 | 31/12 | www.highway-insurance.co.uk |
| Hikma Pharmaceuticals PLC | HIK | Pharmaceuticals & Biotechnology | Mid 250 | 559.2 | 10 | | 25/05/06 | 31/12 | www.hikma.com |
| Hill & Smith Holdings PLC | HILS | Industrial Engineering | S-Cap | 155.4 | 2 | 76.7k | 12/05/06 | 31/12 | www.hsholdings.co.uk |
| Hiscox PLC | HSX | Nonlife Insurance | Mid 250 | 864.0 | 15 | 1.60m | 20/06/06 | 31/12 | www.hiscox.com |
| Hitachi Capital (UK) PLC | HCU | General Financial | S-Cap | 96.6 | 1 | 24.4k | 22/06/06 | 31/03 | www.hitachicapital.co.uk |
| HMV Group PLC | HMV | General Retailers | Mid 250 | 616.1 | 100 | 5.93m | 28/09/05 | 30/04 | www.hmvgroup.com |
| Holidaybreak PLC | HBR | Travel & Leisure | S-Cap | 339.3 | 3 | 101k | 14/03/06 | 30/09 | www.holidaybreak.co.uk |

Source: Hemscott (Hemscott.com)

## Listed Companies

| Company Name | EPIC | Sector | Index | Capital (£m) | NMS | 200D Avg Vol | AGM | Year End | URL |
|---|---|---|---|---|---|---|---|---|---|
| Homeserve PLC | HSV | Support Services | Mid 250 | 1025.7 | 5 | 222k | 28/07/06 | 31/03 | www.homeserve.co.uk |
| Homestyle Group PLC | HME | General Retailers | S-Cap | 310.9 | 5 | 333k | 21/10/05 | 30/04 | www.homestylegroup.com |
| Horizon Technology Group PLC | HOR | Software & Computer Services | | 45.7 | 1 | 43.5k | 05/05/05 | 31/12 | www.horizon.ie |
| Hornby PLC | HRN | Leisure Goods | S-Cap | 82.7 | 3 | 81.2k | 25/07/06 | 31/03 | www.hornby.co.uk |
| House of Fraser PLC | HOF | General Retailers | S-Cap | 331.9 | 50 | 1.53m | 14/06/06 | 28/01 | www.houseoffraser.co.uk |
| Howie Holdings PLC | HOH | Industrial Engineering | Fledge | 2.0 | 0.5 | 11.5k | 05/04/06 | 30/09 | www.howieholdings.co.uk |
| HSBC Holdings PLC | HSBA | Banks | 100 | 110847.5 | 200 | 40.4m | 26/05/06 | 31/12 | www.hsbc.com |
| Hunting PLC | HTG | Oil Equipment; Services & Dist | Mid 250 | 510.8 | 5 | 696k | 26/04/06 | 31/12 | www.hunting.plc.uk |
| Huntleigh Technology PLC | HTL | Health Care Equipment & Services | S-Cap | 194.3 | 2 | 102k | 07/06/06 | 31/12 | www.huntleigh-technology.com |
| Huntsworth PLC | HNT | Media | S-Cap | 172.8 | 10 | 880k | 04/07/06 | 31/12 | www.huntsworth.com |
| Hyder Consulting PLC | HYC | Support Services | S-Cap | 101.7 | 3 | 79.1k | 27/07/06 | 31/03 | www.hyderconsulting.com |
| I S Solutions PLC | ISL | Software & Computer Services | Fledge | 5.6 | 0.5 | 15.1k | 18/05/06 | 31/12 | www.issolutions.co.uk |
| IAWS Group PLC | IAW | Food Producers | | 1259.0 | 0.5 | 21.6m | 30/01/06 | 31/07 | www.iaws.com |
| ICAP PLC | IAP | General Financial | 100 | 2983.0 | 50 | 4.02m | 19/07/06 | 31/03 | www.icap.com |
| ICM Computer Group PLC | ICM | Software & Computer Services | S-Cap | 57.4 | 1 | 12.7k | 15/11/05 | 30/06 | www.icm-computer.co.uk |
| IFG Group PLC | IFP | General Financial | | 84.3 | | 84.0k | 04/07/06 | 31/12 | www.ifgroup.com |
| IFX Group PLC | IXF | General Financial | Fledge | 52.0 | 1 | 85.7k | 04/08/05 | 31/03 | www.ifxgroupplc.com |
| IG Group Holdings PLC | IGG | General Financial | Mid 250 | 720.5 | 25 | 3.00m | 29/09/05 | 31/05 | www.iggroup.com |
| Imagination Technologies Group PLC | IMG | Technology Hardware & Equipment | S-Cap | 136.7 | 10 | 474k | 26/07/06 | 31/03 | www.imgtec.com |
| IMI PLC | IMI | Industrial Engineering | Mid 250 | 1676.8 | 25 | 2.00m | 13/05/05 | 31/12 | www.imiplc.com |
| Imperial Chemical Industries PLC | ICI | Chemicals | 100 | 4275.6 | 150 | 10.9m | 24/05/06 | 31/12 | www.ici.com |
| Imperial Tobacco Group PLC | IMT | Tobacco | 100 | 12022.3 | 50 | 4.33m | 31/01/06 | 30/09 | www.imperial-tobacco.com |
| Inch Kenneth Kajang Rubber PLC | IKK | Food Producers | | 57.9 | 2 | 1.07k | 27/06/06 | 31/12 | |
| Inchcape PLC | INCH | General Retailers | Mid 250 | 2124.2 | 10 | 3.02m | 12/05/05 | 31/12 | www.inchcape.com |
| Incisive Media PLC | INM | Media | S-Cap | 160.6 | 2 | 157k | 05/05/05 | 31/12 | www.incisivemedia.com |
| Independent Media Distribution PLC | IMD | Media | Fledge | 17.8 | 1 | 12.9k | 31/05/06 | 31/12 | www.imdplc.com |
| Independent News & Media PLC | INWS | Media | | 1194.7 | 25 | 2.24m | 08/06/06 | 31/12 | www.inmplc.com |
| Informa PLC | INF | Media | Mid 250 | 1752.8 | 25 | 2.18m | 16/05/06 | 31/12 | www.tfinforma.com |
| Inmarsat PLC | ISAT | Mobile Telecommunications | Mid 250 | 1512.0 | 50 | 5.16m | 26/04/06 | 31/12 | www.inmarsat.com |
| Innovata PLC | IOV | Pharmaceuticals & Biotechnology | Mid 250 | 111.9 | 25 | 1.88m | 15/03/06 | 30/09 | www.innovataplc.com |
| Innovation Group (The) PLC | TIG | Software & Computer Services | S-Cap | 139.3 | 50 | 1.93m | 06/03/06 | 30/09 | www.innovation-group.com |
| Instore PLC | INST | General Retailers | S-Cap | 61.7 | 10 | 177k | 27/07/05 | 25/02 | www.instoreretail.co.uk |
| Intec Telecom Systems PLC | ITL | Software & Computer Services | S-Cap | 97.4 | 25 | 884k | 06/04/06 | 30/09 | www.intec-telecom-systems.com |
| Intelek PLC | ITK | Technology Hardware & Equipment | Fledge | 10.8 | 5 | 125k | 16/09/05 | 31/03 | www.intelek.plc.uk |
| InterContinental Hotels Group PLC | IHG | Travel & Leisure | 100 | 3109.1 | 50 | 4.45m | 01/06/06 | 31/12 | www.ihgplc.com |
| Intermediate Capital Group PLC | ICP | General Financial | Mid 250 | 915.4 | 10 | 418k | 20/07/06 | 31/03 | www.icgplc.com |
| International Power PLC | IPR | Electricity | 100 | 4509.9 | 150 | 13.3m | 17/05/05 | 31/12 | www.ipplc.com |
| Interserve PLC | IRV | Support Services | Mid 250 | 452.2 | 5 | 516k | 17/05/05 | 31/12 | www.interserveplc.co.uk |
| Intertek Group PLC | ITRK | Support Services | Mid 250 | 1037.3 | 25 | 1.71m | 12/05/06 | 31/12 | www.intertek.com |
| Invensys PLC | ISYS | Electronic & Electrical Equipment | Mid 250 | 1387.1 | 200 | 6.79m | 03/08/06 | 31/03 | www.invensys.com |
| Investec PLC | INVP | General Financial | Mid 250 | 2017.9 | 3 | 472k | 11/08/05 | 31/03 | www.investec.com |
| IONA Technologies PLC | IOND | Software & Computer Services | | 71.6 | 12.5 | 159 | 12/08/05 | 31/12 | www.iona.com |
| IP Group PLC | IPO | General Financial | | 281.2 | 2 | 637k | 25/04/06 | 31/12 | www.ip2ipo.com |
| Irish Continental Group PLC | ICGC | Industrial Transportation | | 168.9 | 0.5 | 55.8k | 29/04/05 | 31/12 | www.icg.ie |

## Listed Companies

| Company Name | EPIC | Sector | Index | Capital (£m) | NMS | 200D Avg Vol | AGM | Year End | URL |
|---|---|---|---|---|---|---|---|---|---|
| Irish Life & Permanent PLC | IPM | Banks | S-Cap | 3598.8 | 5 | 390k | 26/05/06 | 31/12 | www.irishlifepermanent.ie |
| iSOFT Group PLC | IOT | Software & Computer Services | S-Cap | 129.1 | 75 | 7.39m | 25/07/05 | 30/04 | www.isoftplc.com |
| Isotron PLC | ISO | Health Care Equipment & Services | S-Cap | 129.1 | 2 | 32.5k | 23/11/05 | 30/06 | www.isotron.com |
| ITE Group PLC | ITE | Media | S-Cap | 303.9 | 10 | 856k | 23/02/06 | 30/09 | www.ite-exhibitions.com |
| ITV PLC | ITV | Media | 100 | 4150.1 | 200 | 42.0m | 10/05/06 | 31/12 | www.itvplc.com |
| Jardine Lloyd Thompson Group PLC | JLT | Nonlife Insurance | Mid 250 | 825.9 | 15 | 1.26m | 27/04/06 | 31/12 | www.jltgroup.com |
| Jarvis PLC | JRVS | Support Services | S-Cap | 83.5 | 5 | 332k | 19/10/05 | 31/03 | www.jarvisplc.com |
| Jasmin PLC | JAS | Software & Computer Services | | 2.1 | 0.5 | | 22/08/05 | 31/03 | www.jasmin.plc.uk |
| Jersey Electricity Company (The) Ltd | JEL | Electricity | Fledge | 24.6 | | 85 | 14/03/06 | 30/09 | www.jec.co.uk |
| Jessops PLC | JSP | General Retailers | S-Cap | 125.5 | 10 | 769k | 27/01/06 | 30/09 | www.jessops.co.uk |
| JJB Sports PLC | JJB | General Retailers | Mid 250 | 408.3 | 25 | 1.59m | 27/07/06 | 29/01 | www.jjbcorporate.co.uk |
| JKX Oil & Gas PLC | JKX | Oil & Gas Producers | Mid 250 | 503.9 | 5 | 586k | 18/05/06 | 31/12 | www.jkx.co.uk |
| John David Group PLC | JD. | General Retailers | S-Cap | 140.2 | 0.5 | 63.7k | 20/07/06 | 28/01 | www.jdsports.co.uk |
| John Wood Group PLC | WG. | Oil Equipment; Services & Dist | Mid 250 | 1237.9 | 50 | 2.35m | 18/05/06 | 31/12 | www.woodgroup.com |
| Johnson Matthey PLC | JMAT | Chemicals | 100 | 2759.9 | 15 | 1.35m | 25/07/06 | 31/03 | www.matthey.com |
| Johnson Service Group PLC | JSG | Support Services | S-Cap | 232.2 | 2 | 106k | 11/05/05 | 31/12 | www.johnsonplc.com |
| Johnston Press PLC | JPR | Media | Mid 250 | 1083.7 | 25 | 1.57m | 28/04/06 | 31/12 | www.johnstonpress.co.uk |
| Kazakhmys PLC | KAZ | Mining | 100 | 5731.2 | 50 | 3.24m | 23/05/06 | 31/12 | www.kazakhmys.com |
| Kelda Group PLC | KEL | Gas; Water & Multiutilities | 100 | 2940.5 | 50 | 2.62m | 25/07/06 | 31/03 | www.keldagroup.com |
| Keller Group PLC | KLR | Construction & Materials | S-Cap | 403.6 | 2 | 209k | 22/06/06 | 31/12 | www.keller.co.uk |
| Kenmare Resources PLC | KMR | Mining | | 261.4 | 25 | 1.63m | 12/07/06 | 31/12 | www.kenmareresources.com |
| Kensington Group PLC | KGN | General Financial | Mid 250 | 457.3 | 10 | 562k | 22/03/05 | 30/11 | www.kensingtongroup.co.uk |
| Kerry Group PLC | KYGA | Food Producers | | 2055.1 | 0.5 | 83.5k | 19/05/06 | 31/12 | www.kerrygroup.com |
| Kesa Electricals PLC | KESA | General Retailers | Mid 250 | 1636.3 | 75 | 6.44m | 24/05/06 | 31/01 | www.kesaelectricals.com |
| Kewill Systems PLC | KWL | Software & Computer Services | Fledge | 49.6 | 5 | 262k | 15/09/05 | 31/03 | www.xewill.com |
| Kier Group PLC | KIE | Construction & Materials | Mid 250 | 565.5 | 2 | 114k | 28/11/05 | 30/06 | www.xier.co.uk |
| Kiln PLC | KIN | Nonlife Insurance | S-Cap | 270.3 | 15 | 655k | 24/05/06 | 31/12 | www.xilnplc.com |
| Kingfisher PLC | KGF | General Retailers | 100 | 5464.3 | 200 | 22.0m | 24/05/06 | 28/01 | www.xingfisher.com |
| Kingfisher PLC | KGFN | General Retailers | 100 | | | | 24/05/06 | 28/01 | www.kingfisher.com |
| Kingspan Group PLC | KGP | Construction & Materials | | 1576.8 | 2 | 501k | 25/05/06 | 31/12 | www.kingspan.com |
| Kingston Communications (Hull) PLC | KCOM | Fixed Line Telecommunications | S-Cap | 288.3 | 50 | 1.40m | 28/07/06 | 31/03 | www.kcom.com |
| Ladbrokes PLC | LAD | Travel & Leisure | Mid 250 | 2429.5 | 25 | 17.5m | 26/05/06 | 31/12 | www.iadbrokesplc.com |
| Laing (John) PLC | LNGO | Support Services | Mid 250 | 685.0 | 15 | 1.07m | 19/05/06 | 31/12 | www.laing.com |
| Laird Group (The) PLC | LARD | Electronic & Electrical Equipment | Mid 250 | 760.9 | 25 | 1.23m | 12/05/06 | 31/12 | www.laird-plc.com |
| Lambert Howarth Group PLC | LMBT | Personal Goods | Fledge | 13.9 | 2 | 90.2k | 02/06/06 | 31/12 | www.lamberthowarth.com |
| Land of Leather Holdings PLC | LAN | General Retailers | S-Cap | 123.9 | 3 | 264k | | 02/04 | www.landofleather.com |
| Land Securities Group PLC | LAND | Real Estate | 100 | 9020.2 | 50 | 2.93m | 19/07/06 | 31/03 | www.landsecurities.com |
| Latchways PLC | LTC | Support Services | Fledge | 84.8 | 0.5 | 13.6k | 02/09/05 | 31/03 | www.latchways.com |
| Lavendon Group PLC | LVD | Support Services | Fledge | 106.4 | 2 | 50.0k | 28/04/05 | 31/12 | www.lavendongroup.com |
| Legal & General Group PLC | LGEN | Life Insurance | 100 | 8132.4 | 200 | 42.6m | 18/05/06 | 31/12 | www.legalandgeneral.com |
| Liberty International PLC | LII | Real Estate | 100 | 3756.0 | 15 | 1.41m | 18/03/06 | 31/12 | www.liberty-international.co.uk |
| Lincat Group PLC | LCT | Industrial Engineering | Fledge | 42.4 | 0.5 | 3.15k | 21/11/05 | 30/06 | www.lincatgroup.co.uk |
| Liontrust Asset Management PLC | LIO | General Financial | S-Cap | 125.0 | 2 | 45.9k | 07/07/06 | 31/03 | www.liontrust.co.uk |
| Litho Supplies PLC | LTS | Support Services | Fledge | 13.6 | 1 | 27.2k | 04/05/05 | 31/12 | www.litho.co.uk |

Source: Hemscott (Hemscott.com)

| Company Name | EPIC | Sector | Index | Capital (£m) | NMS | 200D Avg Vol | AGM | Year End | URL |
|---|---|---|---|---|---|---|---|---|---|
| Lloyds TSB Group PLC | LLOY | Banks | 100 | 28798.5 | 200 | 39.5m | 05/05/05 | 31/12 | www.lloydstsb.com |
| LogicaCMG PLC | LOG | Software & Computer Services | Mid 250 | 1914.2 | 150 | 10.7m | 18/05/05 | 31/12 | www.logicacmg.com |
| LogicaCMG PLC | LOGN | Software & Computer Services | Mid 250 | | | | 18/05/05 | 31/12 | www.logicacmg.com |
| London & Associated Properties PLC | LAS | Real Estate | S-Cap | 86.1 | 2 | 81.3k | 28/06/06 | 31/12 | www.lap.co.uk |
| London Clubs International PLC | LCI | Travel & Leisure | S-Cap | 213.4 | 15 | 935k | 12/09/05 | 27/03 | www.lciclubs.com |
| London Finance & Investment Group PLC | LFI | General Financial | Fledge | 10.9 | 0.5 | 11.0k | 28/09/05 | 30/06 | www.city-group.com |
| London Merchant Securities PLC | LMSO | Real Estate | Mid 250 | 711.4 | 15 | 724k | 27/07/06 | 31/03 | www.lms-plc.com |
| London Merchant Securities PLC | LMSD | Real Estate | Mid 250 | | | 87.6k | 27/07/06 | 31/03 | www.lms-plc.com |
| London Scottish Bank PLC | LSB | General Financial | S-Cap | 165.1 | 10 | 510k | 29/03/06 | 31/10 | www.london-scottish.com |
| London Stock Exchange PLC | LSE | General Financial | Mid 250 | 2358.9 | 25 | 3.94m | 12/07/06 | 31/03 | www.londonstockexchange.com |
| London Stock Exchange PLC | LSEB | General Financial | Mid 250 | | | | 12/07/06 | 31/03 | www.londonstockexchange.com |
| Lonmin PLC | LMI | Mining | 100 | 3840.2 | 15 | 2.03m | 26/01/06 | 30/09 | www.lonmin.com |
| Lookers PLC | LOOK | General Retailers | S-Cap | 279.0 | 1 | 533k | 12/05/05 | 31/12 | www.lookers.co.uk |
| Low & Bonar PLC | LWB | Construction & Materials | S-Cap | 181.1 | 10 | 420k | 24/05/06 | 30/11 | www.lowandbonar.com |
| Luminar PLC | LMR | Travel & Leisure | Mid 250 | 380.4 | 10 | 507k | 18/07/06 | 02/03 | www.luminar.co.uk |
| Macfarlane Group PLC | MACF | Support Services | Fledge | 37.4 | 3 | 195k | 10/05/05 | 31/12 | www.macfarlanegroup.net |
| Macro 4 PLC | MAO | Software & Computer Services | Fledge | 50.0 | 0.5 | 23.8k | 21/10/05 | 30/06 | www.macro4.com |
| Mallett PLC | MAE | General Retailers | Fledge | 34.6 | 0.5 | 19.1k | 23/05/06 | 31/12 | www.mallettantiques.com |
| Man Group PLC | EMG | General Financial | 100 | 7679.0 | 50 | 3.72m | 11/07/06 | 31/03 | www.mangroupplc.com |
| Management Consulting Group PLC | MMC | Support Services | S-Cap | 100.4 | 15 | 828k | 26/04/05 | 31/12 | www.mcgplc.com |
| Manganese Bronze Holdings PLC | MNGS | Industrial Engineering | Fledge | 48.1 | 2 | 85.6k | 22/11/05 | 31/07 | www.manganese.com |
| Mapeley Ltd | MAY | Real Estate | Mid 250 | 824.3 | 2 | 85.8k | 24/05/06 | 31/12 | www.mapeley.com |
| Marchpole Holdings PLC | MPH | General Retailers | Fledge | 28.0 | 15 | 620k | 06/09/05 | 31/03 | www.marchpole.com |
| Marks & Spencer Group PLC | MKS | General Retailers | 100 | 9692.0 | 200 | 15.2m | 11/07/06 | 01/04 | www.marksandspencer.com |
| Marks & Spencer Group PLC | MKSB | General Retailers | 100 | | | 17.4k | 11/07/06 | 01/04 | www.marksandspencer.com |
| Marshalls PLC | MSLH | Construction & Materials | Mid 250 | 452.9 | 10 | 448k | 24/05/06 | 31/12 | www.marshalls.co.uk |
| Marylebone Warwick Balfour Group PLC | MWB | Real Estate | S-Cap | 191.2 | 2 | 554k | 29/11/05 | 30/06 | www.mwb.co.uk |
| Matalan PLC | MTN | General Retailers | Mid 250 | 698.2 | 50 | 3.55m | 05/07/06 | 25/02 | www.matalan.co.uk |
| Mayflower Corporation PLC | MFW | Automobiles & Parts | | 24.1 | 50 | | 15/06/06 | 31/12 | www.mayflowercorp.com |
| McAlpine (Alfred) PLC | MCA | Support Services | Mid 250 | 462.1 | 15 | 464k | 06/06/06 | 31/12 | www.alfredmcalpineplc.com |
| McBride PLC | MCB | Household Goods | S-Cap | 272.8 | 15 | 571k | 31/10/05 | 30/06 | www.mcbride.co.uk |
| McCarthy & Stone PLC | MCTY | Household Goods | Mid 250 | 1121.8 | 10 | 1.19m | 19/12/05 | 31/08 | www.mccarthyandstone.co.uk |
| McInerney Holdings PLC | MCI | Construction & Materials | | 243.0 | 1 | 50.2k | 12/05/05 | 31/12 | www.mcinerney.ie |
| McKay Securities PLC | MCKS | Real Estate | S-Cap | 180.3 | 1 | 78.6k | 27/07/06 | 31/03 | www.mckaysecurities.plc.uk |
| Medical Solutions PLC | MLS | Pharmaceuticals & Biotechnology | Fledge | 13.2 | 25 | 745k | 08/06/06 | 31/12 | www.medical-solutions.co.uk |
| Medisys PLC | MDY | Health Care Equipment & Services | Fledge | 16.5 | 100 | 3.26m | 27/04/05 | 30/09 | www.medisys-group.com |
| Meggitt PLC | MGGT | Aerospace & Defense | Mid 250 | 1235.0 | 50 | 2.72m | 12/05/05 | 31/12 | www.meggitt.com |
| Melrose PLC | MRO | Industrial Engineering | S-Cap | 372.8 | 10 | 1.40m | 24/05/05 | 31/12 | |
| Melrose Resources PLC | MRS | Oil & Gas Producers | S-Cap | 291.5 | 3 | 122k | 20/06/06 | 31/12 | www.melroseresources.com |
| Menzies (John) PLC | MNZS | Support Services | S-Cap | 286.0 | 1 | 89.7k | 25/05/06 | 31/12 | www.johnmenziesplc.com |
| Metal Bulletin PLC | MTLB | Media | S-Cap | 224.1 | 2 | 170k | 23/05/06 | 31/12 | www.metalbulletin.plc.uk |
| Metalrax Group PLC | MRX | Industrial Engineering | S-Cap | 84.5 | 3 | 237k | 23/05/06 | 31/12 | www.metalraxgroup.co.uk |
| MFI Furniture Group PLC | MFI | General Retailers | Mid 250 | 543.3 | 100 | 10.0m | 19/05/06 | 24/12 | www.mfigroup.co.uk |
| MICE Group PLC | MEG | Support Services | Fledge | 60.2 | 15 | 783k | 27/06/06 | 28/02 | www.micegroup.com |

Source: Hemscott (Hemscott.com)

## Listed Companies

| Company Name | EPIC | Sector | Index | Capital (£m) | NMS | 200D Avg Vol | AGM | Year End | URL |
|---|---|---|---|---|---|---|---|---|---|
| Michael Page International PLC | MPI | Support Services | Mid 250 | 1122.3 | 50 | 4.29m | 23/05/06 | 31/12 | www.michaelpage.co.uk |
| Micro Focus International PLC | MCRO | Software & Computer Services | S-Cap | 222.4 | 25 | 523k | 28/09/05 | 30/04 | www.microfocus.com |
| Microgen PLC | MCGN | Software & Computer Services | Fledge | 54.2 | 10 | 245k | 12/04/05 | 31/12 | www.microgen.co.uk |
| Mid-States PLC | MST | Automobiles & Parts | Fledge | 8.1 | 0.5 | 8.91k | 28/06/05 | 31/12 | |
| Millennium & Copthorne Hotels PLC | MLC | Travel & Leisure | Mid 250 | 1234.0 | 10 | 706k | 04/05/06 | 31/12 | www.millenniumhotels.com |
| Minerva PLC | MNR | Real Estate | Mid 250 | 431.6 | 25 | 1.43m | 25/11/05 | 30/06 | www.minervaplc.co.uk |
| Misys PLC | MSY | Software & Computer Services | Mid 250 | 1182.0 | 50 | 5.79m | 13/09/05 | 31/05 | www.misys.com |
| Mitchells & Butlers PLC | MAB | Travel & Leisure | Mid 250 | 2613.9 | 50 | 6.00m | 02/02/06 | 01/10 | www.mbplc.com |
| MITIE Group PLC | MTO | Support Services | Mid 250 | 596.0 | 15 | 1.23m | 27/07/06 | 31/03 | www.mitie.co.uk |
| Molins PLC | MLIN | Industrial Engineering | Fledge | 22.3 | 0.5 | 24.2k | 24/04/06 | 31/12 | www.molins.com |
| Morgan Crucible Company (The) PLC | MGCR | Electronic & Electrical Equipment | Mid 250 | 827.4 | 25 | 1.68m | 21/04/06 | 04/01 | www.morgancrucible.com |
| Morgan Sindall PLC | MGNS | Construction & Materials | Mid 250 | 464.4 | 2 | 151k | 25/04/06 | 31/12 | www.morgansindall.co.uk |
| Morrison (Wm) Supermarkets PLC | MRW | Food & Drug Retailers | 100 | 5831.7 | 200 | 19.4m | 25/05/06 | 29/01 | www.morrisons.co.uk |
| Morse PLC | MOR | Software & Computer Services | S-Cap | 145.3 | 5 | 454k | 01/11/05 | 30/06 | www.morse.com |
| Moss Bros Group PLC | MOSB | General Retailers | S-Cap | 66.0 | 3 | 123k | 25/05/06 | 28/01 | www.mossbros.co.uk |
| Mothercare PLC | MTC | General Retailers | S-Cap | 238.5 | 3 | 200k | 20/07/06 | 01/04 | www.mothercare.com |
| Mouchel Parkman PLC | MCHL | Support Services | S-Cap | 377.0 | 5 | 245k | 09/12/05 | 31/07 | www.mouchelparkman.com |
| Mountview Estates PLC | MTVW | Real Estate | | 184.2 | | 70.6 | 17/08/05 | 31/03 | |
| MS International PLC | MSI | Industrial Engineering | Fledge | 30.7 | 0.5 | 16.9k | 07/08/06 | 29/04 | |
| MSB International PLC | MSB | Support Services | Fledge | 13.0 | 0.5 | 36.3k | 23/05/06 | 31/01 | www.msb.com |
| MTL Instruments Group PLC | MTI | Electronic & Electrical Equipment | Fledge | 80.8 | 0.5 | 23.8k | 05/05/05 | 31/12 | www.mtl-group.com |
| Mucklow (A & J) Group PLC | MKLW | Real Estate | S-Cap | 297.0 | 0.5 | 22.8k | 08/11/05 | 30/06 | www.mucklow.com |
| MyTravel Group PLC | MT.S | Travel & Leisure | Mid 250 | 975.5 | 15 | 4.05m | 13/03/06 | 31/10 | www.mytravelgroup.com |
| Narborough Plantations PLC | NBP | Food Producers | Fledge | 4.3 | 1 | 423 | 16/12/05 | 30/06 | |
| National Express Group PLC | NEX | Travel & Leisure | Mid 250 | 1229.5 | 10 | 1.00m | 24/05/06 | 31/12 | www.nationalexpressgroup.com |
| National Grid PLC | NG. | Gas; Water & Multiutilities | 100 | 16869.0 | 150 | 13.8m | 31/07/06 | 31/03 | www.nationalgrid.com |
| National Grid PLC | NG.B | Gas; Water & Multiutilities | 100 | | | 89.9k | 31/07/06 | 31/03 | www.nationalgrid.com |
| nCipher PLC | NCH | Software & Computer Services | Fledge | 62.5 | 2 | 120k | 30/06/06 | 31/12 | www.ncipher.com |
| Nestor Healthcare Group PLC | NSR | Health Care Equipment & Services | S-Cap | 99.9 | 5 | 293k | 27/04/06 | 31/12 | www.nestorplc.co.uk |
| Network Technology PLC | NTY | Technology Hardware & Equipment | Fledge | 2.5 | 0.5 | 2.13k | 09/09/05 | 31/03 | www.network-technology.com |
| Newcastle United PLC | NCU | Travel & Leisure | Fledge | 77.9 | 1 | 33.0k | 14/12/05 | 31/07 | www.nufc.co.uk |
| Next PLC | NXT | General Retailers | 100 | 3810.5 | 50 | 3.66m | 18/05/05 | 28/01 | www.next.co.uk |
| Nord Anglia Education PLC | NAE | General Retailers | Fledge | 53.0 | 5 | 238k | 27/01/06 | 31/08 | www.nordanglia.com |
| North Midland Construction PLC | NMD | Construction & Materials | Fledge | 28.4 | 1 | 1.61k | 24/05/06 | 31/12 | www.northmid.co.uk |
| Northamber PLC | NAR | Technology Hardware & Equipment | Fledge | 19.8 | 0.5 | 16.2k | 25/11/05 | 30/06 | www.northamber.com |
| Northern Foods PLC | NFDS | Food Producers | Mid 250 | 402.4 | 75 | 5.43m | 19/07/06 | 01/04 | www.northernfoods.com |
| Northern Recruitment Group PLC | NRG | Support Services | Fledge | 21.5 | 1 | 28.2k | 18/10/05 | 30/06 | www.nrgplc.com |
| Northern Rock PLC | NRK | Banks | 100 | 4658.5 | 50 | 4.38m | 26/04/05 | 31/12 | www.northernrock.co.uk |
| Northgate Information Solutions PLC | NIS | Software & Computer Services | Mid 250 | 373.2 | 50 | 2.63m | 29/09/05 | 30/04 | www.northgate-is.com |
| Northgate PLC | NTG | Industrial Transportation | Mid 250 | 707.5 | 10 | 435k | 28/09/05 | 30/04 | www.northgateplc.com |
| Northumbrian Water Group PLC | NWG | Gas; Water & Multiutilities | Mid 250 | 1348.4 | 50 | 2.71m | 27/07/06 | 31/03 | www.nwg.co.uk |
| Novae Group PLC | NVA | Nonlife Insurance | S-Cap | 190.4 | 25 | 924k | 09/05/05 | 31/12 | www.novae.com |
| NSB Retail Systems PLC | NSB | Software & Computer Services | S-Cap | 103.5 | 25 | 1.24m | 05/05/05 | 31/12 | www.nsbgroup.com |
| NXT PLC | NTX | Leisure Goods | Fledge | 31.1 | 15 | 288k | 23/11/05 | 30/06 | www.nxtsound.com |

## Listed Companies

| Company Name | EPIC | Sector | Index | Capital (£m) | NMS | 200D Avg Vol | AGM | Year End | URL |
|---|---|---|---|---|---|---|---|---|---|
| Oakhill Group PLC | OAK | Media | | 3.7 | 1 | 1.80k | 26/07/06 | 31/12 | www.oakhillplc.ie |
| OEM PLC | OEM | Real Estate | Fledge | 1.0 | 0.5 | 3.30k | 12/12/05 | 30/06 | |
| office2office PLC | OFF | Support Services | S-Cap | 77.2 | 2 | 69.2k | 25/04/06 | 31/12 | www.office2office.biz |
| Old Mutual PLC | OML | Life Insurance | 100 | 8657.3 | 200 | 41.9m | 10/05/06 | 31/12 | www.oldmutual.com |
| OPD Group PLC | OPD | Support Services | Fledge | 85.7 | 0.5 | 79.4k | 23/05/06 | 31/12 | www.psdgroup.com |
| Optos PLC | OPTS | Health Care Equipment & Services | S-Cap | 126.3 | | | 31/01/06 | 30/09 | www.optos.com |
| Opus International Group PLC | OPU | General Financial | | 17.4 | 1 | 375 | | 31/12 | |
| Ormonde Mining PLC | ORM | Mining | | 26.4 | 1 | 1.15m | 16/06/06 | 31/12 | www.ormondemining.com |
| Oxford BioMedica PLC | OXB | Pharmaceuticals & Biotechnology | S-Cap | 124.9 | 50 | 2.24m | 10/05/05 | 31/12 | www.oxfordbiomedica.co.uk |
| Oxford Instruments PLC | OXIG | Electronic & Electrical Equipment | S-Cap | 103.1 | 2 | 28.4k | 20/09/05 | 31/03 | www.oxford-instruments.com |
| Pace Micro Technology PLC | PIC | Leisure Goods | S-Cap | 104.7 | 25 | 798k | 06/09/05 | 04/06 | www.pacemicro.com |
| Pacific Media PLC | PCM | Media | Fledge | 1.8 | 200 | 5.92m | 31/07/06 | 31/12 | www.pmplc.com |
| Paddy Power PLC | PAP | Travel & Leisure | | 469.4 | 1 | 166k | 16/05/06 | 31/12 | www.paddypowerplc.com |
| Panther Securities PLC | PNS | Real Estate | | 62.5 | 0.5 | 1.56k | 21/06/06 | 31/12 | |
| Paragon Group of Companies (The) PLC | PAG | General Financial | Mid 250 | 689.1 | 10 | 556k | 09/02/06 | 30/09 | www.paragon-group.co.uk |
| Parity Group PLC | PTY | Software & Computer Services | Fledge | 18.7 | 1 | 66.7k | 28/06/06 | 31/12 | www.parity.net |
| Park Group PLC | PKG | General Financial | Fledge | 33.8 | 1 | 46.5k | 20/09/05 | 31/03 | www.parkgroup.co.uk |
| Parkwood Holdings PLC | PKW | Support Services | Fledge | 14.6 | 0.5 | 24.9k | 28/04/05 | 31/12 | www.parkwood-holdings.co.uk |
| PartyGaming PLC | PRTY | Travel & Leisure | 100 | 4490.0 | 100 | 41.6m | 04/05/06 | 31/12 | www.partygaming.com |
| Patientline PLC | PTL | Fixed Line Telecommunications | Fledge | 9.5 | 25 | 471k | 29/07/05 | 31/03 | www.patientline.co.uk |
| PayPoint PLC | PAY | Support Services | Mid 250 | 379.9 | 2 | 109k | 29/06/06 | 31/03 | www.paypoint.com |
| Pearson PLC | PSON | Media | 100 | 5977.5 | 75 | 6.05m | 21/04/06 | 31/12 | www.pearson.com |
| Pendragon PLC | PDG | General Retailers | Mid 250 | 659.3 | 10 | 808k | 28/04/06 | 31/12 | www.pendragonplc.com |
| Peninsular & Oriental Steam Navigation Co | PO. | Industrial Transportation | | 3927.5 | 100 | 14.3m | 13/05/06 | 31/12 | www.pogroup.com |
| Penna Consulting PLC | PNA | Support Services | Fledge | 16.6 | 0.5 | 12.7k | 15/09/05 | 31/03 | www.e-penna.com |
| Pennon Group PLC | PNN | Gas; Water & Multiutilities | Mid 250 | 1650.3 | 15 | 2.51m | 28/07/06 | 31/03 | www.pennon-group.co.uk |
| Persimmon PLC | PSN | Household Goods | 100 | 3700.9 | 25 | 2.29m | 20/04/06 | 31/12 | www.persimmonhomes.com |
| Petrofac Ltd | PFC | Oil Equipment; Services & Dist | Mid 250 | 1012.2 | 25 | 2.02m | 19/05/06 | 31/12 | www.petrofac.com |
| PGI Group PLC | PGI | Food Producers | Fledge | 49.3 | 2 | 52.6k | 28/06/06 | 31/12 | www.pgi-uk.com |
| Phoenix IT Group PLC | PNX | Software & Computer Services | S-Cap | 164.6 | 3 | 157k | 03/08/06 | 31/03 | www.phoenixitgroup.com |
| Photo-Me International PLC | PHTM | General Retailers | Mid 250 | 373.9 | 75 | 4.44m | 28/09/05 | 30/04 | www.photo-me.co.uk |
| Phytopharm PLC | PYM | Pharmaceuticals & Biotechnology | Fledge | 26.6 | 5 | 269k | 23/01/06 | 31/08 | www.phytopharm.com |
| Pinewood Shepperton PLC | PWS | Media | S-Cap | 96.1 | 5 | 135k | 19/06/06 | 31/12 | www.pinewoodshepperton.com |
| PlaneStation Group PLC | PTG | Industrial Transportation | | 25.7 | 25 | | 14/09/05 | 31/03 | www.planestation.com |
| Plasmon PLC | PLM | Technology Hardware & Equipment | S-Cap | 40.0 | 2 | 114k | 28/07/06 | 31/03 | www.plasmon.co.uk |
| Pochin's PLC | PCH | Construction & Materials | Fledge | 65.5 | 0.5 | 3.70k | 04/11/05 | 31/05 | www.pochins.plc.uk |
| Porvair PLC | PRV | Chemicals | Fledge | 50.1 | 1 | 63.3k | 12/04/06 | 30/11 | www.porvair.com |
| Premier Farnell PLC | PFL | Support Services | Mid 250 | 628.3 | 75 | 4.63m | 13/06/06 | 29/01 | www.premierfarnell.com |
| Premier Foods PLC | PFD | Food Producers | Mid 250 | 784.4 | 50 | 2.21m | 26/05/05 | 31/12 | www.premierfoods.co.uk |
| Premier Oil PLC | PMO | Oil & Gas Producers | Mid 250 | 831.4 | 10 | 537k | 19/05/06 | 31/12 | www.premier-oil.com |
| Primary Health Properties PLC | PHP | Real Estate | S-Cap | 96.0 | 1 | 50.5k | 15/11/05 | 30/06 | www.phpgroup.co.uk |
| Prodesse Investment Ltd | PRD | General Financial | S-Cap | 93.3 | 3 | 221k | 21/06/06 | 31/12 | www.prodesse.co.uk |
| ProStrakan Group PLC | PSK | Pharmaceuticals & Biotechnology | S-Cap | 198.2 | 3 | 125k | 24/07/05 | 31/12 | www.prostrakan.com |
| Protherics PLC | PTI | Pharmaceuticals & Biotechnology | S-Cap | 207.9 | 10 | 588k | 18/07/06 | 31/03 | www.protherics.com |

# Company Directory

## Listed Companies

| Company Name | EPIC | Sector | Index | Capital (£m) | NMS | 200D Avg Vol | AGM | Year End | URL |
|---|---|---|---|---|---|---|---|---|---|
| Provalis PLC | PRO | Pharmaceuticals & Biotechnology | Fledge | 1.0 | 75 | 759k | 01/12/05 | 30/06 | www.provalis.com |
| Provident Financial PLC | PFG | General Financial | Mid 250 | 1493.3 | 50 | 1.96m | 24/05/05 | 31/12 | www.providentfinancial.com |
| Prudential PLC | PRU | Life Insurance | 100 | 13473.9 | 200 | 18.2m | 18/05/06 | 31/12 | www.prudential.co.uk |
| Psion PLC | PON | Technology Hardware & Equipment | S-Cap | 149.1 | 5 | 522k | 19/05/06 | 31/12 | www.psion.com |
| Punch Taverns PLC | PUB | Travel & Leisure | Mid 250 | 2332.7 | 50 | 3.20m | 25/01/06 | 20/08 | www.punchtaverns.com |
| PuriCore PLC | PURI | Pharmaceuticals & Biotechnology | | 123.0 | 10 | 21.4k | 26/09/05 | 31/05 | www.puricore.com |
| PZ Cussons PLC | PZC | Personal Goods | Mid 250 | 661.3 | 0.5 | 7.43k | 26/09/05 | 31/05 | www.pzcussons.com |
| PZ Cussons PLC | PZCA | Personal Goods | Mid 250 | | | | | 31/05 | www.pzcussons.com |
| QinetiQ Group PLC | QQ. | Aerospace & Defense | Mid 250 | 1084.6 | 50 | | 28/07/06 | 31/03 | www.qinwtiq.com |
| Qualceram Shires PLC | QLC | Household Goods | Fledge | 19.1 | 2 | 5.40k | 08/06/06 | 31/12 | www.qualceram-shires.com |
| Quantica PLC | QTA | Support Services | Fledge | 37.9 | 2 | 120k | 18/04/06 | 02/12 | www.quantica.co.uk |
| Quintain Estates & Development PLC | QED | Real Estate | Mid 250 | 860.6 | 5 | 314k | 06/09/05 | 31/03 | www.quintain-estates.com |
| QXL ricardo PLC | QXL | General Retailers | S-Cap | 175.5 | 0.5 | 4.40k | 24/07/06 | 31/03 | www.qxl.com |
| R.E.A. Holdings PLC | RE. | Food Producers | Fledge | 92.3 | 3 | 14.4k | 08/06/06 | 31/12 | www.rea.co.uk |
| Radstone Technology PLC | RST | Technology Hardware & Equipment | S-Cap | 78.9 | 2 | 171k | 07/09/05 | 31/03 | www.radstone.com |
| Randgold Resources Ltd | RRS | Mining | Mid 250 | 834.7 | 100 | 150k | 02/05/06 | 31/12 | www.randgoldresources.com |
| Rank Group (The) PLC | RNK | Travel & Leisure | Mid 250 | 1216.3 | 1 | 9.23m | 26/04/06 | 31/12 | www.rank.com |
| Rathbone Brothers PLC | RAT | General Financial | Mid 250 | 454.5 | 5 | 79.9k | 03/05/06 | 31/12 | www.rathbones.com |
| Raymarine PLC | RAY | Electronic & Electrical Equipment | S-Cap | 308.8 | 50 | 439k | 18/05/06 | 31/12 | www.raymarine.com |
| Reckitt Benckiser PLC | RB. | Household Goods | 100 | 15600.0 | 15 | 3.84m | 04/05/06 | 31/12 | www.reckittbenckiser.com |
| Redrow PLC | RDW | Household Goods | Mid 250 | 771.0 | 100 | 1.08m | 09/11/05 | 30/06 | www.redrow.co.uk |
| Reed Elsevier PLC | REL | Media | 100 | 6871.8 | 10 | 8.57m | 18/04/06 | 31/12 | www.reedelsevier.com |
| Regent Inns PLC | REG | Travel & Leisure | S-Cap | 87.8 | 50 | 490k | 22/11/05 | 02/07 | www.regentinns.co.uk |
| Regus Group PLC | RGU | Support Services | Mid 250 | 920.8 | 2 | 5.92m | 22/05/06 | 31/12 | www.regus.com |
| Renishaw PLC | RSW | Electronic & Electrical Equipment | Mid 250 | 552.8 | 2 | 108k | 14/10/05 | 30/06 | www.renishaw.com |
| Renold PLC | RNO | Industrial Engineering | Fledge | 43.7 | 10 | 160k | 21/07/05 | 31/03 | www.renold.com |
| Renovo Group PLC | RNVO | Pharmaceuticals & Biotechnology | S-Cap | 183.8 | 1 | | 01/08/06 | 31/03 | www.renovo.com |
| Rensburg Sheppards PLC | RBG | General Financial | S-Cap | 279.7 | 150 | 56.6k | 18/05/06 | 31/12 | www.rensburgsheppards.co.uk |
| Rentokil Initial PLC | RTO | Support Services | 100 | 2974.1 | 50 | 11.1m | 17/07/06 | 31/12 | www.rentokil-initial.com |
| Resolution PLC | RSL | Life Insurance | Mid 250 | 2070.9 | 15 | 3.87m | 24/05/06 | 01/01 | www.resolutionplc.com |
| Restaurant Group (The) PLC | RTN | Travel & Leisure | S-Cap | 417.2 | 10 | 677k | 29/04/05 | 31/12 | www.trgplc.com |
| Retail Decisions PLC | RTD | Software & Computer Services | S-Cap | 131.6 | 200 | 431k | 27/04/06 | 31/12 | www.redplc.com |
| Reuters Group PLC | RTR | Media | 100 | 5003.5 | 50 | 15.4m | 05/05/05 | 31/12 | www.reuters.com |
| REXAM PLC | REX | General Industrials | 100 | 2803.4 | | 4.53m | 05/05/05 | 31/12 | www.rexam.com |
| REXAM PLC | REXB | General Industrials | 100 | | | | | | www.rexam.com |
| RHM PLC | RHM | Food Producers | Mid 250 | 989.0 | 75 | 4.39m | 15/08/05 | 30/04 | www.rhm.com |
| Ricardo PLC | RCDO | Support Services | S-Cap | 140.1 | 3 | 463 | 04/11/05 | 30/06 | www.ricardo.com |
| Rightmove PLC | RMV | Media | Mid 250 | 350.8 | 3 | 182k | 30/04/05 | 31/12 | www.rightmove.co.uk |
| Rio Tinto PLC | RIO | Mining | 100 | 28386.6 | 75 | 10.0m | 12/04/06 | 31/12 | www.riotinto.com |
| RM PLC | RM. | Software & Computer Services | S-Cap | 151.3 | 5 | 138k | 23/01/06 | 30/09 | www.rm.com |
| Robert Walters PLC | RWA | Support Services | S-Cap | 172.7 | 3 | 304k | 05/05/05 | 31/12 | www.robertwalters.com |
| Robert Wiseman Dairies PLC | RWD | Food Producers | S-Cap | 285.3 | 1 | 119k | 06/07/06 | 01/04 | www.wiseman-dairies.co.uk |
| ROK PLC | ROK | Construction & Materials | S-Cap | 161.5 | 2 | 70.4k | 28/04/05 | 31/12 | www.rokgroup.com |
| Rolls-Royce Group PLC | RR. | Aerospace & Defense | 100 | 7475.3 | 200 | 17.8m | 03/05/06 | 31/12 | www.rolls-royce.com |

Source: Hemscott (Hemscott.com)

## Listed Companies

| Company Name | EPIC | Sector | Index | Capital (£m) | NMS | 200D Avg Vol | AGM | Year End | URL |
|---|---|---|---|---|---|---|---|---|---|
| Rolls-Royce Group PLC | RR.B | Aerospace & Defense | 100 | 2.7 | 0.5 | 18.4m | 03/05/06 | 31/12 | www.rolls-royce.com |
| Ross Group PLC | RGP | Electronic & Electrical Equipment | Fledge | | | 25.7k | 22/07/05 | 31/12 | www.ross-group.co.uk |
| Rotork PLC | ROR | Industrial Engineering | Mid 250 | 626.6 | 5 | 446k | 21/04/06 | 31/12 | www.rotork.com |
| Royal & Sun Alliance Insurance Group PLC | RSA | Nonlife Insurance | 100 | 3952.6 | 200 | 27.7m | 22/05/06 | 31/12 | www.royal-and-sunalliance.com |
| Royal Bank of Scotland Group (The) PLC | RBS | Banks | 100 | 55619.1 | 200 | 15.5m | 28/04/06 | 31/12 | www.rbs.com |
| Royal Dutch Shell PLC | RDSB | Oil & Gas Producers | 100 | 53807.5 | 100 | 10.7m | 16/05/06 | 31/12 | www.shell.com |
| Royal Dutch Shell PLC | RDSA | Oil & Gas Producers | 100 | | | 8.04m | 16/05/06 | 31/12 | www.shell.com |
| royalblue Group PLC | RYB | Software & Computer Services | S-Cap | 268.9 | 1 | 49.4k | 25/04/06 | 31/12 | www.royalblue.com |
| RPC Group PLC | RPC | General Industrials | S-Cap | 228.6 | 5 | 225k | 19/07/06 | 31/03 | www.rpc-group.com |
| RPS Group PLC | RPS | Support Services | Mid 250 | 437.2 | 10 | 1.11m | 25/05/06 | 31/12 | www.rpsgroup.com |
| Ryanair Holdings PLC | RYA | Travel & Leisure | 100 | 3894.7 | 25 | 4.56m | 22/09/05 | 31/03 | www.ryanair.com |
| S & U PLC | SUS | General Financial | Fledge | 67.5 | 0.5 | 3.42k | 19/05/06 | 31/01 | www.suplc.co.uk |
| SABMiller PLC | SAB | Beverages | 100 | 15308.0 | 75 | 5.69m | 28/07/06 | 31/03 | www.sabmiller.com |
| Safeland PLC | SAF | Real Estate | Fledge | 17.7 | 0.5 | 9.89k | 22/09/05 | 31/03 | www.safeland.co.uk |
| Sage Group (The) PLC | SGE | Software & Computer Services | 100 | 2872.3 | 100 | 9.32m | 02/03/06 | 30/09 | www.sage.com |
| Sainsbury (J) PLC | SBRY | Food & Drug Retailers | 100 | 6056.9 | 150 | 14.0m | 12/07/06 | 25/03 | www.j-sainsburys.co.uk |
| Sainsbury (J) PLC | SBRB | Food & Drug Retailers | 100 | | | 7.05k | 12/07/06 | 25/03 | www.j-sainsburys.co.uk |
| Salvesen (Christian) PLC | SVC | Industrial Transportation | S-Cap | 189.7 | 10 | 463k | 13/07/06 | 31/03 | www.salvesen.com |
| Sanctuary Group (The) PLC | SGP | Media | Fledge | 41.1 | 50 | 1.43m | 28/04/06 | 30/09 | www.sanctuarygroup.com |
| Savills PLC | SVS | Real Estate | Mid 250 | 694.3 | 5 | 474k | 04/05/05 | 31/12 | www.savills.com |
| Scapa Group PLC | SCPA | Chemicals | Fledge | 30.4 | 10 | 326k | 25/07/06 | 31/03 | www.scapa.com |
| Scarborough Minerals PLC | SCRB | Mining | Fledge | 63.4 | 0.5 | 116k | 27/03/06 | 30/09 | www.gr-plc.com |
| Schroders PLC | SDR | General Financial | 100 | 2160.2 | 15 | 1.32m | 26/04/06 | 31/12 | www.schroders.com |
| Schroders PLC | SDRC | General Financial | 100 | | | 266k | 26/04/06 | 31/12 | www.schroders.com |
| SCI Entertainment Group PLC | SEG | Software & Computer Services | Mid 250 | 338.0 | 15 | 811k | 13/02/06 | 30/06 | www.sci.co.uk |
| Scott Wilson Group PLC | SWG | Support Services | S-Cap | 147.0 | 5 | | | 30/04 | www.scottwilson.com |
| Scottish & Newcastle PLC | SCTN | Beverages | 100 | 4976.7 | 75 | 5.51m | 27/04/06 | 31/12 | www.scottish-newcastle.com |
| Scottish & Southern Energy PLC | SSE | Electricity | 100 | 10573.1 | 75 | 4.52m | 27/07/06 | 31/03 | www.scottish-southern.co.uk |
| Scottish Power PLC | SPW | Electricity | 100 | 9027.2 | 100 | 14.0m | 26/07/06 | 31/03 | www.scottishpower.com |
| Scottish Power PLC | SPWB | Electricity | 100 | | | | 26/07/06 | 31/03 | www.scottishpower.com |
| ScS Upholstery PLC | SUY | General Retailers | S-Cap | 163.7 | 1 | 63.8k | 06/02/06 | 30/09 | www.scssofas.co.uk |
| SDL PLC | SDL | Software & Computer Services | S-Cap | 134.4 | 2 | 232k | 28/04/05 | 31/12 | www.sdl.com |
| Senior PLC | SNR | Industrial Engineering | S-Cap | 212.0 | 10 | 563k | 28/04/06 | 31/12 | www.seniorplc.com |
| Serco Group PLC | SRP | Support Services | Mid 250 | 1551.9 | 50 | 2.90m | 29/04/05 | 31/12 | www.serco.com |
| ServicePower Technologies PLC | SVR | Software & Computer Services | Fledge | 17.4 | 5 | 155k | 25/05/06 | 31/12 | www.servicepower.com |
| Severfield-Rowen PLC | SFR | Industrial Engineering | S-Cap | 278.5 | 1 | 82.7k | 15/06/06 | 31/12 | www.sfrplc.com |
| Severn Trent PLC | SVT | Gas; Water & Multiutilities | 100 | 4394.7 | 50 | 2.55m | 25/07/06 | 31/03 | www.severntrent.com |
| Severn Trent PLC | SVTB | Gas; Water & Multiutilities | 100 | | | 1.17k | 25/07/06 | 31/03 | www.severntrent.com |
| Shaftesbury PLC | SHB | Real Estate | Mid 250 | 740.9 | 10 | 496k | 01/02/06 | 30/09 | www.shaftesbury.co.uk |
| Shanks Group PLC | SKS | Support Services | Mid 250 | 406.5 | 15 | 1.07m | 07/07/06 | 31/03 | www.shanks.co.uk |
| Shire PLC | SHP | Pharmaceuticals & Biotechnology | 100 | 4286.3 | 25 | 4.72m | 07/07/06 | 31/12 | www.shire.com |
| SHL Group PLC | SHL | Support Services | S-Cap | 74.8 | 2 | 128k | 12/05/06 | 31/12 | www.shl.com |
| Shore Capital Group PLC | SGR | General Financial | S-Cap | 143.5 | 5 | 235k | 22/05/06 | 31/12 | www.shorecap.co.uk |
| SIG PLC | SHI | Support Services | Mid 250 | 1105.3 | 10 | 532k | 10/05/06 | 31/12 | www.sigplc.co.uk |

Source: Hemscott (Hemscott.com)

# Listed Companies

| Company Name | EPIC | Sector | Index | Capital (£m) | NMS | 200D Avg Vol | AGM | Year End | URL |
|---|---|---|---|---|---|---|---|---|---|
| Signet Group PLC | SIG | General Retailers | Mid 250 | 2004.9 | 200 | 13.3m | 09/06/06 | 28/01 | www.signetgroupplc.com |
| Simon Group PLC | SMON | Industrial Transportation | S-Cap | 97.4 | 5 | 252k | 26/05/06 | 31/12 | www.simongrp.co.uk |
| Sinclair (William) Holdings PLC | SNCL | Household Goods | Fledge | 7.4 | 0.5 | 13.7k | 09/11/05 | 30/06 | www.william-sinclair.co.uk |
| SkyePharma PLC | SKP | Pharmaceuticals & Biotechnology | S-Cap | 171.5 | 100 | 6.42m | 28/06/06 | 31/12 | www.skyepharma.com |
| Slough Estates PLC | SLOU | Real Estate | 100 | 3094.8 | 25 | 2.43m | 16/05/06 | 31/12 | www.sloughestates.com |
| S'mart (J) & Co (Contractors) PLC | SMJ | Real Estate | Fledge | 75.6 | 0.5 | 1.49k | 15/12/05 | 31/07 | www.jsmart.plc.uk |
| SMG PLC | SMG | Media | S-Cap | 231.6 | 25 | 970k | 26/05/06 | 31/12 | www.smg.plc.uk |
| Smith & Nephew PLC | SN. | Health Care Equipment & Services | 100 | 4150.2 | 150 | 8.75m | 27/04/06 | 31/12 | www.smith-nephew.com |
| Smith (DS) PLC | SMDS | General Industrials | Mid 250 | 561.0 | 50 | 3.25m | 05/09/05 | 30/04 | www.dssmith.uk.com |
| Smiths Group PLC | SMIN | Aerospace & Defense | 100 | 4976.1 | 75 | 4.84m | 15/11/05 | 31/07 | www.smiths-group.com |
| SOCO International PLC | SIA | Oil & Gas Producers | Mid 250 | 950.3 | 2 | 332k | 15/06/06 | 31/12 | www.socointernational.co.uk |
| Sondex PLC | SDX | Oil Equipment; Services & Dist | S-Cap | 169.8 | 5 | 238k | 28/06/06 | 28/02 | www.sondex.co.uk |
| Spectris PLC | SXS | Electronic & Electrical Equipment | Mid 250 | 528.5 | 15 |  |  |  |  |
| Speedy Hire PLC | SDY | Support Services | Mid 250 | 741.9 | 10 | 645k | 11/05/05 | 31/12 | www.spectris.com |
| Sperati (C.A.) (Special Agency) PLC | SPR | Personal Goods | Mid 250 | 403.0 | 2 | 102k | 18/07/06 | 31/03 | www.speedyhire.plc.uk |
|  |  |  |  | 1.0 |  | 1.53 | 09/03/05 | 31/10 |  |
| Spirax-Sarco Engineering PLC | SPX | Industrial Engineering | Mid 250 | 660.3 | 3 | 241k | 12/05/06 | 31/12 | www.spiraxsarcoengineering.com |
| Spirent Communications PLC | SPT | Technology Hardware & Equipment | Mid 250 | 386.6 | 150 | 9.27m | 03/05/06 | 31/12 | www.spirent.com |
| Sportech PLC | SPO | Travel & Leisure | Fledge | 59.2 | 15 | 553k | 31/05/06 | 06/01 | www.sportechplc.com |
| Spring Group PLC | SRG | Support Services | S-Cap | 82.8 | 10 | 179k | 30/03/06 | 31/12 | www.spring.com |
| SSL International PLC | SSL | Personal Goods | Mid 250 | 574.7 | 25 | 1.43m | 20/06/06 | 31/03 | www.ssl-international.com |
| St Ives PLC | SIV | Support Services | S-Cap | 219.4 | 10 | 402k | 29/11/05 | 29/07 | www.st-ives.co.uk |
| St James's Place PLC | STJ | Life Insurance | Mid 250 | 1434.3 | 25 | 1.15m | 09/05/06 | 31/12 | www.sjpc.co.uk |
| St Modwen Properties PLC | SMP | Real Estate | Mid 250 | 587.0 | 2 | 150k | 21/04/06 | 30/11 | www.stmodwen.co.uk |
| Stagecoach Group PLC | SGC | Travel & Leisure | Mid 250 | 1224.8 | 100 | 7.32m | 26/08/05 | 30/04 | www.stagecoachgroup.com |
| Standard Chartered PLC | STAN | Banks | 100 | 17263.4 | 100 | 8.07m | 04/05/06 | 31/12 | www.standardchartered.com |
| Standard Life PLC | SL. | Life Insurance |  | 5305.9 | 50 |  | 30/04/05 | 31/12 |  |
| Stanelco PLC | SEO | Industrial Engineering | S-Cap | 48.8 | 150 | 3.74m | 22/04/05 | 31/10 | www.stanelcoplc.com |
| Stanley Leisure PLC | SLY | Travel & Leisure | Mid 250 | 422.6 | 10 | 603k | 08/09/05 | 01/05 | www.stanleyleisure.com |
| Stavert Zigomala PLC | STZ | General Financial | Fledge | 2.5 | 1 | 0.5 | 11/11/05 | 31/05 |  |
| Stewart & Wight PLC | STE | Real Estate | Mid 250 | 11.0 | 1 | 80.3 | 21/09/05 | 31/03 |  |
| SThree PLC | STHR | Support Services | Fledge | 427.0 | 10 | 1.09m | 01/03/06 | 30/11 | www.sthree.com |
| Superscape Group PLC | SPS | Software & Computer Services | S-Cap | 23.4 | 50 | 192k | 08/06/06 | 31/01 | www.superscape.com |
| SurfControl PLC | SRF | Software & Computer Services | Fledge | 111.6 | 5 | 534k | 20/10/05 | 30/06 | www.surfcontrol.com |
| Tadpole Technology PLC | TAD | Software & Computer Services |  | 7.0 | 25 |  | 02/08/06 | 30/09 | www.tadpoletechnology.com |
| Tanjong PLC | TNJ | Travel & Leisure | S-Cap | 52.4 | 1 | 68.6k | 19/04/06 | 31/12 | www.tarsus-group.com |
| Tarsus Group PLC | TRS | Media | 100 | 102.5 | 1 | 5.88m | 19/07/06 | 31/03 | www.tateandlyle.com |
| Tate & Lyle PLC | TATE | Food Producers | Mid 250 | 3363.2 | 75 | 3.12m | 10/05/06 | 31/12 | www.tns-global.com |
| Taylor Nelson Sofres PLC | TNN | Media | Mid 250 | 769.5 | 50 | 5.25m | 03/05/06 | 31/12 | www.taylorwoodrow.com |
| Taylor Woodrow PLC | TWOD | Household Goods | Mid 250 | 1982.7 | 75 | 306k | 09/05/05 | 31/12 | www.tdg.eu.com |
| TDG PLC | TDG | Industrial Transportation | S-Cap | 175.5 | 5 | 674 | 09/05/05 | 31/12 | www.tdg.eu.com |
| TDG PLC | TDGB | Industrial Transportation | S-Cap | 219.1 | 1 | 85.8k | 13/06/06 | 28/01 | www.tedbaker.co.uk |
| Ted Baker PLC | TBK | General Retailers | S-Cap | 108.0 | 2 | 370k | 20/10/05 | 30/06 | www.teesland.com |
| Teesland PLC | TLD | Real Estate | S-Cap |  |  |  |  |  |  |

Source: Hemscott (Hemscott.com)

## Listed Companies

| Company Name | EPIC | Sector | Index | Capital (£m) | NMS | 200D Avg Vol | AGM | Year End | URL |
|---|---|---|---|---|---|---|---|---|---|
| Telecom plus PLC | TEP | Fixed Line Telecommunications | S-Cap | 80.0 | 3 | 175k | 12/07/06 | 31/03 | www.telecomplus.co.uk |
| Telent PLC | TLNT | Technology Hardware & Equipment | S-Cap | 300.4 | 10 | 2.43m | 28/11/05 | 31/03 | www.telent.co.uk |
| Telspec PLC | TSP | Technology Hardware & Equipment | Fledge | 2.4 | 3 | 37.7k | 17/05/06 | 31/12 | www.telspec.co.uk |
| Tesco PLC | TSCO | Food & Drug Retailers | 100 | 28755.8 | 200 | 52.4m | 07/07/06 | 25/02 | www.tesco.com/corporate |
| Tex Holdings PLC | TXH | Industrial Engineering | Fledge | 5.9 | 0.5 | 3.66k | 20/06/06 | 31/12 | www.tex-holdings.co.uk |
| Theratase PLC | THE | Pharmaceuticals & Biotechnology | Fledge | 16.5 | 1 | 89.3k | 20/02/06 | 30/09 | www.theratase.com |
| Thorntons PLC | THT | Food & Drug Retailers | S-Cap | 87.4 | 2 | 114k | 12/10/05 | 25/06 | www.thorntons.co.uk |
| Thus Group PLC | THUS | Fixed Line Telecommunications | S-Cap | 224.1 | 5 | 535k | 27/07/05 | 31/03 | www.thus.net |
| Titon Holdings PLC | TON | Construction & Materials | Fledge | 12.3 | 0.5 | 5.43k | 20/02/06 | 30/09 | www.titon.com |
| Tomkins PLC | TOMK | General Industrials | Mid 250 | 2388.5 | 75 | 8.24m | 22/05/06 | 31/12 | www.tomkins.co.uk |
| Topps Tiles PLC | TPT | General Retailers | Mid 250 | 415.2 | 15 | 1.04m | 10/01/06 | 01/10 | www.toppstiles.co.uk |
| Torotrak PLC | TRK | Automobiles & Parts | Fledge | 33.3 | 10 | 352k | 20/07/06 | 31/03 | www.torotrak.com |
| Total Systems PLC | TTS | Software & Computer Services | Fledge | 3.8 | 0.5 | 3.51k | 08/08/05 | 31/03 | www.totalsystems.co.uk |
| Town Centre Securities PLC | TCSC | Real Estate | S-Cap | 300.7 | 0.5 | 23.1k | 23/11/05 | 30/06 | www.tcs-plc.com |
| Trace Group PLC | TCC | Software & Computer Services | Fledge | 13.9 | 0.5 | 8.94k | 25/11/05 | 31/05 | www.tracegroup.com |
| Trafficmaster PLC | TFC | Media | Fledge | 61.4 | 15 | 942k | 20/06/06 | 31/12 | www.trafficmaster.co.uk |
| Travis Perkins PLC | TPK | Support Services | Mid 250 | 1923.7 | 15 | 1.13m | 24/04/06 | 31/12 | www.travisperkins.co.uk |
| Treatt PLC | TET | Chemicals | Fledge | 33.2 | 0.5 | 5.60k | 27/02/06 | 30/09 | www.treatt.com |
| Triad Group PLC | TRD | Software & Computer Services | Fledge | 3.6 | 0.5 | 5.32k | 26/07/06 | 31/03 | www.triad.co.uk |
| Tribal Group PLC | TRB | Support Services | S-Cap | 149.7 | 3 | 196k | 28/07/06 | 31/03 | www.tribalgroup.co.uk |
| Trifast PLC | TRI | Industrial Engineering | Fledge | 44.9 | 3 | 215k | 20/09/05 | 31/03 | www.trfastenings.com |
| Trinity Mirror PLC | TNI | Media | Mid 250 | 1360.0 | 50 | 3.09m | 04/05/06 | 01/01 | www.trinitymirror.com |
| TT electronics PLC | TTG | Electronic & Electrical Equipment | S-Cap | 274.0 | 10 | 347k | 18/05/05 | 31/12 | www.ttelectronics.com |
| TTP Communications PLC | TTC | Technology Hardware & Equipment | Fledge | 100.9 | 50 | 1.03m | 21/07/05 | 31/03 | www.ttpcom.com |
| Tullow Oil PLC | TLW | Oil & Gas Producers | Mid 250 | 2624.6 | 50 | 5.21m | 31/05/06 | 31/12 | www.tullowoil.com |
| UCM Group PLC | UCM | Chemicals | Fledge | 12.7 | 0.5 | 26.5k | 01/06/06 | 31/12 | www.ucm-group.com |
| UK Coal PLC | UKC | Mining | S-Cap | 288.1 | 15 | 968k | 02/04/06 | 31/12 | www.ukcoal.com |
| Ultra Electronics Holdings PLC | ULE | Aerospace & Defense | Mid 250 | 660.4 | 5 | 259k | 27/04/06 | 31/12 | www.ultra-electronics.com |
| Ultraframe PLC | UTF | Construction & Materials | Fledge | 29.5 | 5 | 435k | 07/02/06 | 30/09 | www.ir.ultraframe.com |
| UMBRO PLC | UMB | Personal Goods | S-Cap | 210.7 | 15 | 576k | 17/05/06 | 31/12 | www.umbro.com |
| UMECO PLC | UMC | Aerospace & Defense | S-Cap | 211.4 | 2 | 85.3k | 25/07/06 | 31/03 | www.umeco.com |
| Unilever PLC | ULVR | Food Producers | 100 | 15774.3 | 75 | 7.31m | 19/05/06 | 31/12 | www.unilever.com |
| Uniq PLC | UNIQ | Food Producers | S-Cap | 195.2 | 10 | 384k | 21/07/06 | 31/03 | www.uniq.com |
| UNITE Group PLC | UTG | Real Estate | Mid 250 | 522.6 | 10 | 538k | 10/05/06 | 31/12 | www.unite-group.co.uk |
| United Business Media PLC | UBM | Media | Mid 250 | 1633.9 | 25 | 2.62m | 04/05/06 | 31/12 | www.unitedbusinessmedia.com |
| United Drug PLC | UDG | Health Care Equipment & Services | 100 | 522.3 | 3 | 103k | 21/02/06 | 30/09 | www.united-drug.ie |
| United Utilities PLC | UU. | Gas; Water & Multiutilities | 100 | 5796.1 | 75 | 5.86m | 28/07/06 | 31/03 | www.unitedutilities.com |
| United Utilities PLC | UU.A | Gas; Water & Multiutilities | 100 | | 1 | 2.13m | 28/07/06 | 31/03 | www.unitedutilities.com |
| Universal Salvage PLC | UVS | Support Services | Fledge | 33.7 | 1 | 26.1k | 28/09/05 | 30/04 | www.universal-services.co.uk |
| UTV PLC | UTV | Media | S-Cap | 192.8 | 3 | 152k | 26/05/06 | 31/12 | www.utvplc.com |
| Vanco PLC | VAN | Fixed Line Telecommunications | S-Cap | 287.9 | 3 | 137k | 26/06/06 | 31/01 | www.vanco.info |
| Vedanta Resources PLC | VED | Mining | 100 | 3611.1 | 25 | 3.64m | 02/08/06 | 31/03 | www.vedantaresources.com |
| VEGA Group PLC | VEG | Software & Computer Services | Fledge | 44.6 | 1 | 41.4k | 08/09/05 | 30/04 | www.vega-group.com |
| Venture Production PLC | VPC | Oil & Gas Producers | Mid 250 | 1086.5 | 10 | 910k | 07/06/06 | 31/12 | www.vpc.co.uk |

Source: Hemscott (Hemscott.com)

## Listed Companies

| Company Name | EPIC | Sector | Index | Capital (£m) | NMS | 200D Avg Vol | AGM | Year End | URL |
|---|---|---|---|---|---|---|---|---|---|
| Vernalis PLC | VER | Pharmaceuticals & Biotechnology | S-Cap | 209.9 | 10 | 511k | 24/05/06 | 31/12 | www.vernalis.com |
| Victoria PLC | VCP | Household Goods | Fledge | 13.8 | 0.5 | 6.16k | 07/08/06 | 01/04 | www.victoria.plc.uk |
| Victrex PLC | VCT | Chemicals | Mid 250 | 583.4 | 5 | 362k | 07/02/06 | 30/09 | www.victrex.com |
| Viridian Group PLC | VRD | Electricity | Mid 250 | 1217.3 | 5 | 577k | 07/07/06 | 31/03 | www.viridiangroup.co.uk |
| Vislink PLC | VLK | Technology Hardware & Equipment | Fledge | 95.0 | 5 | 602k | 24/05/06 | 31/12 | www.vislink.co.uk |
| Vitec Group (The) PLC | VTC | Industrial Engineering | S-Cap | 193.5 | 2 | 84.0k | 24/05/06 | 31/12 | www.vitecgroup.com |
| Vodafone Group PLC | VOD | Mobile Telecommunications | 100 | 67858.4 | 200 | 429m | 25/07/06 | 31/03 | www.vodafone.com |
| Volex Group PLC | VLX | Electronic & Electrical Equipment | Fledge | 56.6 | 3 | 134k | 08/09/05 | 02/04 | www.volex.com |
| Vp PLC | VP. | Support Services | S-Cap | 127.9 | 1 | 50.6k | 08/09/05 | 31/03 | www.vpplc.com |
| VT Group PLC | VTG | Aerospace & Defense | Mid 250 | 848.7 | 15 | 1.19m | 26/07/06 | 31/03 | www.vtplc.com |
| W H Smith PLC | SMWH | General Retailers | Mid 250 | 866.0 | 15 | 1.54m | 02/02/06 | 31/08 | www.whsmithplc.com |
| Wagon PLC | WAGN | Automobiles & Parts | S-Cap | 329.4 | 3 | 183k | 21/07/06 | 31/03 | www.wagonplc.com |
| Walker; Crips; Weddle; Beck PLC | WCW | General Financial | Fledge | 36.0 | 0.5 | 4.81k | 14/07/06 | 31/03 | www.wcwb.co.uk |
| Warner Estate Holdings PLC | WNER | Real Estate | S-Cap | 379.3 | 1 | 98.0k | 08/09/05 | 31/03 | www.warnerestate.co.uk |
| Waterford Wedgwood PLC | WTFU | Household Goods | S-Cap | 162.7 | 25 | 4.43m | 20/10/05 | 31/03 | www.waterfordwedgwood.com |
| Waterman Group PLC | WTM | Support Services | Fledge | 38.9 | 1 | 44.5k | 06/12/05 | 30/06 | www.waterman-group.co.uk |
| Watermark Group PLC | WMK | Support Services | Fledge | 22.1 | 3 | 118k | 29/06/06 | 31/12 | www.watermark.co.uk |
| Weir Group PLC | WEIR | Industrial Engineering | Mid 250 | 872.5 | 25 | 1.48m | 10/05/06 | 30/12 | www.weir.co.uk |
| Wellington Underwriting PLC | WUN | Nonlife Insurance | Mid 250 | 432.1 | 50 | 3.34m | 07/06/06 | 31/12 | www.wellington.co.uk |
| Wetherspoon (J D) PLC | JDW | Travel & Leisure | Mid 250 | 674.5 | 15 | 1.05m | 10/11/05 | 24/07 | www.jdwetherspoon.co.uk |
| Whatman PLC | WHM | Health Care Equipment & Services | Mid 250 | 388.4 | 10 | 626k | 25/05/06 | 31/12 | www.whatman.com |
| Whitbread PLC | WTB | Travel & Leisure | Mid 250 | 2719.1 | 25 | 2.34m | 20/06/06 | 02/03 | www.whitbread.co.uk |
| White Young Green PLC | WHY | Support Services | S-Cap | 154.8 | 2 | 43.2k | 08/11/05 | 30/06 | www.wyg.com |
| William Hill PLC | WMH | Travel & Leisure | Mid 250 | 2168.0 | 75 | 4.52m | 18/05/06 | 27/12 | www.williamhillplc.co.uk |
| Wilmington Group PLC | WIL | Media | S-Cap | 139.2 | 3 | 184k | 09/11/05 | 30/06 | www.wilmington.co.uk |
| Wilson Bowden PLC | WLB | Household Goods | Mid 250 | 1512.5 | 5 | 446k | 26/04/06 | 31/12 | www.wilsonbowden.plc.uk |
| Wimpey (George) PLC | WMPY | Household Goods | Mid 250 | 1835.0 | 50 | 4.44m | 20/04/06 | 31/12 | www.georgewimpeyplc.co.uk |
| Wincanton PLC | WIN | Industrial Transportation | Mid 250 | 386.0 | 10 | 431k | 20/07/06 | 31/03 | www.wincanton.co.uk |
| Windsor PLC | WNDR | Nonlife Insurance | Fledge | 24.2 | 3 | 124k | 08/02/06 | 30/09 | www.windsor.co.uk |
| Wolfson Microelectronics PLC | WLF | Technology Hardware & Equipment | Mid 250 | 514.9 | 15 | 1.75m | 21/04/05 | 31/12 | www.wolfsonmicro.com |
| Wolseley PLC | WOS | Support Services | 100 | 6529.2 | 50 | 4.39m | 17/11/05 | 31/07 | www.wolseley.com |
| Wolverhampton & Dudley Breweries PLC | WOLV | Travel & Leisure | Mid 250 | 1002.2 | 5 | 334k | 20/01/06 | 01/10 | www.wdb.co.uk |
| Woolworths Group PLC | WLW | General Retailers | Mid 250 | 473.6 | 200 | 21.7m | 14/06/06 | 28/01 | www.woolworthsgroupplc.com |
| Workspace Group PLC | WKP | Real Estate | Mid 250 | 642.4 | 10 | 840k | 01/08/06 | 31/03 | www.workspacegroup.co.uk |
| World Trade Systems PLC | WTS | General Financial | Fledge | 3.3 | 0.5 | 1.31k | 21/01/06 | 30/09 | www.worldtradesystems.com |
| Worthington Group PLC | WRN | Personal Goods | Fledge | | 0.5 | 12.1k | 04/08/06 | 31/03 | |
| WPP Group PLC | WPP | Media | 100 | 7590.2 | 100 | 10.1m | 27/06/06 | 31/12 | www.wpp.com |
| WSP Group PLC | WSH | Support Services | S-Cap | 261.1 | 3 | 177k | 03/05/05 | 31/12 | www.wspgroup.com |
| Xaar PLC | XAR | Electronic & Electrical Equipment | S-Cap | 71.7 | 3 | 229k | 24/04/06 | 31/12 | www.xaar.co.uk |
| Xansa PLC | XAN | Software & Computer Services | S-Cap | 234.0 | 25 | 1.23m | 15/09/05 | 30/04 | www.xansa.com |
| XP Power PLC | XPP | Electronic & Electrical Equipment | Fledge | 78.9 | 1 | 72.0k | 20/04/06 | 31/12 | www.xppower.com |
| Xstrata PLC | XTA | Mining | 100 | 14620.3 | 75 | 7.81m | 09/05/05 | 31/12 | www.xstrata.com |
| Yell Group PLC | YELL | Media | 100 | 3968.0 | 75 | 6.08m | 20/07/06 | 31/03 | www.yellgroup.com |
| Yule Catto & Co PLC | YULC | Chemicals | S-Cap | 327.0 | 10 | 547k | 18/05/06 | 31/12 | www.yulecatto.com |
| Zetex PLC | ZTX | Technology Hardware & Equipment | S-Cap | 71.1 | 5 | 209k | 22/04/05 | 31/12 | www.zetex.com |
| Zotefoams PLC | ZTF | Chemicals | Fledge | 34.0 | 0.5 | 24.6k | 16/05/06 | 31/12 | www.zotefoams.com |

Source: Hemscott (Hemscott.com)

- Listed Investment Trusts

# Listed Investment Trusts

| Company Name | EPIC | Index | Capital (£m) | NMS | 200D Avg Vol | AGM | Year End | URL |
|---|---|---|---|---|---|---|---|---|
| Aberdeen Asian Income Fund Ltd | AAIF | | 105.3 | 10 | | | | www.asian-smaller.co.uk |
| Aberdeen Asian Smaller Companies Inv Tr PLC | AAS | Fledge | 87.0 | 1 | 47.4k | 23/11/05 | 31/07 | |
| Aberdeen Development Capital PLC | AVC | Fledge | 13.1 | 2 | 59.7k | 30/09/05 | 31/05 | www.developmentcap.co.uk |
| Aberdeen Growth Opportunities VCT 2 PLC | ABGO | | 8.0 | 0.5 | 210 | 22/05/06 | 31/12 | www.aberdeen-asset.com |
| Aberdeen Growth Opportunities VCT PLC | AGW | | 8.5 | 0.5 | 2.71k | 26/04/06 | 30/11 | www.aberdeen-asset.com |
| Aberdeen Growth VCT I PLC | AGV | S-Cap | 11.5 | 0.5 | 7.61k | 14/06/06 | 31/01 | www.aberdeen-asset.com |
| Aberdeen New Dawn Investment Trust PLC | ABD | Fledge | 110.6 | 1 | 69.7k | 23/08/05 | 30/04 | www.newdawn-trust.co.uk |
| Aberdeen New Thai Investment Trust PLC | ANW | | 25.7 | 0.5 | 39.1k | 20/06/06 | 28/02 | www.newthai-trust.co.uk |
| Aberforth Geared Capital & Income Trust PLC | AFHI | | 27.9 | 3 | 33.1k | 01/03/06 | 31/12 | www.aberforth.co.uk |
| Aberforth Smaller Companies Trust PLC | ASL | Mid 250 | 633.4 | 1 | 166k | 01/03/06 | 31/12 | www.aberforth.co.uk |
| Accelerated Return Fund (The) Ltd | ACF | | 38.8 | 3 | 50.2k | 13/07/05 | 31/03 | www.closefm.com |
| AcenciA Debt Strategies Ltd | ACD | | 66.9 | 1 | | | | www.acencia.co.uk |
| Acorn Income Fund Ltd | AIF | | 52.6 | 10 | 68.6k | 26/06/06 | 31/12 | |
| ACP Mezzanine Ltd | ACPM | | 71.9 | 5 | | | | www.ci.collins-stewart.com |
| Active Capital Trust PLC | AIT | S-Cap | 64.3 | 5 | 260k | 11/10/05 | 31/05 | www.fandc.com |
| Advance Developing Markets Trust PLC | ADD | S-Cap | 230.8 | 1 | 81.4k | 19/10/05 | 31/05 | www.pro-asset.com |
| Advance UK Trust PLC | ADU | Fledge | 80.7 | 0.5 | 57.1k | 14/12/05 | 31/08 | www.pro-asset.com |
| AIM Distribution Trust (The) PLC | AMD | | 9.8 | 0.5 | 7.09k | 06/07/06 | 31/03 | |
| AIM VCT (The) PLC | AIV | | 11.0 | 1 | 12.9k | 28/03/06 | 30/11 | www.theaimvct.co.uk |
| AIM VCT2 PLC | AIC | | 24.6 | 0.5 | 28.7k | 29/03/06 | 30/11 | www.friendsis.com |
| Albany Investment Trust PLC | ABNY | Fledge | 32.1 | 5 | 5.21k | 11/07/06 | 28/02 | |
| Aldgate Capital PLC | AGT | | 7.1 | 10 | | | | |
| Alliance Trust PLC | ATST | Mid 250 | 2301.3 | 0.5 | 668k | 10/05/06 | 31/01 | www.alliancetrusts.com |
| Allianz Dresdner 2nd Endow Policy Tr (2006) PLC | ADR | Fledge | 33.9 | 0.5 | 17.0k | 14/12/05 | 30/09 | www.allianzdresdneram.co.uk |
| Allianz Dresdner 2nd Endow Policy Tr (2009) PLC | ADRK | Fledge | 23.6 | 0.5 | 30.5k | 14/12/05 | 30/09 | www.allianzdresdneram.co.uk |
| Allianz Dresdner Endowment Policy Trust 2010 PLC | AZD | Fledge | 24.3 | 10 | 47.8k | 02/11/05 | 30/06 | www.allianzdresdneram.co.uk |
| Alpha Pyrenees Trust Ltd | ALPH | S-Cap | 121.4 | 1 | | | | www.alphapyreneestrust.com |
| Alternative Asset Opportunities Ltd | TLI | | 46.8 | 3 | | | | |
| Alternative Investment Strategies Ltd | AIS | S-Cap | 212.6 | 3 | | 28/02/06 | 31/10 | www.aisinvest.com |
| American Opportunity Trust PLC | AOP | Fledge | 17.3 | 1 | 243k | 15/06/06 | 31/01 | www.johcm.co.uk |
| Anglo & Overseas PLC | AOT | S-Cap | 96.1 | 3 | 3.23k | 24/05/06 | 31/01 | www.edinburghpartners.co.uk |
| Arc Growth Company VCT PLC | AGCV | | 1.6 | 1 | 92.5k | | | |
| Artemis AiM VCT 2 PLC | AAM | | 41.2 | 0.5 | | 12/01/06 | 30/09 | www.artemisfunds.com |
| Artemis AiM VCT PLC | AAV | | 35.0 | 0.5 | 108 | 30/05/06 | 31/01 | www.artemisonline.com |
| Artemis Alpha Trust PLC | ATS | Fledge | 67.0 | 1 | 25.3k | 12/09/05 | 30/04 | www.artemisonline.co.uk |
| Asset Management Investment Company PLC | AMN | Fledge | 17.6 | 2 | 47.1k | 07/02/06 | 30/09 | www.amicplc.com |
| Athelney Trust PLC | ATY | | 2.3 | 0.5 | 82.3k | 24/05/06 | 31/12 | |
| Atlantis Japan Growth Fund Ltd | AJG | | 269.4 | 0.5 | 569 | 26/09/05 | 30/04 | www.atlantis-investment.com |
| August Equity Trust PLC | AGE | Fledge | 71.4 | 1 | 29.5k | 06/05/05 | 31/12 | www.kleinwortcapital.com |
| Aurora Investment Trust PLC | ARR | Fledge | 32.3 | 0.5 | 65.4k | 01/08/06 | 28/02 | |
| Avanti Capital PLC | AVA | | 10.5 | 1 | 32.8k | 28/11/05 | 30/06 | www.avanticap.com |
| Avarae Global Coins PLC | AVR | | 8.9 | 5 | 16.0k | | | www.gifm.com |
| AXA Property Trust Ltd | APT | S-Cap | 106.8 | 5 | 213k | | | |
| Baillie Gifford Japan Trust (The) PLC | BGFD | S-Cap | 144.9 | 5 | 236k | 06/12/05 | 31/08 | www.bailliegifford.com |

Source: Hemscott (Hemscott.com)

## Listed Investment Trusts

| Company Name | EPIC | Index | Capital (£m) | NMS | 200D Avg Vol | AGM | Year End | URL |
|---|---|---|---|---|---|---|---|---|
| Baillie Gifford Shin Nippon PLC | BGS | Fledge | 62.5 | 2 | 62.2k | 28/04/05 | 31/01 | www.bailliegifford.com |
| Bankers Investment Trust PLC | BNKR | Mid 250 | 426.1 | 3 | 149k | 24/02/06 | 31/10 | www.itshenderson.com |
| Barclays Global Investors Endowment Fund II Ltd | BIF | | 27.2 | 0.5 | 20.6k | 15/12/05 | 31/08 | www.barclaysglobal.com |
| Baring Emerging Europe PLC | BEE | S-Cap | 282.6 | 2 | 98.8k | 26/01/06 | 30/09 | www.bee-plc.com |
| Baronsmead AIM VCT PLC | BAV | | 10.1 | | | | | |
| Baronsmead VCT 2 PLC | BVT | | 41.1 | 0.5 | 11.7k | 19/06/06 | 31/03 | www.fandc.com |
| Baronsmead VCT 3 PLC | BMD | | 36.0 | 0.5 | 16.0k | 16/03/06 | 31/12 | www.fandc.com |
| Baronsmead VCT 4 PLC | BNS | | 33.9 | 0.5 | 7.94k | 09/03/06 | 31/12 | www.baronsmeadvct4.co.uk |
| Baronsmead VCT PLC | BDV | | 35.6 | 0.5 | 11.8k | 05/12/05 | 30/09 | www.fandc.com |
| Bidtimes PLC | BDT | | 0.5 | 2 | 14.8k | 20/09/05 | 28/02 | www.bidtimes.com |
| Billam PLC | BLLM | | 1.9 | 0.5 | 24.0k | 14/07/06 | 31/12 | www.billamplc.co.uk |
| Bionex Investments PLC | BNX | | 3.1 | 3 | 80.2k | 24/01/06 | 30/09 | |
| Blackstar Investors PLC | BLCK | | 40.2 | 1 | 24.6k | 03/08/06 | 31/12 | |
| Blue Chip Value and Income Fund Ltd | BCV | | 16.2 | 5 | 514k | 16/08/05 | 30/04 | www.blu.com |
| Blue Planet Euro Fin Inv Tst PLC | BLP | Fledge | 21.0 | 1 | 50.6k | 04/07/06 | 28/02 | www.blueplanet.eu.com |
| Blue Planet Financials Growth & Inc IT No.1 PLC | BPFA | Fledge | 5.4 | 0.5 | 137 | 02/08/06 | 31/03 | www.blueplanet.eu.com |
| Blue Planet Financials Growth & Inc IT No.10 PLC | BPFS | Fledge | 2.6 | 0.5 | 61.2 | 02/08/06 | 31/03 | www.blueplanet.eu.com |
| Blue Planet Financials Growth & Inc IT No.2 PLC | BPFC | Fledge | 2.6 | 0.5 | 41.2 | 02/08/06 | 31/03 | www.blueplanet.eu.com |
| Blue Planet Financials Growth & Inc IT No.3 PLC | BPFE | Fledge | 2.6 | 0.5 | 51.5 | 02/08/06 | 31/03 | www.blueplanet.eu.com |
| Blue Planet Financials Growth & Inc IT No.4 PLC | BPFG | Fledge | 2.6 | 0.5 | 48.4 | 02/08/06 | 31/03 | www.blueplanet.eu.com |
| Blue Planet Financials Growth & Inc IT No.5 PLC | BPFI | Fledge | 2.6 | 0.5 | 39.7 | 02/08/06 | 31/03 | www.blueplanet.eu.com |
| Blue Planet Financials Growth & Inc IT No.6 PLC | BPFK | Fledge | 2.6 | 0.5 | 48.6 | 02/08/06 | 31/03 | www.blueplanet.eu.com |
| Blue Planet Financials Growth & Inc IT No.7 PLC | BPFM | Fledge | 2.6 | 0.5 | 39.1 | 02/08/06 | 31/03 | www.blueplanet.eu.com |
| Blue Planet Financials Growth & Inc IT No.8 PLC | BPFO | Fledge | 2.6 | 0.5 | 42.1 | 02/08/06 | 31/03 | www.blueplanet.eu.com |
| Blue Planet Financials Growth & Inc IT No.9 PLC | BPFQ | Fledge | 2.6 | 0.5 | 61.5 | 02/08/06 | 31/03 | www.blueplanet.eu.com |
| Blue Planet Worldwide Financials Inv Trust PLC | BPW | Fledge | 22.7 | 1 | 48.6k | 15/11/05 | 31/07 | www.blueplanet.eu.com |
| British & American Investment Trust PLC | BAF | Fledge | 29.0 | 0.5 | 31.3k | 15/06/06 | 31/12 | |
| British Assets Trust PLC | BSET | Mid 250 | 397.2 | 10 | 422k | 19/12/05 | 30/09 | www.british-assets.co.uk |
| British Empire Securities & General Trust PLC | BTEM | Mid 250 | 700.8 | 5 | 294k | 15/12/05 | 30/09 | www.british-empire.co.uk |
| British Portfolio Trust PLC | BPO | Fledge | 70.3 | 0.5 | 34.7k | 10/02/06 | 31/10 | www.allianzglobalinvestors.co.uk |
| British Smaller Companies VCT PLC | BSV | | 11.4 | 0.5 | 7.97k | 01/08/06 | 31/03 | www.yfmprivateequity.co.uk |
| British Smaller Technology Companies VCT 2 PLC | BST | | 7.6 | 0.5 | 6.76k | 10/07/06 | 31/12 | www.yfmprivateequity.co.uk |
| Brunner Investment Trust PLC | BUT | S-Cap | 187.6 | 1 | 39.6k | 23/03/06 | 30/11 | www.brunner.co.uk |
| Caledonia Investments PLC | CLDN | Mid 250 | 1181.5 | 2 | 63.1k | 20/07/06 | 31/03 | www.caledonia.com |
| Caliber Global Investment Ltd | CLBR | | 108.3 | 3 | 86.0k | 09/12/05 | 30/09 | www.caliberglobal.com |
| Candover Investments PLC | CDI | Mid 250 | 379.9 | 1 | 36.6k | 08/05/06 | 31/12 | www.candover.com |
| Capital Gearing Trust PLC | CGT | Fledge | 57.7 | 0.5 | 1.18k | 27/07/06 | 05/04 | |
| Carador PLC | CDO | | 32.9 | 5 | | | | |
| Cayenne Trust (The) PLC | TCT | Fledge | 47.4 | 1 | 51.2k | 20/04/06 | 31/01 | www.cayenneasset.com |
| Chameleon Trust PLC | CHAM | Fledge | 17.2 | 1 | 6.84k | 13/10/05 | 31/05 | |
| Charter Pan-European Trust PLC | CPE | Fledge | 54.8 | 2 | 118k | 21/03/06 | 30/11 | www.charterpaneuropean.co.uk |
| Chelverton Growth Trust PLC | CGW | Fledge | 6.0 | 0.5 | 6.47k | 13/12/05 | 31/08 | www.chelvertonam.com |
| Chrysalis VCT PLC | CYS | | 24.3 | 1 | 14.4k | 23/03/06 | 31/10 | www.downing.co.uk |
| Ciref Ltd | CRF | | 49.7 | 3 | | 31/07/06 | 30/09 | www.ciref.biz |

Source: Hemscott (Hemscott.com)

## Listed Investment Trusts

| Company Name | EPIC | Index | Capital (£m) | NMS | 200D Avg Vol | AGM | Year End | URL |
|---|---|---|---|---|---|---|---|---|
| City Merchants High Yield Trust PLC | EXTP | S-Cap | 0.1 | 2 | 29.1k | 18/10/05 | 31/03 | www.exeter.co.uk |
| City Natural Resources High Yield Trust PLC | CYN | Fledge | 72.9 | 3 | 218k | 27/10/05 | 30/06 | www.ncim.co.uk |
| City of London Investment Trust (The) PLC | CTY | Mid 250 | 573.1 | 5 | 263k | 26/10/05 | 30/06 | www.itshenderson.com |
| Clerkenwell Ventures PLC | CRK | | 3.5 | 1 | 22.8k | 20/12/05 | 30/09 | |
| Climate Exchange PLC | CLE | | 88.5 | 1 | 70.7k | 05/07/06 | 31/12 | |
| Close AllBlue Fund Ltd | CAB | | 134.9 | 2 | | | | |
| Close Brothers AIM VCT PLC | COA | | 23.1 | 1 | 11.9k | 28/06/06 | 28/02 | www.closeventures.co.uk |
| Close Brothers Development VCT PLC | CBD | | 12.0 | 1 | 3.43k | 03/05/06 | 31/12 | www.closeventures.co.uk |
| Close Brothers Protected VCT PLC | CPV | | 20.0 | 0.5 | 9.24k | 12/08/05 | 31/03 | |
| Close Brothers Venture Capital Trust PLC | CVC | | 39.8 | 0.5 | 4.57k | 01/08/06 | 31/03 | www.closeventures.co.uk |
| Close Finsbury EuroTech Trust PLC | CFB | Fledge | 12.7 | 3 | 34.8k | 08/12/05 | 31/08 | www.closefinsbury.com |
| Close High Income Properties PLC | CHI | | 41.4 | 0.5 | 17.9k | 26/05/06 | 31/12 | www.cbil.com |
| Close IHT AIM VCT PLC | CIAA | | 7.2 | 2 | | | | |
| Close Income & Growth VCT PLC | CIG | | 44.2 | 0.5 | 245 | 31/01/06 | 30/09 | www.closeventures.co.uk |
| Close Second AIM VCT PLC | CSA | | 4.3 | 0.5 | 3.75k | 05/07/06 | 28/02 | www.closeventures.co.uk |
| Close Technology & General VCT PLC | CNG | | 14.0 | 3 | 5.85k | 23/05/06 | 31/12 | www.closeventures.co.uk |
| CMA Global Hedge PCC Ltd | CMAU | | 94.6 | 5 | | | | |
| Collective Assets Trust PLC | CAS | | 12.9 | 0.5 | 2.07k | 18/01/06 | 31/10 | |
| Core VCT I PLC | CR. | | 10.9 | 1 | | 06/04/06 | 31/12 | |
| Core VCT II PLC | CR2 | | 16.5 | 0.5 | | | | |
| Core VCT III PLC | CR3 | | 16.5 | 0.5 | | | | |
| Crescent Technology Ventures PLC | CTC | | 1.2 | 2 | 147 | 24/06/06 | | |
| Crown Place VCT PLC | CRWN | | 32.7 | 0.5 | 43.6k | 06/09/05 | 28/02 | www.closeventures.co.uk |
| Danae Investment Trust PLC | DNII | | 1.5 | 3 | 54.1k | 28/09/05 | 31/05 | www.maunbyinvestments.co.uk |
| Defined Capital Return Fund (The) Ltd | DCR | | 30.9 | 1 | 35.7k | 15/06/06 | | |
| DermaSalve Sciences PLC | DRM | | 10.3 | | 107k | 30/06/06 | 31/12 | www.dermasalvesciences.com |
| Dexion Absolute Ltd | DAB | Mid 250 | 416.5 | 15 | 781k | | | www.dexionabsolute.com |
| Dexion Alpha Strategies Ltd | DASL | | 86.0 | 5 | 515k | 15/06/06 | 31/12 | |
| Dexion Equity Alternative Ltd | DEA | S-Cap | 134.8 | 3 | 453k | 28/04/06 | 31/12 | |
| Dexion Trading Ltd | DTL | | 85.3 | 10 | 2.68k | 07/12/05 | 30/06 | www.dexiontrading.com |
| Downing Protected VCT I PLC | DPV1 | | 8.2 | 1 | 233 | 22/06/06 | 31/01 | www.downing.co.uk |
| Downing Protected VCT II PLC | DPV | | 9.5 | 1 | 391 | 22/06/06 | 31/01 | |
| Downing Protected VCT III PLC | DPV3 | | 9.6 | 1 | | | | www.downingcf.co.uk |
| Downing Protected VCT IV PLC | DPV4 | | 21.7 | 10 | | | | |
| Downing Protected VCT V PLC | DPV5 | | 7.1 | | | | | |
| Dunedin Enterprise Investment Trust PLC | DNE | S-Cap | 129.9 | 1 | 34.7k | 07/09/05 | 30/04 | www.dunedin.com |
| Dunedin Income Growth Inv Trust PLC | DIG | S-Cap | 365.0 | 3 | 212k | 27/04/05 | 31/01 | www.dunedinincomegrowth.co.uk |
| Dunedin Smaller Companies Investment Trust PLC | DNDL | S-Cap | 107.3 | 0.5 | 24.9k | 09/02/06 | 31/10 | www.dunedinsmaller.co.uk |
| Eaglet Investment Trust PLC | EIN | S-Cap | 89.2 | 2 | 107k | 09/11/05 | 30/06 | www.unicornam.com |
| Eastern European Trust (The) PLC | EST | S-Cap | 158.5 | 3 | 159k | 16/06/06 | 31/01 | www.teetplc.com |
| Eclipse VCT 2 PLC | ECL2 | | 18.2 | 1 | 54.4 | 24/05/06 | 31/01 | |
| Eclipse VCT 3 PLC | ECL3 | | 26.1 | 1 | 88.4 | | | |
| Eclipse VCT 4 PLC | ECL4 | | 31.0 | | 95.9 | | | |
| Eclipse VCT PLC | ECL | | 24.9 | 1 | 907 | 13/09/05 | 31/05 | |

Source: Hemscott (Hemscott.com)

## Listed Investment Trusts

| Company Name | EPIC | Index | Capital (£m) | NMS | 200D Avg Vol | AGM | Year End | URL |
|---|---|---|---|---|---|---|---|---|
| Ecofin Water & Power Opportunities PLC | ECW | | 130.4 | 2 | 86.9k | 20/07/05 | 31/03 | www.ecofin.co.uk |
| Edge Performance VCT PLC | EDG | | 6.4 | 1 | | | | www.edfd.com/funds/dragontrust.html |
| Edinburgh Dragon Trust PLC | EFM | S-Cap | 272.9 | 10 | 377k | 14/12/05 | 31/08 | www.fidelity.co.uk/its |
| Edinburgh Investment Trust (The) PLC | EDIN | Mid 250 | 977.2 | 5 | 476k | 19/07/06 | 31/03 | www.edinburghnewincome.co.uk |
| Edinburgh New Income Trust PLC | ENI | Fledge | 21.8 | 0.5 | 23.9k | | 30/06 | www.standardlifeinvestments.com |
| Edinburgh Small Companies Trust PLC | EFS | Fledge | 67.4 | 3 | 344k | 03/11/05 | 31/03 | www.edinburgh-uksmalltracker.co.uk |
| Edinburgh UK Smaller Companies Tracker Trust PLC | EDU | | 101.6 | 2 | 180k | 06/07/06 | 31/12 | www.edinburghuktracker.co.uk |
| Edinburgh UK Tracker Trust PLC | EUK | S-Cap | 143.4 | 2 | 61.2k | 21/04/06 | 31/07 | www.edinburghustracker.com |
| Edinburgh US Tracker Trust PLC | EUS | Mid 250 | 410.9 | 5 | 207k | 18/05/06 | 31/10 | www.bailliegifford.com |
| Edinburgh Worldwide Investment Trust PLC | EWI | S-Cap | 100.0 | 2 | 63.2k | 30/01/06 | 28/02 | www.downing.co.uk |
| Elderstreet Millennium Venture Capital Trust PLC | EMV | | 8.0 | 0.5 | 4.75k | 05/07/06 | 21/06/06 | www.elderstreet.co.uk |
| Elderstreet VCT PLC | EDV | | 8.4 | | | | 30/09 | |
| Electra Kingsway VCT 2 PLC | EKW | | 29.4 | 1 | 321 | 13/03/06 | | |
| Electra Kingsway VCT 3 PLC | ELK | | 39.8 | 0.5 | | | 30/09 | www.electraquoted.com |
| Electra Kingsway VCT PLC | EKV | | 19.2 | 1 | 6.75k | 13/03/06 | 30/09 | www.electraequity.com |
| Electra Private Equity PLC | ELTA | Mid 250 | 549.8 | 3 | 112k | 09/02/06 | 31/05 | www.electricandgeneral.com |
| Electric & General Investment Trust PLC | ENG | S-Cap | 244.7 | 2 | 109k | 15/09/05 | 31/05 | www.enterpriseasia.com.hk |
| Emerging UK Investments PLC | EUI | | 0.5 | 1 | 3.79k | 30/09/05 | 31/12 | www.edinburghpartners.co.uk |
| enterpriseAsia PLC | EPA | | 0.5 | 0.5 | 3.49k | 30/06/06 | 31/01 | www.epicip.com |
| EP Global Opportunities Trust PLC | EPG | Fledge | 52.0 | 2 | 45.7k | 19/04/06 | 31/07 | www.epicip.com |
| EPIC Reconstruction PLC | ERN | | 21.6 | 0.5 | 50.5k | 31/07/06 | 31/07 | www.bdtinvest.com |
| Equity Partnership Investment Company (The) PLC | EQPI | | 25.0 | 0.5 | 21.5k | 14/12/05 | 31/03 | www.downing.co.uk |
| Establishment Investment Trust (The) PLC | ET. | Fledge | 30.2 | 0.5 | 6.57k | | 30/09 | |
| Ethical AIM VCT PLC | EAV | | 4.1 | 1 | 3.93k | 22/02/06 | | www.european-trust.co.uk |
| European Equity Tranche Income Ltd | EET | | 70.0 | 5 | | | 30/11 | www.exeter.co.uk |
| European Growth and Income Trust PLC | EURI | | 0.3 | 1 | 3.73k | 14/06/05 | 31/07 | www.fandc.com |
| European Utilities Trust PLC | EUT | Fledge | 17.5 | 0.5 | 14.8k | 18/11/05 | 30/11 | www.focpt.co.uk |
| Exeter Equity Growth & Income Fund Ltd | EXF | | 0.2 | 1 | 56.0k | 23/03/05 | 30/09 | www.fandc.com |
| F&C Capital and Income Investment Trust PLC | FCI | S-Cap | 186.8 | 2 | 71.0k | 31/01/06 | 31/12 | www.fandc.com |
| F&C Commercial Property Trust Ltd | FCPT | Mid 250 | 990.4 | 25 | 1.08m | 28/04/06 | 30/09 | www.fandc.com |
| F&C Emerging Markets Investment Trust PLC | FCT | | 238.3 | 5 | 359k | 30/04/06 | 30/04 | www.fandc.com |
| F&C Global Smaller Companies PLC | FCS | S-Cap | 181.3 | 3 | 429k | 24/07/06 | 31/07 | www.unicornam.com |
| F&C Private Equity Trust PLC | FPEB | Fledge | 102.0 | 2 | 35.2k | 05/12/05 | 30/06 | www.fidelity.co.uk |
| F&C US Smaller Companies PLC | FSC | S-Cap | 59.4 | 1 | 30.6k | 15/11/05 | 30/09 | www.fidelity.co.uk |
| Falcon Investment Trust PLC | FLN | Fledge | 40.3 | 5 | 36.8k | 09/02/06 | 31/07 | www.fidelity.co.uk |
| Fidelity Asian Values PLC | FAS | S-Cap | 88.8 | 2 | 164k | 14/11/05 | 31/12 | www.fidelity.co.uk |
| Fidelity European Values PLC | FEV | Mid 250 | 684.4 | 10 | 102k | 19/05/06 | 31/12 | www.finsbury-asset.com |
| Fidelity Japanese Values PLC | FJV | S-Cap | 81.0 | 2 | 419k | 10/05/05 | 31/08 | www.closefinsbury.com |
| Fidelity Special Values PLC | FSV | S-Cap | 334.3 | 2 | 80.5k | 08/12/05 | 31/03 | www.closefinsbury.com |
| Finsbury Emerging Biotechnology Trust PLC | FEB | Fledge | 69.2 | 2 | 38.7k | 19/07/06 | 30/09 | www.closefinsbury.com |
| Finsbury Growth & Income Trust PLC | FGT | S-Cap | 137.2 | 2 | 61.4k | 26/01/06 | 30/11 | www.firststate.co.uk |
| Finsbury Technology Trust PLC | FTT | Fledge | 47.6 | 2 | 148k | 06/04/06 | 31/03 | |
| Finsbury Worldwide Pharmaceutical Trust PLC | FWP | S-Cap | 278.6 | 2 | 91.9k | 14/07/06 | 28/02 | |
| First State Investments AIM VCT PLC | FSI | | 25.3 | 1 | 327 | 06/06/06 | | |

Source: Hemscott (Hemscott.com)

196

# Listed Investment Trusts

| Company Name | EPIC | Index | Capital (£m) | NMS | 200D Avg Vol | AGM | Year End | URL |
|---|---|---|---|---|---|---|---|---|
| Foreign & Colonial Eurotrust PLC | FCU | S-Cap | 354.2 | 2 | 100k | 15/12/05 | 30/09 | www.fandc.co.uk |
| Foreign & Colonial Investment Trust PLC | FRCL | Mid 250 | 1953.9 | 25 | 1.67m | 19/05/06 | 31/12 | www.foreignandcolonial.com |
| Foresight 2 VCT PLC | FTN | | 22.8 | 1 | 33.5 | 02/02/06 | 30/09 | |
| Foresight 3 VCT PLC | FTD | | 18.9 | 1 | 6.18k | 15/07/05 | 31/03 | www.foresightvct.com |
| Foresight 4 VCT PLC | FTF | | 20.6 | 1 | 4.09k | 04/07/06 | 28/02 | www.foresightvct.com |
| Foresight Technology VCT PLC | FTV | | 6.4 | 0.5 | 7.05k | 09/05/06 | 31/12 | www.vcf.co.uk |
| Framlington AIM VCT 2 PLC | FAMT | | 41.2 | 2 | | | | |
| Framlington AIM VCT PLC | FAME | | 26.2 | 1 | 1.42k | 23/02/06 | 30/09 | www.framlington.co.uk |
| Framlington Global Financial & Income Fund Ltd | FGF | | 0.1 | 2 | 78.4k | 17/04/06 | 30/11 | www.framlington.co.uk |
| Framlington Income & Capital Trust PLC | FRNI | S-Cap | 15.6 | 0.5 | 108k | 25/07/06 | 31/03 | www.framlington.co.uk |
| Framlington Innovative Growth Trust PLC | FIT | S-Cap | 124.5 | 2 | 65.8k | 19/10/05 | 30/06 | www.framlington.co.uk |
| Gartmore Absolute Growth & Income Trust PLC | GTMI | Fledge | 0.2 | 0.5 | 18.5k | 23/02/06 | 31/10 | www.gartmore.co.uk |
| Gartmore Asia Pacific Trust PLC | GAP | Fledge | 33.7 | 0.5 | 32.8k | 26/07/06 | 31/03 | www.gartmore.co.uk |
| Gartmore European Investment Trust PLC | GEO | S-Cap | 291.0 | 2 | 148k | 23/01/06 | 30/09 | www.gartmore.co.uk |
| Gartmore Fledgling Trust PLC | GMF | S-Cap | 79.3 | 0.5 | 24.2k | 05/10/05 | 30/06 | www.gartmore.co.uk |
| Gartmore Global Trust PLC | GGL | S-Cap | 117.6 | 1 | 55.3k | 11/05/06 | 31/01 | www.gartmore.co.uk |
| Gartmore Growth Opportunities PLC | GGOR | Fledge | 31.6 | 0.5 | 17.9k | 18/10/05 | 30/06 | www.gartmore.co.uk |
| Gartmore High Income Trust PLC | GHI | Fledge | 14.4 | 3 | 108k | 20/07/05 | 31/03 | www.gartmore.co.uk |
| Gartmore Irish Growth Fund PLC | GIR | S-Cap | 107.6 | 0.5 | 26.4k | 24/08/05 | 31/03 | www.gartmore.co.uk |
| Gartmore Smaller Companies Trust PLC | GSM | Fledge | 73.5 | 0.5 | 15.3k | 28/11/05 | 31/08 | www.gartmore.co.uk |
| Gateway VCT PLC | GTW | | 5.0 | 1 | 1.85k | 13/09/05 | 31/03 | www.etechnologyvct.co.uk |
| Glasgow Income Trust PLC | GLS | Flecge | 85.8 | 3 | 109k | 13/12/05 | 30/09 | www.glasgowinvestmentmanagers.co.uk |
| Golden Prospect PLC | GOL | | 53.6 | 10 | 434k | 21/04/06 | 31/12 | www.goldenprospectplc.com |
| Goldman Sachs Dynamic Opportunities Ltd | GSDO | | 140.6 | 10 | | | | |
| Graphite Enterprise Trust PLC | GPE | S-Cap | 298.6 | 3 | 96.2k | 25/05/06 | 31/12 | www.fandc.co.uk |
| Greenhouse Fund (The) Ltd | GHF | | 19.4 | 15 | | | | |
| Gresham House PLC | GHE | Fledge | 28.4 | 0.5 | 4.66k | 13/06/06 | 31/12 | |
| GruppeM Investments PLC | GRP | | 0.9 | 1 | 836 | | | |
| Guinness Flight Venture Capital Trust PLC | GFV | | 18.2 | 0.5 | 12.3k | 15/06/05 | 28/02 | www.investec.com |
| Hansa Trust PLC | HAN | S-Cap | 65.6 | 0.5 | 10.2k | 03/08/06 | 31/03 | www.hansagrp.com |
| Harrogate Group PLC | HGP | | 0.6 | 15 | 71.4k | 15/11/05 | 31/03 | www.harrogategroup.com |
| Henderson EuroTrust PLC | HNE | S-Cap | 112.9 | 1 | 63.0k | 08/11/05 | 31/07 | www.itshenderson.co.uk |
| Henderson Far East Income Trust PLC | HFE | S-Cap | 157.4 | 3 | 149k | 09/12/05 | 31/08 | www.hendersonfareastincome.co.uk |
| Henderson High Income Trust PLC | HHI | S-Cap | 110.8 | 2 | 74.8k | 27/04/05 | 31/12 | www.hendersonhighincome.com |
| Henderson Smaller Companies Investment Trust PLC | HSL | S-Cap | 234.6 | 3 | 146k | 30/09/05 | 31/05 | www.itshenderson.com |
| Henderson Strata Investments PLC | HSI | Fledge | 59.6 | 1 | 41.4k | 09/02/06 | 31/10 | www.henderson.co.uk |
| Henderson TR Pacific Investment Trust PLC | HPI | S-Cap | 187.8 | 10 | 358k | 30/03/06 | 31/12 | www.hendersontrpacific.com |
| Herald Investment Trust PLC | HRI | S-Cap | 287.4 | 3 | 246k | 13/04/05 | 31/12 | www.heralduk.com |
| HgCapital Trust PLC | HGT | S-Cap | 163.8 | 1 | 37.9k | 19/04/05 | 31/12 | www.hgcapitaltrust.net |
| Highcroft Investments PLC | HIV | Fledge | 35.3 | 0.5 | 1.18k | 24/05/06 | 31/12 | |
| HSBC Infrastructure Company Ltd | HICL | S-Cap | 271.3 | | 2.46k | 19/04/06 | 31/12 | |
| Hygea VCT PLC | HYG | | 3.4 | 15 | | | | |
| IBIS Media VCT 1 PLC | IBSA | | 5.8 | 1 | | | | |
| iimia Investment Trust PLC | IIM | Fledge | 42.0 | 0.5 | 16.3k | 14/07/05 | 30/04 | www.iimia.co.uk |

Source: Hemscott (Hemscott.com)

## Listed Investment Trusts

| Company Name | EPIC | Index | Capital (£m) | NMS | 200D Avg Vol | AGM | Year End | URL |
|---|---|---|---|---|---|---|---|---|
| Impax Environmental Markets PLC | IEM | S-Cap | 119.1 | 3 | 226k | 04/05/05 | 31/12 | www.impax.co.uk |
| Independent Investment Trust (The) PLC | IIT | | 161.4 | 0.5 | 21.5k | 20/03/06 | 30/11 | www.bailliegifford.com |
| India Capital Growth Fund Ltd | IGC | | 65.1 | | | | | |
| ING UK Real Estate Income Trust Ltd | IRET | S-Cap | 369.8 | 25 | | | | |
| Ingenious Media Active Capital Ltd | IMAC | | 147.8 | 10 | | | | |
| Ingenious Music VCT 2 PLC | IMV | | 33.0 | 1 | | | | |
| Ingenious Music VCT PLC | IGM | | 14.5 | 1 | | 17/05/06 | 31/01 | www.ipft.co.uk |
| Insight Foundation Property Trust Ltd | IFD | Mid 250 | 478.2 | 50 | 2.26m | 25/07/06 | 31/03 | www.internationalbiotrust.com |
| International Biotechnology Trust PLC | IBT | Fledge | 60.1 | 1 | 123k | 11/11/05 | 31/08 | www.invesco.co.uk/investmenttrusts |
| INVESCO Asia Trust PLC | IAT | Fledge | 84.2 | 5 | 167k | 27/07/06 | 30/04 | www.invesco.co.uk/investmenttrusts |
| INVESCO English & International Trust PLC | IEI | S-Cap | 147.3 | 3 | 111k | 26/07/06 | 05/04 | www.invesco.co.uk/investmenttrusts |
| INVESCO Income Growth Trust PLC | IVI | S-Cap | 108.9 | 2 | 84.6k | 04/07/06 | 31/03 | www.invesco.co.uk |
| INVESCO Japan Discovery Trust PLC | IJD | Fledge | 30.7 | 1 | 50.3k | 24/11/05 | 31/07 | www.invescoperpetual.co.uk |
| INVESCO Leveraged High Yield Fund Ltd | ILH | | 23.4 | 2 | 34.5k | 19/01/06 | 30/09 | www.invesco.co.uk/investmenttrusts |
| INVESCO Perpetual AIM VCT PLC | IPA | | 42.1 | 1 | 183 | 21/09/05 | 31/05 | www.invesco.co.uk/investmenttrusts |
| INVESCO Perpetual Euro Absolute Return Trust PLC | IPE | Fledge | 47.6 | 2 | 61.3k | 05/05/05 | 31/12 | |
| INVESCO Perpetual Recovery 2011 PLC | IPRT | Fledge | 17.1 | 1 | | | | |
| INVESCO Perpetual UK Smaller Companies Inv Tst plc | IPU | S-Cap | 107.7 | 0.5 | 14.0k | 24/05/05 | 31/01 | www.invescoperpetual.co.uk |
| INVESCO UK Property Income Trust Ltd | IPI | S-Cap | 188.4 | 10 | 451k | | | www.ukpropertyit.invesco.co.uk |
| Investec Capital Accumulator Trust Ltd | ICA | Fledge | 36.1 | 2 | 42.1k | | | |
| Investec High Income Trust PLC | ICH | Fledge | 20.2 | 2 | 53.0k | 07/07/06 | 31/03 | www.investecfunds.com |
| Investment Company (The) PLC | INV | Fledge | 4.2 | 0.5 | 62.5 | 21/09/05 | 31/03 | |
| Investors Capital Trust PLC | ICAX | | 204.8 | 2 | 166k | 14/12/05 | 30/09 | www.investorscapital.co.uk |
| ISIS Property Trust 2 Ltd | IRP | S-Cap | 156.1 | 5 | 230k | 02/11/05 | 30/06 | www.isispropertytrust.co.uk |
| ISIS Property Trust Ltd | IPT | | 116.9 | 2 | 107k | 26/04/06 | 31/12 | www.isispropertytrust.co.uk |
| ISIS Smaller Companies Trust PLC | ISU | Fledge | 56.4 | 1 | 62.7k | 21/06/06 | 31/03 | www.smaller-cos.co.uk |
| ISIS UK Select Trust PLC | ISI | Fledge | 53.8 | 2 | 55.5k | 05/04/06 | 31/12 | www.isis-trust.co.uk |
| JAB Holdings Ltd | JBH | | 2.0 | 5 | 117k | 29/12/05 | 30/06 | |
| JP Morgan Fleming Claverhouse Investment Tr PLC | JCH | S-Cap | 306.7 | 1 | 54.5k | 27/04/06 | 31/12 | www.jpmfclaverhouse.com |
| JP Morgan Fleming Income & Capital Inv Tr PLC | JPI | Fledge | 84.8 | 1 | 53.3k | 26/07/05 | 28/02 | www.jpmfincomeandcapital.com |
| JP Morgan Fleming Income & Growth Inv Tr PLC | JGIZ | | 67.6 | 3 | 146k | 20/04/06 | 31/12 | www.jpmfincomeandgrowth.com |
| JP Morgan Fleming Japanese Investment Trust PLC | JFJ | Mid 250 | 476.8 | 10 | 551k | 16/12/05 | 30/09 | www.jpmfjapanese.com |
| JP Morgan Fleming Japanese Smaller Cos Inv Tr PLC | JPS | S-Cap | 111.5 | 2 | 140k | 26/07/06 | 31/03 | www.jpmfjapanesesmallercompanies.com |
| JP Morgan Fleming Mercantile Investment Trust PLC | JFM | Mid 250 | 1253.1 | 5 | 297k | 24/05/06 | 31/01 | www.jpmfmercantile.com |
| JP Morgan Fleming Overseas Investment Trust PLC | JMO | S-Cap | 198.6 | 3 | 285k | 30/11/05 | 30/06 | www.jpmfoverseas.com |
| JP Morgan Fleming Smaller Companies Inv Tr PLC | JMI | S-Cap | 114.4 | 0.5 | 30.6k | 28/11/05 | 31/07 | www.jpmfsmallercompanies.com |
| JPMorgan American Investment Trust PLC | JAM | S-Cap | 261.6 | 2 | 97.4k | 27/04/05 | 31/12 | www.jpmfamerican.com |
| JPMorgan Asian Investment Trust PLC | JAI | S-Cap | 199.9 | 5 | 232k | 03/02/06 | 30/09 | www.flemings.co.uk |
| JPMorgan Chinese Investment Trust PLC | JMC | Fledge | 56.6 | 2 | 147k | 13/12/05 | 30/09 | www.jpmfchinese.com |
| JPMorgan Elect PLC | JPE | | 180.0 | 0.5 | 27.5k | 07/12/05 | 31/08 | www.jpmorgan.com |
| JPMorgan Emerging Markets Inv Trust PLC | JMG | S-Cap | 329.3 | 5 | 262k | 08/11/05 | 30/06 | www.jpmfemergingmarkets.com |
| JPMorgan European Fledgeling Investment Trust PLC | JFF | S-Cap | 295.8 | 2 | 132k | 12/07/06 | 31/03 | www.jpmfeuropeanfledgeling.com |
| JPMorgan European Investment Trust PLC | FUT | Mid 250 | 1825.7 | 2 | 142k | 20/07/06 | 31/03 | www.jpmfcontinentaleuropean.com |
| JPMorgan Indian Investment Trust PLC | JII | S-Cap | 249.5 | 10 | 421k | 24/01/06 | 30/09 | www.jpmfindian.com |

Source: Hemscott (Hemscott.com)

Listed Investment Trusts

| Company Name | EPIC | Index | Capital (£m) | NMS | 200D Avg Vol | AGM | Year End | URL |
|---|---|---|---|---|---|---|---|---|
| JPMorgan Mid Cap Investment Trust PLC | JMF | S-Cap | 171.8 | 1 | 86.4k | 02/11/05 | 30/06 | www.jpmfmidcap.com |
| JPMorgan Russian Securities PLC | JRS | S-Cap | 236.4 | 3 | 204k | 01/03/06 | 31/10 | www.flemings.co.uk |
| JPMorgan US Discovery Investment Trust PLC | JPU | S-Cap | 76.7 | 0.5 | 14.5k | 28/04/05 | 31/12 | www.flemings.co.uk |
| Jubilee Investment Trust PLC | JIT | Fledge | 8.5 | 2 | 71.8k | 26/04/06 | 31/12 | |
| Jupiter Dividend & Growth Trust PLC | JDT | Fledge | 37.1 | 5 | 536k | 15/06/06 | 31/12 | www.jupiteronline.co.uk |
| Jupiter European Opportunities Trust PLC | JEO | S-Cap | 127.9 | 3 | 131k | 20/09/05 | 31/05 | www.jupiteronline.co.uk |
| Jupiter Green Investment Trust PLC | JGC | Fledge | 24.8 | 2 | | | | www.jupiteronline.co.uk |
| Jupiter Primadona Growth Trust PLC | JPG | Fledge | 48.0 | 0.5 | 9.74k | 03/10/05 | 30/06 | www.jupiteronline.co.uk |
| Jupiter Second Enhanced Income Trust PLC | JSE | | 28.6 | 3 | 182k | 08/02/06 | 31/10 | www.jupiteronline.co.uk |
| Jupiter Second Split Trust PLC | JSS | | 55.0 | 2 | 86.9k | 23/02/06 | 31/10 | www.jupiteronline.co.uk |
| JZ Equity Partners PLC | JZE | S-Cap | 171.3 | 2 | 116k | 27/07/06 | 31/03 | www.jzep.co.uk |
| KeyData Aim VCT PLC | KEY | | 15.2 | 1 | | 18/01/06 | 30/09 | www.keydataaimvct.com |
| KeyData Income VCT 1 PLC | KIV | | 4.5 | 1 | | 27/06/06 | 28/02 | www.keydataincomevct.co.uk |
| KeyData Income VCT 2 PLC | KIV2 | | 4.5 | 1 | | 27/06/06 | 28/02 | www.keydataincomevct.co.uk |
| Keystone Investment Trust PLC | KIT | S-Cap | 143.4 | 0.5 | 18.2k | 21/12/05 | 30/09 | www.invesco.co.uk/invetmenttrusts |
| KGR Absolute Return PCC Ltd | KGR | | 43.2 | 2 | | | | |
| Langley Park Investment Trust PLC | LPI | Fledge | 10.0 | 5 | 62.8k | 26/04/06 | 31/12 | www.langleyparkinvestmenttrust.com |
| Law Debenture Corporation (The) PLC | LWDB | S-Cap | 357.3 | 3 | 142k | 11/04/06 | 31/12 | www.lawdeb.com |
| Leisure & Media VCT PLC | LEM | | 8.3 | 0.5 | 3.98k | 16/05/05 | 31/12 | www.johcm.co.uk |
| Life Offices Opportunities Trust PLC | LOT | Fledge | 29.9 | 0.5 | 37.7k | 11/04/06 | 31/12 | www.svmonline.co.uk |
| Lindsell Train Investment Trust (The) PLC | LTI | Fledge | 25.9 | | 8.51 | 13/07/06 | 31/03 | www.LindsellTrain.com |
| London & St Lawrence Investment Company PLC | LSLI | Fledge | 77.4 | 0.5 | 6.93k | 29/11/05 | 31/08 | www.londonandstlawrence.com |
| London Asia Capital PLC | LDC | | 43.5 | 15 | 866k | 25/07/06 | 31/12 | www.londonasia.com |
| Lowland Investment Co PLC | LWI | S-Cap | 203.6 | 1 | 22.4k | 15/12/05 | 30/09 | www.lowlandinvestment.com |
| M&G Equity Investment Trust PLC | MEQI | | 42.0 | 3 | 109k | 11/10/05 | 30/06 | www.mandg.co.uk |
| M&G High Income Investment Trust PLC | MGHI | | 37.2 | 0.5 | 34.1k | 04/10/05 | 31/05 | www.mandg.co.uk |
| M&G Income Investment Company Ltd | MIV | | 81.1 | 1 | 75.7k | 28/02/06 | 31/10 | www.mandg.co.uk |
| M&G Recovery Investment Company Ltd | MGR | | 69.2 | 0.5 | 5.26k | 10/08/05 | 30/04 | www.mandg.co.uk |
| Magna Investments PLC | MGN | | 0.5 | 1 | 51.9 | 31/07/06 | | |
| Majedie Investments PLC | MAJE | S-Cap | 173.7 | 0.5 | 23.6k | 18/01/06 | 30/09 | www.majedie.co.uk |
| Man Alternative Investments Ltd | MAIL | | 31.5 | 0.5 | 12.9k | 07/12/05 | 31/05 | www.maninvestments.com |
| Manchester & London Investment Trust PLC | MNL | Fledge | 29.4 | 0.5 | 753 | 24/11/05 | 31/07 | www.midasim.co.uk |
| Martin Currie Enhanced Income Trust PLC | MCN | | 18.3 | 2 | 125k | 26/11/05 | 30/06 | www.martincurrie.com |
| Martin Currie European Inv Trust PLC | MCE | | 25.3 | 1 | 215k | 02/09/05 | 30/04 | www.martincurrie.com |
| Martin Currie Income & Growth Trust PLC | MGTI | | 26.1 | 1 | 53.3k | 25/07/06 | 30/04 | www.martincurrie.com |
| Martin Currie Japan Investment Trust PLC | MCJ | | 56.0 | 3 | 319k | 26/09/05 | 31/05 | www.martincurrie.com |
| Martin Currie Pacific Trust PLC | MCP | S-Cap | 92.9 | 2 | 82.7k | 27/06/06 | 28/02 | www.martincurrie.com |
| Martin Currie Portfolio Investment Trust PLC | MNP | S-Cap | 158.9 | 3 | 166k | 04/05/05 | 31/01 | www.martincurrieportfolio.com |
| Marwyn Value Investors Ltd | MNV | | 17.3 | 3 | | | | |
| Matisse Holdings PLC | MAT | | 0.2 | 2 | 32.6k | 12/08/05 | 30/11 | |
| Matrix Income & Growth 2 VCT PLC | MIG | | 9.2 | 0.5 | 2.65k | 07/09/05 | 30/04 | www.matrixgroup.co.uk |
| Matrix Income & Growth 3 VCT PLC | MIXT | | 23.8 | 2 | | | | |
| Matrix Income & Growth VCT PLC | MIX | | 27.3 | 0.5 | 145 | | | |
| Medical Property Investment Fund (The) Ltd | MPF | | 416.5 | 2 | 354k | 12/04/06 | 31/12 | www.mpif.net |

Source: Hemscott (Hemscott.com)

## Listed Investment Trusts

| Company Name | EPIC | Index | Capital (£m) | NMS | 200D Avg Vol | AGM | Year End | URL |
|---|---|---|---|---|---|---|---|---|
| Melchior Japan Investment Trust PLC | MJT | | 65.2 | 5 | 137k | 09/05/06 | 31/01 | www.merchantstrust.co.uk |
| Merchants Trust (The) PLC | MRCH | Mid 250 | 496.5 | 2 | 44.0k | 21/09/05 | 31/05 | www.mlim.co.uk/its |
| Merrill Lynch Asset Allocator PLC | MLA | | 93.5 | 2 | 72.1k | 05/06/06 | 28/02 | www.mlim.co.uk/its |
| Merrill Lynch British Smaller Companies Trust PLC | MBS | S-Cap | 151.0 | 2 | | | | |
| Merrill Lynch Commodities Income Inv Trust PLC | MLCO | | 80.4 | | | | | |
| Merrill Lynch Greater Europe Investment Trust PLC | MGE | S-Cap | 191.5 | 2 | 232k | 22/11/05 | 31/08 | www.mlim.co.uk/its |
| Merrill Lynch Latin American Investment Trust PLC | MLLA | S-Cap | 171.8 | 3 | 373k | 08/05/06 | 31/12 | www.fandc.com |
| Merrill Lynch New Energy Technology PLC | MNE | Fledge | 100.2 | 15 | 690k | 10/02/06 | 31/10 | www.mlim.co.uk/its |
| Merrill Lynch World Mining Trust PLC | MLW | Mid 250 | 675.7 | 10 | 703k | 17/03/06 | 31/12 | www.mlim.co.uk |
| Mid Wynd International Inv Trust PLC | MWY | Fledge | 38.1 | 0.5 | 4.21k | 03/10/05 | 30/06 | www.bailliegifford.com |
| Midas Income & Growth Trust PLC | MIGT | Fledge | 52.6 | 3 | 73.9k | 19/08/05 | 30/04 | www.midascapital.co.uk |
| Mission Capital PLC | MCAP | | 6.9 | 5 | | | | |
| Mithras Investment Trust PLC | MTH | Fledge | 29.6 | 1 | 16.1k | 11/05/05 | 31/12 | www.legalandgeneralventures.com |
| Monks Investment Trust (The) PLC | MNKS | Mid 250 | 751.1 | 5 | 414k | 01/08/06 | 30/04 | www.bailliegifford.com |
| Montanaro UK Smaller Companies Inv Tr PLC | MTU | Fledge | 87.9 | 2 | 56.5k | 14/07/06 | 31/03 | www.montanaro.co.uk |
| Morant Wright Japan Income Trust Ltd | MWJ | S-Cap | 139.3 | 10 | | | | |
| Murray Income Trust PLC | MUT | Mid 250 | 421.2 | 1 | 73.6k | 26/10/05 | 30/06 | www.murray-income.co.uk |
| Murray International Trust PLC | MYI | Mid 250 | 480.6 | 2 | 94.7k | 27/04/06 | 31/12 | www.murray-intl.co.uk |
| Murray VCT 4 PLC | MUV | | 19.8 | 0.5 | 10.9k | 06/07/06 | 28/02 | www.aberdeen-asset.com |
| Neptune-Calculus Income & Growth VCT PLC | NEP | | 4.9 | 1 | | 01/06/06 | 31/12 | |
| New Century AIM VCT PLC | NCA | | 11.3 | 3 | 12.2 | | | |
| New City High Yield Trust PLC | NCY | Fledge | 50.5 | 2 | 123k | 08/11/05 | 30/06 | www.ncim.co.uk |
| New India Investment Trust PLC | NII | Fledge | 52.9 | 2 | 96.2k | 13/07/05 | 31/03 | www.newindia-trust.co.uk |
| New Star Absolute Return Fund PCC Ltd | NSAG | | 14.0 | 2 | | | | |
| New Star Financial Opp Fund Ltd | NST | | 38.6 | 5 | 241k | 20/03/06 | 30/11 | www.exeter.co.uk |
| New Star Investment Trust PLC | NSI | S-Cap | 102.3 | 1 | 47.4k | 23/11/05 | 30/06 | www.newstaram.com |
| New Zealand Investment Trust (The) PLC | NZL | Fledge | 33.5 | 0.5 | 12.4k | 26/04/06 | 31/10 | www.newzealandinvestmenttrust.co.uk |
| NewMedia SPARK PLC | NMS | | 79.2 | 25 | 1.57m | 15/09/05 | 31/03 | www.newmediaspark.com |
| Noble Income & Growth VCT PLC | NIG | | 3.3 | 0.5 | 1.08k | 21/06/05 | 31/12 | www.teathers.com |
| Noble VCT PLC | | | 7.7 | 0.5 | 1.25k | 03/08/06 | 31/03 | www.noblegp.com |
| North American Banks Fund Ltd | NAM | | 21.1 | 0.5 | 3.84k | 26/06/06 | | |
| North Atlantic Smaller Companies Inv Trust PLC | NAS | S-Cap | 127.5 | 0.5 | 9.83k | 07/07/06 | 31/01 | www.johcm.co.uk |
| Northern 2 VCT PLC | NTV | | 38.3 | 1 | 12.4k | 18/05/06 | 31/01 | www.nvm.co.uk |
| Northern 3 VCT PLC | NTN | | 25.6 | | 6.62k | 18/01/06 | 30/09 | www.nvm.co.uk |
| Northern AIM VCT PLC | NNA | | 12.3 | 1 | 5.01k | 15/02/06 | 31/10 | www.nvm.co.uk |
| Northern Investors Company PLC | NRI | Fledge | 37.6 | 0.5 | 11.8k | 21/06/06 | 31/03 | www.nvm.co.uk |
| Northern Venture Trust PLC | NVT | | 27.1 | 0.5 | 6.68k | 14/12/05 | 30/09 | www.nvm.co.uk |
| Nufcor Uranium Ltd | NU. | | 78.2 | 5 | | | | www.titaniumresources.com/homepage/index.html |
| Old Mutual South Africa Trust PLC | OMT | Fledge | 82.5 | 2 | 45.4k | 07/12/05 | 31/08 | www.omam.com |
| Oryx International Growth Fund Ltd | OIG | | 29.7 | 0.5 | 3.51k | 27/09/05 | 31/03 | |
| Osprey Smaller Companies Income Fund Ltd | OSP | | 20.6 | 0.5 | 33.8k | 07/12/05 | 31/08 | www.ci.collins-stewart.com |
| Ottoman Fund (The) Ltd | OTM | | 158.3 | 10 | | | | |
| Oxford Technology 2 Venture Capital Trust PLC | OXH | | 2.8 | 0.5 | 1.24k | 19/06/06 | 28/02 | www.oxfordtechnology.com |
| Oxford Technology 3 Venture Capital Trust PLC | OTT | | 4.3 | 0.5 | 582 | 19/06/06 | 28/02 | www.oxfordtechnology.com |

Source: Hemscott (Hemscott.com)

# Listed Investment Trusts

| Company Name | EPIC | Index | Capital (£m) | NMS | 200D Avg Vol | AGM | Year End | URL |
|---|---|---|---|---|---|---|---|---|
| Oxford Technology 4 Venture Capital Trust PLC | OXF | | 9.9 | 1 | 25 | 19/06/06 | 28/02 | www.oxfordtechnology.com |
| Oxford Technology Venture Capital Trust PLC | OXT | | 2.4 | 0.5 | 85.5 | 19/06/06 | 28/02 | www.oxfordtechnology.com |
| Pacific Assets Trust PLC | PAC | S-Cap | 99.5 | 5 | 170k | 16/06/06 | 31/01 | www.pacific-assets.co.uk |
| Pacific Horizon Investment Trust PLC | PHI | Fledge | 78.0 | 3 | 85.1k | 12/10/05 | 31/07 | www.bailliegifford.com |
| Pantheon International Participations PLC | PIN | S-Cap | 207.9 | 1 | 48.4k | 22/11/05 | 30/06 | www.pipplc.com |
| Pennine AIM VCT 5 PLC | PNV5 | | 19.4 | 0.5 | 467 | 22/02/06 | 30/09 | www.downing.co.uk |
| Pennine AIM VCT 6 PLC | PNEA | | 27.7 | 0.5 | | | | |
| Pennine AIM VCT PLC | PAV | | 8.9 | 0.5 | 4.57k | 27/07/06 | 31/01 | www.downing.co.uk |
| Pennine Downing AIM VCT 2 PLC | PND | | 8.5 | 0.5 | 4.78k | 27/07/06 | 28/02 | www.downing.co.uk |
| Pennine Downing AIM VCT PLC | PDA | | 5.4 | 0.5 | 3.40k | 28/06/05 | 28/02 | www.downing.co.uk |
| Perpetual Income & Growth Investment Trust PLC | PLI | Mid 250 | 439.3 | 5 | 249k | 19/07/06 | 31/03 | www.invescoperpetual.co.uk |
| Perpetual Japanese Investment Trust PLC | PJI | Flecge | 52.3 | 3 | 164k | 23/11/05 | 31/07 | www.invescoperpetual.co.uk |
| Personal Assets Trust PLC | PNL | S-Cap | 188.6 | | 602 | 14/07/05 | 30/04 | |
| PFI Infrastructure Company (The) PLC | PFI | | 96.4 | 2 | 22.0k | 03/11/05 | 30/06 | www.pfiplc.com |
| Phoenix VCT PLC | PHX | Fledge | 9.8 | 1 | 2.79k | 23/02/06 | 31/10 | www.octopusam.com |
| Platinum Investment Trust PLC | PNI | Fledge | 67.6 | 3 | 34.7k | 09/09/05 | 30/04 | www.platinumfm.co.uk |
| Polar Capital Technology Trust PLC | PCT | S-Cap | 282.8 | 5 | 310k | 21/07/06 | 30/04 | www.polarcapitaltechnologytrust.co.uk |
| Prelude Trust PLC | PDT | Fledge | 41.7 | 1 | 73.5k | 16/08/05 | 31/03 | www.prelude-ventures.com |
| Premier Asian Assets Trust Ltd | PAAI | | 10.0 | 2 | 21.5m | 05/12/05 | 31/07 | www.bfsinvest.co.uk |
| Premier UK Dual Return Trust PLC | PUKI | | 2.0 | 2 | 52.9k | 03/04/06 | 30/11 | www.bfsinvest.co.uk |
| Premier Utilities Trust PLC | PUT | Fledge | 27.4 | 0.5 | 22.9k | 24/04/06 | 31/12 | www.premierfunds.co.uk |
| Premium Trust PLC | PTT | | 29.9 | 2 | 1.48k | 19/12/05 | 31/08 | www.martincurrie.com |
| Principle Capital Investment Trust PLC | PCIT | | 51.9 | 3 | | | | |
| Private Equity Investor PLC | PEQ | Fledge | 78.8 | 1 | 71.0k | 23/09/05 | 31/03 | www.pelplc.com |
| Prospect Japan Fund (The) Ltd | PJF | Fledge | 102.4 | 1 | 155k | 31/05/06 | 31/12 | |
| ProVen Growth & Income VCT PLC | PGO | | 8.9 | 1 | 1.58k | 05/07/05 | 28/02 | www.beringea.com |
| ProVen VCT PLC | PVN | | 28.1 | 1 | 5.61k | 05/07/05 | 28/02 | www.beringea.com |
| Psolve Alternatives PCC Ltd | PSV | | 25.0 | 5 | | | | |
| Parmigan Property Ltd | PPL | | 8.4 | 0.5 | 2.84k | 28/04/06 | 31/12 | |
| PUMA VCT II PLC | PMV | | 8.7 | 1 | | 24/05/06 | 31/12 | |
| PUMA VCT III PLC | PUMC | | 18.5 | 1 | | | | |
| PUMA VCT IV PLC | PUMD | | 18.5 | 1 | | | | |
| PUMA VCT PLC | PUA | | 12.7 | 1 | | | | |
| Quester VCT 4 PLC | QUT | | 26.8 | 0.5 | 11.3k | 24/05/06 | 31/12 | www.quester.co.uk |
| Quester VCT 5 PLC | QUV | | 18.6 | 0.5 | 4.37k | 26/02/06 | 31/12 | www.quester.co.uk |
| Quester VCT PLC | QUR | | 42.5 | 0.5 | 25.8k | 19/04/05 | 31/12 | www.quester.co.uk |
| RAB Special Situations Company Ltd | RSS | | 76.0 | 5 | 372k | 20/06/06 | 28/02 | www.rabcap.com |
| Real Estate Opportunities Ltd | REO | | 253.0 | 3 | 177k | 12/07/06 | 31/12 | www.realestateopportunities.biz |
| Recovery Trust PLC | RVYI | Fledge | 4.0 | 3 | 78.8k | 20/06/06 | 31/07 | www.montanaro.co.uk |
| Red Leopard Holdings PLC | RLH | | 3.9 | 3 | 33.0k | 30/11/05 | | |
| Renaissance US Growth Investment Trust PLC | RUG | Fledge | 55.4 | 1 | 22.3k | 18/07/06 | 31/03 | www.rencapital.com |
| Rensburg AIM VCT PLC | RSB | | 29.8 | 0.5 | 14.1k | 26/07/06 | 28/02 | www.rensburgaimvct.co.uk |
| Resources Investment Trust PLC | REI | Fledge | 47.1 | 0.5 | 67.9k | 13/12/05 | 30/09 | |
| Rights and Issues Inv Trust PLC | RIII | | 20.0 | 0.5 | 3.24k | 16/03/06 | 31/12 | |

Source: Hemscott (Hemscott.com)

## Listed Investment Trusts

| Company Name | EPIC | Index | Capital (£m) | NMS | 200D Avg Vol | AGM | Year End | URL |
|---|---|---|---|---|---|---|---|---|
| RIT Capital Partners PLC | RCP | Mid 250 | 1407.9 | 3 | 178k | 13/07/06 | 31/03 | www.ritcap.co.uk |
| Royal London UK Equity & Income Trust PLC | RLU | Fledge | 14.2 | 3 | 198k | 14/12/05 | 31/08 | www.rlam.co.uk |
| Rutland Trust PLC | RUT | | 113.1 | 2 | 130k | 18/05/06 | 31/12 | www.rutlandtrust.co.uk |
| Schroder AsiaPacific Fund PLC | SDP | S-Cap | 197.7 | 5 | 399k | 27/01/06 | 30/09 | www.schroders.co.uk/its |
| Schroder Income Growth Fund PLC | SCF | S-Cap | 146.6 | 1 | 53.1k | 08/12/05 | 31/08 | www.schroders.co.uk/its |
| Schroder Japan Growth Fund PLC | SJG | S-Cap | 137.5 | 5 | 260k | 10/11/05 | 31/07 | www.schroders.co.uk/its |
| Schroder Oriental Income Fund Ltd | SOI | S-Cap | 148.8 | 10 | 266k | | | www.schroders.co.uk |
| Schroder Split Investment Fund PLC | SCS | Fledge | 43.7 | 1 | 36.9k | 08/03/06 | 31/10 | www.schroders.co.uk/its |
| Schroder UK Growth Fund PLC | SDU | S-Cap | 197.4 | 5 | 236k | 02/08/06 | 30/04 | www.schroders.co.uk |
| Schroder UK Mid & Small Cap Fund PLC | SCP | Fledge | 71.8 | 2 | 49.6k | 23/01/06 | 30/09 | www.schroders.co.uk/its |
| Scottish American Investment Co (The) PLC | SCAM | S-Cap | 296.8 | 3 | 98.4k | 30/03/06 | 31/12 | www.bailliegifford.com |
| Scottish Investment Trust PLC | SCIN | Mid 250 | 605.5 | 3 | 520k | 27/01/06 | 31/10 | www.sit.co.uk |
| Scottish Mortgage Investment Trust PLC | SMT | Mid 250 | 1327.9 | 5 | 449k | 28/06/06 | 31/03 | www.bailliegifford.com |
| Scottish Oriental Smaller Co's Tr (The) PLC | SST | Fledge | 64.0 | 1 | 29.5k | 24/01/06 | 31/08 | www.scottishoriental.co.uk |
| Second London American Trust PLC | SLT | Fledge | 1.6 | 0.5 | 6.73k | 02/08/05 | 31/03 | |
| Securities Trust of Scotland PLC | STS | S-Cap | 122.4 | 5 | 156k | 04/07/06 | 31/03 | www.securitiestrust.com |
| Shires Income PLC | SHRS | S-Cap | 88.7 | 0.5 | 24.1k | 07/07/06 | 31/03 | www.glasgowinvestmentmanagers.co.uk |
| Shires Smaller Companies PLC | SHD | Fledge | 52.8 | 0.5 | 36.2k | 31/03/05 | 31/12 | www.glasgowim.co.uk |
| Singer & Friedlander AIM 3 VCT PLC | SFA | | 37.3 | 0.5 | 28.2k | 06/07/06 | 31/01 | www.sfim.co.uk |
| Sitka Health Fund VCT PLC | STH | | 7.9 | 0.5 | 2.72k | 25/05/06 | 31/01 | www.sitkapartners.com |
| Small Companies Dividend Trust PLC | SDV | Fledge | 35.1 | 0.5 | 27.5k | 25/11/05 | 30/04 | www.chelvertonam.com |
| Smaller Companies Value Trust PLC | SVLI | | 13.0 | 1 | 27.5k | 08/09/05 | 30/04 | www.swipartnership.com |
| SR Europe Investment Trust PLC | SR. | Fledge | 49.0 | 1 | 44.1k | 26/04/06 | 31/12 | www.sreit.co.uk |
| Standard Life Equity Income Trust PLC | SLET | S-Cap | 115.9 | 2 | 71.4k | 20/12/05 | 30/09 | www.standardlife.com |
| Standard Life European Private Equity Trust PLC | SEP | S-Cap | 291.2 | 3 | 136k | 30/01/06 | 30/09 | www.standardlifeinvestments.com |
| Standard Life Investments Property Inc Trust Ltd | SLI | S-Cap | 133.5 | 5 | 253k | 12/07/06 | 31/12 | www.standardlifeinvestments.com |
| Stocks Convertible Trust PLC | SKV | Fledge | 16.8 | 0.5 | 3.43k | 13/10/05 | 31/05 | |
| Strategic Equity Capital PLC | SEC | Fledge | 64.6 | 3 | 116k | | | www.strategicequitycap.com |
| Strathdon Investments PLC | STV | | 13.2 | 1 | 70.1k | 26/07/05 | 31/03 | www.strathdon.com |
| SVG Capital PLC | SVI | Mid 250 | 1014.7 | 3 | 149k | 24/04/06 | 31/12 | www.svgcapital.com |
| SVM Global Fund PLC | SVG | S-Cap | 187.2 | 2 | 80.1k | 13/12/05 | 30/09 | www.svmonline.co.uk |
| SVM UK Active Fund PLC | SVU | S-Cap | 80.2 | 2 | 112k | 11/07/06 | 31/03 | www.svmonline.co.uk |
| SVM UK Emerging Fund PLC | SVM | Fledge | 2.5 | 0.5 | 5.00k | 19/07/06 | 31/03 | www.svmonline.co.uk |
| T2 Income Fund Ltd | T2I | | 35.7 | 2 | 16.6k | | | |
| Talisman First Venture Capital Trust PLC | TFV | Fledge | 1.3 | 0.5 | 6.28k | 25/08/05 | 31/03 | |
| Tea Plantations Investment Trust PLC | TEA | Fledge | 8.3 | 0.5 | 13.4k | 21/02/06 | 30/09 | www.teaplantations.co.uk |
| Teesland Advantage Property Income Trust Ltd | TAP | S-Cap | 154.2 | 5 | 449k | 07/06/06 | 31/12 | |
| Temple Bar Investment Trust PLC | TMPL | Mid 250 | 452.4 | 1 | 67.6k | 27/03/06 | 31/12 | www.itstemplebar.com |
| Templeton Emerging Markets Inv Tr PLC | TEM | Mid 250 | 1425.7 | 25 | 1.42m | 27/09/05 | 30/04 | www.franklintempleton.co.uk |
| Thompson Clive Investments PLC | TCI | Fledge | 7.5 | 0.5 | 872 | 10/05/05 | 31/12 | www.tcvc.com |
| Throgmorton Trust (The) PLC | THRG | S-Cap | 269.1 | 5 | 305k | 28/03/06 | 30/11 | www.framlington.co.uk |
| Tiger Resource Finance PLC | TIR | | 7.3 | 15 | 314k | 07/08/06 | 31/12 | www.tiger-rf.com |
| TR European Growth Trust PLC | TRG | S-Cap | 313.2 | 5 | 171k | 31/10/05 | 30/06 | www.itshenderson.co.uk |
| TR Property Investment Trust PLC | TRY | Mid 250 | 695.4 | 15 | 1.06m | 18/07/06 | 31/03 | www.trproperty.co.uk |

## Listed Investment Trusts

| Company Name | EPIC | Index | Capital (£m) | NMS | 200D Avg Vol | AGM | Year End | URL |
|---|---|---|---|---|---|---|---|---|
| Tribune Trust PLC (Global Managed Fund) | TBE | | 88.7 | 0.5 | 27.8k | 22/04/06 | 31/12 | www.tribunetrust.com |
| Tribune Trust PLC (UK Index Fund) | TBUK | | 224.7 | 1 | 40.3k | 22/04/06 | 31/12 | www.tribunetrust.com |
| Tribune UK Tracker PLC | TBUK | S-Cap | 196.1 | 5 | | | | |
| Trio Finance Ltd | TRIO | | 55.7 | 2 | | | | |
| TriVen VCT PLC | TVV | | 7.3 | 0.5 | 6.38k | 24/05/06 | 31/01 | www.trivestvct.co.uk |
| TriVest VCT PLC | TST | S-Cap | 37.0 | 0.5 | 10.4k | 31/01/06 | 30/09 | www.swipartnership.com |
| UK Balanced Property Trust Ltd (The) | UBR | | 298.6 | 10 | 641k | 28/07/06 | 31/03 | www.swipartnership.com |
| UK Select Trust Ltd | UKT | | 25.8 | 0.5 | 6.12k | 04/05/06 | 31/12 | www.swipartnership.com |
| Ukraine Opportunity Trust PLC | UKRO | | 34.8 | 1 | | | | |
| Unicorn AIM VCT II PLC | UAVT | | 22.4 | 0.5 | 121 | 22/03/06 | 31/12 | www.unicornam.com |
| Unicorn AIM VCT PLC | UAV | | 27.7 | 0.5 | 14.4k | 20/01/06 | 30/09 | www.unicornam.com |
| US Special Opportunities Trust PLC | USPI | | 41.2 | 1 | 115k | 27/09/05 | 31/05 | www.sinclairhenderson.co.uk |
| Utilico Emerging Markets Ltd | UEM | | 81.5 | 5 | 149k | 31/07/06 | 31/03 | www.utilicoemergingmarkets.com |
| Utilico Investment Trust PLC | UILW | S-Cap | 56.3 | 1 | 4.77k | 11/10/05 | 30/06 | www.utilico.co.uk |
| Value & Income Trust PLC | VIN | S-Cap | 97.7 | 1 | 38.7k | 07/07/06 | 31/03 | |
| Ventus 2 VCT PLC | VEN2 | | 12.8 | 1 | | | | |
| Ventus 3 VCT PLC | VEN3 | | 11.2 | 1 | | | | |
| Ventus VCT PLC | VEN | | 14.8 | 1 | | | | |
| Welsh Industrial Investment Trust PLC | WII | Fledge | 5.3 | 0.5 | 5 | 12/07/06 | 28/02 | www.ventusvct.com |
| Westbury Property Fund (The) Ltd | WPF | | 145.7 | 2 | 129 | 01/09/05 | 05/04 | |
| Western Selection PLC | WSE | | 6.6 | 0.5 | 66.8k | 19/05/06 | 31/12 | www.berringtonfm.com |
| Witan Investment Trust PLC | WTAN | Mid 250 | 1072.5 | 15 | 6.14k | 28/09/05 | 30/06 | www.westernselection.co.uk |
| Witan Pacific Investment Trust PLC | WPC | S-Cap | 125.0 | 3 | 639k | 24/04/06 | 31/12 | www.witan.com |
| Zero Preference Growth Trust (The) PLC | ZPG | Fledge | 1.3 | 2 | 120k | 22/06/06 | 31/01 | www.witan.com |
| | | | | | 77.1k | 08/12/05 | 31/07 | www.bfsinvest.co.uk |

- Members of AIM

## Members of AIM

| Company Name | EPIC | Sector | Capital (£m) | NMS | 200D Avg Vol | AGM | Year End | URL |
|---|---|---|---|---|---|---|---|---|
| @UK PLC | ATUK | Software & Computer Services | 20.7 | 5 | | 15/06/06 | 31/12 | www.ukplc.net |
| 1pm PLC | OPM | General Financial | 4.2 | 5 | | | | |
| 1st Dental Laboratories PLC | FDT | Health Care Equipment & Services | 5.9 | 2 | 64.9k | 04/07/06 | 30/11 | www.1stdental.co.uk |
| 2 ergo Group PLC | RGO | Mobile Telecommunications | 58.3 | 1 | 38.0k | 30/01/06 | 31/08 | www.2ergo.co.uk |
| 3DM Worldwide PLC | TDM | Chemicals | 7.9 | 10 | 349k | 13/09/05 | 31/12 | www.3dmworldwide.com |
| 4Less Group (The) PLC | FL. | General Financial | 1.9 | 1 | 5.79k | 30/05/06 | 31/03 | www.the4lessgroup.com |
| 9999 PLC | NNN | General Financial | 1.4 | 2 | 7.21k | | | |
| Abbey PLC | ABBY | Construction & Materials | 172.8 | 0.5 | 12.0k | 07/10/05 | 30/04 | www.abbeyplc.ie |
| Abcam PLC | ABC | General Retailers | 92.1 | 2 | | 15/10/05 | 30/06 | www.abcam.com |
| Abraxus Investments PLC | AXU | Real Estate | 1.4 | 1 | 12.7k | 27/10/05 | 31/03 | |
| Access Intelligence PLC | ACC | Software & Computer Services | 4.3 | 3 | 133k | 20/06/06 | 30/11 | |
| Accident Exchange Group PLC | ACE | General Financial | 219.4 | 3 | 145k | 20/07/06 | 30/04 | www.accidentexchange.com |
| Accsys Technologies PLC | AXS | General Industrials | 114.1 | 5 | | 20/11/05 | 31/03 | www.accsysplc.com |
| Accuma Group PLC | ACG | General Financial | 78.1 | 2 | 108k | 25/01/06 | 31/07 | www.accumagroup.com |
| Acertec PLC | ACER | Industrial Metals | 75.0 | | | | | |
| ACP Capital Ltd | APL | General Financial | 66.4 | 3 | | | | www.actifgroup.com |
| ACP Mezzanine Ltd | ACPM | Equity Investment Instruments | 71.9 | 10 | | | | |
| Actif Group PLC | ACT | General Retailers | 1.2 | 3 | 30.6k | 20/12/05 | 30/07 | www.actifgroup.com |
| ADDleisure PLC | ADE | Leisure Goods | 2.9 | 5 | 92.9k | 16/12/05 | 31/07 | www.addleisure.co.uk |
| Addworth PLC | ADW | General Financial | 1.9 | 3 | 118k | 23/07/06 | 31/12 | www.addworth.co.uk |
| AdEPT Telecom PLC | ADT | Fixed Line Telecommunications | 32.0 | 2 | 30.6k | 31/07/05 | 31/03 | www.adept-telecom.co.uk |
| Adeste Investments PLC | AET | General Financial | 0.1 | 3 | 81.8k | 19/07/06 | 31/10 | |
| ADL PLC | AD. | Health Care Equipment & Services | 5.0 | 0.5 | 2.59k | 07/09/05 | 31/03 | www.adlcare.com |
| Adorian PLC | ADP | Media | 1.0 | 0.5 | 7.39k | 29/03/05 | 31/12 | |
| AdVal Group PLC | ADL | Support Services | 0.7 | 1 | 22.7k | 25/10/05 | 31/03 | www.advalgroup.co.uk |
| Advance Visual Communications PLC | ACV | Software & Computer Services | 0.2 | 1 | 241k | 30/12/05 | 30/06 | |
| Advanced Fluid Connections PLC | AFC | Industrial Engineering | 9.9 | 100 | 1.49m | 26/05/06 | 31/12 | www.advancedfluidconnections.co.uk |
| Advanced Medical Solutions Group PLC | AMS | Health Care Equipment & Services | 14.6 | 10 | 305k | 31/05/06 | 31/12 | www.admedsol.com |
| Advanced Power Components PLC | APC | Electronic & Electrical Equipment | 4.1 | 0.5 | 59.9k | 20/01/06 | 31/08 | www.apc-plc.co.uk |
| Advanced Smartcard Technologies PLC | SMRT | Software & Computer Services | 8.3 | 5 | | 02/01/06 | 30/09 | |
| Advent Capital (Holdings) PLC | ADV | Nonlife Insurance | 112.7 | 3 | 14.6k | 02/05/06 | 31/12 | www.adventgroup.co.uk |
| Adventis Group PLC | ATG | Media | 13.7 | 0.5 | 43.1k | 01/06/06 | 31/12 | www.adventis.co.uk |
| ADVFN PLC | AFN | General Financial | 15.7 | 50 | 1.72m | 06/12/05 | 30/06 | www.advfn.com |
| Adwalker PLC | AWR | Media | 3.8 | 2 | 137k | 31/03/05 | 28/02 | www.adwalker.co.uk |
| AEC Education PLC | AEC | Support Services | 2.6 | 0.5 | 10.7k | 01/08/06 | 31/12 | www.aeceduplc.co.uk |
| Aero Inventory PLC | AI. | Aerospace & Defense | 150.3 | 2 | 196k | 21/11/05 | 30/06 | www.aero-inventory.com |
| AeroBox PLC | ARX | Chemicals | 2.5 | 25 | 663k | 20/06/06 | 31/12 | www.aeroboxplc.com |
| Afren PLC | AFR | Oil & Gas Producers | 86.6 | 10 | 1.45m | 29/06/06 | 31/12 | www.afren.com |
| African Consolidated Resources PLC | AFCR | Mining | 22.7 | 5 | | | | |
| African Copper PLC | ACU | Industrial Metals | 92.8 | 5 | 270k | 06/07/06 | 31/12 | www.africancopper.com |
| African Diamonds PLC | AFD | Mining | 125.5 | 5 | 402k | 23/01/06 | 30/06 | www.afdiamonds.com |
| African Eagle Resources PLC | AFE | Mining | 19.5 | 15 | 435k | 29/06/06 | 31/12 | www.africaneagle.co.uk |
| African Platinum PLC | APP | Mining | 154.5 | 25 | 2.41m | 25/11/05 | 31/03 | www.afplats.com |
| AfriOre Ltd | AFO | Mining | 140.9 | 2 | 8.74k | 01/06/06 | 28/02 | www.afriore.com |

Source: Hemscott (Hemscott.com)

## Members of AIM

| Company Name | EPIC | Sector | Capital (£m) | NMS | 200D Avg Vol | AGM | Year End | URL |
|---|---|---|---|---|---|---|---|---|
| AGI Therapeutics PLC | AGI | Pharmaceuticals & Biotechnology | 76.2 | 5 | | 15/06/06 | 31/12 | www.agitherapeutics.com |
| AI Claims Solutions PLC | ACS | Travel & Leisure | 9.8 | 2 | | 18/11/05 | 26/06 | www.autoindemnity.co.uk |
| Air Music & Media Group PLC | AMU | Media | 11.3 | 0.5 | 33.6k | 23/09/05 | 31/03 | www.airmusicandmedia.co.uk |
| Airsprung Furniture Group PLC | APG | Household Goods | 5.5 | 2 | 26.5k | 07/09/05 | 31/03 | www.airsprung-furniture.co.uk |
| Alba Mineral Resources PLC | ALBA | Mining | 5.1 | 2 | 10.5k | 10/05/06 | 30/11 | www.albamineralresources.com |
| Albemarle & Bond Holdings PLC | ABM | General Financial | 91.6 | 1 | 104k | 04/11/05 | 30/06 | www.albemarlebond.com |
| Aldgate Capital PLC | AGT | Equity Investment Instruments | 7.1 | 5 | 40.4k | | | |
| Alexander Mining PLC | AXM | Mining | 31.6 | 15 | 640k | 30/05/05 | 31/12 | www.alexandermining.com |
| Alkane Energy PLC | ALK | Oil & Gas Producers | 14.2 | 25 | 717k | 10/05/06 | 31/12 | www.alkane.co.uk |
| All IPO PLC | ALP | General Financial | 6.5 | 0.5 | 22.1k | 06/12/05 | 30/06 | www.allipo.com |
| All New Video PLC | ANV | Mobile Telecommunications | 3.0 | 3 | 92.0k | | | |
| Allergy Therapeutics PLC | AGY | Pharmaceuticals & Biotechnology | 83.6 | 2 | 152k | 02/11/05 | 30/06 | www.allergytherapeutics.com |
| Alliance Pharma PLC | APH | Pharmaceuticals & Biotechnology | 21.9 | 10 | 106k | 12/05/06 | 31/12 | www.alliancepharma.co.uk |
| Alltracel Pharmaceuticals PLC | AP. | Pharmaceuticals & Biotechnology | 11.8 | 10 | 434k | 19/06/06 | 31/12 | www.alltracel.com |
| Alltrue Investments PLC | ATR | General Financial | 1.8 | 3 | 94.7k | 08/08/06 | 31/12 | |
| Alpha Strategic PLC | APS | General Financial | 3.3 | 0.5 | 4.39k | | | |
| Alternative Networks PLC | AN. | Fixed Line Telecommunications | 47.3 | 0.5 | 82.1k | 27/01/06 | 30/09 | www.alternativenetworks.com |
| Altona Resources PLC | ANR | Mining | 18.7 | 15 | 848k | 28/07/06 | | |
| Amarin Corporation PLC | AMRN | Pharmaceuticals & Biotechnology | 110.4 | 5 | | | | |
| Amazing Holdings PLC | AMZ | Travel & Leisure | 24.1 | 3 | | 30/09/05 | 31/05 | www.amazing.co.im |
| Amberley Group PLC | AMB | Software & Computer Services | 4.7 | 0.5 | 19.8k | 25/05/06 | 30/04 | |
| Amco Corporation PLC | ARP | Construction & Materials | 44.9 | 0.5 | 2.06k | 01/06/06 | 31/12 | www.amco-corporation.plc.uk |
| Amino Technologies PLC | AMO | Technology Hardware & Equipment | 42.8 | 2 | 199k | 22/04/05 | 30/11 | www.aminocom.com |
| Amphion Innovations PLC | AMP | General Financial | 26.7 | 2 | 14.3k | 08/06/06 | 31/12 | www.amphionplc.com |
| Amteus PLC | AUS | Technology Hardware & Equipment | 32.9 | 2 | | 15/01/06 | 30/09 | www.amteus.com |
| Andor Technology PLC | AND | Electronic & Electrical Equipment | 21.3 | 1 | 19.8k | 05/01/06 | 30/09 | www.andor.com |
| Andrews Sykes Group PLC | ASY | Support Services | 64.6 | 0.5 | 10.5k | 07/06/06 | 31/12 | www.andrews-sykes.com |
| Angel Biotechnology Holdings PLC | ABH | Pharmaceuticals & Biotechnology | 4.5 | 25 | | 19/06/06 | 31/12 | www.angelbio.com |
| ANGLE PLC | AGL | Support Services | 24.3 | 0.5 | 51.0k | 25/08/05 | 30/04 | www.angletechnology.com |
| Anglo Asian Mining PLC | AAZ | Mining | 24.5 | 5 | 201k | 26/01/06 | 31/12 | www.aamining.com |
| Angus & Ross PLC | AGU | Mining | 29.9 | 5 | 393k | 31/08/05 | 28/02 | www.angusandross.com |
| Ant PLC | ANTP | Software & Computer Services | 13.2 | 5 | 35.4k | 23/05/06 | 31/12 | www.antplc.com |
| Antonov PLC | ATV | Automobiles & Parts | 16.5 | 0.5 | 15.5k | 22/07/05 | 31/12 | www.antonov-transmission.com |
| AorTech International PLC | AOR | General Financial | 15.0 | 0.5 | 12.3k | 26/10/05 | 31/03 | www.aortech.com |
| Apace Media PLC | APA | Media | 11.6 | 2 | 108k | 29/07/06 | 31/12 | www.apacemedia.co.uk |
| Appian Technology PLC | APN | Electronic & Electrical Equipment | 12.7 | 5 | | 30/11/05 | 30/09 | |
| Applied Optical Technologies PLC | ALT | Support Services | 24.6 | 3 | 198k | 27/07/06 | 31/03 | www.aotgroup.com |
| Aquilo PLC | AQL | Support Services | 8.3 | 10 | 286k | 06/09/05 | 31/12 | www.aquiloplc.co.uk |
| Arbuthnot Banking Group PLC | ARBB | General Financial | 83.1 | 0.5 | 14.2k | 23/05/06 | 31/12 | www.arbuthnotgroup.com |
| Arc Fund Management Holdings PLC | AFM | General Financial | 4.3 | 5 | | | | |
| ARC Risk Management Group PLC | ARC | Support Services | 3.0 | 10 | 892k | 07/07/05 | 31/03 | www.arcrisk.com |
| Archimedia Ventures PLC | ARV | General Financial | 0.3 | 1 | 7.15k | 28/07/06 | | |
| Archipelago Resources PLC | AR. | Mining | 51.2 | 1 | 65.5k | 25/07/06 | 31/12 | www.mining-investor.com/arch |
| Arden Partners PLC | ARDN | General Financial | 40.9 | 3 | | | | www.vimio.com |

Source: Hemscott (Hemscott.com)

## Members of AIM

| Company Name | EPIC | Sector | Capital (£m) | NMS | 200D Avg Vol | AGM | Year End | URL |
|---|---|---|---|---|---|---|---|---|
| Ardent Group PLC | ARN | General Financial | 13.3 | 0.5 | 42.2k | 28/02/06 | 30/06 | www.arianaresources.com |
| Ariana Resources PLC | AAU | Mining | 6.0 | 2 | 114k | 19/07/06 | 31/12 | www.aricom.plc.uk |
| Aricom PLC | TIO | Chemicals | 203.0 | 2 | 1.28m | 06/06/06 | 31/12 | |
| Arko Holdings PLC | AKO | Electricity | 9.9 | 2 | 88.4k | 20/07/05 | 31/12 | |
| Armour Group PLC | AMR | Automobiles & Parts | 22.9 | 2 | 240k | 09/12/05 | 31/08 | www.armourgroup.uk.com |
| Arthro Kinetics PLC | AKI | Pharmaceuticals & Biotechnology | 30.8 | 3 | | | | www.arthro-kinetics.com |
| Artisan (UK) PLC | ART | Household Goods | 11.9 | 10 | 343k | 07/09/05 | 31/03 | www.artisan-plc.co.uk |
| Ascent Resources PLC | AST | Oil & Gas Producers | 22.9 | 10 | 956k | 14/02/06 | 30/06 | www.ascentresources.com |
| Ascribe PLC | ASP | Software & Computer Services | 35.4 | 3 | 266k | 26/10/05 | 30/06 | www.ascribe.com |
| Asfare Group PLC | ASF | Industrial Engineering | 4.1 | 0.5 | 4.53k | 18/07/06 | 31/03 | www.as-fire.co.uk |
| Ashton Penney Holdings PLC | ASHT | Support Services | 1.8 | 3 | 29.2k | 16/12/05 | 31/03 | |
| Asia Capital PLC | ASI | General Financial | 0.3 | 3 | 66.2k | 22/09/05 | 31/12 | |
| Asia Energy PLC | AEN | Mining | 160.5 | 15 | 557k | 20/12/05 | 30/06 | www.asia-energy.com |
| ASITE PLC | ASE | Software & Computer Services | 2.1 | 1 | 24.4k | 27/07/06 | 31/12 | www.asite.com |
| ASOS PLC | ASC | General Retailers | 57.9 | 10 | 443k | 17/10/05 | 31/03 | www.asos.com |
| Aspen Clean Energy PLC | ACEP | General Financial | 3.3 | 2 | 81.3k | 26/07/06 | | www.atc.co.uk |
| AT Communications Group PLC | ATCG | Software & Computer Services | 26.8 | 2 | 128k | 02/06/06 | 31/12 | www.ata-group.co.uk |
| ATA Group PLC | ATP | Support Services | 5.6 | 0.5 | 9.05k | 19/05/06 | 31/12 | |
| Atelis PLC | ATEL | Technology Hardware & Equipment | 5.0 | 3 | | | | |
| ATH Resources PLC | ATH | Mining | 81.0 | 1 | 35.6k | 09/01/06 | 02/10 | www.ath.co.uk |
| Atheiney Trust PLC | ATY | Equity Investment Instruments | 2.3 | 0.5 | 569 | 24/05/06 | 31/12 | |
| Atlantic Global PLC | ATL | Software & Computer Services | 3.5 | 1 | 7.29k | 19/04/06 | 31/12 | www.atlantic-global.com |
| Atlas Estates Ltd | ATLS | Real Estate | 128.6 | | | | | |
| Augean PLC | AUG | Support Services | 98.9 | 10 | 303k | 31/05/06 | 31/12 | www.augeanplc.com |
| Auket Fitzroy Robinson Group PLC | AUK | Support Services | 5.4 | 3 | 116k | 23/03/06 | 30/09 | www.auketfitzroyrobinson.com |
| Aurora Russia Ltd | AURR | General Financial | 66.4 | 3 | | | | |
| Aurum Mining PLC | AUR | Mining | 11.2 | 3 | 70.4k | 28/10/05 | 31/03 | www.aurummining.net |
| Autoclenz Holdings PLC | ACZ | General Retailers | 11.4 | 3 | | 30/04/05 | 31/12 | www.autoclenz.co.uk |
| Avacta Group PLC | AVCT | Food Producers | 24.2 | 3 | 83.4k | 21/10/05 | 30/04 | |
| Avanti Capital PLC | AVA | Equity Investment Instruments | 10.5 | 1 | 16.0k | 28/11/05 | 30/06 | www.avanticap.com |
| Avanti Screenmedia Group PLC | ASG | Media | 61.8 | 1 | 56.5k | 14/10/05 | 30/06 | www.avanti-screenmedia.co.uk |
| Avarae Global Coins PLC | AVR | Nonequity Investment Instruments | 8.9 | 5 | | | | |
| Avesco PLC | ASO | Media | 18.1 | 1 | 21.2k | 08/09/05 | 31/03 | www.avesco.co.uk |
| Avid Holdings PLC | AVD | Support Services | 4.4 | 10 | 622k | 04/08/06 | 31/12 | |
| Avingtrans PLC | AVG | Industrial Engineering | 21.0 | 0.5 | 29.3k | 05/10/05 | 31/05 | www.avingtrans.plc.uk |
| Avocet Mining PLC | AVM | Mining | 218.5 | 3 | 431k | 27/09/05 | 31/03 | www.avocet.co.uk |
| Axeon Holdings PLC | AXE | Technology Hardware & Equipment | 15.9 | 3 | 17.8k | 13/06/06 | 31/12 | |
| AxisMobile PLC | AXIS | General Financial | 18.1 | 1 | 1.38k | | | |
| Azman PLC | AMAN | General Financial | 0.8 | 10 | 75.9k | 16/06/06 | | |
| Azure Holdings PLC | AZH | Support Services | 0.1 | 5 | 101k | 28/07/06 | 31/12 | |
| B.P. Marsh & Partners PLC | BPM | General Financial | 36.5 | 2 | | 28/06/06 | 31/01 | www.bpmarsh.co.uk |
| Bailey (C H) PLC | BLEY | Industrial Engineering | 6.8 | 1 | 2.35k | 23/11/05 | 31/03 | www.chbaileyplc.co.uk |
| Bakery Services PLC | BKE | Food & Drug Retailers | 0.3 | 5 | 306k | 02/12/05 | 31/03 | www.bakeryservices.co.uk |
| Baltic Oil Terminals PLC | BTC | Oil & Gas Producers | 67.8 | 2 | | | | |

Source: Hemscott (Hemscott.com)

# Company Directory

## Members of AIM

| Company Name | EPIC | Sector | Capital (£m) | NMS | 200D Avg Vol | AGM | Year End | URL |
|---|---|---|---|---|---|---|---|---|
| Baltimore PLC | BLM | General Financial | 20.1 | 1 | | 31/05/06 | 31/12 | www.baltimoreplc.com |
| Bango PLC | BGO | Software & Computer Services | 31.9 | 2 | 58.7k | 12/07/06 | 31/03 | www.bango.com |
| Bank Restaurant Group PLC | BKR | Travel & Leisure | 1.5 | 1 | 52.0k | 28/03/06 | 31/10 | www.bankrestaurants.com |
| Bartercard PLC | BRTR | Support Services | 21.4 | 3 | 129k | 19/10/05 | 31/03 | www.bartercard.com |
| Base Group PLC | BS. | Travel & Leisure | 0.6 | 25 | 1.24m | 16/12/05 | 28/02 | www.base-group.com |
| BBI Holdings PLC | BBI | Pharmaceuticals & Biotechnology | 24.2 | 2 | 50.7k | 23/09/05 | 31/03 | www.british-biocell.co.uk |
| Beaufort PLC | BFRD | Electronic & Electrical Equipment | 0.1 | 10 | 21.7m | 26/08/05 | 31/12 | www.beauford.co.uk |
| Beaufort International Group PLC | BFG | Support Services | 0.6 | 0.5 | 3.08k | 05/06/06 | 30/09 | |
| Begbies Traynor Group PLC | BEG | Support Services | 122.1 | 2 | 148k | 01/09/05 | 30/04 | www.begbies-traynor.com |
| Belgravium Technologies PLC | BVM | Technology Hardware & Equipment | 9.8 | 5 | 200k | 25/05/06 | 31/12 | www.belgraviuminvestorrelations.com |
| Bella Media PLC | BLL | Software & Computer Services | 1.0 | 200 | 5.67m | 14/03/06 | 30/06 | |
| Beowulf Mining PLC | BEM | General Financial | 3.0 | 10 | 60.8k | 21/04/06 | 31/12 | www.beowulfmining.com |
| Berkeley Scott Group PLC | BGP | Support Services | 1.5 | 0.5 | 3.50k | 21/02/06 | 30/09 | www.berkeley-scott.com |
| Betex Group PLC | BTX | Travel & Leisure | 64.5 | 3 | | 27/07/06 | | |
| betinternet.com PLC | BET | Travel & Leisure | 11.1 | 5 | 161k | 11/01/06 | 29/05 | www.betinternet.com |
| BETonSPORTS PLC | BSS | Travel & Leisure | 110.2 | 10 | 1.03m | 14/07/06 | 06/02 | www.betonsports.co.uk |
| Bidtimes PLC | BDT | Equity Investment Instruments | 0.5 | 2 | 14.8k | 20/09/05 | 28/02 | www.bidtimes.com |
| Billam PLC | BLLM | Equity Investment Instruments | 1.9 | 0.5 | 24.0k | 14/07/06 | 31/12 | www.billamplc.co.uk |
| Biofuels Corporation PLC | BFC | Chemicals | 46.3 | 10 | 728k | 02/03/05 | 31/03 | www.biofuelscorp.com |
| Biofusion PLC | BFN | Pharmaceuticals & Biotechnology | 32.5 | 0.5 | 10.9k | 18/11/05 | 31/07 | www.biofusion.co.uk |
| Biofutures International PLC | BIP | General Financial | 10.3 | 3 | | | | |
| Bioganix PLC | BGX | Support Services | 8.6 | 2 | | | | |
| Bionex Investments PLC | BNX | Equity Investment Instruments | 3.1 | 3 | 80.2k | 24/01/06 | 30/09 | |
| BioProgress PLC | BPRG | Chemicals | 54.1 | 25 | 1.18m | 22/06/06 | 31/12 | www.bioprogress.com |
| Birmingham City PLC | BMC | Travel & Leisure | 15.7 | 0.5 | 9.55k | 05/04/06 | 31/08 | www.bcfc.com |
| Black Arrow Group PLC | BLKA | Household Goods | 15.1 | 0.5 | 5.30k | 06/10/05 | 31/03 | www.logic-office.co.uk |
| Black Raven Properties PLC | BRP | General Financial | 3.6 | 2 | 43.6k | 26/06/06 | 30/11 | |
| Black Rock Oil & Gas PLC | BLR | Oil & Gas Producers | 7.7 | 75 | 3.54m | 19/12/05 | 30/06 | www.blackrockoilandgasplc.co.uk |
| Black Sea Property Fund (The) Ltd | BKSA | Real Estate | 53.9 | 10 | 544k | 26/04/06 | 31/12 | www.dcmanagement.com |
| Blackrock International Land PLC | BLK | Real Estate | 151.6 | 15 | | | | www.bilplc.com |
| Blackstar Investors PLC | BLCK | Equity Investment Instruments | 40.2 | 1 | 24.6k | 03/08/06 | 31/12 | |
| Blavod Extreme Spirits PLC | BES | Beverages | 12.0 | 10 | 134k | 18/07/06 | 31/03 | www.blavod.com |
| Block Shield Corporation PLC | BLS | Electronic & Electrical Equipment | 39.8 | 2 | 70.9k | 18/07/05 | 28/02 | www.blockshield.com |
| Blooms of Bressingham Holdings PLC | BBR | General Retailers | 23.2 | 1 | 54.0k | 05/07/06 | 29/01 | www.bloomsofbressingham.com |
| Blue Star Capital PLC | BLU | General Financial | 11.3 | 2 | 118k | 23/05/06 | 30/09 | |
| Blue Star Mobile Group PLC | BTR | Mobile Telecommunications | 3.6 | 1 | 50.6k | 15/06/06 | 26/02 | www.bluestarmobile.com |
| Blueheath Holdings PLC | BLH | Food Producers | 18.3 | 5 | 89.6k | 26/07/06 | 31/12 | www.blueheath.co.uk |
| BNB Recruitment Solutions PLC | BNB | Support Services | 16.4 | 0.5 | 12.5k | 30/11/05 | 31/07 | www.bnbgroup.co.uk |
| BNS Telecom Group PLC | BTP | Mobile Telecommunications | 20.4 | 3 | | | | www.bnstele.com |
| Bond International Software PLC | BDI | Software & Computer Services | 39.0 | 1 | 40.5k | 19/05/05 | 31/12 | www.bondadapt.com |
| Borders & Southern Petroleum PLC | BOR | Oil & Gas Producers | 58.7 | 5 | 267k | 08/12/05 | 28/02 | www.bordersandsouthern.com |
| BowLeven PLC | BLVN | Oil & Gas Producers | 63.7 | 10 | 219k | 25/11/05 | 30/06 | www.bowleven.com |
| Brady PLC | BRY | Software & Computer Services | 7.1 | 1 | 29.5k | 04/05/06 | 31/12 | www.bradyplc.co.uk |
| Braemar Group PLC | BRG | Real Estate | 2.4 | 5 | 263k | | | |

Source: Hemscott (Hemscott.com)

# Members of AIM

| Company Name | EPIC | Sector | Capital (£m) | NMS | 200D Avg Vol | AGM | Year End | URL |
|---|---|---|---|---|---|---|---|---|
| Braemore Resources PLC | BRR | Mining | 32.5 | 25 | 575k | 28/07/06 | | www.brainspark.com |
| Brainspark PLC | BSP | General Financial | 2.1 | 50 | 944k | 31/07/06 | 31/12 | |
| Bridgewell Group PLC | BWL | General Financial | 46.8 | 3 | | | | |
| Bright Futures Group PLC | BRF | General Retailers | 0.6 | 5 | 72.3k | 25/07/06 | 31/12 | |
| Bright Things PLC | BGT | Leisure Goods | 0.9 | 3 | 76.0k | 07/12/05 | 31/03 | www.brightthings.com |
| Brinkley Mining PLC | BRM | Industrial Metals | 78.5 | 10 | | | | |
| Bristol & London PLC | BTL | General Financial | 12.9 | 0.5 | 18.2k | 02/05/06 | 31/01 | www.bristolandlondon.com |
| Broker Network Holdings PLC | BNH | Support Services | 25.9 | 1 | 41.7k | 10/08/05 | 30/04 | www.brokernetworkholdingsplc.co.uk |
| Brooks Macdonald Group PLC | BRK | General Financial | 20.3 | 0.5 | 8.42k | 13/10/05 | 30/06 | www.brooksmacdonald.com |
| Buckland Group PLC | BUC | Electronic & Electrical Equipment | 0.6 | 25 | 3.52m | 01/08/05 | 31/12 | www.buckland-grp.com |
| Bulgarian Land Development PLC | BLD | Real Estate | 22.6 | 3 | | | | |
| Bulgarian Property Developments PLC | BPD | Real Estate | 41.0 | 2 | 24.4k | 05/01/06 | 30/06 | |
| Business Control Solutions Group PLC | BCT | Software & Computer Services | 21.0 | 5 | 70.6k | 23/06/06 | 31/12 | www.bcsplc.com |
| Business Direct Group PLC | BDG | Support Services | 6.0 | 0.5 | 24.3k | 23/05/06 | 31/12 | www.bdpx.com |
| Business Systems Group Holdings PLC | BSG | Software & Computer Services | 9.1 | 5 | 149k | 03/08/06 | 31/03 | www.bsg.co.uk |
| BWA Group PLC | BWA | General Financial | 0.0 | 0.5 | | 08/12/05 | 30/04 | |
| Byotrol PLC | BYOT | Chemicals | 20.4 | 1 | 64.8k | 27/07/06 | 31/03 | www.byotrol.com |
| C.I.Traders Ltd | CI. | Travel & Leisure | 187.3 | 3 | 145k | 28/06/06 | 28/01 | www.citraders.com |
| Cagney PLC | CGNY | Media | 4.9 | 5 | | 22/06/06 | | |
| Caldwell Investments PLC | CDW | Personal Goods | 2.0 | 1 | 18.0k | 27/07/05 | 28/02 | www.caldwellinvestmentsplc.com |
| Caledon Resources PLC | CDN | Mining | 19.9 | 25 | 1.45m | 27/07/06 | 31/12 | www.caledonresources.com |
| Caledonian Trust PLC | CNN | Real Estate | 20.9 | 0.5 | 468 | 20/01/06 | 30/06 | |
| CamAxys Group PLC | CAX | Software & Computer Services | 0.3 | 0.5 | 6.49k | 23/01/06 | 30/06 | www.camaxys.com |
| Cambrian Mining PLC | CBM | Mining | 118.6 | 10 | 545k | 29/11/05 | 30/06 | www.cambrianmining.com |
| Cambrian Oil & Gas PLC | COIL | Oil & Gas Producers | 4.4 | 10 | 410k | 31/10/05 | 30/06 | |
| Cambridge Mineral Resources PLC | CMR | Mining | 6.4 | 15 | 553k | 02/08/06 | 31/12 | www.cambmin.co.uk |
| Camco International Ltd | CAO | Support Services | 70.1 | 5 | | 31/03/06 | 31/12 | www.camco-international.com |
| Camelot Capital PLC | CMT | General Financial | 1.0 | 1 | 17.2k | 27/07/06 | 31/12 | |
| Canisp PLC | CN. | Fixed Line Telecommunications | 0.5 | 5 | 114k | 02/11/05 | 31/03 | |
| Capcon Holdings PLC | CPC | General Financial | 0.3 | 0.5 | 26.4k | 26/04/06 | 30/09 | www.capconplc.com |
| Cape Diamonds PLC | CAPE | Mining | 47.1 | 2 | | | | |
| Cape PLC | CIU | Support Services | 140.3 | 3 | 290k | 19/06/06 | 31/12 | www.capeplc.com |
| Capital Ideas PLC | CAPT | Travel & Leisure | 0.9 | 10 | 485k | 13/12/05 | 30/04 | |
| Capital Management and Investment PLC | CMIP | General Financial | 77.5 | 5 | 227k | 25/07/05 | 31/01 | |
| Caplay PLC | CLY | Travel & Leisure | 2.5 | 25 | 315k | 17/01/06 | 31/05 | |
| Capricorn Resources PLC | CIR | General Financial | 1.6 | 0.5 | 44.3k | 16/12/05 | 31/12 | |
| CAP-XX Ltd | CPX | Electronic & Electrical Equipment | 47.4 | 3 | | 29/07/05 | 30/06 | www.cap-xx.com |
| Cardinal Resources PLC | CDL | Oil & Gas Producers | 17.5 | 15 | 460k | 27/07/06 | 31/12 | www.cardinal-uk.com |
| Cardpoint PLC | CASH | Support Services | 83.7 | 25 | 1.16m | 28/02/06 | 30/09 | www.cardpointplc.com |
| CareCapital Group PLC | CARE | Real Estate | 28.0 | 5 | | | | |
| Careforce Group PLC | CFG | Health Care Equipment & Services | 11.3 | 1 | 25.5k | 13/12/05 | 31/07 | www.careforcegroup.co.uk |
| CareTech Holdings PLC | CTH | Health Care Equipment & Services | 102.5 | 2 | 33.3k | 23/02/06 | 30/09 | www.caretech-uk.com |
| Carluccio's PLC | CARL | Travel & Leisure | 86.3 | 2 | | 31/01/06 | 25/09 | www.carluccios.com |
| Cartucho Group PLC | CTGP | General Retailers | 8.8 | 5 | | | | |

Source: Hemscott (Hemscott.com)

## Members of AIM

| Company Name | EPIC | Sector | Capital (£m) | NMS | 200D Avg Vol | AGM | Year End | URL |
|---|---|---|---|---|---|---|---|---|
| Cashbox PLC | CBOX | Support Services | 14.3 | 3 | 674k | 31/10/05 | 30/06 | www.caspianoil.co.uk |
| Caspian Holdings PLC | CSH | Oil & Gas Producers | 14.8 | 10 | 1.00k | 26/07/05 | 31/12 | www.casdon.co.uk |
| Cassidy Brothers PLC | CDY | Leisure Goods | 2.1 | 0.5 | 77 | 05/08/05 | 30/04 | |
| Castle Acquisitions PLC | CAQ | General Financial | 7.1 | | 35.2k | 11/04/06 | 30/09 | |
| Castor Investments PLC | CSI | General Financial | 1.3 | 2 | 1.49m | | | www.cmg-plc.com |
| Catalyst Media Group PLC | CMX | Media | 21.2 | 25 | 169 | 30/08/05 | 31/10 | www.cavanagh.co.uk |
| Catalyst New Opportunities PLC | CNW | General Financial | 0.2 | 1 | 2.29k | 30/09/05 | 31/05 | www.cbg-group.co.uk |
| Cavanagh Group PLC | CVH | General Financial | 13.6 | 0.5 | 9.14k | 29/06/06 | 31/12 | www.cch-international.com |
| CBG Group PLC | CB. | Nonlife Insurance | 9.4 | 0.5 | 11.6k | 10/05/06 | 31/12 | www.cdsogg.com |
| CCH International PLC | CCH | General Financial | 22.3 | 0.5 | 196k | 10/05/05 | 31/12 | www.cellcast.com |
| CDS Oil & Gas Group PLC | CDS | Oil & Gas Producers | 6.3 | 5 | 45.4k | 27/07/06 | 31/12 | www.cellogroup.co.uk |
| Cellcast PLC | CLTV | Media | 3.7 | 2 | 74.7k | 30/04/05 | 31/12 | www.celltalk.co.uk |
| Cello Group PLC | CLL | Media | 40.6 | 1 | 6.38k | 23/05/06 | 31/12 | www.celoxica.com |
| Celltalk Group (The) PLC | CLT | General Retailers | 0.4 | 0.5 | | 26/09/05 | 31/03 | www.celticfc.net |
| Celoxica Holdings PLC | CXA | Technology Hardware & Equipment | 14.2 | 3 | 40.1k | 24/05/06 | 31/12 | www.celticresources.com |
| Celtic PLC | CCP | Travel & Leisure | 19.4 | | 484k | 07/10/05 | 30/06 | www.cenes.com |
| Celtic Resources Holdings PLC | CER | Mining | 116.5 | 10 | 1.29m | 20/09/05 | 31/12 | |
| CeNeS Pharmaceuticals PLC | CEN | Pharmaceuticals & Biotechnology | 19.5 | 50 | 446k | 13/07/06 | 31/12 | www.camec-plc.com |
| Central African Gold PLC | CAN | General Financial | 37.2 | 2 | 4.17m | 30/08/05 | 31/12 | www.ccgoldfields.com |
| Central African Mining & Exploration | CFM | Mining | 580.8 | 25 | 990k | 20/12/05 | 31/03 | www.centrom.com |
| Central China Goldfields PLC | GGG | Mining | 12.8 | 10 | 43.1k | 30/04/05 | 31/12 | www.ceplc.net |
| Centrom Group PLC | CET | Software & Computer Services | 4.2 | 3 | 12.6k | 28/02/05 | 31/12 | |
| Centurion Electronics PLC | CUC | Automobiles & Parts | 6.2 | 15 | 153k | 28/05/06 | 30/09 | www.cerespower.com |
| CEPS PLC | CEPS | Personal Goods | 1.8 | 5 | 485k | 10/06/05 | 31/12 | www.chacoplc.com |
| Ceres Power Holdings PLC | CWR | Electronic & Electrical Equipment | 152.2 | 5 | 4.38m | 21/11/05 | 30/06 | www.thecharacter.net |
| Chaco Resources PLC | CHP | Oil & Gas Producers | 69.4 | 50 | 159k | 05/10/05 | 31/03 | www.chariot.org.uk |
| Character Group (The) PLC | CCT | Media | 32.8 | 3 | 5.85k | 22/02/06 | 31/08 | www.cafc.co.uk |
| Chariot (UK) PLC | CRT | Travel & Leisure | 3.0 | 3 | 158k | 15/08/04 | 30/04 | www.themoneypages.com |
| Charlton Athletic PLC | CLO | Travel & Leisure | 24.4 | 0.5 | 8.31k | 18/02/06 | 30/06 | www.charteris.com |
| Charterhouse Communications PLC | CHO | Media | 4.0 | 1 | 302k | 20/10/05 | 31/05 | www.cheerfulscout.com |
| Charteris PLC | CAE | Software & Computer Services | 6.7 | 0.5 | 11.4k | 28/11/05 | 31/07 | www.chelfordgroup.com |
| CheekyMoon Entertainment PLC | CHKY | Travel & Leisure | 7.4 | 10 | 24.0k | 03/04/06 | 31/12 | |
| Cheerful Scout PLC | CLS | Media | 2.0 | 15 | 17.5k | 22/12/05 | 30/06 | www.chieftaingroup.co.uk |
| Chelford Group PLC | CHR | Software & Computer Services | 13.9 | 0.5 | | 20/07/06 | 31/12 | www.chinashoto.com |
| Chian Resources PLC | CHN | Mining | 1.0 | 5 | 6.89k | | | |
| Chieftain Group PLC | CFT | Support Services | 9.5 | 0.5 | 50.8k | 19/05/06 | 31/12 | www.hecplc.com |
| China Goldmines PLC | CGM | Mining | 26.8 | 2 | 31.6k | | | www.christiegroup.com |
| China Shoto PLC | CHNS | Electronic & Electrical Equipment | 44.4 | 3 | 42.1k | 20/06/06 | 31/12 | www.chromogenex.com |
| China Wonder Ltd | CWO | Industrial Engineering | 2.5 | 1 | 9.00k | 05/11/01 | 31/12 | www.churchillchina.com |
| ChoicesUK PLC | CHUK | General Retailers | 11.6 | 0.5 | 77.5k | 29/09/05 | 04/06 | |
| Christie Group PLC | CTG | Support Services | 39.3 | 0.5 | | 28/06/06 | 31/12 | |
| Chromogenex PLC | CGX | Health Care Equipment & Services | 5.5 | 3 | | 06/06/06 | 31/12 | |
| Churchill China PLC | CHH | Household Goods | 24.3 | 0.5 | | 17/05/06 | 31/12 | |
| Churchill Mining PLC | CHL | General Financial | 11.8 | 15 | | 31/10/05 | 30/06 | |

Source: Hemscott (Hemscott.com)

# Members of AIM

| Company Name | EPIC | Sector | Capital (£m) | NMS | 200D Avg Vol | AGM | Year End | URL |
|---|---|---|---|---|---|---|---|---|
| Circle Oil PLC | COP | Oil & Gas Producers | 39.0 | 25 | 2.09m | 08/09/05 | 31/12 | www.circleoil.com |
| Ciref Ltd | CRF | Real Estate | 49.7 | 3 | | 31/07/06 | 30/09 | www.ciref.biz |
| Citel PLC | CITE | Fixed Line Telecommunications | 23.3 | | | | | |
| City Lofts Group PLC | CTF | Real Estate | 44.8 | 1 | 36.5k | 28/06/06 | 31/12 | www.citylofts.co.uk |
| City of London Investment Group PLC | CLIG | General Financial | 47.8 | | | | | |
| CityBlock PLC | CLK | Real Estate | 7.6 | 2 | 4.15k | 23/09/05 | 31/03 | www.cityblock.co.uk |
| Civica PLC | CIV | Software & Computer Services | 122.0 | 2 | 169k | 01/03/06 | 30/09 | www.civica.co.uk |
| Claimar Care Group PLC | CCGP | Health Care Equipment & Services | 17.3 | 30 | | 15/01/06 | 30/09 | www.claimar.co.uk |
| Claims People Group (The) PLC | CLM | Support Services | 1.0 | 10 | 183k | 31/05/06 | 31/12 | www.theclaimspeople.com |
| Clan Homes PLC | CNH | Real Estate | 1.1 | 0.5 | 16.7 | 21/10/05 | 31/03 | |
| Clapham House Group (The) PLC | CPH | Travel & Leisure | 74.1 | 1 | 83.2k | 09/09/05 | 31/03 | www.claphamhouse.com |
| Clarity Commerce Solutions PLC | CCS | Software & Computer Services | 11.6 | 0.5 | 12.7k | 25/08/05 | 31/03 | www.claritycommerce.com |
| Clarkson Hill Group (The) PLC | CLKH | General Financial | 8.8 | 3 | | 15/11/04 | 31/07 | |
| ClearDebt Group PLC | CLEA | General Financial | 10.0 | 3 | 293k | 15/06/05 | 31/12 | www.cleardebtgroup.co.uk |
| ClearSpeed Technology PLC | CSD | Technology Hardware & Equipment | 91.1 | 1 | 110k | 26/05/06 | 31/12 | www.clearspeed.com |
| Clerkenwell Ventures PLC | CRK | Nonequity Investment Instruments | 3.5 | 1 | 22.8k | 20/12/05 | 30/09 | |
| Climate Exchange PLC | CLE | Equity Investment Instruments | 88.5 | 1 | 70.7k | 05/07/06 | 31/12 | |
| Clipper Ventures PLC | CLV | Travel & Leisure | 9.2 | 1 | 92.8k | 23/12/05 | 30/04 | www.clipper-ventures.com |
| Clipper Windpower PLC | CWP | Electricity | 475.5 | 5 | 311k | 31/05/06 | 31/12 | www.clipperwind.com |
| Close AllBlue Fund Ltd | CAB | Nonequity Investment Instruments | 134.9 | 2 | | | | |
| Cluff Gold PLC | CLF | Mining | 34.8 | 2 | 48.9k | 18/05/06 | 31/12 | www.cluffgold.com |
| Clyde Process Solutions PLC | CPSP | Industrial Engineering | 14.7 | 15 | 282k | | | |
| CMR Fuel Cells PLC | CMF | Electronic & Electrical Equipment | 31.6 | 3 | | 30/05/06 | | www.cmrfuelcells.com |
| CMS WebView PLC | CWV | Media | 1.2 | 10 | 183k | 15/06/06 | 31/12 | www.cms.co.uk |
| CNG Travel Group PLC | CTV | Travel & Leisure | 6.0 | 3 | 331k | 22/06/05 | 31/12 | www.cngplc.com |
| Coal International PLC | CLN | Mining | 33.0 | 5 | 130k | 16/01/06 | 30/06 | |
| Cobra Bio-Manufacturing PLC | CBF | Pharmaceuticals & Biotechnology | 9.3 | 2 | 47.8k | 07/04/05 | 30/09 | www.cobrabio.com |
| Cobra Capital Ltd | COC | General Financial | 2.7 | 0.5 | 6.93k | 27/04/06 | 31/12 | |
| Coburg Group PLC | CGG | Beverages | 2.3 | 0.5 | 8.85k | 14/09/05 | 30/04 | |
| CODASciSys PLC | CSY | Software & Computer Services | 126.5 | 0.5 | 25.8k | 25/05/06 | 31/12 | www.codascisys.co.uk |
| COE Group PLC | COE | Electronic & Electrical Equipment | 0.5 | 0.5 | 5.48k | 17/01/06 | 30/06 | www.coe.co.uk |
| Coffee Republic PLC | CFE | Travel & Leisure | 11.3 | 75 | 3.56m | 02/11/05 | 27/03 | www.coffeerepublic.co.uk |
| coffeeheaven international PLC | COH | Travel & Leisure | 27.6 | 5 | 442k | 02/12/05 | 31/03 | www.coffeeheaven.eu.com |
| Cohen (A) & Co PLC | CHEN | Industrial Metals | 0.3 | 0.5 | 22.9k | 15/08/05 | 31/12 | |
| Cohort PLC | CHRT | Aerospace & Defense | 40.8 | | 60.3k | 31/05/06 | 30/04 | |
| Colefax Group PLC | CFX | Household Goods | 32.3 | 0.5 | 5.49k | 13/09/05 | 30/04 | www.colefaxgroupplc.com |
| Colliers CRE PLC | COL | Real Estate | 76.8 | 2 | 119k | 15/05/06 | 31/12 | www.collierscre.com |
| Collins and Hayes Group PLC | CIY | Household Goods | 0.6 | 0.5 | 9.20k | 04/07/06 | 31/01 | www.collinsandhayesgroup.co.uk |
| Comland Commercial PLC | COM | Real Estate | 18.8 | 0.5 | 130 | 30/09/05 | 31/03 | www.comland.co.uk |
| Compact Power Holdings PLC | CPO | Support Services | 9.3 | 1 | | 17/11/05 | 31/03 | www.compactpower.co.uk |
| Company Health Group PLC | CHT | Health Care Equipment & Services | 1.9 | 0.5 | 21.4k | 23/01/05 | 31/12 | www.companyhealthgroup.com |
| Compass Finance Group PLC | CAF | General Financial | 36.5 | 1 | 149k | 23/02/06 | 30/09 | www.compassfinancegroupplc.co.uk |
| Computer Software Group PLC | CSW | Software & Computer Services | 56.5 | 2 | 206k | 27/09/05 | 28/02 | www.computersoftware.com |
| ComputerLand UK PLC | CPU | Software & Computer Services | 18.7 | 0.5 | 16.9k | 02/09/05 | 30/04 | www.computerland.co.uk |

Source: Hemscott (Hemscott.com)

## Members of AIM

| Company Name | EPIC | Sector | Capital (£m) | NMS | 200D Avg Vol | AGM | Year End | URL |
|---|---|---|---|---|---|---|---|---|
| Concateno PLC | COT | General Financial | 3.7 | 0.5 | 7.75k | 12/07/06 | 31/12 | www.cct.co.uk |
| Concurrent Technologies PLC | CNC | Technology Hardware & Equipment | 24.0 | 2 | 93.6k | 28/04/06 | 31/12 | |
| Conder Environmental PLC | CDE | Industrial Engineering | 4.2 | 2 | 15.3k | 23/08/05 | 30/04 | |
| Condor Resources PLC | CNR | General Financial | 15.6 | 5 | | | | |
| Conister Trust PLC | CTU | General Financial | 23.9 | 0.5 | 78.2k | 26/06/06 | 31/12 | www.conistertrust.com |
| Conival PLC | CVL | Food Producers | 5.0 | 15 | 816k | | | |
| Connaught PLC | CNT | Support Services | 192.9 | 5 | 313k | 21/01/06 | 31/08 | www.connaught.plc.uk |
| Conroy Diamonds & Gold PLC | CDG | Mining | 3.1 | 5 | 240k | 12/12/05 | 31/05 | www.conroydiamondsandgold.com |
| Consolidated Communications Corp PLC | CCM | Fixed Line Telecommunications | 4.2 | 15 | 101k | 26/09/05 | 31/12 | www.3cplc.com |
| Contemporary Enterprises PLC | CPY | Support Services | 3.7 | 0.5 | 454 | 06/02/06 | 30/09 | www.ausped.net |
| ContentFilm PLC | CFL | Media | 19.5 | 5 | 491k | 01/11/05 | 31/03 | www.contentfilm.com |
| Conygar Investment Company (The) PLC | CIC | General Financial | 22.2 | 0.5 | 7.61k | 01/02/06 | 30/09 | |
| Coolabi PLC | COO | Media | 3.7 | 3 | 155k | 06/01/06 | 30/06 | www.ccolabi.co.uk |
| Corac Group PLC | CRA | Industrial Engineering | 27.9 | 5 | 197k | 18/05/06 | 31/12 | www.corac.co.uk |
| Cordillera Resources PLC | CLA | General Financial | 8.4 | 15 | 206k | 24/07/06 | | |
| Core Business (The) PLC | CORE | Personal Goods | 2.2 | 3 | | 29/09/05 | 31/05 | www.thecorebusiness.co.uk |
| Cornwell Management Consultants PLC | CWM | Support Services | 7.8 | 5 | 21.7k | 12/06/06 | 31/12 | www.cornwell.co.uk |
| Corpora PLC | CP. | Software & Computer Services | 10.3 | 5 | 282k | 17/01/06 | 30/06 | www.corporaplc.com |
| Corporate Synergy Group PLC | CSG | General Financial | 28.3 | 1 | 149k | 01/03/06 | 31/12 | www.corporatesynergy.co.uk |
| Corsie Group PLC | CEG | Travel & Leisure | 6.9 | 5 | | 01/07/06 | 31/12 | www.corsiegroup.com |
| Corvus Capital Inc | CVS | General Financial | 32.6 | 15 | 567k | 08/11/05 | 31/03 | |
| Cosentino Signature Wines PLC | MCOZ | Beverages | 31.8 | 0.5 | | 28/05/06 | 31/12 | www.cosentinowinery.com |
| County Contact Centres PLC | CUY | Support Services | 4.7 | 0.5 | 8.39k | 20/09/05 | 30/06 | www.countycontactcentres.com |
| Cozart PLC | CZT | Health Care Equipment & Services | 29.2 | 5 | 201k | 09/11/05 | 31/05 | www.cozart.biz |
| CPL Resources PLC | CPS | Support Services | 102.9 | 0.5 | 16.7k | 01/10/05 | 30/06 | www.cpl.ie |
| Cradley Group Holdings PLC | CDLY | Support Services | 1.5 | 0.5 | 2.70k | 27/01/06 | 30/06 | www.cradleygp.co.uk |
| CRC Group PLC | CCG | Software & Computer Services | 7.1 | 1 | 69.9k | 26/05/06 | 31/12 | www.crc-group.com |
| Creative Education Corporation (The) PLC | CEC | General Retailers | 2.7 | 15 | 132k | 23/02/06 | 31/07 | www.cecplc.com |
| Creon Corporation PLC | CRO | General Financial | 4.5 | 1 | 1.23k | 26/04/06 | 31/01 | |
| Crescent Hydropolis Resorts PLC | CRES | General Financial | 25.1 | 2 | 5.12k | | 31/12 | www.crescent-hydropolis.com |
| Crescent Technology Ventures PLC | CTC | Equity Investment Instruments | 1.2 | 5 | 147 | 24/06/06 | | |
| Croma Group PLC | CMG | Aerospace & Defense | 5.2 | 5 | 330k | 28/01/05 | 30/06 | www.cromadefence.com |
| Crucial Plan PLC | CPN | Travel & Leisure | 5.8 | 0.5 | 32.5 | 31/08/05 | 30/04 | |
| Crystalband PLC | CRYB | Construction & Materials | 1.2 | 3 | 26.4k | 15/06/06 | 30/09 | |
| CSS Stellar PLC | CSS | Media | 8.0 | 0.5 | 72.0k | 16/05/06 | 31/12 | www.css-stellar.com |
| Cubus Lux PLC | CBX | Travel & Leisure | 11.9 | 0.5 | 6.49k | 31/03/05 | 31/12 | |
| Cue Energy PLC | CUE | General Financial | 6.3 | 5 | | | | |
| Curidium Medica PLC | CUR | Pharmaceuticals & Biotechnology | 12.0 | 3 | 276k | 09/06/06 | 31/10 | www.curidium.com |
| CustomVis PLC | CUS | Health Care Equipment & Services | 1.9 | 1 | 24.3k | 14/12/05 | 30/06 | www.customvis.com |
| CW Residential PLC | CWE | Real Estate | 5.7 | 0.5 | 1.17k | 06/06/06 | 31/12 | |
| Cyan Holdings PLC | CYAN | Technology Hardware & Equipment | 11.9 | 5 | | 18/04/06 | 31/12 | www.cyantechnology.com |
| CybIT Holdings PLC | CYH | Industrial Transportation | 8.3 | 2 | 57.0k | 30/08/05 | 31/03 | www.cybit.co.uk |
| CYC Holdings PLC | CYC | General Financial | 2.0 | 25 | 514k | 14/07/06 | 31/10 | www.cycholdings.com |
| Cyprotex PLC | CRX | Pharmaceuticals & Biotechnology | 9.3 | 5 | 123k | 01/06/06 | 31/12 | www.cyprotex.com |

Source: Hemscott (Hemscott.com)

## Members of AIM

| Company Name | EPIC | Sector | Capital (£m) | NMS | 200D Avg Vol | AGM | Year End | URL |
|---|---|---|---|---|---|---|---|---|
| Cytomyx Holdings PLC | CYX | Pharmaceuticals & Biotechnology | 1.5 | 3 | 113k | 28/04/06 | 30/09 | www.cytomyx-holdings.com |
| D1 Oils PLC | DOO | Chemicals | 71.3 | 3 | 259k | 25/05/06 | 31/12 | www.d1plc.com |
| DA Group PLC | DAG | Software & Computer Services | 8.8 | 3 | 79.9k | 31/07/06 | 31/03 | www.dagroupplc.com |
| Daniel Stewart Securities PLC | DAN | General Financial | 40.9 | 10 | 655k | 23/08/05 | 31/03 | www.danielstewart.co.uk |
| Dart Group PLC | DTG | Industrial Transportation | 154.1 | 2 | 296k | 03/08/06 | 31/03 | www.dartgroup.co.uk |
| DataCash Group PLC | DATA | Support Services | 169.9 | 5 | 160k | 17/05/06 | 31/12 | www.datacash.com |
| Datong Electronics PLC | DTE | Electronic & Electrical Equipment | 12.1 | 1 | 30.7k | 17/10/05 | 31/03 | www.datong.co.uk |
| Davenham Group PLC | DAV | General Financial | 78.9 | 2 |  | 31/10/04 | 30/06 | www.davenhamdirect.co.uk |
| DawMed Systems PLC | DSY | Health Care Equipment & Services | 1.9 | 0.5 | 19.5k | 10/03/06 | 30/09 | www.dawmed.com |
| Dawnay; Day Carpathian PLC | DDC | Real Estate | 144.0 | 10 | 490k |  |  |  |
| Dawnay; Day Treveria PLC | DTR | Real Estate | 346.7 | 15 |  |  |  |  |
| Dawson International PLC | DWSN | Personal Goods | 9.9 | 10 | 201k | 29/06/05 | 31/12 | www.dawson-international.co.uk |
| DCD Media PLC | DCD | Media | 50.2 | 100 | 5.45m | 30/11/05 | 30/06 | www.digitalclassics.co.uk |
| DDD Group PLC | DDD | Software & Computer Services | 6.9 | 5 | 152k | 20/06/06 | 31/12 | www.ddd.com |
| Deal Group Media PLC | DGM | Media | 16.6 | 100 | 1.24m | 06/06/06 | 31/12 | www.dealgroupmediaplc.com |
| Dealogic (Holdings) PLC | DL | Software & Computer Services | 98.1 | 1 | 14.3k | 09/05/05 | 31/12 | www.dealogic.com |
| Debt Free Direct Group PLC | DFD | General Financial | 178.3 | 3 | 275k | 04/08/06 | 30/04 | www.debtfreedirect.co.uk |
| Debtmatters Group PLC | DEBT | General Financial | 93.5 | 2 | 130k | 31/07/06 | 31/03 |  |
| Debts.co.uk PLC | DETS | General Financial | 37.1 | 2 |  |  |  |  |
| Deep-Sea Leisure PLC | DSL | Travel & Leisure | 11.2 | 0.5 | 123 | 22/02/06 | 31/10 | www.deepseaworld.com |
| Delcam PLC | DLC | Software & Computer Services | 19.3 | 0.5 | 3.67k | 04/05/05 | 31/12 | www.delcam.com |
| Deiling Group PLC | DLG | Media | 11.8 | 5 | 144k | 28/11/05 | 31/12 | www.dellinggroup.com |
| Deltex Medical Group PLC | DEMG | Health Care Equipment & Services | 12.6 | 5 | 231k | 03/05/06 | 31/12 | www.deltexmedical.com |
| Densitron Technologies PLC | DSN | Electronic & Electrical Equipment | 4.6 | 2 | 52.7k | 04/08/06 | 31/12 | www.densitron.com |
| DermaSalve Sciences PLC | DRM | Equity Investment Instruments | 10.3 | 1 | 107k | 30/06/06 | 31/12 | www.dermasalvesciences.com |
| Designer Vision Group PLC | DVS | Automobiles & Parts | 6.5 | 10 | 472k | 21/07/06 | 31/12 | www.designervision.co.uk |
| Desire Petroleum PLC | DES | Oil & Gas Producers | 84.6 | 25 | 841k | 24/05/06 | 31/12 | www.desireplc.co.uk |
| Deutsche Land PLC | DLD | Real Estate | 75.9 | 5 |  | 30/05/06 |  |  |
| Develica Deutschland Ltd | DDE | Real Estate | 172.6 |  |  |  |  |  |
| Dewhurst PLC | DWHT | Electronic & Electrical Equipment | 7.5 | 0.5 | 1.33k | 02/02/06 | 30/09 | www.dewhurst.co.uk |
| Diablo Group PLC | DBLO | Media | 2.0 | 1 | 44.6k | 15/07/05 | 31/03 |  |
| Dillistone Group PLC | DSG | Software & Computer Services | 7.5 | 2 |  |  |  |  |
| Dipford Group PLC | DIP | General Financial | 6.5 | 0.5 | 3.58k | 15/09/05 | 30/04 | www.dipford.com |
| Disperse Group PLC | DGP | Personal Goods | 9.1 | 2 | 49.1k | 28/04/06 | 31/12 | www.disperseplc.com |
| DM PLC | DMP | Media | 16.3 | 0.5 | 27.5k | 27/06/06 | 31/12 | www.dmplc.com |
| Dobbies Garden Centres PLC | DGC | General Retailers | 97.2 | 0.5 | 22.3k | 19/04/05 | 31/10 | www.dobbies.com |
| Domino's Pizza UK & IRL PLC | DOM | Travel & Leisure | 244.6 | 2 | 124k | 21/04/05 | 01/01 | www.dominos.co.uk |
| Dowgate Capital PLC | DGT | General Financial | 4.7 | 75 | 3.74m | 29/03/06 | 31/12 |  |
| Dowlis Corporate Solutions PLC | DWL | Media | 17.6 | 2 |  | 31/07/05 | 30/06 |  |
| Draganfly Investments Ltd | DRG | General Financial | 3.0 | 3 | 146k |  |  |  |
| Dream Direct Group PLC | DDG | General Retailers | 4.2 | 0.5 | 3.41k | 30/09/05 | 31/03 | www.edream.co.uk |
| Driver Group PLC | DRV | Construction & Materials | 19.7 | 1 | 17.6k | 01/03/06 | 30/09 | www.drivergroupplc.com |
| E Wood Holdings PLC | EWD | Industrial Engineering | 26.0 | 0.5 | 10.4k | 26/04/05 | 31/12 |  |
| Eagle Eye Telematics PLC | EIT | Industrial Transportation | 2.9 | 1 | 5.21k | 30/06/06 | 30/11 | www.eagle-eye.co.uk |

## Members of AIM

| Company Name | EPIC | Sector | Capital (£m) | NMS | 200D Avg Vol | AGM | Year End | URL |
|---|---|---|---|---|---|---|---|---|
| Earthport PLC | EPO | Software & Computer Services | 7.2 | 3 | 163k | 23/12/05 | 30/06 | www.earthport.com |
| Eastern European Property Fund Ltd | EEP | Real Estate | 19.8 | 3 | | | | |
| EBT Mobile China PLC | EBT | General Retailers | 46.7 | 5 | 593k | 26/05/06 | 31/12 | www.ebtmobile.com |
| EBTM PLC | EBTM | General Retailers | 2.8 | 5 | 101k | | | |
| Eckoh Technologies PLC | ECK | Support Services | 33.4 | 15 | 971k | 21/09/05 | 31/03 | www.eckoh.com |
| Econergy International PLC | ECG | General Financial | 77.0 | | | | 31/12 | |
| EcoSecurities Group PLC | ECO | General Financial | 142.0 | | 291k | 31/05/06 | 31/12 | www.edipic.com |
| Education Development International PLC | EDD | General Retailers | 5.4 | 1 | 13.2k | 26/01/06 | 30/09 | www.eguk.co.uk |
| EG Solutions PLC | EGS | Software & Computer Services | 20.5 | 1 | 261k | 06/06/06 | 31/01 | www.egdon-resources.com |
| Egdon Resources PLC | EDR | Oil & Gas Producers | 106.6 | 5 | 2.74k | 09/12/05 | 31/07 | www.eicom.co.uk |
| Eicom PLC | EIC | Media | 70.2 | 25 | 6.35m | 19/12/05 | 30/06 | www.eirxtherapeutics.com |
| EiRx Therapeutics PLC | ERX | Pharmaceuticals & Biotechnology | 4.2 | 5 | | 27/01/06 | 30/06 | www.ekayadvertising.com |
| Ekay PLC | EKY | Media | 13.5 | 3 | 2.57k | 31/10/05 | 30/06 | www.eloro.co.uk |
| El Oro and Exploration Company PLC | ELX | General Financial | 60.4 | 0.5 | 136k | 14/06/05 | 31/12 | www.eleco.com |
| Eleco PLC | ELCO | Construction & Materials | 34.1 | 2 | 238k | 16/11/05 | 30/06 | www.electricwordplc.com |
| Electric Word PLC | ELE | Media | 12.4 | 5 | 10.8k | 28/03/06 | 30/11 | |
| Eleksen Group PLC | ELG | Electronic & Electrical Equipment | 19.3 | 1 | 92.6k | | | www.elektronplc.com |
| Elektron PLC | EKT | Electronic & Electrical Equipment | 12.9 | 1 | | 03/08/06 | 31/01 | www.elephantloans.co.uk |
| Elephant Loans & Mortgages PLC | ELEP | General Financial | 8.1 | 10 | 94.8k | 11/07/06 | 31/03 | www.elevationevents.co.uk |
| Elevation Events Group PLC | EEG | Media | 1.2 | 2 | 54.3k | 27/04/06 | 30/09 | www.elyproperty.ie |
| Elite Strategies PLC | ETS | General Financial | 2.5 | 2 | 379k | 27/01/06 | 30/06 | |
| Ely Property Group PLC | ELY | Real Estate | 12.6 | 5 | 3.79k | 21/06/06 | 31/10 | www.emess.co.uk |
| Emerging UK Investments PLC | EUI | Equity Investment Instruments | 0.5 | 1 | 141k | 30/09/05 | 31/05 | www.empireinteractive.com |
| Emess PLC | WTC | Household Goods | 33.8 | 10 | 151k | 27/07/06 | 31/12 | www.empresaria.com |
| Empire Interactive PLC | EMP | Software & Computer Services | 3.1 | 5 | 36.5k | 31/07/05 | 31/12 | www.empyreanenergy.com |
| Empresaria Group PLC | EMR | Support Services | 19.6 | 0.5 | 855k | 09/06/06 | 31/12 | www.encoreoil.co.uk |
| Empyrean Energy PLC | EME | Oil & Gas Producers | 11.8 | 3 | 704k | 07/07/06 | 31/03 | |
| EnCore Oil PLC | EO. | Oil & Gas Producers | 42.0 | 5 | 356k | 27/10/05 | 30/06 | |
| Energy Asset Management PLC | EAM | Support Services | 2.5 | 5 | 425k | 19/07/06 | | www.energytechniqueplc.co.uk |
| Energy Technique PLC | ETQ | Industrial Engineering | 3.3 | 25 | 3.56m | 26/10/05 | 31/03 | |
| Enition PLC | ENT | Software & Computer Services | 3.0 | 15 | 3.68k | 25/07/06 | 31/12 | www.ensor.co.uk |
| Enola Resources PLC | ENR | General Financial | 1.3 | | 9.58k | 15/07/06 | | |
| Ensor Holdings PLC | ESR | Support Services | 6.9 | 0.5 | 12.3k | 19/07/06 | 31/03 | www.enterpriseasia.com.hk |
| Enterprise North PLC | ENTH | General Financial | 0.3 | 0.5 | 3.49k | 21/07/05 | 31/03 | |
| enterpriseAsia PLC | EPA | Equity Investment Instruments | 0.5 | 0.5 | 21.7 | 30/06/06 | 31/12 | www.epicip.com |
| EP&F Capital PLC | ECA | General Financial | 1353.3 | 0.5 | 50.5k | 06/09/04 | 31/12 | www.eqgroup.co.uk |
| EPIC Reconstruction PLC | ERN | Equity Investment Instruments | 21.6 | 0.5 | 697 | 31/07/06 | 31/01 | www.equestbalkan.com |
| eq group PLC | EQI | Media | 5.8 | 10 | | 24/04/06 | 31/12 | |
| Equest Balkan Properties PLC | EBP | Real Estate | 145.6 | 2 | 13.4k | | | |
| Equity Pre-IPO Investments Ltd | EIL | General Financial | 5.5 | 0.5 | 2.15k | 24/10/05 | 31/03 | www.eredene.com |
| Equity Special Situations Ltd | EQS | General Financial | 21.3 | 1 | 26.7k | | | |
| Eredene Capital PLC | ERE | Real Estate | 69.7 | 5 | | | | www.erumaplc.com |
| Eros International PLC | EROS | Media | 191.5 | | 157k | 28/02/05 | 31/12 | |
| Eruma PLC | ERU | Support Services | 6.1 | | | | | |

Source: Hemscott (Hemscott.com)

| Company Name | EPIC | Sector | Capital (£m) | NMS | 200D Avg Vol | AGM | Year End | URL |
|---|---|---|---|---|---|---|---|---|
| Essentially Group Ltd | ESN | Media | 10.8 | 3 | | | | www.essentiallygroup.com |
| Eurasia Mining PLC | EUA | Mining | 6.8 | 5 | 452k | 14/07/06 | 31/12 | www.eurasia-mining.plc.uk |
| Eureka Mining PLC | EKA | Mining | 20.6 | 2 | 81.3k | 13/06/06 | 31/12 | www.eurekamining.co.uk |
| Europa Oil & Gas (Holdings) PLC | EOG | Oil & Gas Producers | 17.6 | 3 | 146k | 14/12/05 | 31/07 | www.europaoil.co.uk |
| Europasia Education PLC | EPE | General Financial | 2.8 | 2 | 177k | 26/08/05 | 31/12 | www.europasiaeducation.com |
| Europe Vision PLC | EVN | General Financial | 170.1 | | | | | |
| European Business Jets PLC | EBJ | Travel & Leisure | 2.1 | 25 | 577k | | | www.europeanbusinessjets.com |
| European Convergence Property Comp plc | ECPC | Real Estate | 43.2 | 5 | 80.0k | | | |
| European Diamonds PLC | EPD | Mining | 11.7 | 10 | 316k | 08/12/05 | 30/06 | www.europeandiamondsplc.com |
| European Equity Tranche Income Ltd | EET | Equity Investment Instruments | 70.0 | 5 | | | | |
| European Islamic Investment Bank PLC | EIIB | Banks | 205.4 | 15 | | | | |
| European Nickel PLC | ENK | Mining | 143.8 | 5 | 672k | 23/03/06 | 30/09 | www.enickel.co.uk |
| Eurovestech PLC | EVT | General Financial | 56.5 | 10 | 464k | 25/10/05 | 31/03 | www.eurovestech.com |
| Everfor Diamonds PLC | EVE | Mining | 3.7 | 5 | | 27/07/06 | | |
| Evolutec Group PLC | EVC | Pharmaceuticals & Biotechnology | 28.0 | 0.5 | 46.6k | 26/04/06 | 31/12 | www.evolutec.co.uk |
| EXC PLC | EXC | Support Services | 7.0 | 5 | 61.8k | 04/08/06 | 31/12 | |
| Expomedia Group PLC | EXP | Media | 56.6 | 0.5 | 13.2k | 19/05/06 | 31/12 | www.expomediagroup.com |
| Fairground Gaming Holdings PLC | FGH | General Financial | 21.8 | 3 | 29.3k | | 30/06 | www.fairplace.com |
| Fairplace Consulting PLC | FCO | Support Services | 1.5 | 0.5 | 37.4k | 24/11/05 | 31/03 | www.flhplc.com |
| Falkland Islands Holdings PLC | FKL | Food & Drug Retailers | 26.2 | 1 | 8.21k | 25/07/05 | 31/03 | www.fogi.com |
| Falkland Oil & Gas Ltd | FOGL | Oil & Gas Producers | 102.8 | 5 | 248k | 30/07/05 | 31/03 | www.farleyandco.co.uk |
| Farley Group PLC | FGR | Real Estate | 23.9 | 0.5 | 33.2k | 15/12/05 | 30/09 | www.faroe-petroleum.com |
| Faroe Petroleum PLC | FPM | Oil & Gas Producers | 90.3 | 2 | 142k | 17/07/06 | 31/12 | www.farsight.co.uk |
| Farsight PLC | FAR | Support Services | 2.0 | 2 | 35.9k | 22/12/05 | 31/05 | www.fayrewood.co.uk |
| Fayrewood PLC | FWY | Technology Hardware & Equipment | 37.2 | 5 | 160k | 15/05/06 | 31/12 | www.fdmgroup.com |
| FDM Group PLC | FDMG | Software & Computer Services | 18.2 | 1 | 16.1k | 19/05/06 | 31/12 | www.feedback.plc.uk |
| Feedback PLC | FDBK | Electronic & Electrical Equipment | 0.7 | 0.5 | 4.73k | 26/09/05 | 31/03 | www.felixgroupplc.com |
| Felix Group PLC | FLX | Media | 19.6 | 15 | 711k | 01/12/05 | 31/05 | www.ffastfill.com |
| FFastFill PLC | FFA | Software & Computer Services | 10.1 | 5 | 341k | 20/06/05 | 31/03 | www.finobj.com |
| Financial Objects PLC | FIO | Software & Computer Services | 17.8 | 3 | 77.2k | 05/05/05 | 31/12 | |
| Financial Payment Systems Ltd | FPS | Support Services | 9.6 | 5 | | | | www.finsburyfoods.co.uk |
| Finsbury Food Group PLC | FIF | Food Producers | 16.8 | 1 | 47.2k | 30/11/05 | 30/06 | www.firestonediamonds.com |
| Firestone Diamonds PLC | FDI | Mining | 50.2 | 3 | 94.6k | 27/01/06 | 30/06 | www.firstartist.com |
| First Artist Corporation PLC | FAN | Media | 7.5 | 5 | 274k | 29/03/06 | 31/10 | www.firstderivatives.com |
| First Derivatives PLC | FDP | Software & Computer Services | 19.4 | 0.5 | 8.79k | 01/06/06 | 28/02 | www.fprop.com |
| First Property Group PLC | FPO | Real Estate | 16.2 | 2 | 87.5k | 06/09/05 | 31/03 | www.firstafricaoil.com |
| FirstAfrica Oil PLC | FAO | Oil & Gas Producers | 92.3 | 100 | 4.85m | 23/09/05 | 30/11 | www.fishworks.co.uk |
| FishWorks PLC | FSH | Travel & Leisure | 13.7 | 2 | 64.6k | 08/12/05 | 31/07 | www.fiskeplc.com |
| Fiske PLC | FKE | General Financial | 6.3 | 0.5 | 5.28k | 22/09/05 | 31/05 | |
| Flightstore Group PLC | FLG | Software & Computer Services | 0.2 | 10 | 162k | 07/09/05 | 31/12 | |
| Flomerics Group PLC | FLO | Software & Computer Services | 20.3 | 1 | 43.1k | 25/04/06 | 31/12 | www.flomerics.com |
| Floors 2 Go PLC | FGO | General Retailers | 23.6 | 15 | 456k | 18/05/06 | 31/12 | www.floors2go.co.uk |
| Focus Solutions Group PLC | FSG | Software & Computer Services | 4.9 | 0.5 | 22.4k | 02/08/06 | 31/03 | www.focus-solutions.co.uk |
| Fonebak PLC | FON | Technology Hardware & Equipment | 24.7 | 1 | 71.1k | 27/11/05 | 30/06 | www.fonebak.com |

Source: Hemscott (Hemscott.com)

**Company Directory**

## Members of AIM

| Company Name | EPIC | Sector | Capital (£m) | NMS | 200D Avg Vol | AGM | Year End | URL |
|---|---|---|---|---|---|---|---|---|
| Food & Drink Group (The) PLC | FDG | Travel & Leisure | 7.8 | 0.5 | 9.06k | 30/03/06 | 24/09 | www.hartfordgroup.co.uk |
| Forbidden Technologies PLC | FBT | Software & Computer Services | 14.8 | 0.5 | 17.2k | 27/06/06 | 31/12 | www.forbidden.co.uk |
| Formation Group PLC | FRM | Media | 21.6 | 3 | 359k | 15/12/05 | 31/08 | www.formationgroupplc.com |
| Formjet PLC | FMJ | Software & Computer Services | 2.3 | 25 | 490k | 03/05/06 | 31/12 | www.formjetplc.com |
| Formscan PLC | FSA | Technology Hardware & Equipment | 1.7 | 0.5 | 9.81k | 23/01/06 | 31/07 | www.formscan.com |
| Fortfield Investments PLC | FIV | Electronic & Electrical Equipment | 1.4 | 15 | 169k | 31/07/05 | 31/03 | www.forumenergyplc.com |
| Forum Energy PLC | FEP | Oil & Gas Producers | 20.7 | 2 | 41.3k | 30/06/06 | 31/12 | www.forumenergyplc.com |
| fountains PLC | FNT | Support Services | 13.7 | 1 | 30.6k | 14/02/06 | 30/09 | www.fountainsplc.com |
| Freeplay Energy PLC | FRE | General Retailers | 16.2 | 1 | 7.21k | 17/07/06 | 30/12 | www.freeplayenergy.com |
| Frenkel Topping Group PLC | FEN | General Financial | 7.5 | 0.5 | 850 | 30/05/06 | 31/12 | www.frenkeltopping.co.uk |
| Fujin Technology PLC | FJN | Software & Computer Services | 23.9 | 5 | 130k | 10/05/06 | 31/10 | www.mxcplc.com |
| Fulcrum Pharma PLC | FUL | Pharmaceuticals & Biotechnology | 4.8 | 5 | 145k | 19/12/05 | 31/08 | www.fulcrumpharma.com |
| Fundamental-e Investments PLC | FEI | Electronic & Electrical Equipment | 4.2 | 5 | 280k | 23/08/05 | 30/09 | www.feiplc.com |
| Futura Medical PLC | FUM | Pharmaceuticals & Biotechnology | 37.1 | 3 | 258k | 04/07/06 | 31/12 | www.futuramedical.co.uk |
| FuturaGene PLC | FGN | Chemicals | 14.9 | 3 | 110k | 19/07/06 | 31/12 | www.futuragene.com |
| Future Internet Technologies PLC | FTI | General Financial | 64.7 | 3 | 607k | 12/01/06 | 30/06 | |
| G.R. (Holdings) PLC | GRH | General Financial | 4.0 | 0.5 | 11.5k | 10/11/05 | 30/06 | |
| Galahad Gold PLC | GLA | Mining | 67.8 | 50 | 1.28m | 27/06/06 | 31/12 | www.galahadgold.com |
| Galleon Holdings PLC | GON | Media | 3.1 | 5 | 88.6k | 22/02/06 | 30/09 | www.galleonplc.com |
| Gaming Corporation PLC | GMC | Travel & Leisure | 25.4 | 75 | 2.54m | 27/03/06 | 30/09 | www.gamingcorp.net |
| Gamingking PLC | GGK | Travel & Leisure | 3.0 | 25 | 203k | 10/10/05 | 30/04 | www.gamingking.co.uk |
| Garner PLC | GAR | Support Services | 0.8 | 25 | 32.2k | 03/07/06 | 31/12 | www.constellationcorporation.com |
| Gas Turbine Efficiency PLC | GTE | General Industrials | 21.4 | 5 | | 05/06/06 | 31/12 | |
| GASOL PLC | GAS | General Financial | 10.3 | 5 | 362k | 30/06/06 | | |
| Gemfields Resources PLC | GEM | Mining | 36.0 | 5 | | 28/06/06 | 30/06 | |
| Genesis Petroleum Corporation PLC | GPC | Oil & Gas Producers | 14.2 | 75 | 101k | 15/11/05 | 31/12 | www.genesis-petroleum.com |
| Genetix Group PLC | GTX | Health Care Equipment & Services | 35.8 | 1 | 39.2k | 30/04/05 | 31/12 | www.genetix.com |
| Genosis PLC | GNOS | Health Care Equipment & Services | 3.4 | 1 | | 08/06/06 | 31/12 | www.genosis.com |
| Genus PLC | GNS | Pharmaceuticals & Biotechnology | 241.7 | 2 | 95.9k | 18/08/05 | 31/03 | www.genusplc.com |
| Geong International Ltd | GNG | Software & Computer Services | 5.7 | 2 | | | | |
| Georgica PLC | GGA | Travel & Leisure | 143.5 | 2 | 340k | 26/04/06 | 01/01 | |
| GET Group PLC | GTG | Electronic & Electrical Equipment | 24.1 | 0.5 | 16.8k | 24/02/06 | 31/08 | www.getplc.co.uk |
| GETECH Group PLC | GTC | Oil Equipment; Services & Dist | 10.7 | 2 | 40.9k | 22/10/05 | 31/07 | |
| Getmobile Europe PLC | GETM | Mobile Telecommunications | 5.9 | 10 | 38.3k | 16/05/06 | 31/12 | |
| Gladstone PLC | GLD | Software & Computer Services | 12.1 | 3 | 181k | 24/02/06 | 31/08 | www.gladstoneplc.com |
| Glen Group PLC | GLN | Software & Computer Services | 3.0 | 15 | 1.58m | 13/02/06 | 30/09 | www.glengroup.co.uk |
| Glencar Mining PLC | GEX | Mining | 25.7 | 10 | 1.70m | 14/06/06 | 31/12 | www.glencarmining.ie |
| Glisten PLC | GLI | Food Producers | 45.4 | 0.5 | 34.1k | 03/11/05 | 30/06 | www.glisten.plc.uk |
| Global Energy Development PLC | GED | Oil & Gas Producers | 63.4 | 0.5 | 51.7k | 16/06/06 | 31/12 | www.globalenergyplc.com |
| Global Gaming Technologies PLC | GGT | Software & Computer Services | 1.6 | 5 | 277k | 23/01/06 | 31/07 | |
| Global Marine Energy PLC | GME | Oil Equipment; Services & Dist | 12.7 | 1 | 181k | 24/10/05 | 31/03 | www.mosplc.com |
| Global Natural Energy PLC | GNE | General Retailers | 11.4 | 0.5 | 15.3k | 10/07/06 | 31/12 | www.gnegroup.co.uk |
| Global Oceanic Carriers Ltd | GOC | Industrial Transportation | 13.0 | 2 | 264k | | | www.gocarriers.com |
| GMA Resources PLC | GMA | Mining | 34.9 | 25 | 907k | 18/07/06 | 31/12 | www.gmaresources.plc.uk |

Source: Hemscott (Hemscott.com)

| Company Name | EPIC | Sector | Capital (£m) | NMS | 200D Avg Vol | AGM | Year End | URL |
|---|---|---|---|---|---|---|---|---|
| Goals Soccer Centres PLC | GOAL | Travel & Leisure | 92.4 | 0.5 | 105k | 20/04/06 | 31/12 | www.goalsplc.com |
| GoIndustry PLC | GOI | Support Services | 31.4 | 3 | 47.9k | 26/07/06 | | www.goindustryplc.com |
| Gold Oil PLC | GOO | General Financial | 29.4 | 25 | 2.13m | 07/10/05 | 30/04 | www.goldoilplc.com |
| Golden Prospect PLC | GOL | Equity Investment Instruments | 53.6 | 10 | 434k | 21/04/06 | 31/12 | www.goldenprospectplc.com |
| Goldplat PLC | GDP | Mining | 8.6 | 3 | | | | |
| GoldStone Resources Ltd | GRL | Mining | 1.8 | 25 | 157k | 28/05/04 | 29/02 | www.goldstoneresources.com |
| Gooch & Housego PLC | GHH | Industrial Engineering | 61.6 | 0.5 | 35.5k | 15/02/06 | 30/09 | www.goochandhousego.com |
| Gourmet Holdings PLC | GRM | Travel & Leisure | 8.6 | 0.5 | 37.5k | 02/12/05 | 26/06 | www.gourmetholdings.co.uk |
| Granby Oil and Gas PLC | GOIL | Oil & Gas Producers | 21.1 | 1 | 39.2k | | | www.granbyoil.com |
| Greatfleet PLC | GFG | Support Services | 6.8 | 1 | 40.2k | 27/07/06 | 31/12 | www.greatfleet.com |
| Greatland Gold PLC | GGP | Mining | 2.8 | | | | | |
| Greenfield Construction Group PLC | GFC | Construction & Materials | 0.7 | 3 | 58.3k | 02/12/05 | 31/03 | www.greenfieldconstruction.co.uk |
| Greenhouse Fund (The) Ltd | GHF | Equity Investment Instruments | 19.4 | 15 | | | | |
| Griffin Group PLC | GFF | General Financial | 1.5 | 10 | 381k | 06/04/06 | 30/09 | www.griffingroupplc.co.uk |
| Group NBT PLC | NBT | Software & Computer Services | 27.9 | 0.5 | 34.6k | 27/10/05 | 30/06 | www.netbenefit.com |
| GruppeM Investments PLC | GRP | Equity Investment Instruments | 0.9 | 1 | 836 | | | |
| GSH Group PLC | GSH | Support Services | 55.1 | 0.5 | 850 | 19/01/06 | 31/07 | www.gshgroup.com |
| GTL Resources PLC | GTL | Oil & Gas Producers | 54.5 | 75 | 9.54m | 19/12/05 | 31/03 | www.gtlresources.com |
| Gulfsands Petroleum PLC | GPX | Oil & Gas Producers | 108.8 | 5 | 350k | 15/09/05 | 31/12 | www.gulfsands.net |
| GW Pharmaceuticals PLC | GWP | Pharmaceuticals & Biotechnology | 103.9 | 15 | 393k | 21/03/06 | 30/09 | www.gwpharm.com |
| H&T Group PLC | HAT | General Retailers | 57.8 | | | | | |
| Halladale Group PLC | HDG | Real Estate | 56.9 | 1 | 78.5k | 13/09/05 | 30/04 | www.halladale.co.uk |
| Hallin Marine Subsea International PLC | HMS | Oil Equipment; Services & Dist | 26.3 | 1 | 19.1k | 26/04/06 | 31/12 | www.hallinmarine.com |
| Hambledon Mining PLC | HMB | Mining | 56.8 | 10 | 712k | 17/07/06 | 31/12 | www.hambledon-mining.com |
| Hamsard Group PLC | HMSD | Software & Computer Services | 9.1 | 1 | 20.6k | 15/07/04 | 31/05 | www.hamsard.com |
| Hamworthy PLC | HMY | Industrial Engineering | 164.9 | 3 | 155k | 27/07/06 | 31/03 | www.hamworthy.com |
| HandMade PLC | HMF | Media | 7.2 | 2 | 4.72k | 08/06/06 | 31/12 | |
| Hansteen Holdings PLC | HSTN | Real Estate | 148.8 | 10 | | | | www.hansteen.co.uk |
| Harbinger Capital PLC | HBC | General Financial | 0.5 | 2 | 5.32k | 30/05/06 | | |
| Hardide PLC | HDD | Chemicals | 17.6 | 5 | 266k | 31/01/06 | 30/09 | www.hardide.com |
| Hardy Amies PLC | HRD | General Retailers | 6.2 | 2 | 29.7k | 29/06/06 | 31/12 | www.hardyamies.co.uk |
| Hardy Oil & Gas PLC | HDY | Oil & Gas Producers | 175.9 | 2 | 65.7k | 28/06/06 | 31/12 | www.hardyoil.com |
| Hardys & Hansons PLC | HDYS | Travel & Leisure | 209.7 | 1 | 77.0k | 02/02/06 | 30/09 | www.hardysandhansons.co.uk |
| Hargreaves Services PLC | HSP | Support Services | 95.3 | 3 | | | | www.hargreavesservices.co.uk |
| Harrier Group PLC | HRR | Software & Computer Services | 4.6 | 1 | 28.6k | 01/06/06 | 31/12 | www.harrier.com |
| Harrogate Group PLC | HGP | Equity Investment Instruments | 0.6 | 15 | 71.4k | 15/11/05 | 31/03 | www.harrogategroup.com |
| Hartest Holdings PLC | HTH | Industrial Engineering | 5.2 | 50 | 1.55m | 10/08/05 | 31/03 | www.hartest-holdings.com |
| Hat Pin PLC | HTP | Support Services | 12.1 | 0.5 | 56.9k | 10/05/06 | 31/12 | www.hatpin.co.uk |
| Hawtin PLC | HTI | Real Estate | 12.0 | 2 | 69.0k | 20/06/06 | 31/12 | www.hawtin.co.uk |
| Hay (Norman) PLC | HNN | Industrial Engineering | 10.2 | 0.5 | 5.44k | 23/06/06 | 31/12 | www.normanhay.com |
| Healthcare Enterprise Group PLC | HCEG | Health Care Equipment & Services | 11.9 | 15 | 767k | 27/07/06 | 28/02 | www.hcegroup.com |
| Healthcare Locums PLC | HLO | Support Services | 35.2 | 3 | | 14/06/06 | 31/12 | www.healthcarelocums.com |
| Healthy Living Centres PLC | HLC | Travel & Leisure | 0.5 | 0.5 | 13.6k | 04/08/06 | 31/12 | www.motorcise.com |
| Heath (Samuel) & Sons PLC | HSM | Construction & Materials | 12.3 | 0.5 | 194 | 19/08/05 | 31/03 | www.samuel-heath.com |

## Members of AIM

| Company Name | EPIC | Sector | Capital (£m) | NMS | 200D Avg Vol | AGM | Year End | URL |
|---|---|---|---|---|---|---|---|---|
| Heavitree Brewery PLC | HVTA | Travel & Leisure | 21.8 | 0.5 | 199 | 13/04/05 | 31/10 | |
| Hemisphere Properties PLC | HPE | Real Estate | 12.6 | 2 | 245k | 10/11/05 | 31/03 | |
| Hemscott PLC | HEM | Media | 24.0 | 0.5 | 10.6k | 20/06/06 | 31/12 | www.hemscottplc.com |
| Henderson Morley PLC | HML | Pharmaceuticals & Biotechnology | 15.4 | 15 | 7.20m | 18/10/05 | 30/04 | www.henderson-morley.com |
| Herencia Resources PLC | HER | Mining | 4.1 | 2 | 201k | 26/07/06 | | |
| Heritage Underwriting Agency PLC | HUA | General Financial | 44.5 | 3 | | | | |
| HHK PLC | HHK | General Financial | 1.3 | 0.5 | 1.38k | 23/08/05 | 31/12 | www.hichens.com |
| Hichens; Harrison & Co PLC | HICH | General Financial | 27.4 | 0.5 | 18.6k | 12/07/06 | 31/12 | www.hidefield.co.uk |
| Hidefield Gold PLC | HIF | Mining | 22.1 | 10 | 312k | 12/08/05 | 31/03 | www.highams.co.uk |
| Highams Systems Services Group PLC | HSS | Support Services | 1.5 | 1 | 36.8k | 07/06/06 | 31/12 | www.highlandgold.com |
| Highland Gold Mining Ltd | HGM | Mining | 303.5 | 15 | 370k | 20/04/06 | 31/12 | www.honeycombe.co.uk |
| Highland Timber PLC | HTB | Forestry & Paper | 7.4 | 0.5 | 2.71k | 16/03/06 | 31/12 | www.hillstation.cc.uk |
| Hill Station PLC | HLL | Food Producers | 13.4 | 5 | 198k | | 31/10 | |
| HML Holdings PLC | HMLH | Real Estate | 2.1 | 5 | | | | |
| Holders Technology PLC | HDT | Electronic & Electrical Equipment | 3.9 | 0.5 | 1.83k | 26/04/05 | 30/11 | www.holders.co.uk |
| Homebuy Group PLC | HBG | General Retailers | 90.9 | 3 | 210k | 10/11/05 | 17/04 | www.homebuyit.com |
| Honeycombe Leisure PLC | HCL | Travel & Leisure | 4.9 | 1 | 27.5k | 28/09/05 | 01/05 | www.honeycombe.co.uk |
| Horizonte Minerals PLC | HZM | Mining | 7.4 | 3 | | | | www.horizonteminerals.com |
| Hot Tuna (International) PLC | HTT | Personal Goods | 13.8 | 2 | 48.2k | | | |
| Hot Corporation (The) PLC | HCP | Travel & Leisure | 68.0 | 0.5 | 43.1k | 05/06/06 | 31/12 | |
| Hurlingham PLC | HRL | Real Estate | 1.7 | 0.5 | 676 | 15/04/05 | 30/09 | www.huveauxplc.com |
| Huveaux PLC | HVX | Media | 65.2 | 10 | 491k | 12/04/05 | 31/12 | www.hydro-international.biz |
| Hydro International PLC | HYD | Industrial Engineering | 16.4 | 1 | 21.1k | 19/05/06 | 31/12 | www.hydrodec.com |
| Hydrodec Group PLC | HYR | Oil & Gas Producers | 51.8 | 10 | 575k | 26/05/06 | 31/12 | www.iafgroup.com |
| IAF Group PLC | IAF | General Financial | 12.3 | 0.5 | 36.4k | 21/12/05 | 30/06 | www.ibsopensystems.com |
| IBS OPENSystems PLC | OPN | Software & Computer Services | 70.8 | 2 | 109k | 25/04/06 | 31/12 | www.id-date.co.uk |
| ID Data PLC | IDD | Electronic & Electrical Equipment | 6.9 | 75 | 1.96m | 28/10/05 | 31/03 | www.idealshoppingdirect.co.uk |
| Ideal Shopping Direct PLC | IDS | General Retailers | 79.6 | 2 | 131k | 04/05/05 | 31/12 | www.idmos.com |
| IDMoS PLC | IDO | Health Care Equipment & Services | 24.0 | 1 | 8.61k | 12/12/05 | 31/07 | www.idn.co.uk |
| IDN Telecom PLC | IDN | Fixed Line Telecommunications | 8.2 | 25 | 1.14m | 30/03/06 | 31/10 | www.idoxplc.com |
| IDOX PLC | IDOX | Software & Computer Services | 12.9 | 5 | 284k | 22/02/06 | 31/10 | www.igmmobile.com |
| IGM Ltd | IGMG | Mobile Telecommunications | 11.7 | 3 | | | | www.iimia.co.uk |
| iimia Investment Group PLC | IIG | General Financial | 33.6 | 0.5 | 24.8k | 08/06/05 | 31/12 | www.ilxgroup.com |
| iLX Group PLC | ILX | Support Services | 17.9 | 0.5 | 15.7k | 27/07/05 | 31/03 | www.ish.co.uk |
| Image Scan Holdings PLC | IGE | Electronic & Electrical Equipment | 6.6 | 1 | 92.5k | 23/03/06 | 30/09 | www.imagesound.co.uk |
| Imagesound PLC | ISD | General Financial | 6.3 | 3 | 100k | 19/06/06 | 31/12 | www.imate.com |
| i-mate PLC | IMTE | Technology Hardware & Equipment | 213.4 | 10 | 212k | 30/06/06 | 31/03 | www.immediabroadcasting.com |
| Immedia Broadcasting PLC | IME | Media | 1.8 | 0.5 | 8.85k | 26/05/06 | 31/12 | www.idsltd.com |
| Immunodiagnostic Systems Holdings PLC | IDH | Health Care Equipment & Services | 20.4 | 1 | 36.9k | 06/09/05 | 31/03 | www.immupharma.com |
| ImmuPharma PLC | IMM | Pharmaceuticals & Biotechnology | 48.0 | 1 | 6.90k | 28/07/05 | 31/03 | |
| Impact Holdings (UK) PLC | IHUK | General Financial | 10.6 | 5 | 11.3k | 19/06/06 | 31/03 | |
| Impax Group PLC | IPX | General Financial | 18.1 | 2 | 124k | 03/02/06 | 30/09 | www.impax.co.uk |
| Imperial Energy Corporation PLC | IEC | Oil & Gas Producers | 426.1 | 2 | 264k | 25/05/06 | 31/12 | www.imperialenergy.com |
| Imperial Innovations Group PLC | IVO | General Financial | 189.9 | 5 | | | | |

Source: Hemscott (Hemscott.com)

Members of AIM

| Company Name | EPIC | Sector | Capital (£m) | NMS | 200D Avg Vol | AGM | Year End | URL |
|---|---|---|---|---|---|---|---|---|
| Imprint PLC | IMP | Support Services | 93.0 | 2 | 93.1k | 10/05/06 | 31/12 | www.imprintplc.com |
| IMS Maxims PLC | IMX | General Financial | 7.0 | 2 | 106k | 22/11/05 | 31/03 | www.imsmaxims.com |
| In Cup Plus PLC | ICU | Industrial Engineering | 3.0 | 10 | 71.0k | 30/04/05 | 31/12 | www.incupplus.com |
| IncaGold PLC | IGD | Media | 2.7 | 5 | 14.7k | 30/05/06 | 31/12 | www.incagold.com |
| Indago Petroleum Ltd | IPL | Oil & Gas Producers | 134.7 | 15 | | 31/07/06 | 31/12 | www.indagopetroleum.com |
| Independent International Invest Research | IIR | General Retailers | 1.9 | 0.5 | 2.83k | 22/08/05 | 28/02 | www.iirgroup.com |
| Independent Media Support Group PLC | IMS | Media | 3.3 | 0.5 | 31.3k | 16/05/06 | 31/12 | www.ims-media.com |
| Independent Resources PLC | IRG | Oil & Gas Producers | 16.0 | 5 | | | | |
| India Capital Growth Fund Ltd | IGC | Equity Investment Instruments | 65.1 | | | | | |
| India Outsourcing Services PLC | IOS | General Financial | 2.7 | 5 | 14.3k | 22/05/06 | 30/09 | www.indiaoutsourcingservices.com |
| India Star Energy PLC | INDY | General Financial | 1.6 | 5 | 184k | 31/01/06 | 30/06 | |
| IndigoVision Group PLC | IND | Software & Computer Services | 38.4 | 5 | 32.2k | 22/11/05 | 31/07 | www.indigovision.com |
| Inditherm PLC | IDM | Chemicals | 3.7 | 2 | 50.0k | 28/04/06 | 31/12 | www.indithermplc.com |
| Infoscreen Networks PLC | INFO | Media | 11.3 | 1 | 116 | 05/12/05 | 30/06 | |
| Infoserve Group PLC | INFS | Software & Computer Services | 5.7 | 2 | | | | |
| Ingenious Media Active Capital Ltd | IMAC | Equity Investment Instruments | 147.8 | 10 | | | | |
| Ingenious Music VCT 2 PLC | IMV | Equity Investment Instruments | 33.0 | 1 | | | | |
| Ingenta PLC | IGA | Media | 3.4 | 10 | 291k | 19/05/06 | 31/12 | www.ingenta.com |
| Innobox PLC | INO | General Financial | 0.6 | 10 | 74.6k | 20/12/05 | 30/04 | www.innobox.co.uk |
| Innovision Research & Technology PLC | INN | Electronic & Electrical Equipment | 19.3 | 3 | 161k | 07/09/05 | 31/03 | www.innovision-group.com |
| Inova Holding PLC | INA | Software & Computer Services | 15.1 | 3 | | | | |
| Inspace PLC | INSP | Support Services | 70.5 | 2 | 98.2k | 18/05/06 | 31/12 | www.inspace.co.uk |
| Inspicio PLC | INP | Support Services | 73.0 | 3 | 129k | 21/06/06 | 31/12 | www.inspicioplc.com |
| Inspired Gaming Group PLC | INGG | Software & Computer Services | 113.8 | 5 | | | | www.inspiredgaminggroup.com |
| Intandem Films PLC | IFM | Media | 2.5 | 3 | 184k | 01/02/06 | 31/12 | |
| InTechnology PLC | ITO | Software & Computer Services | 52.2 | 3 | 49.3k | 09/08/05 | 31/03 | www.intechnology.co.uk |
| Integrated Asset Management PLC | IAM | General Financial | 14.2 | 1 | 45.6k | 22/06/06 | 31/12 | www.integratedam.com |
| Intellego Holdings PLC | IHP | Support Services | 1.7 | 0.5 | 107k | 29/10/05 | 31/03 | www.intellego-holdings.com |
| Intelligent Environments Group PLC | IEN | Software & Computer Services | 7.9 | 5 | 335k | 29/06/06 | 31/12 | www.ie.com |
| Inter Link Foods PLC | ITF | Food Producers | 52.4 | 0.5 | 49.8k | 09/09/05 | 07/05 | www.interlinkfoods.co.uk |
| Interactive Digital Solutions PLC | IGL | Software & Computer Services | 1.9 | 10 | 74.5k | 12/05/06 | 30/09 | www.ids-plc.com |
| Interactive Gaming Holdings PLC | IGH | Travel & Leisure | 3.7 | 5 | 145k | 05/06/06 | 30/11 | www.igh.com |
| Interactive Prospect Targeting Holdings PLC | IPH | Media | 84.7 | 2 | 97.6k | 10/05/00 | 31/12 | www.ipt-ltd.co.uk |
| Interactive World PLC | ITW | Software & Computer Services | 31.9 | 3 | | | | |
| Interbulk Investments PLC | INB | General Financial | 18.6 | 10 | 94.5k | 13/07/06 | 31/03 | www.intercedegroup.com |
| Intercede Group PLC | IGP | Software & Computer Services | 10.1 | 0.5 | 15.1k | 30/04/06 | 31/12 | www.intercytex.com |
| Intercytex Group PLC | ICX | Pharmaceuticals & Biotechnology | 55.7 | 2 | | 07/12/05 | 30/06 | www.isgplc.com |
| Interior Services Group PLC | ISG | Support Services | 70.4 | 1 | 87.5k | 22/04/05 | 31/12 | www.intermodalresource.com |
| Intermodal Resource PLC | IMR | Industrial Engineering | 5.1 | 1 | 39.4k | 06/09/05 | 31/12 | |
| International Brand Licensing PLC | IBL | General Financial | 7.6 | 2 | 59.4k | | | www.ifml.com |
| International Ferro Metals | IFL | Industrial Metals | 146.7 | 15 | 549k | | | |
| International Greetings PLC | IGR | Media | 197.1 | 0.5 | 20.3k | 21/09/05 | 31/03 | www.internationalgreetings.co.uk |
| International Marketing & Sales Group PLC | IMSG | Media | 57.2 | 5 | | 12/06/06 | 31/12 | www.imsg.co.uk |
| International Medical Devices PLC | INT | Health Care Equipment & Services | 12.9 | 1 | 167k | 16/12/05 | 31/08 | www.imd-plc.com |

Source: Hemscott (Hemscott.com)

## Members of AIM

| Company Name | EPIC | Sector | Capital (£m) | NMS | 200D Avg Vol | AGM | Year End | URL |
|---|---|---|---|---|---|---|---|---|
| International Molybdenum PLC | IMY | Mining | 9.2 | 2 | 94.1k | 28/06/06 | 31/12 | www.intermoly.com |
| International Nuclear Solutions PLC | INS | Support Services | 24.5 | 5 | | | | |
| International Real Estate PLC | IRE | Real Estate | 13.4 | 0.5 | 3.53k | 10/07/06 | 31/12 | www.ireplc.com |
| Internet Business Group PLC | IBG | Software & Computer Services | 23.2 | 5 | 247k | 17/05/06 | 31/10 | www.ibg.co.uk |
| InterQuest Group PLC | ITQ | Support Services | 26.7 | 0.5 | 13.5k | 22/06/06 | 31/12 | www.interquestgroup.com |
| Intimas Group PLC | IAG | Personal Goods | 14.8 | 5 | 132k | 16/06/06 | 31/12 | www.sherwoodgroup.co.uk |
| Inveresk PLC | IVS | Forestry & Paper | 27.0 | 5 | 211k | 26/05/05 | 31/12 | www.inveresk.co.uk |
| InvestinMedia PLC | IVM | Media | 25.8 | 0.5 | 15.0k | 03/03/06 | 30/09 | www.investinmedia.com |
| Invocas Group PLC | INVO | General Financial | 49.7 | 2 | | 17/03/06 | 31/03 | |
| Invox PLC | INX | Fixed Line Telecommunications | 6.6 | 3 | 128k | 04/11/05 | 30/06 | |
| Iomart Group PLC | IOM | Software & Computer Services | 56.7 | 1 | 140k | 21/06/06 | 31/03 | www.iomart.com |
| IP Live PLC | IPV | General Financial | 3.2 | 1 | 7.47k | 21/07/05 | 31/03 | www.ipliveplc.com |
| IPSA Group PLC | IPSA | Electricity | 19.9 | 2 | 120k | | | |
| IQE PLC | IQE | Technology Hardware & Equipment | 51.5 | 25 | 1.61m | 31/05/06 | 31/12 | www.iqep.com |
| IQ-Ludorum PLC | IQL | Software & Computer Services | 34.8 | 2 | 537k | 08/11/05 | 31/12 | www.iq-l.com |
| Irish Estates PLC | IERG | Support Services | 56.2 | 0.5 | 1.38k | 30/05/06 | 31/12 | |
| Irvine Energy PLC | IVE | General Financial | 6.8 | 10 | | | | |
| ISIS Medical Technology PLC | IST | General Financial | 0.9 | 0.5 | 260 | 15/08/05 | 30/04 | |
| Isis Resources PLC | ISS | General Financial | 2.4 | 2 | 13.8k | 24/05/06 | | |
| Islamic Bank of Britain PLC | IBB | General Financial | 68.1 | 10 | 205k | 26/04/06 | 31/12 | www.islamic-bank.com |
| Island Oil & Gas PLC | IOG | Oil & Gas Producers | 72.8 | 1 | 553k | 01/03/06 | 31/07 | www.islando-landgas.com |
| ITIS Holdings PLC | ITH | Industrial Transportation | 46.0 | 10 | 245k | 14/09/05 | 31/03 | www.itisholdings.com |
| ITM Power PLC | ITM | Electronic & Electrical Equipment | 163.9 | 10 | 583k | 30/09/05 | 30/04 | www.itm-power.com |
| iTrain PLC | IRN | Support Services | 2.5 | 5 | 114k | 02/09/05 | 31/12 | www.itrain-nat.com |
| IX Europe PLC | IXE | Support Services | 50.9 | 5 | | | | |
| JAB Holdings Ltd | JBH | Equity Investment Instruments | 2.0 | 5 | 117k | 29/12/05 | 30/06 | |
| Jacques Vert PLC | JQV | General Retailers | 33.7 | 5 | 228k | 06/09/05 | 30/04 | |
| James Halstead PLC | JHD | Construction & Materials | 190.0 | 0.5 | 27.1k | 02/12/05 | 30/06 | www.jacques-vert.co.uk |
| James R. Knowles (Holdings) PLC | JRK | Support Services | 6.9 | 0.5 | 11.4k | 15/12/05 | 31/07 | www.jrknowes.com |
| Jarlway Holdings PLC | JWY | Industrial Engineering | 2.9 | 2 | 9.10k | 30/04/03 | 31/12 | www.jarlway.com |
| Jarvis Porter Group PLC | JVP | Construction & Materials | 1.0 | 1 | 13.9k | 07/07/05 | 28/02 | www.jarvisporter.co.uk |
| Jarvis Securities PLC | JIM | General Financial | 11.6 | 0.5 | 7.16k | 24/04/06 | 31/12 | www.jarvissecurities.co.uk |
| Jelf Group PLC | JLF | General Financial | 40.8 | 0.5 | 24.2k | 21/03/06 | 30/09 | www.jelfgroup.com |
| John Lewis of Hungerford PLC | JLH | Household Goods | 2.1 | 1 | 21.5m | 17/03/06 | 31/08 | www.john-lewis.co.uk |
| Jourdan PLC | JDR | Household Goods | 5.7 | 0.5 | 695 | 27/10/05 | 30/06 | |
| JS Real Estate PLC | JSRE | Real Estate | 108.7 | 0.5 | 15.2k | 13/07/06 | 24/03 | www.jsrealestate.co.uk |
| Jubilee Platinum PLC | JLP | Mining | 47.9 | 5 | 509k | 25/11/05 | 30/06 | www.jubileeplatinum.com |
| Judges Capital PLC | JDG | Industrial Engineering | 3.4 | 0.5 | 134 | 17/06/06 | 31/12 | |
| Just Car Clinics Group PLC | JCR | General Retailers | 5.4 | 0.5 | 19.1k | 24/05/06 | 31/12 | www.justcar-clinics.co.uk |
| K3 Business Technology Group PLC | KBT | Software & Computer Services | 17.2 | 1 | 31.6k | 24/05/06 | 31/12 | www.k3btg.com |
| Kalahari Minerals PLC | KAH | Mining | 14.2 | 5 | | | | |
| Karelian Diamond Resources PLC | KDR | Mining | 2.1 | 1 | 37.3k | 31/08/05 | 31/05 | |
| KBC Advanced Technologies PLC | KBC | Oil Equipment; Services & Dist | 16.7 | 2 | 84.8k | 25/05/06 | 31/12 | www.kbcat.com |
| KGR Absolute Return PCC Ltd | KGR | Equity Investment Instruments | 43.2 | 2 | | | | |

Source: Hemscott (Hemscott.com)

# Members of AIM

| Company Name | EPIC | Sector | Capital (£m) | NMS | 200D Avg Vol | AGM | Year End | URL |
|---|---|---|---|---|---|---|---|---|
| KimCor Diamonds PLC | KIM | Mining | 9.6 | 2 | 18.5k | 11/07/06 | 31/12 | www.kimcordiamonds.com |
| Kiotech International PLC | KIO | Pharmaceuticals & Biotechnology | 3.6 | 2 | | 25/05/06 | | |
| KleenAir Systems International PLC | KSI | Automobiles & Parts | 5.7 | 2 | | 28/11/05 | 30/06 | www.ktsplc.com |
| Knowledge Technology Solutions PLC | KTS | Media | 1.5 | 10 | 148k | 31/07/06 | 31/12 | www.kprenewables.com |
| KP Renewables PLC | KPR | Electricity | 10.9 | 2 | 6.83k | 12/07/06 | 31/12 | www.kryso.com |
| Kryso Resources PLC | KYS | Mining | 4.9 | 5 | 77.6k | 30/11/05 | 31/03 | www.kuju.com |
| Kuju PLC | KUJ | Software & Computer Services | 1.1 | 0.5 | 16.7k | 08/09/05 | 30/04 | www.latascagroup.com |
| La Tasca Group PLC | LAT | Travel & Leisure | 61.8 | 3 | 102k | 23/05/06 | 31/12 | www.landore.com |
| Landore Resources Ltd | LND | Mining | 8.4 | 15 | 311k | 09/06/06 | 31/01 | www.landround.com |
| Landround PLC | LDR | Media | 1.7 | 0.5 | 29.8k | | | |
| Lansdowne Oil & Gas PLC | LOGP | Oil & Gas Producers | 13.4 | 2 | | 24/04/05 | 31/12 | www.lapp-plats.com |
| Lapp Plats PLC | LPP | Mining | 2.2 | 1 | 5.55k | 11/08/05 | 31/03 | www.lathamtimber.co.uk |
| Latham (James) PLC | LTHM | Support Services | 37.3 | 1 | 10.9k | 24/01/06 | 30/06 | www.latituderesources.com |
| Latitude Resources PLC | LTR | Mining | 14.6 | 10 | 458k | 29/09/05 | 31/03 | www.lawrenceplc.com |
| Lawrence PLC | LAC | Chemicals | 75.0 | 1 | 33.9k | 26/01/06 | 30/09 | www.leedsgroup.plc.uk |
| Leeds Group PLC | LDSG | General Financial | 7.7 | 1 | 47.1k | 23/05/06 | 31/12 | www.leesofscotland.co.uk |
| Lees Foods PLC | LEE | Food Producers | 5.6 | 0.5 | 472 | 21/10/05 | 31/03 | www.legendaryinvestmentsplc.com |
| Legendary Investments PLC | LEG | General Financial | 0.4 | 25 | 469k | 22/06/06 | 31/12 | www.lngplc.com |
| Leisure & Gaming PLC | LNG | Travel & Leisure | 48.9 | 3 | 118k | 26/07/06 | 31/12 | www.lennoxholdings.com |
| Lennox Holdings PLC | LNX | Food Producers | 1.1 | 2 | 27.6k | 31/07/06 | | www.leocapitalplc.com |
| Leo Capital PLC | LEOC | General Financial | 230.3 | 10 | | | | |
| Leo Insurance Services PLC | LEO | Nonlife Insurance | 2.0 | | | | | |
| Lewis Charles Sofia Property Fund Ltd | LCSS | Real Estate | 35.5 | 5 | 112k | 16/06/06 | | |
| LHP Investments PLC | LHP | General Financial | 1.3 | 1 | 910 | 30/06/06 | | |
| Libertas Capital Group PLC | LBR | General Financial | 14.1 | 2 | 46.1k | 27/06/06 | 31/12 | www.libertascapital.com |
| Liberty PLC | LBE | General Retailers | 58.8 | 0.5 | 673 | 22/11/05 | 30/06 | www.mwb.co.uk |
| Libra Natural Resources PLC | LNR | General Financial | 14.3 | 15 | 538k | 28/07/06 | 31/12 | |
| LiDCO Group PLC | LID | Health Care Equipment & Services | 24.2 | 2 | 139k | 15/06/06 | 31/01 | www.lidco.com |
| Lighthouse Group PLC | LGT | General Financial | 13.6 | 2 | 73.2k | 25/05/06 | 31/12 | www.lighthouseifa.com |
| Lipoxen PLC | LPX | Pharmaceuticals & Biotechnology | 24.5 | 3 | 167k | 28/04/06 | 31/12 | www.lipoxen.co.uk |
| Litcomp PLC | LIN | Nonlife Insurance | 1.8 | 2 | | 12/06/05 | 31/03 | www.litcomp-plc.com |
| Loades PLC | LOD | Automobiles & Parts | 13.0 | | 13.5k | 25/01/06 | 30/06 | www.loades.com |
| Local Radio Company (The) PLC | TLR | Media | 9.9 | 3 | 44.8k | 02/02/06 | 30/09 | www.thelocalradiocompany.com |
| Lok'n Store Group PLC | LOK | Support Services | 38.7 | 1 | 59.3k | 01/12/05 | 31/07 | www.loknstore.co.uk |
| Lombard Medical Technologies PLC | LMT | Health Care Equipment & Services | 55.7 | 5 | | 09/05/06 | 31/12 | www.lombardmedical.com |
| Lombard Risk Management PLC | LRM | Software & Computer Services | 9.5 | 2 | 25.1k | 15/09/05 | 31/03 | www.lombardrisk.com |
| London Asia Capital PLC | LDC | Equity Investment Instruments | 43.5 | 15 | 866k | 25/07/06 | 31/12 | www.londonasia.com |
| London Asia Chinese Private Equity Fund Ltd | LCP | General Financial | 53.0 | 3 | | | | |
| London Capital Group Holdings Plc | LCG | General Financial | 45.4 | 5 | | 25/05/06 | 31/12 | www.londoncapitalgroup.co.uk |
| London Security PLC | LSC | Support Services | 141.7 | | | 07/06/06 | 31/12 | www.londonsecurity.org |
| London Town PLC | LTW | Real Estate | 6.3 | 0.5 | 19.8 | 07/07/06 | 31/12 | www.londontownplc.co.uk |
| Longmead Group (The) PLC | LGM | Household Goods | 0.6 | 0.5 | 1.59k | 29/05/06 | 29/10 | www.longmead-group.co.uk |
| Lonrho Africa PLC | LAF | Travel & Leisure | 46.1 | 15 | 1.48m | 28/04/06 | 30/09 | |
| Lo-Q PLC | LOQ | Travel & Leisure | 2.4 | 0.5 | 30.9k | 10/05/05 | 31/12 | www.lo-q.com |

Source: Hemscott (Hemscott.com)

## Members of AIM

| Company Name | EPIC | Sector | Capital (£m) | NMS | 200D Avg Vol | AGM | Year End | URL |
|---|---|---|---|---|---|---|---|---|
| Lorien PLC | LRG | Support Services | 6.3 | 1 | 18.7k | 04/07/06 | 27/11 | www.lorien.co.uk |
| LPA Group PLC | LPA | Electronic & Electrical Equipment | 2.1 | 0.5 | 8.07k | 08/03/06 | 30/09 | www.lpa-group.com |
| LTG Technologies PLC | LTG | Industrial Engineering | 16.1 | 5 | 205k | 29/05/06 | 31/12 | www.ltg-technologies.com |
| Ludorum PLC | LUD | General Financial | 6.8 | 2 | | 28/05/06 | 28/02 | |
| Lupus Capital PLC | LUP | General Financial | 80.1 | 10 | 741k | 17/05/06 | 31/12 | www.lupuscapital.co.uk |
| M&C Saatchi PLC | SAA | Media | 55.3 | 3 | 69.1k | 07/06/06 | 31/12 | www.mcsaatchi.com |
| M.P. Evans Group PLC | MPE | Food Producers | 139.1 | 1 | 24.5k | 13/06/06 | 31/12 | www.mpevans.co.uk |
| Macau Property Opportunities Fund Ltd | MPO | General Financial | 102.4 | 5 | | | | |
| Maelor PLC | MLR | Health Care Equipment & Services | 2.4 | 3 | 100k | 02/08/06 | 31/03 | www.maelor.plc.uk |
| Maghreb Minerals PLC | MMS | Mining | 4.7 | 5 | 146k | 19/10/05 | 30/06 | www.maghrebminerals.com |
| Magna Investments PLC | MGN | Equity Investment Instruments | 0.5 | 1 | 51.9 | 31/07/06 | | |
| Maintel Holdings PLC | MAI | Support Services | 21.8 | 0.5 | 14.0k | 22/04/05 | 31/12 | www.maintel.co.uk |
| Maisha PLC | MSA | Software & Computer Services | 0.4 | 0.5 | 2.97k | 09/02/06 | 31/08 | www.maishasystems.com |
| Majestic Wine PLC | MJW | Food & Drug Retailers | 190.4 | 3 | 184k | 04/08/06 | 27/03 | www.majestic.co.uk |
| Mama Group PLC | MAMA | Media | 14.1 | 2 | 38.8k | 07/02/06 | 31/07 | www.campusmedia.org |
| Manpower Software PLC | MNS | Software & Computer Services | 7.7 | 2 | 29.8k | 15/12/05 | 31/05 | www.manpowersoftware.com |
| Marakand Minerals Ltd | MKD | Mining | 12.9 | 2 | 152k | 25/11/05 | 30/06 | www.marakand.co.uk |
| Mariana Resources Ltd | MARL | Mining | 5.4 | 5 | | | | www.marianaresources.com |
| Marwyn Value Investors Ltd | MNV | Equity Investment Instruments | 17.3 | 3 | | | | |
| Matisse Holdings PLC | MAT | Equity Investment Instruments | 0.2 | 2 | 32.6k | 12/08/05 | 30/11 | |
| Matra Petroleum PLC | MTA | Oil & Gas Producers | 7.9 | 10 | 544k | 28/07/06 | | |
| Mattioli Woods PLC | MTW | General Financial | 36.4 | 2 | | 30/08/05 | 31/05 | www.mattioli-woods.com |
| Maverick Entertainment Group PLC | MVK | Media | 2.0 | 25 | 1.66m | 28/06/06 | 31/12 | www.maverickentertainment.co.uk |
| Mavinwood PLC | MVW | Support Services | 59.7 | 10 | 313k | 25/04/06 | 31/12 | www.mavinwoodplc.com |
| Max Petroleum PLC | MXP | Oil & Gas Producers | 335.9 | 25 | | | | www.maxpetroleum.com |
| Maxima Holdings PLC | MXM | Software & Computer Services | 24.6 | 1 | 6.89k | 20/10/05 | 31/05 | www.maximaholdings.com |
| May Gurney Integrated Services PLC | MAYG | Construction & Materials | 169.6 | 3 | | | | www.maygurney.co.uk |
| Maypole Group PLC | MPG | Travel & Leisure | 1.5 | 5 | | | | |
| Mears Group PLC | MER | Support Services | 157.6 | 3 | 207k | 07/06/06 | 31/12 | www.mearsgroup.co.uk |
| Mecom Group PLC | MEC | Media | 50.0 | 15 | 24.4k | 16/12/05 | 31/07 | www.mecom.co.uk |
| Medal Entertainment & Media PLC | MME | General Financial | 9.6 | 0.5 | 22.6k | 27/10/05 | 31/03 | www.mem-plc.com |
| Media Square PLC | MSQ | Media | 75.7 | 15 | 839k | 11/04/05 | 31/10 | www.mediasquare.co.uk |
| Media Steps Group PLC | STEP | Media | 0.2 | 3 | 14.6k | | | |
| Mediasurface PLC | MSR | Software & Computer Services | 10.0 | 3 | 315k | 01/03/06 | 30/09 | www.mediasurface.co.uk |
| MediaZest PLC | MDZ | Media | 2.7 | 0.5 | 36.5k | 08/08/05 | 31/12 | |
| Medical House (The) PLC | MLH | Health Care Equipment & Services | 21.8 | 2 | 23.0k | 11/11/05 | 30/06 | www.themedicalhouse.com |
| Medical Marketing International Group PLC | MMG | Pharmaceuticals & Biotechnology | 79.2 | 3 | 164k | 02/11/05 | 31/03 | www.mmigroup.co.uk |
| Medici Bioventures PLC | MEB | General Financial | 1.1 | 2 | 31.2k | 24/06/06 | | |
| Mediterranean Oil & Gas PLC | MOG | Oil & Gas Producers | 53.7 | 3 | | | | www.medoilgas.com |
| Mediwatch PLC | MDW | Health Care Equipment & Services | 8.6 | 5 | 220k | 29/07/05 | 30/04 | www.mediwatch.com |
| MedOil PLC | MDL | Oil & Gas Producers | 8.8 | 2 | 86.6k | 23/02/06 | 30/09 | www.medoilplc.com |
| Medsea Estates Group PLC | MEA | Real Estate | 11.7 | 0.5 | 23.3k | 16/06/06 | 31/12 | www.medseaestates-ir.com |
| Melchior Japan Investment Trust PLC | MJT | Equity Investment Instruments | 65.2 | 5 | | | | |
| Mercator Gold PLC | MCR | Mining | 43.6 | 1 | 144k | 26/10/05 | 30/06 | www.mercatorgold.com |

Source: Hemscott (Hemscott)

Members of AIM

| Company Name | EPIC | Sector | Capital (£m) | NMS | 200D Avg Vol | AGM | Year End | URL |
|---|---|---|---|---|---|---|---|---|
| Merchant House Group PLC | MHG | General Financial | 1.6 | 3 | 294k | 25/08/05 | 31/12 | www.merchant-capital.com |
| Mercury Group PLC | MGP | Support Services | 4.4 | 1 | 257k | 24/04/06 | 30/09 | www.mgplc.co.uk |
| Mercury Recycling Group PLC | MRG | Support Services | 8.0 | 1 | 23.7k | 19/06/06 | 31/12 | www.mercuryrecycling.co.uk |
| Meriden Group PLC | MRD | Support Services | 0.4 | 15 | 444k | 01/03/05 | 31/07 | www.meriden-group.co.uk |
| Meridian Petroleum PLC | MRP | Oil & Gas Producers | 12.0 | 15 | 1.61m | 27/07/06 | 31/12 | www.meridianpetroleum.com |
| Messaging International PLC | MES | Mobile Telecommunications | 3.7 | 2 | 96.4k | 29/06/06 | 31/12 | www.telemessage.com |
| Metals Exploration PLC | MTL | Mining | 19.3 | 15 | 1.07m | 31/07/06 | 30/09 | www.metalsexploration.com |
| Metnor Group PLC | MTG | General Industrials | 42.0 | 0.5 | 14.2k | 26/05/06 | 31/12 | www.metnor.co.uk |
| Metrodome Group PLC | MRM | Media | 2.8 | 0.5 | 28.9k | 11/07/06 | 31/12 | www.metrodomegroup.com |
| MG Capital PLC | MAP | General Financial | 2.4 | 0.5 | 799 | 09/12/05 | 30/06 | www.micap.biz |
| Micap PLC | MIC | Pharmaceuticals & Biotechnology | 1.5 | 2 | 83.3k | 12/12/05 | 31/03 | www.micap.biz |
| Michelmersh Brick Holdings PLC | MBH | Construction & Materials | 43.0 | 0.5 | 21.5k | 26/04/06 | 31/12 | www.michelmersh.com |
| Microcap Equities PLC | MEQ | General Financial | 0.2 | 5 | 29.7k | 27/09/05 | 31/12 | |
| MicroEmissive Displays Group PLC | MED | Electronic & Electrical Equipment | 6.3 | 0.5 | 13.1k | 23/05/06 | 31/12 | www.microemissive.com |
| MicroFuze International PLC | MFZ | General Industrials | 8.9 | 5 | | | | |
| Milestone Group PLC | MSG | Media | 1.4 | 0.5 | 11.4k | 28/04/06 | 30/09 | www.milestone.co.uk |
| Millbrook Scientific Instruments PLC | MBK | Electronic & Electrical Equipment | 2.4 | 5 | 162k | 01/08/06 | 31/03 | www.millbrook-instruments.com |
| Millfield Group PLC | MIL | General Financial | 1.5 | 15 | 709k | 12/10/05 | 31/03 | www.millfield-partnership.co.uk |
| Millwall Holdings PLC | MWH | Travel & Leisure | 9.9 | 150 | 10.8m | 29/12/05 | 31/05 | www.millwallfc.co.uk |
| Minco PLC | MIO | Mining | 17.6 | 1 | 773k | 22/06/05 | 31/12 | www.minco.ie |
| Mincorp PLC | MOP | Mining | 2.0 | 2 | 82.8k | | 31/05 | |
| Minmet PLC | MNT | Mining | 7.4 | 15 | 1.92m | 20/07/06 | 31/12 | www.minmet.ie |
| Minorplanet Systems PLC | MPS | Electronic & Electrical Equipment | 10.8 | 2 | 76.3k | 26/01/06 | 31/08 | www.minorplanet.com |
| Minster Pharmaceuticals PLC | MPM | Pharmaceuticals & Biotechnology | 22.3 | 75 | 3.51m | 26/10/05 | 31/03 | www.minsterpharma.com |
| Mission Capital PLC | MCAP | Real Estate | 6.9 | 5 | | | | |
| Mission Marketing Group (The) PLC | TMMG | Media | 24.1 | 2 | | | | |
| MKM Group PLC | MKM | Media | 2.2 | 0.5 | 20.1k | 24/10/05 | 31/03 | www.mkm-promotions.com |
| Mobestar Holdings PLC | MOBS | Mobile Telecommunications | 7.6 | 3 | | 15/04/06 | 31/12 | www.mobestar.com |
| Mobile Streams PLC | MOS | Mobile Telecommunications | 14.7 | 2 | | 30/04/05 | 31/12 | www.mobilestreams.com |
| Mobile Tornado Group PLC | MBT | General Financial | 6.3 | 2 | 18.0k | 30/10/05 | 30/06 | www.tmtgroup.com |
| Mondas PLC | MDS | Software & Computer Services | 4.9 | 2 | 102k | 24/11/05 | 31/12 | www.mondas.com |
| Monsoon PLC | MSN | General Retailers | 698.7 | 2 | 183k | 30/09/05 | 28/05 | www.monsoon.co.uk |
| Monstermob Group PLC | MOB | Media | 38.6 | 3 | 512k | 22/06/06 | 31/12 | www.monstermobgroup.plc.uk |
| Monterrico Metals PLC | MNA | Mining | 50.0 | 3 | 121k | 19/06/06 | 31/12 | www.monterrico.com |
| Morson Group PLC | MRN | Support Services | 79.1 | 3 | | 15/03/06 | 31/12 | www.morson.com |
| Motivcom PLC | MCM | Media | 21.0 | 0.5 | 4.33k | 04/05/05 | 31/12 | www.motivcom.com |
| Motive Television PLC | MTV | Media | 0.9 | 5 | 46.0k | 30/06/06 | 31/12 | |
| Mulberry Group PLC | MUL | General Retailers | 85.8 | 1 | 24.0k | 27/07/05 | 31/03 | www.mulberry.com |
| Multi Group PLC | MLT | Support Services | 3.4 | 10 | 304k | 08/06/05 | 31/12 | www.multiplc.com |
| MultiMedia Television PLC | MTM | Media | 1.6 | 0.5 | 11.8k | 27/01/06 | 30/04 | www.mtmplc.com |
| Murgitroyd Group PLC | MUR | Support Services | 24.1 | 0.5 | 4.93k | 28/09/05 | 31/05 | www.murgitroyd.com |
| Music Copyright Solutions PLC | MCS | Media | 1.7 | 0.5 | 6.90k | 01/12/05 | 31/12 | www.musiccopyrightsolutions.co.uk |
| Mwana Africa PLC | MWA | Mining | 91.7 | 3 | 357k | 25/10/05 | 31/03 | www.mwanaafrica.com |
| MWB Business Exchange PLC | MBE | Support Services | 68.1 | 5 | | 07/06/06 | 31/12 | www.mwbex.com |

Source: Hemscott (Hemscott.com)

## Members of AIM

| Company Name | EPIC | Sector | Capital (£m) | NMS | 200D Avg Vol | AGM | Year End | URL |
|---|---|---|---|---|---|---|---|---|
| Myratech.net PLC | MYA | Software & Computer Services | 1.0 | 15 | 403k | 05/12/05 | 30/06 | www.myratech.net |
| Nadlan PLC | NAD | Real Estate | 0.8 | 25 | 2.52m | 29/09/05 | 30/04 | www.nadlan.co.uk |
| Namibian Resources PLC | NBR | Mining | 9.8 | 2 | 28.5k | 28/10/05 | 28/02 | |
| Nardina Resources PLC | NRR | General Financial | 7.5 | 10 | | | | |
| Nasstar PLC | NASA | Software & Computer Services | 3.2 | 2 | | 31/01/06 | 30/09 | www.nasstar.com |
| Nationwide Accident Repair Services PLC | NARS | Support Services | 61.5 | | | | | www.narsplc.com |
| Nature Technology Solutions Ltd | NSO | Support Services | 3.5 | 5 | 464k | 29/06/05 | 31/12 | www.naturetechsolution.com |
| Nautical Petroleum PLC | NPE | Oil & Gas Producers | 120.6 | 15 | 1.19m | 21/07/05 | 31/12 | www.nautica.petroleum.com |
| NBA Quantum PLC | NAQ | Construction & Materials | 2.5 | 0.5 | 3.61k | 16/01/06 | 30/06 | www.nbagro-jp.com |
| NCC Group PLC | NCC | Software & Computer Services | 84.8 | 3 | 112k | 21/09/05 | 31/05 | www.nccgroup.com |
| Neptune Minerals PLC | NPM | Mining | 8.9 | 2 | 33.0k | | | |
| Netb2b2 PLC | NEB | Software & Computer Services | 0.9 | 0.5 | 14.5k | 18/01/06 | 30/06 | www.netb2b2.com |
| Netcall PLC | NET | Software & Computer Services | 7.6 | 2 | 78.4k | 15/11/05 | 30/06 | www.netcall.com |
| Netcentric Systems PLC | NCS | Software & Computer Services | 1.4 | 10 | 896k | 30/06/06 | 30/09 | |
| NETeller PLC | NLR | General Financial | 482.1 | 50 | 2.53m | 11/05/06 | 31/12 | www.netelle:.com |
| NetServices PLC | NSV | Software & Computer Services | 7.9 | 2 | | 15/12/04 | 31/08 | www.netservicesplc.com |
| NetStore PLC | NES | Software & Computer Services | 45.0 | 5 | 158k | 23/12/05 | 30/06 | www.netstore.co.uk |
| NETTEC PLC | NTC | Software & Computer Services | 15.4 | 2 | 18.0k | 19/05/06 | 31/12 | www.nettecplc.com |
| Nettworx PLC | NTWX | General Financial | 9.4 | 15 | | | | |
| Networkers International PLC | NWKI | Support Services | 29.9 | 0.5 | 26.5k | 31/10/05 | 31/03 | |
| NeuTec Pharma PLC | NTP | Pharmaceuticals & Biotechnology | 305.4 | 2 | 120k | 11/11/05 | 30/06 | www.neutecpharma.com |
| NeutraHealth PLC | NUT | Food & Drug Retailers | 15.9 | 3 | 116k | 19/04/06 | 31/12 | www.neutrahealthplc.com |
| New Media Lottery Services PLC | NMLS | Travel & Leisure | 14.6 | 2 | | | | www.nmlsplc.com |
| New Star Absolute Return Fund PCC Ltd | NSAG | Equity Investment Instruments | 14.0 | 2 | | | | |
| New Star Asset Management Group PLC | NSAM | General Financial | 1010.3 | 10 | | 24/05/06 | 31/12 | www.newstaram.com |
| Newcourt Group PLC | NEW | Support Services | 68.6 | 0.5 | | | 31/12 | |
| Newmark Security PLC | NWT | Support Services | 4.2 | 25 | 510k | 12/10/05 | 30/04 | www.newmarksecurity.com |
| Newmarket Investments PLC | NWN | Travel & Leisure | 1.9 | 0.5 | 2.80k | 01/09/05 | 31/03 | www.newmediaspark.com |
| NewMedia SPARK PLC | NMS | Equity Investment Instruments | 79.2 | 25 | 1.57m | 15/09/05 | 31/03 | |
| Newport Networks Group PLC | NNG | Technology Hardware & Equipment | 10.0 | 5 | 508k | 02/06/06 | 31/12 | www.newport-networks.com |
| Next Fifteen Communications Group PLC | NFC | Media | 31.7 | 2 | 69.8k | 24/01/06 | 31/07 | www.nextfifteen.com |
| NextGen Group PLC | NGG | Pharmaceuticals & Biotechnology | 8.0 | 15 | | 28/06/06 | 31/12 | www.nextgensciences.com |
| Nexus Management PLC | NXS | Software & Computer Services | 4.7 | 10 | 2.07m | 24/08/05 | 31/03 | www.nexusmgmt.com |
| Niche Group (The) PLC | NGP | General Financial | 0.4 | 10 | 36.2k | 28/03/06 | 30/06 | |
| Nichols PLC | NICL | Beverages | 84.5 | 1 | 34.0k | 16/05/06 | 31/12 | www.nichosplc.co.uk |
| Nikanor PLC | NKR | Industrial Metals | 865.2 | | | | | www.nikanor.co.uk |
| Nipson Digital Printing Systems PLC | NDP | Media | 14.4 | 3 | 88.4k | 24/05/06 | 31/12 | www.nipson.com |
| NMI Security PLC | NMI | Electronic & Electrical Equipment | 8.1 | 25 | 2.85m | 16/12/05 | 30/04 | www.nmisecurity.com |
| NMT Group PLC | NMT | Health Care Equipment & Services | 4.3 | 3 | 29.7k | 23/06/06 | 31/12 | www.newmedicaltechnology.com |
| Noble Investments (UK) PLC | NBL | General Financial | 18.7 | 0.5 | 42.0k | 28/11/05 | 31/08 | www.nobleinvestmentsplc.com |
| Norkom Group PLC | NORK | Software & Computer Services | 73.0 | 3 | | | | |
| North American Banks Fund Ltd | NAM | Equity Investment Instruments | 21.1 | 0.5 | 3.84k | 26/06/06 | | |
| Northacre PLC | NTA | Real Estate | 2.6 | 1 | 48.0k | 28/09/05 | 28/02 | www.northacre.com |
| Northbridge Industrial Services PLC | NBI | Industrial Engineering | 8.6 | 1 | | 15/04/05 | 31/12 | |

# Members of AIM

| Company Name | EPIC | Sector | Capital (£m) | NMS | 200D Avg Vol | AGM | Year End | URL |
|---|---|---|---|---|---|---|---|---|
| Northern Lynx PLC | NLX | Real Estate | 46.0 | 5 | 741k | | 31/12 | www.northpet.com |
| Northern Petroleum PLC | NOP | Oil & Gas Producers | 90.7 | 10 | 4.53k | 26/07/06 | 31/12 | www.northernracing.co.uk |
| Northern Racing PLC | NOR | Travel & Leisure | 46.7 | 0.5 | | 19/05/06 | | www.titaniumresources.com/homepage/index.html |
| Nutcor Uranium Ltd | NU. | Equity Investment Instruments | 78.2 | 5 | | | | www.numiscorp.com |
| Numis Corporation PLC | NUM | General Financial | 284.9 | 3 | 195k | 07/02/06 | 30/09 | www.nwdgroup.co.uk |
| NWD Group PLC | NWD | Media | 1.0 | 50 | 912k | 15/09/05 | 31/12 | www.nwf.co.uk |
| NWF Group PLC | NWF | Support Services | 77.9 | 0.5 | 6.91k | 30/09/05 | 31/05 | |
| O Twelve Estates Ltd | OTE | Real Estate | 120.7 | 5 | | | | www.oakholdings.co.uk |
| Oak Holdings PLC | OAH | Real Estate | 13.1 | 10 | 346k | 25/05/06 | 31/10 | www.oakdene-homes.co.uk |
| Oakdene Homes PLC | OKD | Household Goods | 45.1 | 2 | 98.0k | 27/06/06 | 31/12 | www.oasis-healthcare.com |
| Oasis Healthcare PLC | OSH | Health Care Equipment & Services | 22.7 | 1 | 164k | 20/09/05 | 31/03 | www.oceanresources.co.uk |
| Ocean Resources Capital Holdings PLC | OCE | General Financial | 18.8 | 2 | 15.4k | 05/07/06 | 31/12 | |
| Off-Plan Fund (The) Ltd | OPF | Real Estate | 7.8 | 1 | | 13/01/06 | 30/09 | www.ohmsurveys.com |
| Offshore Hydrocarbon Mapping PLC | OHM | Oil Equipment; Services & Dist | 33.4 | 1 | 70.5k | 01/12/05 | 31/08 | www.omegaplc.co.uk |
| Omega International Group PLC | OME | Household Goods | 60.7 | 0.5 | 18.2k | 07/06/06 | 31/12 | www.omegaunderwriting.co.uk |
| Omega Underwriting Holdings PLC | OUH | General Financial | 148.0 | 5 | 283k | 19/06/06 | 31/12 | www.omg3d.com |
| OMG PLC | OMG | Software & Computer Services | 21.6 | 3 | 146k | 22/02/06 | 30/09 | www.oneclickhr.com |
| OneClickHR PLC | OCR | Software & Computer Services | 5.8 | 5 | 117k | 15/06/05 | 31/12 | www.on-line.co.uk |
| On-Line PLC | ONL | Software & Computer Services | 2.2 | 0.5 | 8.41k | 08/12/05 | 30/06 | |
| Optimisa PLC | OPS | Media | 7.8 | 0.5 | 301 | 08/07/05 | 31/12 | www.oeplc.com |
| Optimistic Entertainment PLC | OEP | Media | 1.8 | 1 | 26.5k | | | www.orbisplc.com |
| Orbis PLC | OBS | Support Services | 0.3 | 0.5 | 13.4k | 06/09/05 | 31/03 | www.orielresources.com |
| Oriel Resources PLC | ORI | Mining | 72.1 | 15 | 651k | 27/07/06 | 31/12 | www.bioprojects.com |
| Original Investments PLC | OIP | General Financial | 14.0 | 15 | 632k | 28/09/05 | 31/03 | www.osmetech.com |
| Osmetech PLC | OMH | Pharmaceuticals & Biotechnology | 38.0 | 10 | 913k | 03/05/06 | 31/12 | |
| Ottoman Fund (The) Ltd | OTM | Equity Investment Instruments | 158.3 | 10 | | | | www.ovocagold.com |
| Ovoca Gold PLC | OVG | Mining | 12.6 | 3 | 546k | 29/09/05 | 28/02 | www.ovum.com |
| Ovum PLC | OVM | Software & Computer Services | 20.3 | 2 | | 20/07/06 | 31/03 | |
| Oxford Catalysts Group PLC | OCG | Chemicals | 51.7 | 2 | | | | www.oxonica.co.uk |
| Oxonica PLC | OXN | Chemicals | 47.7 | 0.5 | 11.8k | 30/05/06 | 31/12 | www.oxusgold.co.uk |
| Oxus Gold PLC | OXS | Mining | 84.8 | 50 | 1.23m | 25/11/05 | 30/06 | |
| Pactolus Hungarian Property PLC | PHU | Real Estate | 10.5 | 3 | | | | www.palladex.co.uk |
| Palladex PLC | PLX | Mining | 2.3 | 10 | 115k | 14/01/05 | 30/09 | www.palmariscapital.com |
| Palmaris Capital PLC | PMS | Support Services | 15.3 | 3 | 155k | 17/11/05 | 30/06 | www.panafricanresources.com |
| Pan African Resources PLC | PAF | Mining | 29.1 | 15 | 1.41m | 27/07/06 | 31/03 | www.panandeanresources.com |
| Pan Andean Resources PLC | PRE | Oil & Gas Producers | 14.3 | 5 | 302k | 25/10/05 | 31/03 | www.panagg.com |
| Pan Pacific Aggregates PLC | PPA | Mining | 32.7 | 3 | | 12/06/06 | | www.panmure.com |
| Panmure Gordon & Co PLC | PMR | General Financial | 91.5 | 3 | 137k | 08/06/05 | 31/12 | |
| Pannal PLC | PAN | General Financial | 2.7 | 3 | 4.00k | | | |
| Pantheon Leisure PLC | PLEI | Travel & Leisure | 1.8 | 10 | 91.3k | 15/04/05 | 31/12 | |
| Pantheon Resources PLC | PANR | Oil & Gas Producers | 19.7 | 2 | | | | www.parallelmediagroup.com |
| Parallel Media Group PLC | PAA | Media | 0.6 | 0.5 | 16.8k | 02/08/06 | 31/12 | www.interregnum.com |
| Parkmead Group (The) PLC | PMG | Support Services | 22.6 | 5 | 144k | 20/12/05 | 30/06 | |

**Company Directory**

## Members of AIM

| Company Name | EPIC | Sector | Capital (£m) | NMS | 200D Avg Vol | AGM | Year End | URL |
|---|---|---|---|---|---|---|---|---|
| ParOS PLC | PARO | Technology Hardware & Equipment | 14.8 | 10 | 454k | 22/06/06 | 31/12 | www.parostech.com |
| Patagonia Gold PLC | PGD | Mining | 19.1 | 10 | 22.1k | 09/09/05 | 31/12 | www.patagoniagold.com |
| Pathfinder Properties PLC | PFP | Real Estate | 7.8 | 0.5 | 326k | 05/04/06 | 31/12 | www.pathfinderplc.com |
| Patsystems PLC | PTS | Software & Computer Services | 25.0 | 10 | 69.5k | 24/05/05 | 31/12 | www.patsystems.com |
| Pavilion Insurance Network PLC | PVL | Nonlife Insurance | 2.6 | 2 | 390k | 30/10/05 | 30/06 | www.pinplc.co.uk |
| Pearl Street Holdings PLC | PSH | General Financial | 3.7 | 15 | 9.96k | 12/05/06 | 12/02 | |
| Peel Hotels PLC | PHO | Travel & Leisure | 18.5 | 0.5 | 20.4k | 30/03/06 | 31/08 | www.peelhotel.com |
| Peninsular Gold Ltd | PGL | Mining | 22.0 | 2 | 51.9k | 24/05/05 | 31/12 | www.peninsulargold.com |
| Penmc PLC | PNC | General Financial | 0.1 | 5 | | | 30/09 | |
| Pennant International Group PLC | PEN | Software & Computer Services | 4.3 | 0.5 | 45.9k | 29/03/05 | 31/12 | www.pennantplc.co.uk |
| Pentagon Protection PLC | PPR | Support Services | 3.6 | 15 | 318k | 27/07/06 | 31/12 | www.pentagonglasstech.com |
| Persian Gold PLC | PNG | Mining | 15.3 | 10 | 16.9k | 25/04/06 | 31/12 | www.persiangoldplc.com |
| Personal Group Holdings PLC | PGH | Nonlife Insurance | 82.0 | 0.5 | 16.1k | 30/04/05 | 31/12 | www.personal-group.com |
| Personal Screening PLC | PSP | Health Care Equipment & Services | 2.5 | 10 | 342 | 27/07/06 | 31/12 | www.personalscreening.com |
| Perspective Capital PLC | PER | General Financial | 0.7 | | | | | |
| Petards Group PLC | PEG | Support Services | 5.1 | 15 | 849k | 22/06/06 | 30/06 | www.petards.com |
| Peter Hambro Mining PLC | POG | Mining | 1054.2 | 10 | 557k | 02/12/05 | 31/12 | www.peterhambro.com |
| Petra Diamonds Ltd | PDL | Mining | 146.7 | 10 | 503k | 26/07/06 | 31/12 | www.petradiamonds.com |
| Petrel Resources PLC | PET | Oil & Gas Producers | 30.7 | 10 | 281k | 28/07/06 | 31/12 | www.petrelresources.com |
| Petroceltic International PLC | PCI | Oil & Gas Producers | 136.4 | 50 | 7.11m | 24/05/06 | 30/06 | www.petroceltic.com |
| PetroLatina Energy PLC | PELE | Oil & Gas Producers | 27.2 | 3 | 21.6m | 03/11/05 | 31/12 | www.taghmenenergy.com |
| Petsome PLC | PSM | General Financial | 0.3 | 2 | | | | |
| PFI Infrastructure Company (The) PLC | PFI | Equity Investment Instruments | 96.4 | 2 | 41.0k | 15/06/06 | 31/03 | www.pfiplc.com |
| Phoqus Group PLC | PQS | Pharmaceuticals & Biotechnology | 44.7 | 0.5 | 22.0k | 28/03/06 | 30/09 | www.phoqus.com |
| PHSC PLC | PHSC | Support Services | 5.6 | 0.5 | 2.53k | 22/12/05 | 30/06 | www.phscplc.co.uk |
| Phynova Group PLC | PYN | Pharmaceuticals & Biotechnology | 14.1 | 3 | | | | |
| Physiomics PLC | PYC | Health Care Equipment & Services | 0.9 | 10 | 330k | 01/06/06 | 31/12 | www.physiomics-plc.com |
| Pilat Media Global PLC | PGB | Software & Computer Services | 29.9 | 2 | 96.3k | 14/12/05 | 31/12 | www.pilatmedia.com |
| PipeHawk PLC | PIP | Construction & Materials | 5.1 | 1 | 84.6k | 07/06/06 | 30/04 | www.pipehawk.com |
| PIPEX Communications PLC | PXC | Fixed Line Telecommunications | 191.6 | 150 | 14.6m | 21/07/06 | 30/04 | www.pipex.net |
| Pittards PLC | PTD | Personal Goods | 13.4 | 3 | 53.3k | 26/07/06 | 31/12 | www.pittardsleather.com |
| Pixel Interactive Media Ltd | PIXL | Media | 17.2 | 2 | 54.5k | 27/09/05 | 31/07 | www.pixelinteractivemedia.com |
| Pixology PLC | PIX | Software & Computer Services | 5.6 | 1 | 84.8k | 30/09/05 | 31/12 | www.pixology.com |
| PKL Holdings PLC | PKL | Support Services | 8.8 | 3 | 98.0k | 09/06/06 | 31/03 | www.pkl.co.uk |
| Planit Holdings PLC | PLN | Software & Computer Services | 24.9 | 3 | 80.0k | 23/02/06 | 31/12 | www.planitholdingsplc.com |
| Plant Health Care PLC | PHC | Chemicals | 35.2 | 0.5 | 159k | 30/08/05 | 31/12 | www.planthealthcare.co.uk |
| Platinum Mining Corporation of India PLC | PMCI | Mining | 21.5 | 5 | 17.9k | 22/11/05 | 31/12 | www.pmciplc.com |
| Playgolf (Holdings) PLC | PLG | Travel & Leisure | 4.6 | 1 | | | | |
| Playtech Ltd | PTEC | Travel & Leisure | 522.7 | 10 | | | | |
| Playwize PLC | PLW | Software & Computer Services | 5.3 | 15 | 748k | 11/05/06 | 31/03 | www.bitscorp.com |
| Plectrum Petroleum PLC | PPE | Oil & Gas Producers | 22.5 | 10 | 795k | 05/06/06 | 31/12 | www.plectrum.co.uk |
| Plethora Solutions Holdings PLC | PLE | Pharmaceuticals & Biotechnology | 43.4 | 1 | 50.8k | 31/10/05 | 31/12 | www.plethorasolutions.co.uk |
| Plexus Holding PLC | POS | Oil Equipment; Services & Dist | 53.3 | 5 | | | 30/06 | |
| PLUS Markets Group PLC | PMK | General Financial | 35.7 | 15 | 1.04m | 20/04/06 | 31/12 | www.ofex.com |

Source: Hemscott (Hemscott.com)

| Company Name | EPIC | Sector | Capital (£m) | NMS | 200D Avg Vol | AGM | Year End | URL |
|---|---|---|---|---|---|---|---|---|
| PlusNet PLC | PNT | Software & Computer Services | 28.7 | 5 | 286k | 20/04/05 | 31/12 | www.plus.net |
| PM Group PLC | PGP | Support Services | 33.6 | 0.5 | 21.7k | 24/11/05 | 30/06 | www.pmgroup-plc.uk |
| PNC Telecom PLC | PTC | Fixed Line Telecommunications | 0.8 | 50 | 663k | 15/10/05 | 31/03 | www.polaron.com |
| Polaron PLC | POL | Electronic & Electrical Equipment | 10.2 | 1 | 24.7k | 02/11/05 | 30/06 | |
| Poly Information PLC | PLY | Software & Computer Services | 0.5 | 15 | 300k | 04/08/06 | | www.polyinformation.com |
| Poole Investments PLC | PIV | Construction & Materials | 5.3 | 3 | 77.7k | 14/10/05 | 31/05 | www.portmeirion.com |
| Portmeirion Group PLC | PMP | Household Goods | 23.2 | 0.5 | 3.39k | 23/05/06 | 31/12 | www.portraitsoftware.com |
| Portrait Software PLC | PST | Software & Computer Services | 15.9 | 3 | 129k | 15/09/05 | 31/03 | www.potentialfinance.com |
| Potential Finance Group PLC | POT | General Financial | 5.1 | 0.5 | 14.9k | 04/05/06 | 31/09 | www.powerleague.co.uk |
| Powerleague Group PLC | PWR | Travel & Leisure | 56.9 | 3 | 182k | 25/11/05 | 02/07 | www.premierfunds.co.uk |
| Premier Asset Management PLC | PAM | General Financial | 21.7 | 0.5 | 31.2k | 26/01/06 | 30/09 | www.premierdirectgroup.co.uk |
| Premier Direct Group PLC | PDR | General Retailers | 6.0 | 0.5 | 204k | 14/12/05 | 31/07 | www.premierplc.com |
| Premier Management Holdings PLC | PMA | Travel & Leisure | 0.3 | 5 | 182k | 18/11/05 | 31/01 | www.premier-research.com |
| Premier Research Group PLC | PRG | Pharmaceuticals & Biotechnology | 102.1 | 3 | 180k | 14/06/06 | 31/01 | www.prestbury.com |
| Prestbury Holdings PLC | PBH | General Financial | 5.6 | 0.5 | 33.1k | 18/03/06 | 31/10 | www.pne.com |
| Preston North End PLC | PNE | Travel & Leisure | 3.7 | 0.5 | 497 | 24/10/05 | 30/06 | www.prezzoplc.co.uk |
| Prezzo PLC | PRZ | Travel & Leisure | 112.2 | 2 | 85.0k | 09/06/06 | 01/01 | www.prime-people.co.uk |
| Prime People PLC | PRP | Support Services | 13.0 | 2 | 7.93k | 04/07/06 | 31/03 | |
| Principle Capital Investment Trust PLC | PCIT | Equity Investment Instruments | 51.9 | 3 | | | | |
| Printing.com PLC | PDC | Media | 23.4 | 2 | 132k | 03/08/05 | 31/03 | www.printing.com |
| Private & Commercial Finance Group PLC | PCF | General Financial | 4.3 | 1 | 31.7k | 23/05/06 | 31/12 | www.pcfg.co.uk |
| Proactis Holdings PLC | PHD | Software & Computer Services | 14.0 | 2 | | | | www.proactis.com |
| Probus Estates PLC | PBE | Real Estate | 0.7 | 1 | 51.9k | 20/02/06 | 31/12 | |
| Prologic PLC | PGC | Software & Computer Services | 8.5 | 0.5 | 1.34k | 25/07/06 | 31/03 | www.prologic.net |
| Promethean PLC | PTH | General Financial | 51.9 | 1 | 3.66k | | | |
| Property Recycling Group PLC | PROP | Real Estate | 24.4 | 2 | 29.5k | 15/06/06 | 31/12 | |
| Prosperity Minerals Holdings Ltd | PMHL | Construction & Materials | 199.4 | 5 | | | | www.proteome.co.uk |
| Proteome Sciences PLC | PRM | Pharmaceuticals & Biotechnology | 53.2 | 25 | 506k | 27/07/06 | 31/12 | www.proventecplc.com |
| Proventec PLC | PROV | Chemicals | 23.4 | 10 | 281k | 24/08/05 | 31/03 | www.provexis.com |
| Provexis PLC | PXS | Food Producers | 15.7 | 15 | 563k | 23/08/05 | 31/03 | www.providenceresources.com |
| Providence Resources PLC | PVR | Oil & Gas Producers | 110.7 | 15 | 1.24m | 20/06/06 | 31/12 | www.proximagen.com |
| Proximagen Neuroscience PLC | PRX | Pharmaceuticals & Biotechnology | 24.6 | 1 | 10.7k | 05/07/06 | 30/11 | www.psgsols.com |
| PSG Solutions PLC | PGS | Support Services | 15.3 | 2 | 20.0k | 07/08/06 | 31/03 | |
| Ptarmigan Property Ltd | PPL | Equity Investment Instruments | 8.4 | 0.5 | 2.84k | 28/04/06 | 31/12 | www.publicrecruitmentgroup.com |
| Public Recruitment Group PLC | PUG | Support Services | 12.3 | 2 | 57.1k | 30/05/05 | 31/12 | www.pubsnbars.co.uk |
| Pubs 'N' Bars PLC | PNB | Travel & Leisure | 11.1 | 1 | 31.3k | 16/06/06 | 31/12 | www.punchgraphix.com |
| Puma Brandenburg Ltd | PUMA | Real Estate | 193.3 | 5 | | | | www.purewafer.com |
| Punch Graphix PLC | PGX | Media | 106.9 | 5 | 203k | 24/05/06 | 31/12 | www.pursuitdynamics.com |
| Pure Wafer PLC | PUR | Technology Hardware & Equipment | 64.9 | 1 | 27.5k | 15/11/05 | 30/06 | www.qonnectis.com |
| Pursuit Dynamics PLC | PDX | Industrial Engineering | 60.4 | 5 | 227k | 27/01/06 | 30/09 | www.quadnetics.com |
| Qonnectis PLC | QTI | Software & Computer Services | 4.1 | 25 | 417k | 22/02/06 | 30/06 | www.quayle.co.uk |
| Quadnetics Group PLC | QDG | Support Services | 36.6 | 0.5 | 22.7k | 29/11/05 | 31/05 | |
| Quadrise Fuels International PLC | QFI | Chemicals | 103.8 | 5 | 157k | | 31/12 | |
| Quayle Munro Holdings PLC | QYM | General Financial | 37.9 | 0.5 | 1.47k | 04/11/05 | 30/06 | |

## Members of AIM

| Company Name | EPIC | Sector | Capital (£m) | NMS | 200D Avg Vol | AGM | Year End | URL |
|---|---|---|---|---|---|---|---|---|
| Queen's Walk Investment Ltd | QWIL | General Financial | 299.0 | 3 | | 31/07/06 | 31/12 | |
| Quintessentially English PLC | QES | General Financial | 0.8 | 0.5 | 29.9 | | 31/12 | |
| RAB Capital PLC | RAB | General Financial | 416.7 | 15 | 1.91m | 16/04/05 | 31/12 | www.rabcap.com |
| RAB Special Situations Company Ltd | RSS | Equity Investment Instruments | 76.0 | 5 | 372k | 12/07/06 | 31/03 | www.rabcap.com |
| Radicle Projects PLC | RDP | General Financial | 14.7 | 1 | 21.4k | 31/10/05 | 31/03 | |
| Ragusa Capital PLC | USA | General Financial | 13.9 | 2 | 37.9k | 10/09/05 | 31/05 | |
| RAM Investment Group PLC | RAM | Electronic & Electrical Equipment | 1.4 | 0.5 | 4.02k | 28/09/05 | 31/05 | |
| Rambler Media Ltd | RMG | Media | 190.3 | 0.5 | 43.0k | 15/06/06 | 31/12 | www.ramblermedia.com |
| Rambler Metals and Mining PLC | RMM | Mining | 19.4 | 2 | 71.7k | 16/11/05 | 31/08 | www.ramblermines.com |
| Ramco Energy PLC | ROS | Oil & Gas Producers | 8.9 | 3 | 159k | 31/07/06 | 31/12 | www.ramco-plc.com |
| Ransom (William) & Son PLC | RNSM | Pharmaceuticals & Biotechnology | 38.4 | 3 | 136k | 16/09/05 | 31/03 | www.williamransom.com |
| Raven Mount PLC | RAV | Household Goods | 135.6 | 0.5 | 89.4k | 05/06/06 | 31/12 | www.theravengroup.co.uk |
| Raven Russia Ltd | RUS | Real Estate | 437.4 | 10 | 447k | 31/05/06 | 31/12 | www.ravenrussia.co.uk |
| RDF Group PLC | RFG | Software & Computer Services | 6.0 | 0.5 | 6.06k | 19/07/06 | 31/03 | www.rdfgroup.com |
| RDF Media Group PLC | RDF | Media | 72.8 | 1 | 120k | 24/07/06 | 31/01 | www.rdfmedia.com |
| Real Affinity PLC | RAF | Media | 3.5 | 50 | 9.67m | 21/07/06 | 31/03 | www.realaffinity.co.uk |
| Real Estate Investors PLC | RLE | Real Estate | 7.9 | 3 | 66.8k | 10/05/06 | 31/12 | www.reiplc.com |
| Real Good Food Company (The) PLC | RGD | Food Producers | 50.6 | 3 | 156k | 24/05/06 | 31/12 | |
| Red Leopard Holdings PLC | RLH | Equity Investment Instruments | 3.9 | 3 | 33.0k | | | |
| Red Rock Resources PLC | RRR | Mining | 3.8 | 2 | 171k | | | www.rrrplc.com |
| Red Squared PLC | RDS | Software & Computer Services | 1.3 | 1 | 37.2k | 07/03/06 | 30/09 | www.red2plc.com |
| Redhall Group PLC | RHL | Industrial Engineering | 10.7 | 1 | 62.2k | 05/04/06 | 30/09 | www.booth-industries.co.uk |
| Redstone PLC | RED | Technology Hardware & Equipment | 59.9 | 25 | 1.57m | 02/08/06 | 31/03 | www.redstone.co.uk |
| ReEnergy Group PLC | RGY | Support Services | 25.2 | 50 | | 27/07/06 | 31/12 | www.reenergygroup.com |
| Reflec PLC | REF | Chemicals | 5.0 | 50 | 1.18m | 04/07/06 | 28/02 | www.reflec.com |
| Reflexion Cosmetics PLC | RFX | General Financial | 0.1 | 0.5 | 1.77k | 25/05/06 | | www.reflexioncosmetics.com |
| Regal Petroleum PLC | RPT | Oil & Gas Producers | 107.9 | 50 | 2.08m | 02/08/06 | 31/12 | www.regalpetroleum.com |
| ReGen Therapeutics PLC | RGT | Pharmaceuticals & Biotechnology | 6.4 | 50 | 2.83m | 13/06/06 | 31/12 | www.regentherapeutics.com |
| Regency Mines PLC | RGM | Mining | 2.3 | 3 | 54.5k | 21/12/05 | 30/06 | www.regency-mines.com |
| Reliance Security Group PLC | RSG | Support Services | 130.0 | 0.5 | 31.6k | 07/09/05 | 29/04 | www.reliancesecurity.co.uk |
| ReNeuron Group PLC | RENE | Pharmaceuticals & Biotechnology | 9.5 | 3 | 63.4k | 31/07/05 | 31/03 | www.reneuron.com |
| Renew Holdings PLC | RNWH | Household Goods | 31.7 | 2 | 395k | 22/03/06 | 30/09 | www.renewholdings.com |
| Renewable Energy Generation Ltd | RWE | Gas; Water & Multiutilities | 31.8 | 2 | 133k | | | |
| Renewable Energy Holdings PLC | REH | Electricity | 20.1 | 1 | 65.0k | 25/01/06 | 30/06 | www.reh-plc.com |
| Renova Energy PLC | RVA | Chemicals | 59.9 | 1 | 69.5k | 08/06/05 | 31/03 | www.renovaenergy.com |
| Research Now PLC | RNOW | Media | 28.8 | 0.5 | 20.3k | 15/03/06 | 31/10 | www.researchnow.co.uk |
| Rheochem PLC | RHEP | Oil Equipment; Services & Dist | 14.4 | 2 | 75.2k | 20/01/06 | 30/06 | www.rheochem.com.au |
| Ridge Mining PLC | RDG | Mining | 20.1 | 3 | 316k | 13/07/06 | 31/12 | www.ridgemining.com |
| Rift Oil PLC | RIFT | Oil & Gas Producers | 18.3 | 3 | | | | |
| RingProp PLC | RPP | Industrial Engineering | 1.5 | 1 | 40.3k | 14/12/05 | 30/09 | www.ringprop.com |
| River Diamonds PLC | RVD | Mining | 4.7 | 50 | 982k | 13/06/06 | 31/08 | www.riverdiamonds.co.uk |
| Robinson PLC | RBN | General Industrials | 13.4 | 0.5 | 1.32k | 05/05/05 | 31/12 | www.r1son.co.uk |
| Robotic Technology Systems PLC | RTS | Support Services | 9.8 | 2 | 105k | 30/05/06 | 31/12 | www.rts-group.com |
| Rockhopper Exploration PLC | RKH | Oil & Gas Producers | 26.6 | 3 | 106k | 25/07/05 | 31/03 | www.rockhopperexploration.co.uk |

Source: Hemscott (Hemscott.com)

## Members of AIM

| Company Name | EPIC | Sector | Capital (£m) | NMS | 200D Avg Vol | AGM | Year End | URL |
|---|---|---|---|---|---|---|---|---|
| Roeford Properties PLC | ROE | General Financial | 3.4 | 2 | 24.9k | 21/04/06 | 31/12 | www.roeford.com |
| Romag Holdings PLC | ROM | Construction & Materials | 49.8 | 2 | 93.4k | 23/02/06 | 30/09 | www.romag.co.uk |
| Ross Home Builders PLC | ROSS | Real Estate | 10.9 | 5 | | | | |
| Rotala PLC | ROL | Travel & Leisure | 5.1 | 10 | 322k | | 30/11 | |
| Rugby Estates PLC | RES | Real Estate | 56.5 | 0.5 | 45.7k | 21/06/06 | 31/01 | www.rugbyestates.plc.uk |
| Rurelec PLC | RUR | Electricity | 27.7 | 1 | 39.5k | 12/12/05 | 31/12 | www.rurelec.com |
| RWS Holdings PLC | RWS | Support Services | 111.2 | 1 | 52.7k | 09/02/06 | 30/09 | www.rws.com |
| Sagittarius Professional Services PLC | SGT | General Financial | 0.5 | | | | | |
| samedaybooks.co.uk PLC | SDK | General Retailers | 0.4 | 10 | 197k | 15/07/06 | 31/03 | www.samedaybooks.co.uk |
| Sanderson Group PLC | SND | Software & Computer Services | 19.0 | 0.5 | 21.0k | 12/01/06 | 30/09 | www.sanderson.com |
| Sarantel Group PLC | SLG | Technology Hardware & Equipment | 8.4 | 5 | 103k | 03/02/06 | 30/09 | www.sarantel.com |
| Sareum Holdings PLC | SAR | Pharmaceuticals & Biotechnology | 4.7 | 25 | 1.62m | 07/11/05 | 30/06 | www.sareum.co.uk |
| SatCom Group Holdings PLC | SGH | Mobile Telecommunications | 18.6 | 2 | 13.6k | 31/10/02 | 30/06 | www.satcom.nic.in/ |
| SBS Group PLC | SBG | Support Services | 0.4 | 0.5 | 1.51k | 01/08/05 | 10/03 | |
| Scott Tod PLC | SCD | Support Services | 6.6 | 2 | 41.9k | 30/11/05 | 30/06 | www.scotty-tod.com |
| SCOTTY Group PLC | SCO | Technology Hardware & Equipment | 10.2 | 100 | 4.67m | 03/02/06 | 31/07 | www.scottygroup.com |
| Screen FX PLC | SFX | Media | 7.0 | 25 | 1.25m | 01/06/06 | 31/12 | www.screenfx.com |
| Screen Technology Group PLC | SCT | Electronic & Electrical Equipment | 15.4 | 0.5 | 12.9k | 12/06/06 | 31/12 | www.screentechnology.com |
| SectorGuard PLC | SGD | Support Services | 12.4 | 10 | 250k | 16/02/06 | 30/09 | www.sectorguard.plc.uk |
| Serabi Mining PLC | SRB | Mining | 35.4 | 2 | 132k | 01/06/06 | 31/12 | www.serabimining.com |
| Serica Energy PLC | SQZ | Oil & Gas Producers | 171.1 | 3 | | 30/04/05 | 31/12 | www.serica-energy.com |
| Serviced Office Group PLC | SVO | Real Estate | 9.0 | 1 | 131k | 18/07/06 | 31/12 | |
| Servision PLC | SEV | Support Services | 5.6 | 0.5 | 2.49k | 07/08/06 | 31/12 | www.servision.net |
| Servocell Group PLC | SERV | Electronic & Electrical Equipment | 24.3 | 3 | | | | |
| Seven Arts Pictures PLC | SVA | Media | 1.4 | 0.5 | 657 | 09/10/05 | 31/03 | www.7artspictures.com |
| Shanta Gold Ltd | SHG | Mining | 51.2 | 2 | 75.4k | 05/07/06 | 31/12 | www.shantagold.com |
| Shed Productions PLC | SHDP | Media | 82.7 | 2 | 21.5m | 18/01/06 | 31/08 | www.shedproductions.com |
| Sheffield United PLC | SUT | Travel & Leisure | 28.6 | 2 | 118k | 12/12/05 | 30/06 | www.sufc.co.uk |
| Shoprite Group PLC | SHO | Food & Drug Retailers | 9.7 | 0.5 | 6.37k | 12/06/06 | 31/12 | www.shoprite.co.za |
| Sibir Energy PLC | SBE | Oil & Gas Producers | 1356.5 | 10 | 709k | 08/12/05 | 31/12 | www.sibirenergy.com |
| Sigma Capital Group PLC | SGM | General Financial | 11.5 | 0.5 | 22.7k | 08/06/06 | 31/12 | www.sigmatech.co.uk |
| Silentpoint PLC | SLP | General Financial | 1.2 | 0.5 | 26.8k | 06/06/06 | 31/12 | |
| Silverdell PLC | SID | Construction & Materials | 30.6 | 2 | | | 31/10 | |
| silverjet PLC | SIL | Travel & Leisure | 34.3 | 3 | | | | |
| Sinclair Pharma PLC | SPH | Pharmaceuticals & Biotechnology | 110.4 | 2 | 73.4k | 28/11/05 | 30/06 | www.sinclairpharma.com |
| Sino-Asia Mining & Resources Company plc | SNO | Mining | 0.6 | 1 | 2.59k | 04/05/06 | | |
| Sinosoft Technology PLC | SFT | Software & Computer Services | 33.1 | 5 | 82.1k | 12/06/06 | 31/12 | www.sinosoft-technology.net |
| Sirdar PLC | SRDR | Personal Goods | 17.3 | 2 | 84.1k | 08/11/05 | 30/06 | www.sirdar.co.uk |
| Sirius Exploration PLC | SXX | Mining | 2.9 | 3 | | | | www.siriusexploration.com |
| Sirius Financial Solutions PLC | SIR | Software & Computer Services | 24.0 | 0.5 | 9.81k | 31/05/06 | 31/12 | www.siriusfs.com |
| SiRVIS IT PLC | SRV | Software & Computer Services | 3.4 | 5 | 91.6k | 29/09/05 | 31/05 | www.sirvisit.com |
| Slimma PLC | SLM | Personal Goods | 6.5 | 0.5 | 35.8k | 03/02/06 | 30/09 | www.slimma.com |
| Slingsby (H O) PLC | SLNG | Industrial Engineering | 11.4 | 0.5 | 215 | 15/06/06 | 31/12 | www.slingsby.com |
| Smallbone PLC | SML | Household Goods | 22.4 | 0.5 | 18.9k | 01/07/05 | 31/12 | www.smallbone.co.uk |

**Company Directory**

## Members of AIM

| Company Name | EPIC | Sector | Capital (£m) | NMS | 200D Avg Vol | AGM | Year End | URL |
|---|---|---|---|---|---|---|---|---|
| Smart Telecom PLC | SMR | Fixed Line Telecommunications | 37.1 | 15 | 3.51m | 31/07/06 | 31/12 | www.smarttelecom.ie |
| smartFOCUS Group PLC | STF | Software & Computer Services | 14.4 | 3 | 93.4k | 23/05/06 | 31/12 | www.smartfocus.com |
| SMC Group PLC | SMC | Construction & Materials | 57.2 | 1 | 95.5k | 13/06/06 | 31/12 | www.smcgroupplc.com |
| Soccercity PLC | SOC | Travel & Leisure | 1.5 | 1 | 22.8k | 13/10/05 | 31/01 | |
| Software Radio Technology PLC | SRT | Technology Hardware & Equipment | 40.2 | 2 | | 07/08/06 | 31/03 | www.softwarerad.com |
| Solid State PLC | SSP | Electronic & Electrical Equipment | 2.4 | 0.5 | 2.23k | 02/08/06 | 31/03 | www.ssplc.com |
| Solomon Gold PLC | SOLG | Mining | 6.3 | 3 | | | | |
| Songbird Estates PLC | SBDB | Real Estate | 390.1 | 10 | 348k | 20/07/05 | 31/12 | www.songbirdestates.com |
| Sopheon PLC | SPE | Software & Computer Services | 25.4 | 2 | 30.2k | 17/06/06 | 31/12 | www.sopheon.com |
| Sound Oil PLC | SOU | General Financial | 53.5 | 10 | 669k | 30/04/06 | 31/12 | |
| South China Resources PLC | SCR | Mining | 33.5 | 15 | 1.08m | 25/01/06 | 30/06 | www.southchinaresources.com |
| Southampton Leisure Holdings PLC | SOO | Travel & Leisure | 12.4 | 1 | 68.3k | 01/11/05 | 31/05 | www.saintsfc.co.uk |
| Southern Bear PLC | CVN | General Financial | 1.1 | 10 | 57.8k | 16/07/06 | | |
| Sovereign Oilfield Group PLC | SOGP | Oil Equipment; Services & Dist | 41.1 | 1 | 9.32k | 30/11/05 | 31/03 | |
| Sovereign Reversions PLC | SVN | Real Estate | 46.4 | 0.5 | 11.8k | 13/09/05 | 30/04 | www.sovereign-reversions.co.uk |
| SovGEM Ltd | SOV | General Financial | 3.5 | 2 | 206k | 20/04/06 | 31/12 | www.sovgem.com |
| SpaceandPeople PLC | SAL | Media | 7.1 | 0.5 | 5.99k | 28/02/06 | 31/10 | www.spaceandpeople.com |
| Spectrum Interactive PLC | SIN | Fixed Line Telecommunications | 8.1 | 2 | 38.0k | 28/11/05 | 30/06 | www.spectruminteractive.co.uk |
| Speymill Deutsche Immobilien Company plc | SDIC | Real Estate | 163.2 | 10 | | | | |
| Speymill Group PLC | SYG | Support Services | 29.4 | 5 | 301k | 22/05/06 | 31/12 | www.speymill.com |
| SPG Media Group PLC | SPM | Media | 6.7 | 2 | 42.5k | 04/08/05 | 31/03 | www.spgmedia.com |
| SPI Lasers PLC | SPIL | Electronic & Electrical Equipment | 46.9 | 0.5 | | 15/04/05 | 31/12 | www.spilasers.com |
| Spice Holdings PLC | SPI | Support Services | 143.5 | 1 | 149k | 07/09/05 | 30/04 | www.spiceholdings.co.uk |
| Spiritel PLC | STP | Mobile Telecommunications | 6.7 | 10 | 455k | 13/10/05 | 30/04 | www.spiritelplc.com |
| Sportingbet PLC | SBT | Travel & Leisure | 1147.1 | 75 | 6.72m | 16/12/05 | 31/07 | www.sportingbet.com |
| Sports Cafe Holdings PLC | SCA | Travel & Leisure | 10.9 | 1 | 41.5k | 09/05/06 | 31/12 | www.sportscafeholdings.com |
| Sports Network Group PLC | SOP | Media | 3.8 | 10 | 155k | 05/06/06 | 31/12 | |
| SR Pharma PLC | SPA | Pharmaceuticals & Biotechnology | 10.9 | 5 | 250k | 03/08/06 | 31/12 | www.srpharma.com |
| SRS Technology Group PLC | SGY | Leisure Goods | 1.1 | 10 | 444k | 30/11/05 | 30/06 | www.srstechnology.co.uk |
| St James's Energy Group PLC | SJA | Electricity | 7.7 | 10 | | | | |
| Stadium Group PLC | SDM | Electronic & Electrical Equipment | 19.0 | 1 | 65.2k | 20/04/06 | 31/12 | www.stadium.co.uk |
| Staffline Recruitment Group PLC | STAF | Support Services | 27.0 | 0.5 | 26.6k | 25/05/06 | 31/12 | www.staffline.cc.uk |
| Stagecoach Theatre Arts PLC | STA | General Retailers | 3.8 | 0.5 | 6.67k | 13/09/05 | 31/05 | www.stagecoach.co.uk |
| Stanley Gibbons Group (The) Ltd | SGI | General Retailers | 37.1 | 2 | 205k | 13/04/05 | 31/12 | www.stanleygibbons.com |
| Star Energy Group PLC | STAR | Oil & Gas Producers | 273.8 | 5 | 343k | 22/05/06 | 31/12 | www.starenergy.co.uk |
| Starvest PLC | SVE | General Financial | 6.8 | 2 | 126k | 11/10/05 | 31/07 | www.starvest.co.uk |
| StatPro Group PLC | SOG | Software & Computer Services | 35.2 | 1 | 61.9k | 18/05/05 | 31/12 | www.statpro.com |
| Stem Cell Sciences PLC | STEM | Pharmaceuticals & Biotechnology | 12.3 | 2 | 14.4k | 30/05/06 | 31/12 | www.stemcellsciences.com |
| Stepquick PLC | SQK | General Financial | 10.8 | 0.5 | 62.9 | 08/01/06 | 30/06 | www.champion-accountants.co.uk |
| Sterling Energy PLC | SEY | Oil & Gas Producers | 336.7 | 100 | 6.87m | 15/06/06 | 31/12 | www.sterlingenergyplc.com |
| Stilo International PLC | STL | Software & Computer Services | 1.9 | 3 | 176k | 18/05/05 | 31/12 | www.stilo.com |
| Stockcube PLC | SKC | General Financial | 4.0 | 1 | 10.3k | 24/05/06 | 31/12 | www.stockcube.com |
| Stonemartin PLC | SOA | Support Services | 8.8 | 3 | 40.7k | 27/07/06 | 31/03 | www.stonemartin.co.uk |
| Straight PLC | STT | General Industrials | 30.4 | 0.5 | 18.5k | 22/06/06 | 31/12 | www.straight.co.uk |

Source: Hemscott (Hemscott.com)

Members of AIM

| Company Name | EPIC | Sector | Capital (£m) | NMS | 200D Avg Vol | AGM | Year End | URL |
|---|---|---|---|---|---|---|---|---|
| Strategic Global Investments PLC | SGB | General Financial | 0.7 | 3 | 50 | 24/01/06 | 30/06 | |
| Strategic Retail PLC | SRR | General Retailers | 1.8 | 0.5 | 18.4k | 19/07/05 | 26/02 | |
| Strategic Thought Group PLC | STR | Software & Computer Services | 47.3 | 1 | 34.6k | 15/05/05 | 31/03 | www.strategicthought.com |
| Stratex International PLC | STI | Mining | 11.3 | 3 | | | | www.stratexexploration.com |
| Strathdon Investments PLC | STV | Equity Investment Instruments | 13.2 | 1 | 70.1k | 26/07/05 | 31/03 | www.strathdon.com |
| Stream Group PLC | SEA | Media | 8.2 | 10 | 221k | 06/04/06 | 31/12 | www.streamgroup.co.uk |
| Strontium PLC | STTM | Support Services | 2.4 | 2 | | 10/10/05 | 30/06 | www.strontiumplc.com |
| Stylo PLC | STYL | General Retailers | 22.7 | 0.5 | 6.39k | 26/06/06 | 28/01 | www.stylo.co.uk |
| SubSea Resources PLC | SUB | Industrial Transportation | 45.0 | 5 | 274k | | 31/03 | www.subsearesources.com |
| Summit Germany Ltd | SGL | Real Estate | 54.0 | 5 | | | | |
| Summit Resources PLC | SUMR | General Financial | 6.4 | 10 | | | | |
| Sumus PLC | SUMU | General Financial | 8.4 | 0.5 | 15.9k | 30/01/06 | 30/09 | www.sumus.co.uk |
| Sun TV Shop PLC | SNTS | General Financial | 63.9 | | | | | |
| Sunrise Diamonds PLC | SDS | Mining | 2.4 | 3 | 217k | 31/01/06 | 30/09 | www.sunrisediamonds.com |
| Supercart PLC | SC. | Support Services | 3.4 | 1 | 38.0k | 17/05/05 | 31/12 | www.supercart.com |
| Supporta PLC | SOR | Support Services | 51.2 | 0.5 | 71.6k | 03/11/05 | 31/03 | www.supportaplc.com |
| Surface Technology Systems PLC | SRTS | Technology Hardware & Equipment | 6.8 | 1 | 44.3k | 23/05/06 | 31/12 | www.stsystems.com |
| Surface Transforms PLC | SCE | Industrial Engineering | 1.9 | 0.5 | 15.0k | 20/10/05 | 31/05 | www.surface-transforms.com |
| Surgical Innovations Group PLC | SUN | Health Care Equipment & Services | 6.5 | 5 | 282k | 27/06/06 | 31/12 | www.sigroupplc.com |
| Sutton Harbour Holdings PLC | SUH | Industrial Transportation | 64.3 | 0.5 | 11.0k | 26/07/06 | 31/03 | www.sutton-harbour.co.uk |
| Swallowfield PLC | SWL | Personal Goods | 4.6 | 0.5 | 37.1k | 24/10/05 | 30/06 | www.swallowfield.com |
| Swan (John) & Sons PLC | SWJ | General Retailers | 7.8 | 0.5 | 122 | 25/10/05 | 30/04 | www.johnswan.co.uk |
| SWP Group PLC | SWP | Construction & Materials | 10.6 | 0.5 | 31.9k | 24/01/06 | 30/06 | |
| Symphony Plastic Technologies PLC | SYM | General Industrials | 7.8 | 10 | 272k | 14/07/06 | 31/12 | www.symphonyplastics.com |
| Symphony Telecom Holdings PLC | SMY | Technology Hardware & Equipment | 16.6 | 1 | 34.0k | 15/06/05 | 31/03 | www.symphony.com |
| Synairgen PLC | SNG | Pharmaceuticals & Biotechnology | 23.0 | 0.5 | 2.24k | 30/11/05 | 30/06 | www.synairgen.com |
| Synchronica PLC | SYNC | Technology Hardware & Equipment | 5.2 | 25 | 441k | 31/05/06 | 31/12 | www.synchronica.com |
| Syndicate Asset Management PLC | SAM | General Financial | 75.3 | 3 | 68.2k | | | |
| Synergy Healthcare PLC | SYR | Health Care Equipment & Services | 208.6 | 2 | 97.7k | 21/07/06 | 02/04 | www.synergyhealthcare.plc.uk |
| Synexus Clinical Research PLC | SNX | Pharmaceuticals & Biotechnology | 23.5 | 1 | | 27/07/06 | 31/03 | www.synexus.com |
| Synigence PLC | SYE | General Financial | 0.5 | 0.5 | | 28/07/06 | 31/12 | |
| Syntopix Group PLC | SYN | Pharmaceuticals & Biotechnology | 10.1 | 2 | | | | www.syntopix.com |
| System C Healthcare PLC | SYS | Software & Computer Services | 25.9 | 10 | 215k | 22/11/05 | 31/05 | www.systemc.com |
| T2 Income Fund Ltd | T2I | Equity Investment Instruments | 35.7 | 2 | 16.6k | | | |
| Talarius PLC | TLS | Travel & Leisure | 82.5 | 3 | 185k | | 31/12 | www.talarius.com |
| Talent Group PLC | TTV | Media | 2.5 | 0.5 | 3.51k | 21/02/06 | 30/09 | www.talenttv.com |
| Tandem Group PLC | TND | Leisure Goods | 3.6 | 2 | 41.2k | 27/06/06 | 31/01 | |
| Tanfield Group PLC | TAN | Support Services | 69.2 | 10 | 855k | 17/09/05 | 31/12 | www.tanfieldgroup.com |
| Tangent Communications PLC | TNG | Support Services | 13.4 | 5 | 200k | 06/07/06 | 28/02 | www.tangentuk.com |
| Target Resources PLC | TGT | Mining | 44.2 | 3 | | | | www.target-resources.co.uk |
| Tarquin Resources PLC | TQN | General Financial | 2.8 | 1 | 27.5k | 30/07/05 | 31/12 | |
| Tasty PLC | TAST | Travel & Leisure | 23.1 | 2 | | | | |
| Taurus Storage PLC | TAS | General Financial | 0.5 | | | 24/05/06 | | |
| Techcreation PLC | TCH | General Financial | 1.6 | 10 | 302k | 03/05/06 | 30/09 | www.techcreation.com |

Source: Hemscott (Hemscott.com)

## Members of AIM

| Company Name | EPIC | Sector | Capital (£m) | NMS | 200D Avg Vol | AGM | Year End | URL |
|---|---|---|---|---|---|---|---|---|
| Tecteon PLC | TEO | Technology Hardware & Equipment | 5.9 | 15 | 532k | 27/01/06 | 30/06 | www.tecteon.com |
| TEG Environmental PLC | TEG | Industrial Engineering | 25.1 | 1 | 30.4k | 19/05/06 | 31/12 | www.tegenvironmental.co.uk |
| Telephone Maintenance Group PLC | TEL | Fixed Line Telecommunications | 1.8 | 5 | 79.2k | 28/02/06 | 31/07 | www.tmgtelecom.co.uk |
| Telephonetics PLC | TPH | Software & Computer Services | 21.0 | 1 | 52.0k | | | www.telephonetics.co.uk |
| Telford Homes PLC | TEF | Household Goods | 78.8 | 0.5 | 71.2k | 06/07/06 | 31/03 | www.telfordhomes.plc.uk |
| Telit Communications PLC | TCM | Technology Hardware & Equipment | 14.0 | 2 | 41.0k | 24/07/06 | 31/12 | www.telit.com |
| Tellings Golden Miller Group PLC | TGM | Travel & Leisure | 5.2 | 2 | 12.6k | 09/05/06 | 31/12 | www.tellingsgoldenmiller.co.uk |
| Ten Alps PLC | TAL | Media | 36.9 | 3 | 159k | 29/07/05 | 31/03 | www.tenalps.com |
| Tenon Group PLC | TNO | General Financial | 39.4 | 5 | 451k | 22/11/05 | 30/06 | www.tenongroup.com |
| TEP Exchange Group PLC | TEX | General Financial | 1.1 | 1 | 137k | 27/06/06 | 31/12 | www.tepexchange.com |
| Tepnel Life Sciences PLC | TED | Pharmaceuticals & Biotechnology | 17.0 | 25 | 467k | 01/08/06 | 31/12 | www.tepnel.com |
| Terrace Hill Group PLC | THG | Real Estate | 114.2 | 1 | 93.3k | 10/03/06 | 31/10 | www.terracehill.co.uk |
| Tersus Energy PLC | TER | General Financial | 14.3 | 1 | 21.2k | 26/06/06 | 31/12 | www.tersusenergy.com |
| Tertiary Minerals PLC | TYM | Mining | 6.1 | 2 | 165k | 31/01/06 | 30/09 | www.tertiaryminerals.com |
| TG21 PLC | TGP | Support Services | 4.3 | 10 | 277k | 19/06/06 | 31/12 | www.tg21plc.com |
| THB Group PLC | THB | Nonlife Insurance | 25.7 | 0.5 | 26.9k | 05/10/05 | 30/04 | www.thbgroup.com |
| themutual.net PLC | TMN | Media | 31.1 | 3 | 354k | 12/10/05 | 30/04 | www.themutual.net |
| Theo Fennell PLC | TFL | Personal Goods | 11.5 | 0.5 | 24.7k | 06/10/05 | 31/03 | www.theofennell.com |
| Third Advance Value Realisation UK) Ltd | TAR | General Financial | 21.8 | 1 | | | | |
| ThirdForce PLC | THF | Support Services | 23.6 | 2 | 12.7k | 24/05/06 | 31/12 | www.thirdforceplc.com |
| Thomson Intermedia PLC | THN | Media | 65.0 | 1 | 77.5k | 07/07/06 | 31/01 | www.thomson-intermedia.com |
| Thor Mining PLC | THR | Mining | 6.5 | 10 | 366k | 26/10/05 | 30/06 | www.thormining.com |
| Thorpe (F W) PLC | TFW | Household Goods | 57.6 | 0.5 | 7.15k | 10/11/05 | 30/06 | www.thorlux.com |
| Tiger Resource Finance PLC | TIR | Equity Investment Instruments | 7.3 | 15 | 314k | 07/08/06 | 31/12 | www.tiger-rf.com |
| Tikit Group PLC | TIK | Software & Computer Services | 25.9 | 0.5 | 14.6k | 28/04/05 | 31/12 | www.tikit.com |
| Timestrip PLC | TIME | General Industrials | 23.1 | 10 | 334k | 28/06/06 | 31/12 | www.timestrip.com |
| Tinopolis PLC | TIN | Media | 31.1 | 1 | 21.6m | 29/12/05 | 30/09 | www.tinopolis.com |
| Tissue Science Laboratories PLC | TSL | Health Care Equipment & Services | 36.5 | 1 | 30.7k | 04/07/06 | 31/12 | www.tissuescience.com |
| Titan Europe PLC | TSW | Industrial Engineering | 164.2 | 1 | 79.7k | 08/05/06 | 31/12 | www.titaneurope.com |
| Titan Move PLC | TNM | Travel & Leisure | 6.2 | 3 | 172k | 12/08/05 | 30/04 | |
| Toledo Mining Corporation PLC | TMC | General Financial | 28.2 | 2 | 126k | 07/11/05 | 31/03 | www.toledomining.com |
| Tolent PLC | TLT | Construction & Materials | 29.8 | 0.5 | 7.24k | 01/06/06 | 31/12 | www.tolent.co.uk |
| ToLuna PLC | TOL | Media | 58.9 | 1 | 41.5k | 24/05/06 | 31/12 | www.tolunapro.com |
| Top Ten Holdings PLC | TTH | Travel & Leisure | 28.9 | 0.5 | 18.9k | 20/07/05 | 26/03 | www.toptenbingo.info |
| Torex Retail PLC | TRX | Software & Computer Services | 230.5 | 50 | 4.05m | 25/05/06 | 31/12 | www.torexretail.com |
| Totally PLC | TLY | Media | 2.1 | 2 | 64.5k | 03/07/06 | 31/12 | www.totallyplc.com |
| Tottenham Hotspur PLC | TTNM | Travel & Leisure | 45.6 | 10 | 30.3k | 25/11/05 | 30/06 | www.tottenhamhotspur.com |
| Touch Group PLC | TOU | Media | 4.2 | 10 | 128k | 06/06/06 | 31/12 | www.touchgroupplc.com |
| Touchstone Group PLC | TSE | Software & Computer Services | 16.5 | 0.5 | 20.5k | 08/08/05 | 31/03 | www.touchstone.co.uk |
| Tower PLC | TWR | Technology Hardware & Equipment | 2.5 | 50 | 463k | 02/07/05 | 31/12 | www.vykecorporate.com |
| Tower Resources PLC | TRP | Mining | 10.2 | 10 | 202k | 15/10/05 | 30/06 | www.towerresources.co.uk |
| Toye & Co PLC | TOYE | Personal Goods | 0.7 | 0.5 | 115 | 12/06/06 | 31/12 | www.toye.com |
| Trading Emissions PLC | TRE | General Financial | 232.8 | 10 | 435k | | | |
| Trading New Homes PLC | TNH | Real Estate | 1.2 | 0.5 | 729 | 28/10/05 | 31/03 | |

Source: Hemscott (Hemscott.com)

## Members of AIM

| Company Name | EPIC | Sector | Capital (£m) | NMS | 200D Avg Vol | AGM | Year End | URL |
|---|---|---|---|---|---|---|---|---|
| Trakm8 Holdings PLC | TRAK | Technology Hardware & Equipment | 10.2 | 0.5 | | 31/07/05 | 31/03 | www.trakm8.com |
| Transense Technologies PLC | TRT | Automobiles & Parts | 30.3 | 5 | 207k | 19/05/06 | 31/12 | www.transense.co.uk |
| Transport Systems PLC | TSY | Industrial Transportation | 1.8 | 0.5 | 31.1k | 09/09/05 | 31/03 | |
| Trans-Siberian Gold PLC | TSG | Mining | 36.6 | 2 | 260k | 01/08/06 | 31/12 | www.trans-siberiangold.com |
| Transvision Resources PLC | TVR | General Financial | 0.8 | 0.5 | 4.12k | 15/08/05 | 30/04 | |
| Travelzest PLC | TVZ | Travel & Leisure | 14.8 | 1 | 1.46k | 27/04/06 | 31/10 | www.travelzestplc.com |
| Tricorn Group PLC | TCN | Industrial Engineering | 5.4 | 1 | 45.8k | 06/09/05 | 31/03 | www.tricorn.uk.com |
| Trinity Capital PLC | TRC | Real Estate | 218.4 | 10 | | | | |
| Triple Plate Junction PLC | TPJ | Mining | 15.8 | 3 | 133k | 01/10/06 | 31/03 | www.tripleplatejunction.com |
| TripleArc PLC | TPA | Support Services | 6.2 | 50 | 608k | 28/06/05 | 31/12 | www.triplearc.com |
| Tristel PLC | TSTL | Health Care Equipment & Services | 11.0 | 2 | 44.1k | 15/11/05 | 30/06 | www.tristel.com |
| Turbotec Products PLC | TRBO | Industrial Engineering | 10.8 | 2 | | | | |
| TV Commerce Holdings PLC | TVC | Media | 2.3 | 2 | 19.9k | | | |
| Twenty PLC | TWE | Media | 7.2 | 2 | | 26/07/06 | | www.twentyplc.com |
| TXO PLC | TXO | Oil & Gas Producers | 7.8 | 10 | 250k | 26/09/05 | 31/03 | www.txoplc.com |
| UBC Media Group PLC | UBC | Media | 38.4 | 5 | 91.6k | 04/08/06 | 31/03 | www.ubcmedia.com |
| ubet2win PLC | UBT | Travel & Leisure | 3.8 | 10 | 132k | 05/07/05 | 31/12 | www.ubet2win.co.uk |
| Ubiquity Software Corporation PLC | UBQ | Software & Computer Services | 37.9 | 10 | 560k | 02/05/06 | 31/12 | www.ubiquitysoftware.com |
| ukbetting PLC | UKB | Travel & Leisure | 69.7 | 10 | 409k | 07/06/06 | 31/12 | www.ukbettingplc.com |
| UKproduct Group Ltd | UKR | Food Producers | 17.1 | 2 | 50.9k | 22/06/06 | 31/12 | www.ukrproduct.com |
| Ultima Networks PLC | UTN | Software & Computer Services | 1.5 | 3 | 65.1k | 30/06/06 | 31/12 | www.ultima-networks.co.uk |
| Ultimate Finance Group PLC | UFG | General Financial | 4.3 | 0.5 | 23.6k | 19/10/05 | 30/06 | www.ultimatefinance.net |
| Ultimate Leisure Group PLC | ULG | Travel & Leisure | 50.1 | 5 | 95.3k | 25/11/05 | 30/06 | www.ultimateleisure.com |
| Ultrasis PLC | ULT | Software & Computer Services | 22.4 | 200 | 14.2m | 09/02/06 | 31/07 | www.ultrasis.com |
| UMC Energy PLC | UEP | Mining | 5.0 | 1 | 33.0k | 18/07/06 | | |
| United Carpets Group PLC | UCG | General Retailers | 6.9 | 3 | 94.7k | 31/10/05 | 31/03 | www.unitedcarpet.com |
| Universe Group PLC | UNG | Support Services | 8.2 | 5 | 64.4k | 12/05/06 | 31/12 | www.universe-group.co.uk |
| Uranium Resources PLC | URA | General Financial | 4.5 | 10 | 324k | | | www.uraniumresources.co.uk |
| Utilico Emerging Markets Ltd | UEM | Equity Investment Instruments | 81.5 | 5 | 149k | 31/07/06 | 31/03 | www.utilicoemergingmarkets.com |
| Van Dieman Mines PLC | VDM | Mining | 16.5 | 5 | 23.0k | 30/04/05 | 31/12 | www.vandiemanmines.com |
| Vane Minerals PLC | VML | Mining | 14.2 | 5 | 224k | 12/05/05 | 31/12 | www.vaneminerals.com |
| Vantis PLC | VTS | General Financial | 116.1 | 1 | 40.5k | 29/09/05 | 30/04 | www.vantisplc.com |
| VASTox PLC | VOX | Pharmaceuticals & Biotechnology | 56.8 | 0.5 | 13.7k | 08/06/06 | 31/01 | www.vastox.com |
| Vebnet (Holdings) PLC | VBT | Support Services | 13.8 | 0.5 | 7.84k | 30/11/05 | 30/06 | www.vebnet.com |
| Vectura Group PLC | VEC | Pharmaceuticals & Biotechnology | 155.7 | 5 | 423k | 12/09/05 | 31/03 | www.vectura.com |
| Velti PLC | VEL | Software & Computer Services | 18.9 | 2 | | | | www.velti.net |
| Venteco PLC | VTO | General Financial | 3.5 | 5 | | | | |
| Venturia PLC | VRA | Media | 0.2 | 1 | 61.5k | 28/07/06 | 31/12 | |
| Venue Solutions Holdings PLC | VSH | Support Services | 6.6 | 2 | | 19/05/06 | 30/11 | www.venue-solutions.com |
| VI Group PLC | VIG | Software & Computer Services | 3.4 | 2 | 36.6k | 15/06/06 | 31/12 | www.vero-software.com |
| Vianet Group PLC | VIA | Technology Hardware & Equipment | 7.5 | 10 | 123k | 22/06/06 | 31/12 | www.vianet.co.uk |
| Victoria Oil & Gas PLC | VOG | Oil & Gas Producers | 79.5 | 15 | 2.48m | 17/11/05 | 31/05 | www.victoriaoilandgas.com |
| Victory Corporation PLC | VRY | Personal Goods | 9.6 | 0.5 | 1.57k | 16/09/05 | 31/03 | www.virgincosmetics.com |
| Vimio PLC | VIM | Software & Computer Services | 17.7 | 1 | 20.9k | | | www.vimio.com |

Source: Hemscott (Hemscott.com)

## Members of AIM

| Company Name | EPIC | Sector | Capital (£m) | NMS | 200D Avg Vol | AGM | Year End | URL |
|---|---|---|---|---|---|---|---|---|
| Vindon Healthcare PLC | VDN | Support Services | 15.0 | 3 | 69.6k | 25/05/05 | 31/12 | www.vindon.co.uk |
| Vista Group PLC | VST | Construction & Materials | 2.8 | 0.5 | 1.77k | 12/06/06 | 31/12 | www.vista-panels.co.uk |
| Vitesse Media PLC | VIS | Media | 4.9 | 0.5 | 2.34k | 07/07/06 | 31/01 | www.vitessemedia.com |
| Vividas Group PLC | VDS | Software & Computer Services | 7.6 | 2 | 75.1k | 01/12/05 | 30/06 | www.vividas.com |
| Voller Energy Group PLC | VLR | Electronic & Electrical Equipment | 8.7 | 2 | 133k | 20/10/05 | 30/06 | www.voller-energy.com |
| Volvere PLC | VLE | General Financial | 6.9 | 0.5 | 226 | 19/07/06 | 31/12 | www.volvere.co.uk |
| Voss Net PLC | VOS | Software & Computer Services | 7.5 | 50 | 769k | 24/11/05 | 30/06 | www.vossnet.com |
| VTR PLC | VTR | Media | 9.0 | 2 | 20.2k | 27/01/06 | 31/08 | www.vtrplc.com |
| W.H. Ireland Group PLC | WHI | General Financial | 20.6 | 1 | 30.5k | 12/04/05 | 30/11 | www.wh-ireland.co.uk |
| Walker (Thomas) PLC | WKT | Industrial Engineering | 1.7 | 0.5 | 1.11k | 04/11/05 | 30/06 | www.thomaswalker.co.uk |
| Walker Greenbank PLC | WGB | Household Goods | 14.5 | 3 | 379k | 25/07/06 | 31/01 | www.walkergreenbank.com |
| Warthog PLC | WHOG | Software & Computer Services | 0.4 | 200 | 2.16m | 17/11/05 | 31/03 | |
| Water Hall Group PLC | WTH | Support Services | 2.5 | 0.5 | 16.5k | 18/04/06 | 31/12 | www.waterhallgroupplc.com |
| Waterline Group PLC | WTL | General Retailers | 9.8 | 1 | 31.1k | 23/08/05 | 31/03 | |
| Watford Leisure PLC | WFC | Travel & Leisure | 3.9 | 0.5 | 3.07k | 19/12/05 | 30/06 | www.watfordfc.com |
| Weatherly International PLC | WTI | Mining | 78.0 | 2 | 225k | 15/07/06 | 31/12 | www.weatherlyplc.com |
| Wensum Company (The) PLC | WNS | Personal Goods | 7.8 | 0.5 | 7.07k | 15/06/06 | 28/01 | www.wensum.co.uk |
| Western & Oriental PLC | WEST | Travel & Leisure | 6.8 | 3 | | 20/02/06 | 30/09 | www.westernoriental.com |
| Western Selection PLC | WSE | Equity Investment Instruments | 6.6 | 0.5 | 6.14k | 28/09/05 | 30/06 | www.westernselection.co.uk |
| Westmount Energy Ltd | WTE | Oil & Gas Producers | 9.4 | 0.5 | 13.9k | 10/11/05 | 30/06 | |
| Westside Acquisitions PLC | WST | General Financial | 4.2 | 2 | 30.1k | 26/07/06 | 31/12 | |
| WHAM Energy PLC | WAM | Oil & Gas Producers | 12.8 | 1 | 33.8k | 10/04/06 | 31/12 | www.whamenergy.com |
| White Nile Ltd | WNL | Oil & Gas Producers | 411.3 | 3 | 221k | 16/12/05 | 30/06 | |
| White Star Property Holdings PLC | WSPH | Real Estate | 2.9 | 1 | 48.1k | 08/06/06 | 30/09 | |
| Whitehead Mann Group PLC | WHT | Support Services | 19.3 | 5 | 211k | 06/07/06 | 31/03 | www.wmann.com |
| Wichford PLC | WICH | Real Estate | 189.1 | 1 | 171k | | 30/09 | |
| Widney PLC | WDNY | Industrial Engineering | 6.6 | 3 | 99.8k | 17/01/06 | 30/09 | www.widney.plc.uk |
| Wilshaw PLC | WSW | Automobiles & Parts | 1.9 | 3 | 133k | 18/11/05 | 31/03 | www.wilshawplc.com |
| WIN PLC | WNN | Mobile Telecommunications | 11.4 | 1 | 27.7k | 13/07/06 | 31/12 | www.winplc.com |
| Wogen PLC | WGN | General Financial | 39.3 | 1 | | 09/03/06 | 30/09 | www.wogen.com |
| Work Group PLC | WORK | Support Services | 19.9 | 3 | | 30/04/05 | 31/12 | |
| Workplace Systems International PLC | WSI | Software & Computer Services | 6.8 | 5 | 176k | 02/08/05 | 31/03 | www.workplacesystemsinternational.com |
| Works Media Group (The) PLC | WKS | Media | 1.9 | 2 | 54.0k | 25/07/06 | 31/12 | www.civiliancontent.com |
| World Careers Network PLC | WOR | Support Services | 11.2 | 0.5 | 1.00k | 14/12/05 | 31/07 | www.wcn.co.uk |
| World Gaming PLC | WGP | Software & Computer Services | 38.2 | 5 | 257k | 02/02/05 | 31/12 | www.worldgaming.com |
| World Television Group PLC | WTV | Software & Computer Services | 5.1 | 25 | 1.27m | 25/07/06 | 31/12 | www.world-television.com |
| Worthington Nicholls Group PLC | WNG | General Retailers | 39.6 | 2 | | | | www.worthington-nicholls.co.uk |
| Wraith PLC | WRT | Support Services | 23.8 | 1 | 6.69k | 02/10/05 | 31/03 | www.wraith.co.uk |
| Wyatt Group PLC | WYT | General Financial | 1.0 | 0.5 | 2.59k | 02/11/05 | 31/03 | www.wyattgroup.co.uk |
| Wynnstay Group PLC | WYN | Food Producers | 24.7 | 0.5 | 21.5m | 23/03/06 | 31/10 | www.wynnstay.co.uk |
| Wynnstay Properties PLC | WSP | Real Estate | 11.1 | 0.5 | 789 | 27/07/06 | 25/03 | |
| Xceldiam Ltd | XLD | Mining | 22.5 | | | | | |
| XKO Group PLC | XKO | Software & Computer Services | 39.1 | 3 | 114k | 26/07/06 | 31/03 | www.xko.co.uk |
| Xpertise Group PLC | XPG | Support Services | 2.3 | 0.5 | 4.90k | 23/03/06 | 31/12 | www.xpertise-group.com |

Source: Hemscott (Hemscott.com)

| Company Name | EPIC | Sector | Capital (£m) | NMS | 200D Avg Vol | AGM | Year End | URL |
|---|---|---|---|---|---|---|---|---|
| Xtract Energy PLC | XTR | General Financial | 15.5 | 5 | 510k | 24/05/06 | 31/12 | www.yoomedia.com |
| YooMedia PLC | YOO | Media | 11.0 | 100 | 2.44m | 24/07/06 | 31/12 | www.yorkpharma.com |
| York Pharma PLC | YRK | Pharmaceuticals & Biotechnology | 19.1 | 2 | 43.4k | 26/01/06 | 30/09 | www.yougov.com |
| YouGov PLC | YOU | Media | 65.5 | 0.5 | 44.8k | 12/12/05 | 31/07 | www.youngs.co.uk |
| Young & Co's Brewery PLC | YNGN | Travel & Leisure | 165.3 | 0.5 | 1.85k | 11/07/06 | 01/04 | www.yourspaceplc.com |
| Your Space PLC | YSP | Real Estate | 10.8 | 1 | 39.5k | 28/10/05 | 31/03 | www.zgroupplc.com |
| Z Group PLC | ZGP | Software & Computer Services | 20.6 | 1 | 66.6k | 05/07/06 | 28/02 | www.zhgplc.com |
| Zenith Hygiene Group PLC | ZHG | Support Services | 27.1 | 0.5 | 21.0k | 20/01/06 | 31/08 | |
| Zest Group PLC | ZEST | Media | 6.4 | 10 | 163k | 30/03/06 | 30/09 | |
| Zetar PLC | ZTR | Food Producers | 48.3 | 0.5 | 20.8k | | | |
| Zi Medical PLC | ZIM | Health Care Equipment & Services | 9.0 | 10 | 156k | 31/07/06 | 31/12 | www.zi-medical.com |
| ZincOx Resources PLC | ZOX | Mining | 102.0 | 1 | 103k | 20/06/06 | 31/12 | www.zincox.com |
| Zirax PLC | ZRX | Chemicals | 25.0 | 5 | | 28/12/05 | 31/12 | www.zirax.com |
| Zoo Digital Group PLC | ZOO | Software & Computer Services | 4.8 | 50 | 1.18m | 26/07/05 | 31/03 | www.zoodigitalgroup.com |
| Zytronic PLC | ZYT | Electronic & Electrical Equipment | 37.8 | 0.5 | 18.1k | 28/02/06 | 30/09 | www.zytronic.co.uk |
| Zyzygy PLC | ZYZ | General Financial | 3.0 | 50 | 959k | 31/10/05 | 30/06 | |

# 5.

# Books

# Harriman House Titles

## About Harriman House

Harriman House is a UK-based publisher which specialises in publishing books about money – how to make it, how to keep it, how to live with it, how to live without it. Harriman House offers an extensive catalogue of titles covering a variety of subjects, including: stock market investing, trading, personal finance, spread betting, and charting.

For bulk ordering or more information call +44 (0) 1730 269 809

### Investing with Anthony Bolton – 2nd Edition

**The anatomy of a stock market phenomenon**

by Jonathan Davis

In this important book, Jonathan Davis, investment columnist of *The Independent*, takes an in-depth look at the way that Bolton goes about his business and analyses in detail the performance of the fund over the past 25 years.

ISBN: 1905641117, ISBN 13: **9781905641116, Hardback, 176pp, 2006,** Code: **23867,** RRP: **£12.99**
www.harriman-house.com/anthonybolton

### Fundology

**The Secrets of Successful Fund Investing**

by John Chatfeild-Roberts

The award-winning manager at one of the UK's best fund management firms explains in simple language what it takes to buy and sell investment funds successfully.

ISBN: 189759770, ISBN 13: **9781897597774, Hardback, 166pp, 2006,** Code: **22930,** RRP: **£16.99**
www.harriman-house.com/fundology

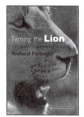

### Taming the Lion

100 Secret Strategies for Investing

by Richard Farleigh

Richard Farleigh reveals the 100 secret strategies that he developed to enable him to succeed in the markets.

ISBN: 1897597622, ISBN 13: **9781897597620, Hardback, 224pp, 2005,** Code: **21815,** RRP: **£12.99**
www.harriman-house.com/tamingthelion

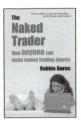

## The Naked Trader

**How anyone can make money trading shares**

by Robbie Burns

In this revealing book, top trader Robbie Burns cuts through the jargon to give you the lowdown on the strategies you need to make money from share dealing.

ISBN: 1897597452, ISBN 13: 9781897597453, Paperback, 276pp, 2005, Code: 19682, RRP: £12.99
www.harriman-house.com/nakedtrader

## The Book of Investing Rules

**Invaluable advice from 150 master investors**

Edited by Philip Jenks and Stephen Eckett

Never before has so much quality advice been packed into a single book. If you want to increase your wealth through investing, this is an unmissable opportunity to acquire knowledge and skills from the best in the world.

ISBN: 1897597215, ISBN 13: 9781897597217, Paperback, 502pp, 2002, Code: 14870, RRP: £19.99
www.harriman-house.com/rules

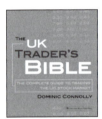

## The UK Trader's Bible

**The Complete Guide to Trading the UK Stock Market**

by Dominic Connolly

This is the only comprehensive UK-published guide to short-term trading, combining detailed reference information with the author's advice on strategy and tactics. Every serious trader in the UK needs this book – not a nice-to-have, but a must-have!

ISBN: 1897597398, ISBN 13: 9781897597392, Paperback, 330pp, 2005, Code: 16702, RRP: £29.99
www.harriman-house.com/tradersbible

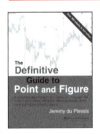

## The Definitive Guide to Point and Figure

A Comprehensive Guide to the Theory and Practical Use of the Point and Figure Charting Method

by Jeremy du Plessis

For the first time this book thoroughly demystifies the world of Point and Figure charting, with a detailed explanation of the history and development of the technique from its invention to the modern day. The book covers the makeup of the chart patterns, why they are created, and their interpretation.

ISBN: 1897597630, ISBN 13: 9781897597637, Hardback, 550pp, 2005, Code: 21822, RRP: £59.95
www.harriman-house.com/definitivepandf

## The Midas Touch

The strategies that have made Warren Buffett the world's most successful investor

by John Train

This is the book that tells readers how to invest like the man known as 'the Wizard of Omaha' (*Forbes*) and the investor with 'the Midas Touch' . John Train introduces the remarkable story of Warren Buffett in his classic text.

ISBN: 1897597290, ISBN 13: 9781897597293, Hardback, 208pp, 2003, Code: 15842, RRP: £14.00
www.harriman-house.com/midas

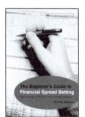

## The Beginner's Guide to Financial Spread Betting

Step-by-step instructions and winning strategies

by Michelle Baltazar

The aim of this book is to give you a basic understanding of how spread betting works, so that, with a little time and effort, you can find out how to turn a pauper's budget into a king's ransom.

ISBN: 1897597355, ISBN 13: 9781897597354, Paperback, 140pp, 2004, Code: 16699, RRP: £12.99
www.harriman-house.com/spreadbetting

## The Way to Trade

Discover Your Successful Trading Personality

by John Piper

Never before has so much quality advice been packed into a single book. If you want to increase your wealth through investing, this is an unmissable opportunity to acquire knowledge and skills from the best in the world.

ISBN: 1897597940, ISBN 13: 9781897597941, Paperback, 320pp, 2006, Code: 23371, RRP: £39.99
www.harriman-house.com/twtt

## Extraordinary Popular Delusions and the Madness of Crowds

by Charles MacKay

First published in 1841, Extraordinary Popular Delusions and the Madness of Crowds is often cited as the best book ever written about market psychology. This Harriman House edition includes Charles Mackay's account of the three infamous financial manias - John Law's Mississipi Scheme, the South Sea Bubble, and Tulipomania.

ISBN: 1897597320, ISBN 13: 9781897597323, Hardback, 96pp, 2003, Code: 16347, RRP: £11.00
www.harriman-house.com/epd

## Ichimoku Charts

### An Introduction to Ichimoku Kinko Clouds

by Nicole Elliott

Candlestick charts, although originating in Japan, now play an important role in technical analysis worldwide. Now, for the first time in English, this book presents the next stage of candlestick analysis - Ichimoku Kinko Hyo. Sometimes called Cloud Charts, this analysis adds moving averages to candlestick charts.

ISBN: 1897597843, ISBN 13: 9781897597842, Paperback, end of 2006, Code: 22962, RRP: £39.99
www.harriman-house.com/ichimoku

## Bets and the City

### Sally Nicolls Spread Betting Diary

by Sally Nicolls

Bets and the City is based on Sally's enormously popular column for *Finspreads*. It takes you inside the dealing room of the UK's leading spread betting firm as Sally begins her transformation from naive beginner to hardened pessimist. Her Spread Betting Diary is frank, factual (these are all real trades) and fun.

ISBN: 1905641060, ISBN 13: 9781905641062, paperback, end of 2006, Code: 25792, RRP: £9.99

# Order your copy of The UK Stock Market Almanac 2008

As a special offer to our readers, we are offering you the chance to pre-order your copy of *The UK Stock Market Almanac 2008* at the discounted price of £11.99 (R.R.P. £19.99).

As you know, the Almanac is a unique reference work for all UK investors, and next year's edition promises to be even more informative and entertaining. You will find articles filled with even more information, covering a broader range of topics, as well as even more up to date company and stock market information.

So don't miss out on your essential guide to the next financial year – order your copy now to receive your exclusive discount, only available in *The UK Stock Market Almanac 2007*.

---

## Ordering information

**By phone:**
+44 (0)1730 233870

**By fax:**
+44 (0)1730 233880

**Email:**
bookshop@harriman-house.com

**Online:**
www.harriman-house.com

**By post:**
Harriman House Ltd
43 Chapel Street
Petersfield
Hampshire
GU32 3DY
UK

Name ....................................................
Address ....................................................
....................................................
Town ....................................................
Postcode ....................................................
Country ....................................................
Telephone ....................................................
Email ....................................................

| Qty | Title | Price | Total |
|-----|-------|-------|-------|
| | **The UK Stock Market Almanac 2008** | **£11.99** | |

UK: £2.00 per book ( max £4.00 )
Europe : £4.00 for the first book, £2.00 for each extra book
ROW: £6.00 for the first book, £3.00 for each extra book

Postage

TOTAL

I enclose a cheque made payable to 'Harriman House Ltd' ☐

Charge my :   Visa ☐   Mastercard ☐   Maestro ☐   Amex ☐

valid from ☐☐ to ☐☐ issue # ☐

Three digit security number ☐☐☐